Dewey, Pragmatism, and Economic Methodology

The writings of the American philosopher John Dewey contend systematically with metaphysics, epistemology, logic, philosophy education, aesthetics, social problems, and public policy. Given the recent revival of Dewey's legacy, it is surprising that the ramifications of his thought have not been explored in relation to economic theory and the philosophy of economics.

This book brings together, for the first time, philosophers of pragmatism and economists interested in methodological questions. The main theoretical thrust of Dewey is to unite inquiry with behavior, and this book's contributions assess this insight in the light of developments in modern American philosophy, social and legal theories, and the theoretical orientation of economics.

This unique book contains impressive contributions from a range of different perspectives and its unique nature will make it required reading for academics involved with philosophy and economics.

Elias L. Khalil is a member of the faculty of Vassar College. His main research interests are behavioral economics and organizational economics. His recent publications include *Trust* (Edward Elgar, 2003), "Information, Knowledge and the Close of Friedrich Hayek's System" (*Eastern Economic Journal*, 2002), and 'Is Adam Smith Liberal?' (*Journal of Institutional and Theoretical Economics*, 2002).

Routledge INEM Advances in Economic Methodology

Edited by D. Wade Hands
Professor of Economics, University of Puget Sound,
Tacoma, USA

The field of economic methodology has expanded rapidly during the last few decades. This expansion has occurred in part because of changes within the discipline of economics, in part because of changes in the prevailing philosophical conception of scientific knowledge, and also because of various transformations within wider society. Research in economic methodology now reflects not only developments in contemporary economic theory, the history of economic thought, and the philosophy of science; it also reflects developments in science studies, historical epistemology, and social theorizing more generally. The field of economic methodology still includes the search for rules for the proper conduct of economic science, but it also covers a vast array of other subjects and accommodates a variety of different approaches to those subjects.

The objective of this series is to provide a forum for the publication of significant works in the growing field of economic methodology. Since the series defines methodology quite broadly, it will publish books on a wide range of different methodological subjects. The series is also open to a variety of different types of works: original research monographs, edited collections, as well as re-publication of significant earlier contributions to the methodological literature. The International Network for Economic Methodology (INEM) is proud to sponsor this important series of contributions to the methodological literature.

Foundations of Economic Method, 2nd Edition
A Popperian perspective
Lawrence A. Boland

Applied Economics and the Critical Realist Critique
Edited by Paul Downward

Dewey, Pragmatism and Economic Methodology
Edited by Elias L. Khalil

Dewey, Pragmatism, and Economic Methodology

Edited by Elias L. Khalil

Routledge
Taylor & Francis Group

LONDON AND NEW YORK

First published 2004
by Routledge
2 Park Square, Milton Park, Abingdon, Oxfordshire OX14 4RN

Simultaneously published in the USA and Canada
by Routledge
711 Third Avenue, New York, NY 10017

Routledge is an imprint of the Taylor & Francis Group, an informa business

First issued in paperback 2012

© 2004 American Insitute for Economic Research

Typeset in Bembo by
Taylor & Francis Books Ltd

British Library Cataloguing in Publication Data
A catalogue record for this book is available from the British Library

Library of Congress Cataloging in Publication Data
A catalog record for this title has been requested

ISBN13: 978-0-415-70014-6 hardback
ISBN13: 978-0-415-64722-9 paperback

Contents

Contributors

Richard J. Bernstein is Vera List Professor of Philosophy at the Graduate Faculty, New School University. He specializes in the study of American pragmatism, social and political philosophy, and critical theory. His most recent books include *The New Constellation: The Ethical–Political Horizons of Modernity/Postmodernity* (MIT Press, 1991), *Hannah Arendt and the Jewish Question* (1996), *Freud and the Vexed Legacy of Moses* (Cambridge University Press, 1998), and *Radical Evil: A Philosophical Interrogation* (Polity Press, 2002).

Peter J. Boettke is a Professor of Economics at George Mason University. Prior to joining GMU, Boettke taught at New York University and was a National Fellow at the Hoover Institution at Stanford University. He is the author of *The Political Economy of Soviet Socialism: The Formative Years, 1918–1928* (Kluwer Academic, 1990), *Why Perestroika Failed* (Routledge, 1993), and *Calculation and Coordination* (Routledge, 2001). He is the co-author of *The Economic Way of Thinking* (Prentice Hall, 2002).

Tom Burke is Associate Professor in the Department of Philosophy at the University of South Carolina. He is co-editor of *Dewey's Logical Theory: New Studies and Interpretations* (Vanderbilt University Press, 2002) and is author of *Dewey's New Logic: A Reply to Russell* (University of Chicago Press, 1994).

Vincent Colapietro is Professor of Philosophy at Penn State University. His current projects include the study of psyches and their vicissitudes, and the relation between pragmatism and psychoanalysis. His recent publications include "The Speculative Reconsidered" (*Journal of Speculative Philosophy*, 2002), "Robust Realism and Real Externality: The Complex Commitments of a Convinced Pragmaticist" (*Semiotica*, 2000), "Let's All Go To The Movies: Two Thumbs Up for Hugo Munsterberg's The Photoplay (1916)" (*Transactions of Charles S. Peirce Society*, 2000), and *Fateful Shapes of Human Freedom* (Vanderbilt University Press, 2003).

Stanley Fish is Dean of the College of Liberal Arts and Sciences at the University of Illinois at Chicago. He is the author of many books, including: *Surprised by Sin: The Reader in Paradise Lost* (1967; and a 30th anniversary edition, Harvard University Press 1997); *The Living Temple: George Herbert and Catechizing* (University of California Press, 1978); *Is There a Text in This Class? Interpretive Communities and the Sources of Authority* (Harvard University Press, 1980); *There's No Such Thing as Free Speech, and It's a Good Thing, Too* (Oxford University Press, 1994); *The Trouble with Principle* (Harvard University Press, 1999); and *How Milton Works* (Harvard University Press, 2001). *The Stanley Fish Reader*, edited by H. Aram Veeser, was published by Blackwell in 1999.

D. Wade Hands is Professor of Economics at the University of Puget Sound in Tacoma, WA. He has published widely on various topics in the history of economic thought and economic methodology. His most recent book is *Reflection Without Rules* (Cambridge University Press, 2001). He is also one of the editors (along with John Davis and Uskali Mäki) of *The Handbook of Economic Methodology* (Edward Elgar, 1998). The second edition of his text-book *Introductory Mathematical Economics* was published by Oxford University Press in 2003.

Peter H. Hare is State University of New York Distinguished Service Professor of Philosophy Emeritus. Since 1974 he has edited the *Transactions of the C.S. Peirce Society: A Quarterly Journal in American Philosophy*. He is a past president of the C.S. Peirce Society and of the Society for the Advancement of American Philosophy. In 2003 Prometheus Books published a volume of essays in his honor, *Pragmatic Naturalism and Realism*, edited by John R. Shook.

Larry A. Hickman is Director of the Center for Dewey Studies and Professor of Philosophy at Southern Illinois University, Carbondale. He is the author of *Modern Theories of Higher Level Predicates* (Philosophia Verlag, 1980), *John Dewey's Pragmatic Technology* (Indiana University Press, 1990), and *Philosophical Tools for Technological Culture* (Indiana University Press, 2001), as well as being the editor of *Technology as a Human Affair* (McGraw-Hill, 1990), *Reading Dewey* (Indiana University Press, 1998), *The Essential Dewey* (with Thomas Alexander, Indiana University Press, 1998), and *The Correspondence of John Dewey* (NLX, 1999 and 2001).

David L. Hildebrand is assistant professor of philosophy at the University of Colorado at Denver and is the author of *Beyond Realism and Antirealism: John Dewey and the Neopragmatists* (Vanderbilt University Press, 2003). He has also published articles on other American figures (including Hilary Putnam, Richard Rorty, A.N. Whitehead, Charles Peirce, and Kenneth Burke) and on the connections among philosophy, literary criticism, historiography, and classroom pedagogy. He maintains a website (www.davidhildebrand.org).

Elias L. Khalil is a member of the faculty of Vassar College. His main research interests are behavioral economics and organizational economics. His recent publications include *Trust* (Edward Elgar, 2003), "Information, Knowledge and the Close of Friedrich Hayek's System" (*Eastern Economic Journal*, 2002) and "Is Adam Smith Liberal?" (*Journal of Institutional and Theoretical Economics*, 2002).

Don Lavoie was the Charles and David Koch Chair of Economics in the School of Public Policy at George Mason University. He was the author of *Rivalry and Central Planning* (Cambridge University Press, 1985) and *National Economic Planning: What is Left?* (Ballinger, 1985), and the co-author (with Emily Chamlee-Wright) of *Culture and Enterprise* (Routledge, 2001). Don specialized in the field of history of economic thought and methodology, and in his last years of research devoted himself to work in epistemology, and the interdisciplinary study of culture and political economy. He was a teacher revered by his students and a devoted family man. He tragically died at the age of 50 after battling cancer, and is survived by his wife Mary and their three children Jon, Marc, and Gabby.

Michael S. Lawlor is a Professor of Economics and Public Health at the Department of Economics, Wake Forest University, and the Department of Public Health Sciences, Wake Forest University School of Medicine. His research has concerned the history of economics, especially the development of Keynes's economics and the history of monetary theory. He also writes on the economics of health care institutions, most recently publishing papers on academic medical centers and the role of public funding in biotechnology research.

Isaac Levi has been a Professor of Philosophy at Columbia University since 1970 and John Dewey Professor since 1992. His most recent book is *The Covenant of Reason* (Columbia University Press, 1997). He has written on epistemology, philosophy of probability, induction and statistical reasoning, decision making, belief change and value conflict. His ideas and projects have been controlled by an abiding interest in the models of inquiry proposed by Charles Peirce and John Dewey. He has written about both Peirce's views of ampliative reasoning and Dewey's approach to value conflict.

Joseph Margolis is currently Laura H. Carnell Professor of Philosophy at Temple University. His forthcoming books include *The Unraveling of Scientism: American Philosophy at the End of the Twentieth Century* (Cornell University Press, 2003) and *The Advantages of a Second-best Morality: Moral Philosophy after 9/11 (XXXX)*.

William Milberg is Associate Professor of Economics at the Graduate Faculty of New School University in New York. His recent publications include "The Changing Structure of Trade Linked to Global Production Systems: What are the Policy Implications?" (*International Labor Organization*, 2003), "Deindustrialization and Changes in Manufacturing Trade: Factor Content Calculations for 1978–1995," (*Weltwirtschaftliches Archiv*, 2003, with David Kucera), and *The Making of Economic Society* (11th edition, Prentice-Hall, 2001, with Robert Heilbroner).

Sami Pihlström (PhD from the University of Helsinki in 1996) is Docent and University Lecturer of Theoretical Philosophy at the University of Helsinki, Finland. He is the author of *Structuring the World* (Acta Philosophica Fennica, 1996), *Pragmatism and Philosophical Anthropology* (Peter Lang, 1998), and *Naturalizing the Transcendental: A Pragmatic View* (Prometheus Books, 2003), as well as four books in Finnish and dozens of articles on, for example, pragmatism, transcendental arguments, and the realism issue in international and Finnish philosophical journals.

Richard A. Posner is a judge of the US Court of Appeals for the Seventh Circuit and a senior lecturer at the University of Chicago Law School. He is the author of many articles and books applying economic analysis to law, most recently the sixth edition of his textbook treatise *Economic Analysis of Law* (Aspen, 2003); and he has also written extensively on the theory of judicial decision making, with particular reference to the application of pragmatism to adjudication, most recently in his book *Law, Pragmatism, and Democracy* (Harvard University Press, 2003).

Sandra B. Rosenthal is Provost Distinguished Professor of Philosophy at Loyola University, New Orleans. She has published eleven books and over 200 articles on pragmatism and on its relation to other areas of philosophy. She has given a formal lecture series on pragmatism in China, Germany, and Poland; delivered over 200 papers/lectures at conferences and universities in the US and abroad; served as president of several major philosophical societies; and is a member of numerous editorial boards of journals and book series. Her publications include *Speculative Pragmatism* (University of Massachusetts Press, 1986), *Charles Peirce's Pragmatic Pluralism* (SUNY Press, 1994), and *Time, Continuity and Indeterminacy* (SUNY Press, 2000).

Frank X. Ryan is Associate Professor in the Department of Philosophy, Kent State University. His research interests include American philosophy and epistemology. His recent publications include *Darwin and Theology in America: 1850–1930* (4 volumes, Thoemmes Press, 2002) and "Scholastic Realism and Pragmatic Contextualism" in John R. Shook (ed.) *The Future of Realism in the American Tradition of Pragmatic Realism* (Prometheus Press, 2002).

John E. Smith is Clark Professor Emeritus of Philosophy at Yale University where he has taught since 1952. He received an MDiv in 1945 from the Union Theological Seminary in New York and a PhD from Columbia University in 1948. Between 1945 and 1952 he held appointments in the Departments of Philosophy and Religion at Vassar and Barnard Colleges. He is a past President of the American Philosophical Association, Eastern Division, of the Metaphysical Society of America and of the Charles S. Peirce Society. Among other works, he is the author of *Reason and God* (Yale University Press, 1961), *The Spirit of American Philosophy* (Oxford University Press, 1963), *Experience and God* (Oxford University Press, 1968), *The Analogy of Experience* (Harper & Row, 1973), *Purpose and Thought: The Meaning of Pragmatism* (Yale University Press, 1978), *America's Philosophical Vision* (University of Chicago Press, 1992), *Jonathan Edwards: Puritan, Preacher, Philosopher* (University of Notre Dame Press, 1992), and *Quasi-Religions: Humanism, Marxism, Nationalism* (St. Martin's Press, 1994). He is General Editor, Emeritus, of the Yale Edition of *The Works of Jonathan Edwards* (Yale University Press, 1957-2003).

Virgil Henry Storr is the Chief Information Officer for TSD, a consulting firm. He received his PhD in Economics from George Mason University. His academic writings have been published and are forthcoming in several scholarly journals and edited volumes, including the *American Journal of Economics and Sociology*.

John J. Stuhr is W. Alton Jones Professor of Philosophy and American Studies at Vanderbilt University. His research focuses on ethics, politics, contemporary culture, European philosophy, and pragmatism. His recent books include *Pragmatism, Postmodernism, and the Future of Philosophy* (Routledge, 2003), *Pragmatism and Classical American Philosophy* (Oxford University Press, 2000), and *Genealogical Pragmatism: Philosophy, Experience, and Community* (State University of New York Press, 1997). He is editor of the American Philosophy Series (Indiana University Press) and co-editor of *The Journal of Speculative Philosophy*.

Alex Viskovatoff is a Visiting Assistant Professor at the Department of Economics at the University of Pittsburgh. Recent publications include "Rationality as Optimal Choice versus Rationality as Valid Inference" (*Journal of Economic Methodology*, 2001), "Critical Realism and Kantian Transcendental Arguments" (*Cambridge Journal of Economics*, 2002), and "Searle, Rationality, and Social Reality" (*American Journal of Economics and Sociology*, 2003). He is currently working on a book exploring the philosophical presuppositions of mainstream economics.

Introduction

John Dewey, the transactional view, and the behavioral sciences

Elias L. Khalil

The essays in this volume were presented at a conference that took place in July 2001 in Great Barrington, Massachusetts. The Behavioral Research Council (BRC), a division of the American Institute for Economic Research (AIER), sponsored the conference to assess the recent revitalization of John Dewey in relation to debates surrounding postmodernism in philosophy, on one hand, and to methodological controversies in economics, on the other.

History and purpose

When BRC invited the contributors to this volume, many were surprised to learn that John Dewey's philosophy, especially his collaboration with Arthur Bentley, has informed and guided for many decades the work of AIER. In fact, AIER uses Dewey and Bentley's *Knowing and the Known* as the backbone of its workshops and summer school. Colonel E.C. Harwood, the founder of AIER, came to value and promote Dewey and Bentley's theory of inquiry as early as 1950, about the time when pragmatism was eclipsed by analytical philosophy in major departments of philosophy in the United States.

Harwood (1900–1981), a self-educated man, founded AIER in 1933 in Cambridge, Massachusetts, as a non-profit, educational organization. Harwood wanted to spread economic education so that the average citizen could protect himself from such economic hardships as those experienced by many during the Great Depression. AIER is wholly supported by subscriptions to its newsletter, sales of its publications, and contributions by individuals. According to its bylaws, AIER cannot accept any funding from corporations, foundations, or government agencies.

When Harwood started to read the books and pamphlets written by economists in the 1920s, he was struck by how far apart they were in their explanations of such core disciplinary concepts as the nature of money, the business cycle, and economic growth. As he tried to decipher such divergent views, he was surprised by the scant use of empirical findings, not to mention the lack of a common terminology and a common set of procedures for communicating differences in views. In Dewey's and Bentley's only major work together, the aforementioned *Knowing and the Known*, he found the transactional view of human scientific inquiry a guiding principle on how to proceed and inquire about the state of the economy. For Dewey and Bentley, one should avoid starting from a priori axioms that lead us into force-fitting the world to suit our preconceived attitudes and into taking our truth claims based on this one-sided projection as scientific truth. One should rather temper one's pronouncements as "warranted assertions," subject to revision if further findings call for it.

Inquiry as action

However, on the face of it, this methodology does not yet point to any partic- ularly unique conclusions. For instance, the great majority of economists have read Milton Friedman's (1953) classic essay on method in graduate school. They generally adhere, at least ostensibly, to Popperian or other positivist views of science. They usually qualify their models as approximations whose predictions are subject to testing. They couch the findings of their econo- metric testing as tentative and subject to change in light of new or better data. Maxims about verifiable assertions and the centrality of empirical evidence are also entertained by diverse positivist views of inquiry ranging from logical positivism to Popperian falsificationism.

So, what differentiates Dewey's and Bentley's maxims from positivist maxims about evidence and verification? First and foremost, Dewey and Bentley denied that the aim of verification is a wholly complete, final, and inquiry-independent "reality," even in principle. Positivism was certainly one of the schools of inquiry that upheld the distinction between inquiry and reality. For Dewey and Bentley, a fulfilled hypothesis is warranted rather than verified – while the hypothesis resolves the problem under focus, it invites indefinite revision and modification. Action is not merely an external imple- ment to the acquisition of "knowledge," regarded as a sheer "beholding" of truth. Instead, action is integral to whatever we claim to know. As Dewey and Bentley put it, the process of knowing helps constitute what is known; stated otherwise, inquiry is action.

This means that true inquiry cannot take place within an ivory tower, and inquirers cannot pretend to be above the fray of their own interests, beliefs, passions, and imagination. Dewey and Bentley argued that humans gain knowledge by transacting with the environment, an environment that they partly constitute. Knowing is acting with imagination, interests, and beliefs. However, such imagination and beliefs are phases of inquiry that are warranted; they are not immovable starting points as some postmodern and poststructuralist linguistic thinkers suppose. Nonetheless, as part of the process of inquiry, imagination and beliefs are as intrinsic to statements about "reality" as empirical evidence is. Such statements do not simply reflect "reality," but rather mold reality according to the imagination and beliefs that are warranted. As long as the actor is alive, i.e., directed by imagination and beliefs, statements are inherently revisable and thus contingent – contingent even if there is no more empirical evidence to be uncovered or discovered in the world. Thus, as long as imagination and beliefs are warranted assertions and, in turn, constitutive of statements, statements cannot be final by definition.

Statements also cannot be final by the simple appeal to empirical evidence. As long as the actor is alive, i.e., directed by imagination, beliefs, and theoretical constructs, no direct appeal to empirical evidence can univocally determine either the meaning of a statement or the reality it denotes: depending upon the context of use and background of beliefs, even a simple act of pointing at a brown table could indicate, e.g., a table, a rectangular surface, the color brown, or a finger. The noted philosopher W.V.O. Quine had something like this in mind when he later insisted that such statements are invariably undetermined by empirical evidence.

In contrast, for positivists, statements are revisable only because of accidental or hypothetical grounds. There is always the possibility of a new observation that may upset the current statement. So, the true meaning of a statement is doubted only because of some unforeseen, hidden evidence. If there was a Genie that assured us that there was no such hidden evidence ever to be unearthed, the true meaning of a statement could not be doubted in principle. For positivists, given the element of surprise, it is only out of prudence that the investigator does not claim his statement is the final truth about the matter at hand.

In order to perceive surprises, however, an imaginative agent must be on the lookout, ready to capture them, or, to emphasize the transactional quality of inquiry, be captured by them. It is not the phenomenon of accidental surprises – if there is such a thing – that makes statements contingently warranted assertions. Rather, for Dewey, the skeptical element in statements, what Charles Peirce called "fallibilism," arises from the nature of inquiry *qua* action – whereas action involves beliefs and imagination. This means that the products of inquiry, i.e., statements, are as open to revision as one's beliefs and imagination. Put tersely, the positivist philosopher tempers his excitement for a statement because of some possible surprises of hidden evidence. In contrast, the transactionist philosopher tempers his excitement for a statement because it is the product of transaction between the knower (as an actor with beliefs and imagination) and the known (as ends sought in light of the beliefs and imagination). Thus, when the transactionist qualifies statements as tentative, the qualification arises from an understanding of inquiry as action, rather than from some possible encounter with new facts.

Action as inquiry

Aside from the theory of inquiry, what ramifications does Dewey and Bentley's transactional view have on the theory of action? Dewey and Bentley, in fact, were critical of a host of theories of action in the behavioral sciences. What sets the transactional view apart from such theories is the view of action as inquiry.

In light of this view, inquiry transforms the agent. Action is not a mediation between supposedly given ends (the preferences and beliefs of the actor/knower) and supposedly given means (the known or environment). Dewey and Bentley maintained that the preferences and beliefs of the actor/knower are never deposited as data, given independently of the means. If action is inquiry conducted by the actor, the actor's preferences and beliefs are transformed in the process of trying to satisfy them. Dewey and Bentley's theory of action *qua* inquiry undermines secular and religious foundationalist views of action. The transactional theory of action entails that there is no absolute rock, some supposed prior structures of thought, upon which the actor stands and determines the unmistaken and clear means to achieve an unmistaken and clear end. While refuting the possibility of such a rock, the transactional view is not an invitation to subjectivism, relativism, or other modes of postmodernism – transactional inquiry does not proceed as if reality is out there, providing ends that are given, but one cannot determine the proper means because one is hopelessly the slave of passions and prejudices. The transactional view is rather an invitation to see reality as vague and indeterminate, which allows for various specifications of means and ends as one experiences reality. Given that such ends gain greater specificity when the agent acts, we are justified in saying reality becomes more specific. So, action does not stand outside reality but rather is partially constitutive of it. In this manner, the transactional view of action is not an invitation to relativism and solipsism, but rather an invitation to careful action, where one realizes that the end is formulated as one transacts with it through varying means.

The task is to study action as inquiry, i.e., a transaction between the knower (actor with beliefs) and the known (environment or incentives). This entails that action cannot be fully explained in terms of ends and beliefs only, as if means and the environment in general do not matter, or in terms of the environment only, as if beliefs do not matter. It is a mistake to view the environment and the actor as separate. If the theory focuses only on the actor and his beliefs, it amounts to appealing to some ingrained dispositions or instincts, such as cultural or personality traits, while ignoring the environment or the incentives that make the particular context. Dewey and Bentley (1973) called such an explanation the "self-actional" view. The self-actional view, broadly speaking, reduces behavior to prior structures such as religious creeds, civilizational attitudes, instincts, deep preferences, habits, or, in short, beliefs. To be clear, beliefs do matter. However, they only matter or even mean anything, or gain significance, in light of a particular current context or incentive that challenges the actor. The self-actional view disregards the context and, in turn, attributes to the belief under focus a separate life of its own.

Modern economics is a triumph over such culturalist, self-actional theories. Many scholars have celebrated the success of modern economics over the past two decades for accounting for actions in terms of incentives, what economists call the set of constraints defined by budgets and prices. The modern economist perspective, what Dewey and Bentley call generally the "interactionist" view, starts with the premise that people may have different preferences and beliefs. While such preferences and beliefs partially account for behavior, they definitely do not account for the change in such behavior. For the modern economist, it would be *ad hoc* to explicate the change in behavior as the result of some change in preferences or beliefs. The change in behavior, as argued by George Stigler and Gary Becker (1977) in a famous article, is better elucidated by the change of incentives, or stimuli according to behaviorism, rather than by an appeal to supposed change in preferences or tastes.

Dewey recognized the validity of the interactionist view, a view mainly promoted by behaviorism. But he did not regard it to be a comprehensive description of human action. For one thing, as Dewey noted in his classic 1896 article, "The Reflex Arc Concept in Psychology," the actor does not sit passively *vis-à-vis* the incentive or stimulus. The actor, when acting with intentionality, appropriates the relevant environment after an image or a belief. The image is a product of imagination, whereas imagination is not "imagistic" in the sense of being a mirror or a representation of nature. Rather, imagination involves intentionality in the sense that there is a creative interpretation of the environment and projection of ends-in-view. In this manner, the transaction view involves intentionality, which distinguishes it from the interactionist underpinning of mechanistic, representational theories of the mind. The image, what other disciplines call belief, is formed in light of one's particular standpoint, desires, and goals – all of which are the fruition of an agent's past experience and current intention. So, the incentives presented are not "objectively" defined in the sense of a naïve or direct realism. Stated differently, incentives are not defined independently of the individual's own desires, tastes, or beliefs in terms of a transcendent reality. In fact, the inquiring agent – while communicating with and learning from the experience of other agents – behaving to overcome obstacles encountered in an environment, is the only one who can understand such incentives.

This transactional view highlights how action as inquiry is shaped by the transaction or union of the knower and the known: the knower with the particular belief that cannot be alive independent of the incentive and the known as the incentive that cannot be defined independently of the knower. In this light, the transactional view can be seen as a synthesis of the self-actional view entrenched in anthropology and sociology – which stresses beliefs while discounting incentives – and the interactional view entrenched in economics – which emphasizes incentives while treating beliefs as given data. For Dewey, beliefs (the subject) and incentive (the object) cannot be separated from each other. This view resolves the subject–object dichotomy so deep-seated in Western philosophy.

The transactional view can serve as a general theory of human behavior to help transcend traditional boundaries among academic disciplines. In economics, the transactional view may provide much-needed theories of entrepreneurship, context-dependent behavior, and trustworthiness – which mainstream neoclassical economics and interactionist social theories in general cannot explain (see Khalil 1997, 2003a, b, c). In political science, the transactional view may contribute to an explanation of the origin of authority and political order – which political theorists have generally not answered satisfactorily. Political theorists employ interactionist models regularly to get their normative programs off the ground, a tradition as old as Grotius' social contract theory. In psychology, the transactional view may highlight the biological basis of cognition and the emotional aspect of rationality – which most psychologists have ignored. Psychologists usually treat cognition as a representation of some objective reality, basically as a sub-discipline of neurophysiology or as "serial processing" gleaned from early work in artificial intelligence. Only recently have a few psychologists and neurologists become interested in "embedded" cognition, where cognition is seen as the activity of a brain embedded in the life-history of the organism that is motivated by desires and tastes (see Damasio 1994; Lakoff and Johnson 1999). In sociology and anthropology, the transactional view may emphasize the contextual nature of action in a more robust and descriptively adequate way than even those empirical accounts of human action that agree with Dewey and Bentley on its contextual nature. Thereby it avoids the pitfalls inherent in the writings of traditional sociologists and anthropologists who usually reduce behavior to some inherited cultural norms or functional roles, supposedly designed (by whom?) to guarantee the stability of the social structure.

The Behavioral Research Council seeks to advance the transactional approach by providing a forum for students, academics, and independent scholars to pursue research and to debate central questions in the social sciences in a free intellectual environment in the true tradition of American philosophy. This volume hopefully will serve as a chapter in the ongoing development of Dewey's theory of inquiry, especially in relation to economic methodology.

Organization of the volume

The volume is organized into four parts. Part I discusses how to read Dewey, and classical pragmatism in general, in light of the rise of postmodernism in the last three decades of the twentieth century. Part II discusses more closely John Dewey's theory of inquiry, especially his collaboration with Arthur Bentley, in relation to language and nature. Part III draws some important implications of Dewey's theory of inquiry with regard to wide ranging social issues. Part IV criticizes and reconstructs current economic methodology in light of Dewey's theory of inquiry.

Part I

Part I, focusing on pragmatism in general, starts with Frank Ryan's panoramic view of the achievements of pragmatism. The milestones Ryan charts are: the method of doubt-belief and the pattern of inquiry, the prag-matic theory of truth, the ontology of primary experience, the fact-value relation, and transactionism. Dewey developed his theory of inquiry, transac-tionism, to see the subject and object together, as a solution to what Richard Bernstein called the "deep crack" in Dewey's metaphysics. In turn, Bernstein challenges the standard story that pragmatism was eclipsed by analytic philos-ophy by the middle of the last century. While this standard story is generally accurate, it doesn't tell the whole story. Indeed, as Bernstein demonstrates, some of the great figures in the rise of analytic philosophy's predominance in America are themselves in agreement with some of pragmatism's most famous and important philosophical contributions. These heroes of analytic philosophy, then, are truly a continuation of the living pragmatic tradition. For example, Hilary Putnam appropriated many themes from Dewey and, like Dewey, rejected all traditional forms of scientific and epistemological realism. And we should not forget W.V.O. Quine's critique of the analytic-synthetic dichotomy and Wilfrid Sellars' rejection of the "myth of the given." Further, John McDowell tried to develop a richer notion of natu-ralism that accounts for human spontaneity. And Robert Brandom, following the later Wittgenstein, recognized that norms are embedded in social prac-tices. Norms are not explicit rules that tell us what the norms are or how they are to be applied in any given situation.

In a tone similar to Bernstein's, Sami Pihlström adopts a broad definition of pragmatism that includes neo-pragmatists such as Hilary Putnam and Richard Rorty. Pihlström contrasts Putnam and Rorty on truth, rationality, and normativity. He also compares Putnam's and Rorty's views of James and Dewey and shows how to avoid falling into the trap of a Rortyan anti-realistic type of pragmatism.

Joseph Margolis adopts a more restricted criterion in defining pragmatism. Margolis challenges Brandom's notion, endorsed by Sellars and Rorty, that the fundamental form of the conceptual is the propositional or the linguistic. Margolis argues that, for Dewey, the "paradigmatic pragmatist," the linguistic cannot precede the experiential. David Hildebrand continues Margolis' theme and distinguishes between classical pragmatism and what he calls "linguistic pragmatism" as typified by Rorty. Rorty salutes the "good" Dewey for attacking certainty, foundationalism, and a host of dualisms. But Rorty criti-cizes Dewey for residual metaphysics such as his investigation of "experience." Such a criticism, according to Hildebrand, misses the main thrust of pragma-tism, namely, the priority of the practical (or experiential) standpoint over the linguistic. Larry Hickman goes further and maintains that Dewey traveled the road that postmodernists, such as Foucault and Deleuze, took later. But Dewey's pragmatism goes beyond the postmodernist road, through his commitments to logic, a theory of living inquiry, and evolutionary naturalism.

In turn, Vincent Colapietro criticizes Rorty's assessment that Charles Peirce should not be included in the pragmatist camp. Colapietro maintains that a better way to understand Peirce's theory of signs as thoroughly pragmatic is to examine it through Dewey's *Logic: The Theory of Inquiry*. In fact, Dewey regarded his own theory of logic as a theory of inquiry that builds on Peirce's theory of signs and symbols. As Dewey stresses, it is important to avoid Peirce's occasional use of dichotomies such as thoughts and signs – as if the latter are accidental clothing of the former. For Peirce and Dewey, it is crucial to think of signs as more than language – one form of symbolization so important in our lives – if one is to avoid the "linguistic turn." Signs originate and develop from publicly observable processes involving intersubjectively shared meaning. For Peirce and Dewey, the pragmatic turn encompasses the linguistic turn because language is part of a wide range of human practices.

Part II

Part II focuses on Dewey's theory of inquiry. It commences with John Smith's evaluation of *Knowing and the Known*, the collaborative work of Dewey and Bentley, as well as Dewey's and Bentley's neglected *A Philosophical Correspondence, 1932–1951*. Smith emphasizes that communication for Dewey is the central role of language and that Dewey dismissed the epistemological approach to knowing in favor of inquiry.

Peter Hare also focuses on *Knowing and the Known*. Hare welcomes Dewey's and Bentley's focus on terminology, which goes to show that there are some common grounds shared by some analytic epistemologists and Dewey and Bentley in their respective metaphysics. For Hare, analytic epistemology does not need to be pitted against either Deweyan metaphysics or empirical science. Hare notes that Dewey and Bentley offer a theory of inquiry that still calls for an assessment in light of recent developments in neurobiology – a necessary task given that Dewey and Bentley are committed to the idea that philosophy is an empirical inquiry. Sandra Rosenthal also stresses the biological roots of their theory of inquiry. Inquiry expresses the transactional unity between the organism and the natural environment. Therefore, for Rosenthal, the emergent meaning of the transactional unity between the knower and the known is neither reducible to what is antecedently there in nature nor to some social construction.

Part III

Part III, exposing the ramifications of Dewey's theory of inquiry, commences with Richard Posner's explication of Dewey's notions of democracy and law. Posner finds that Dewey conflates "epistemic democracy" and "political democracy." While Posner welcomes epistemic democracy to generate the most warranted assertions, political democracy is not, as Dewey claims following the Aristotelian tradition, about the "good." The "good" is not transparent: issues confronting modern governments are so complex and ordinary people have little interest and little aptitude in deciphering them. For

Posner, following Joseph Schumpeter's notion of democracy, people are more passive than Dewey wishes to be the case. In fact, Posner welcomes such passivity because people tend to make better judgments in light of their self-interest rather than in light of some lofty notions of the "good." Posner also discusses Dewey's pragmatic theory of law, where the application of principles has to take into account how they work themselves out in current circumstances. Such experimentation implies, for Posner, judicial restraint, where judges should allow legislations to be experimented with.

Stanley Fish tackles what Posner calls "political democracy" from another angle. Fish argues that one's overarching, abstract belief does not inform one on how to act in mundane, particular situations. To put it in the opposite way, people involved in practical situations do not make better decisions if they adopt some metaphysical standpoint. From the pragmatic standpoint, the normative project of the Enlightenment – where general principles are supposed to guide us in practical contexts – is a non-starter. On this basis, Fish takes issue with Jürgen Habermas' notion of "communicative reason" or "discourse ethics" – as if there is a metaphysical foundation that can supersede conflicting interests and upon which differences can be adjudicated according to universal norms of validation.

Contrary to Fish, Tom Burke argues that systems of universals inform and guide practical activities even if they do not fully determine it. Universals in Dewey's sense denote ways of acting or modes of being. In this sense they are abstract but also instrumental in guiding one's behavior in particular situations. Burke employs various formal techniques in conjunction with Dewey's logical theory to characterize ideologies as systems of universals. Burke argues that Dewey's theory of inquiry entails the indispensability of ideologies. For Burke, once the fallible and functional nature of universal terms and propositions is understood, ideologies would be admitted as an essential aspect of inquiry as conceived by Dewey.

Aside from ideology, John Stuhr investigates another implication of Dewey's theory of inquiry, namely, criticism as discrimination and appraisal of matters that concern values. Given its generality, philosophy is criticism of criticism – an exercise that is neither exactly science nor exactly literature. For Stuhr, criticism is the inquiry into relations that occasions the experience of values. Criticism is not a method to find values because values are presupposed by inquiry. Criticism is rather transformative; it turns values into valuables or what should be made into priorities.

In turn, Isaac Levi articulates the importance of one of the original concepts of the pragmatic theory of inquiry: fallibilism. One should not undertake inquiry in order to justify one's held beliefs. Otherwise, one would slip into foundationalism. Rather, one should accept one's held belief, and undertake inquiry in order to find out whether it is warranted to change that belief. To make this clear, Levi stresses the difference between fallibilism and corrigibilism. Despite their protestations to the contrary, pragmatists generally are non-fallibilists – i.e., they do not doubt their current beliefs, and thus tolerate dissenters' views out of friendship, politeness, or a refusal to engage in cruel repression. That is, contrary to Rorty, pragmatists do not tolerate the views of others out of the possibility that they are wrong. However, pragmatists are corrigibilists – i.e., ready to doubt and change their beliefs for good reasons and, hence, may start respecting the views of dissenters if they offer plausibly good reasons. Levi notes that in the case of doubt or conflict of beliefs, the issue of solidarity with one community rather than another cannot explain why the conflict is resolved in one way and not the other. For Levi, Rorty's appeal to solidarity begs the question: why not side with the opposing community?

Part IV

Part IV, relating Dewey's theory to economic methodology, starts with Wade Hands' review of the changes in contemporary philosophy of science that resulted in the dismissal of the received, positivist approach. Such changes offer a great opportunity for the recent revival of pragmatism. He, in turn, evaluates and finds parallels between pragmatism and recent developments of economic methodology. Hands then asks the question of whether the endorsement of pragmatic economic methodology leads one necessarily to endorse Dewey's advocacy of wide-scale social engineering and economic planning. Alex Viskovatoff extends, beyond Hands, Dewey's theory of science to criticize neoclassical economic theory *in toto*. Viskovatoff argues that while Dewey's rejection of the ontological standing of laws does not apply to physics, it applies to human society. At best, human society is characterized by "rules" or what economists call "institutions." A comparative study of institutions is the best that economists can achieve. The economist's commitments to free trade, laissez faire and markets unconstrained by moral values, stem from the dubious belief that human society embodies absolute laws such as those that govern physical nature.

Michael Lawlor next exposes Dewey's views of reality and knowledge, drawing mainly from his middle period writings. Lawlor focuses on Dewey's notion of inquiry as action – i.e., where knowledge, since it is experimental knowledge, modifies the world. Lawlor then illustrates Dewey's notion of experimental knowledge by examining the breakdown of the relationship between the money supply and gross domestic product. The example illustrates how the theory of money updates itself in pursuit of its subject. Lawlor ends by using this example, and its display of multiple understandings of monetary events by different communities, to explore the relationship between Dewey's views and postmodernism. Moving from a field of economics to a heterodox school of economics called the Austrian school, Peter J. Boettke, Don Lavoie, and Virgil Henry Storr discuss the affinity between the methodology of Austrian economics, called "subjectivism," and Dewey's theory of inquiry. The chapter tries to make two distinct but related points. First, it clarifies what "subjectivism" really means. Subjectivism can be understood as a challenge to the "objectivistic" attitude of mainstream economics, the attitude that the Austrians argue is what is keeping economics too disconnected with the everyday world. Second, they try to show that the confusions that have arisen around the Austrians' own method might be cleared up if they were to draw from Dewey's work.

Finally William Milberg identifies a recent, empiricist, turn in mainstream economics, a backlash against the unrobust "New Economics" of the 1980s and 1990s that was itself a response to the aridity and irrelevance of general equilibrium analysis of the post-Second World War era. After placing this recent empiricist turn in historical and methodological perspective, Milberg explores the theoretical possibilities this development creates. He argues that one outcome of this intellectual shift and the theoretical opening it has created is the existence today of various tendencies in economics – both within and outside the mainstream – each of which claims as a strength its pragmatist methodology. Milberg maintains that it is not obvious which of these tendencies, if any, will become the mainstream of a future economics. In any case, economics may be headed for a more pluralist era, in which debates over the most appropriate form of pragmatism figure prominently.

This volume became possible because the contributors undertook their tasks with vigor and dedication. I would like to thank each one of them. I would like especially to thank Frank Ryan, Fred Harwood, Charles Murray, James Garrison, Brendan Hogan, Paul Saka, Michael Lawlor, Cornelis de Waal, and anonymous reviewers who provided useful comments. Finally, the idea of this volume would never have materialized if it was not for the infectious enthusiasm of Robert Gilmour, President Emeritus of AIER, and the wholehearted support of the Board of Trustees of the American Institute for Economic Research, especially its chairman, C. Lowell Harriss.

References

Damasio, A.R. (1994) *Descartes' Error: Emotion, Reason, and the Human Brain*, New York: G.P. Putnam's Sons.

Dewey, J. (1896) "The reflex arc concept in psychology," *Psychological Review*, 3: 357–70.

Dewey, J. and Bentley, A.F. (1973) *Knowing and the Known*, in R. Handy and E.C. Harwood (eds), *Useful Procedures of Inquiry*, Great Barrington, MA: Behavioral Research Council.

Friedman, M. (1953) "The methodology of positive economics," in *Friedman's Essays in Positive Economics*, Chicago: University of Chicago Press.

Khalil, E.L. (1997) "Buridan's ass, uncertainty, risk, and self-competition: a theory of entrepreneurship," *Kyklos*, 50: 147–163.

—— (2003a) "The context problematic, behavioral economics and the transactional view: an introduction to 'Symposium: John Dewey and economic theory'," *Journal of Economic Methodology*, 10: 107–130.

—— (2003b) "A transactional view of entrepreneurship: a Deweyan approach," *Journal of Economic Methodology*, 10: 161–179.

—— (2003c) "Why does trustworthiness pay? Three answers: an introduction," in E.L. Khalil (ed.), *Trust*, Cheltenham, UK: Edward Elgar.

Lakoff, G. and Johnson, M. (1999) *Philosophy in the Flesh: The Embodied Mind and Its Challenge to Western Thought*, New York: Basic Books.

Stigler, G.J. and Becker, G.S. (1977) "*DE Gustibus Non Est Disputandum*," *American Economic Review*, 67: 76–90.

Part I

Pragmatism and postmodernism

1 Five milestones of pragmatism

Frank X. Ryan

Introduction

A quarter of a century ago, Willard Quine presented "The Pragmatists' Place in Empiricism" at a symposium at the University of South Carolina. In it he identifies "five milestones" of a pragmatic empiricism (Quine 1981: 67–75). Intriguingly, the great classical pragmatists, Charles S. Peirce, William James, and John Dewey are nowhere in sight here – the quarrymen of Quine's milestones are J.H. Tooke, Jeremy Bentham, Auguste Comte, Gottlob Frege, and Bertrand Russell. Their great achievement is the progressive broadening of the unit of meaning from idea to word, word to sentence, sentence to sentence set, and sentence set to theory. No longer a mental power or self-contained unit of information, meaning is naturalized as the malleable and context-dependent product of our social and scientific theories.

While not diminishing the genuine worth of such advances, it seems to me these are more yardsticks than milestones toward a pragmatically enlightened empiricism. The "linguistic turn" in philosophy began with the recognition of the inseparable bond between context and meaning: empiricists overcame the folly of hooking sentences to context-free objects in the world by delimiting the reference of sentences to other sentences. The classical pragmatists equally disdained "context-free objects," but they refused to accept a vacuous nominalism where in the end we only talk about talk. Instead, our world itself is continually contextualized and re-contextualized in ongoing dynamic problem-solving activity – its objects the attained objectives of directed inquiry. Thus, from the very outset Peirce loses the linguistic tethers of "sentence sets" by insisting upon an integral connection between meaning and doing, doing and reality.

This is just one of a series of revolutionary advances I propose as five milestones of pragmatism. Classical pragmatism, as conceived here, is not Quine's moderate empiricism that dodges thorny "metaphysical" questions, but a radically reconstructed empiricism that reaches from an ontology of primary experience to the transactional "cosmos of fact."

The milestones we will consider are:

1   doubt-belief and the pattern of inquiry;
2   the pragmatic theory of truth;
3   the ontology of primary experience;
4   the fact–value relation; and
5   transaction.

There is, of course, no claim to having recovered the five milestones of pragmatism. If there are five, there are fifty. Consider, as merely representative,
Peirce's categories and theory of signs; James's psychology, radical empiricism,
and critique of consciousness; Dewey's generic traits of existences, having an
experience, the theory of propositions, and "a common faith"; Mead's social
self – the "I" and "me"; Lewis's pragmatic a priori. Hopefully, however, these
focal five are sufficient to justify classical pragmatism's current renaissance – a
wellspring even Quine, despite his aspiration to a "more thorough pragmatism" (Quine 1953: 46), left largely untapped.

Milestone 1: doubt–belief and the pattern of inquiry

Unlike Quine, whose "unregenerate scientific realism" led him to dismiss
"traditional" problems of philosophy, Peirce reports that his genuine experience of "laboratory life" drew him to metaphysics. Early on he immersed
himself in scholastic realism in an effort to resolve the venerable problem of
mind and reality. Duns Scotus's insistence upon "real generals" helped Peirce
see that relations and inferences are as real as the things related. As we shall
see, this prevents nominalism's perilous slide toward the radical separation of
thing and thought: for if only physical substances "out there" are real, and
ideas, concepts, or relations about them are mere phenomenal manifestations
in our minds, then reality as it is "in-itself" is locked away from our cognitive
ability to grasp it.

   This result is intolerable, but to avoid it Peirce had to turn the entire
paradigm around: reality must be brought within experience such that "the
phenomenal manifestation of the substance is the substance" (Peirce 1868).[1]
But how is this possible? Scotus insisted there must be real generals, such as
"human," that (to avoid self-sustaining platonic "forms") exist only as they are
"contracted" within individuals. Though suggestive of a genuine solution,
Peirce finds "contraction" unsatisfactory – beyond the antiquated and implausible metaphysics of "contracted forms," the problem of "real for us" versus
"real in itself" is simply recycled into the distinction between "contracted"
and "uncontracted" states.

   But if real generals are not metaphysical forms contracted into particulars,
is there another way to think about them so as not to offend the sensibilities
of a "laboratory man"? Scotus left Peirce a valuable clue in noting that
beyond real generals cognitively grasped are generals that operate *habituliter* –
that is, as noncognitive feelings or predispositions to actual states of awareness.
Scotus could only speculate that this *habituliter* is an inexplicable "intellectual

intuition." Peirce's scientific bent, however, drew him to the modern sense of "habit," and with it a way to bring the uncontracted and contracted into an integral system of "doubt-belief."

The recognized function of habit undermines the old view of association-alist psychology that concepts are formed by piecing together images of discrete particulars. We don't normally develop the conception of red by recapturing images of red patches from memory. Indeed, Peirce goes so far as to claim "we have no images even in actual [current] perception" (5.303).[2] What we typically begin with is not the image of red, but the habit of red – the disposition to act upon, report, or recognize, the actual quality of "red" in response to some problem that requires us to do so.[3] Peirce thus transforms Scotus's uncontracted form into the habituated disposition for action in the face of the onset of doubt. He also calls this firstness – a "permanent possi-bility of sensation."

Belief, for Peirce, is an expression of habit: "the feeling of believing is a more or less sure indication of there being established in our nature some habit which will determine our actions" (5.371). As James later points out, even the most open-minded among us are extremely conservative about our beliefs (James 1981: 31). Even so, belief is invariably challenged by the "irrita-tion of doubt": an "uneasy and dissatisfied state from which we struggle to free ourselves" to achieve a new state of belief (5.372). This directed struggle, says Peirce, is inquiry: indeed, the resolution of doubt is "the sole end of inquiry" (5.375). We think so that we may overcome doubt.

A belief, then, is a general assertion of what we take to be real.[4] But the gap between what we take to be real and what is real is not the contraction of the real into the individual. Instead, beliefs approach reality via experimenta-tion, where successful "adjustments" forge new beliefs. As such, doubt-belief differs from mere contraction in two key ways: First, instead of the contain-ment of one thing in another, or the mere association of similar properties, the movement of inquiry in doubt-belief is inferential: e.g. the predicate expression "is a man" is realized in a fulfilled or verified hypothesis (5.292).[5] Second, and coordinate with this, reality is not an antecedent state lurking behind its phenomenal manifestation, but a continually unfolding conse-quence or achievement of ongoing inquiry.

For Peirce, doubt-belief permeates human experience – it designates "any question, no matter how small or how great, and the resolution of it." For Peirce, even hunting for a cab fare is an exercise of doubt-belief (5.394).

All grown up, doubt-belief is Dewey's method of inquiry (Dewey 1976: 360).[6] The initial state of secure belief, the matrix of habit, is recast as settled or primary experience, a milestone in itself. The onset of doubt is Dewey's problematic situation – shock or interruption that calls forth a hypothesis and implementing tools that diagnose the problem then propose a solution. A hypothesis is a sort of "clutch" between imposed danger and instinctive reac-tion – it's smarter to lead with one's mind than one's chin. The outcome of a successful hypothesis is an attained objective or object. In subsequently returning to and enriching primary experience, a settled object becomes a secure tool for the resolution of future problems.

Dewey reminds us that inquiry is a pattern, not a prescription – nothing is gained quibbling about five, or seven, or nine distinct stages. Sometimes we start in the middle, or with a solution to which there is no clear problem. Many, perhaps most, problems are cut off without recourse to inquiry by calling upon "banked" solutions that need no hypothesis. Contrary to Peirce's claim about cab fare, when the solution is easy or obvious the full pattern of inquiry is unnecessary.

Milestone 2: the pragmatic theory of truth

Best known of the five milestones, in the lean years this was pragmatism's survivor – holding out against rival "coherence" and "correspondence" theories in basic texts. Its premise is clear: truth is a relation between beliefs and the world, and thus we require more than the mere coherence or consistency of ideas. But if an idea or statement must correspond to an unknowable thing-in-itself, no purported reference from thought to thing is justified. The pragmatic alternative preserves the notion of correspondence, but recasts it as the experienced relation between an encountered problem and its successful solution. Truth, recast as warranted assertability, is an achievement of inquiry; and since inquiry is open-ended and revisable, there is no pretense of final truth. Instead truth grows, proliferates, flourishes with new discoveries.

James provides the most recognizable account of the pragmatic theory of truth. Where Peirce and Dewey focus upon the incoherence of corresponding to an unknowable thing-in-itself,[7] James stresses the interpretive role of the human subject, the "trail of the human serpent" that subordinates truth to personal needs, desires, and satisfactions. "A new opinion is 'true,' " he tells us, to the extent it "gratifies the individual's desire to assimilate the novel in his experience to his beliefs in stock" (James 2001: 124).

James skillfully handles the charge that truth is capricious – each new candidate must survive a gauntlet of obstinate existing beliefs. He also deflects the notion that one generation's truth is as good as another's. Modern science, for instance, has not merely replaced the Ptolemaic earth-centered "truth" with a heliocentric truth, but declares, retroactively, the Ptolemaic view absolutely false – false for that era as well as our own.[8] But he is less successful in establishing an objective basis for truth. That ideas become true by helping "us get into satisfactory relation with other parts of experience" (James 1981: 30) smacks of coherence. And when these relations are elaborated as an orchestration of "concepts and percepts" we again worry about nominalism, and ask ourselves: "what has become of the world in all of this?"[9]

Here Dewey's guidance is helpful. Dewey never lets us forget that inquiry underlies both what is experienced and who experiences it. As such, satisfaction is not primarily a personal feeling, but a satisfactory adjustment of hypotheses to consequences (MW 6: 4–5). Dewey goes beyond James in realizing that truth is a process of social adaptation to nature:

knowing is not the condescension of reduplicating a nature that already is, but is the turning of that nature to account in behalf of consequences. And objective truth is the free outworking of nature so interpreted into an intercourse more secure, more varied, and more free.

(MW 6: 68)

Milestone 3: the ontology of primary experience

We sometimes hear that Peirce founded pragmatism as a theory of meaning, James added truth, and Dewey evolved an ontology and a naturalistic metaphysics. Though this is an oversimplification, Dewey's 1905 essay "The Postulate of Immediate Empiricism" is a distinct ontological watershed; for here is boldly proclaimed – "things are what they are experienced to be" (MW 3: 159). Eight apocalyptic words – so direct, yet so enigmatic! What is Dewey saying? I inadvertently carry a nine two places in my account ledger, and experience an unexpected boon to my balance. Am I suddenly wealthier? Do I find the best deal to Kansas by closing my eyes, clicking my heels, and experiencing myself as being in Kansas?

If the experience of things made them so in the world, we'd live as infallible gods, creating realities at will. Clearly this is not what Dewey means by "things are what they are experienced to be." But, again, what is he saying? I suggest tackling this on two fronts. First, relieve the word "thing" from any requisite concreteness or particularity: for Dewey, "thing" is more an indefinite "something" or "subject matter" than a discrete "object."[10] Second, add this qualification: "What is is what it is experienced as – in *primary* experience." Primary experience is the qualitative immediacy of any experience – the feel or sense of what it is. This holds both for cognitive knowing as well as for what Dewey calls noncognitive having. In the case of the two account balances, both experiences are cognitive. I have the qualitative immediacy of a certain balance; later I experience the "true" balance. In this instance, "what is is what it is experienced as" reminds us that the comparison between the initial balance and the revised balance is between two reals of experience, not between an "appearance" and a "reality":[11] I did experience the initial balance just as I experienced it. Ontologically, however, this isn't very interesting, for it's just the tautology that my experience of the initial balance was indeed just that experience.

But different, and really more instructive for getting to the heart of "what is," is primary experience as the qualitative immediacy of the noncognitive "fringe and background" that is far more pervasive than any focal awareness.[12] For example, throughout my travails with my account book, what was the status of … my desk light? the ink flowing from my pen? the tactile sense of paper-edge on fingertip? Certainly these experiences were there, they were had, but were they experienced as had by *me*? To be experienced as had by *me* would have involved some disruption, some intervening problem – the light blown out with a pop, the pen running dry, a nasty paper cut. Then I find myself having to do something – I must devise a plan of action – albeit a very simple plan of replacing the bulb or pen, or treating the wound.

The brilliance in the postulate of immediate empiricism – applied to noncognitive primary experience – is that it undercuts – yea, dare I say "solves?" – the dualism of subject versus object, and with it the problem of how "mind" gets to "reality." The experience of the unanalyzed totality is fully real – as are the subsequent discriminations of "myself" and "the desk light" made for specific purposes within inquiry (LW 16: 288–289). Of course, cognitively I not only recognize "myself" and "the desk light," but quite rightly say, "both were there, as separate existences, all along." This subsequent judgment is more informative about the circumstances of my original experience – it cites relations between cognitively discrete objects. But this judgment does not make the experience of the unanalyzed totality any less real. Nor, unlike the account book example, does it falsify this experience – not because having is an ultimate truth, but because truth and falsity fall within the realm of cognitive judgment, not noncognitive having.[13]

Still, have we not taken leave of Kansas, if not our senses? Is Dewey really saying that self and object magically spring to existence with the onset of a problem, then meld back into an amorphous glob when the job is done? Emphatically, and thankfully, no. Dewey isn't talking about the described contents of the physical world. Instead, he means a way or a method: a how, not a what; a relational reality, not a concrete existence. Directed inquiry is how we get to objective knowledge; it is, to risk allegiance with Kant, a condition of objectivity in general, and a self is a discriminated means to this end.

Kenneth Chandler once predicted that primary experience would one day be recognized as the "alpha and omega of all theorizing" (Chandler 1977: 51), and we should note that Dewey's postulate predates Heidegger's tools "ready to hand" by two decades. But even among pragmatists Dewey's so-called "struggle with the ineffable" has produced lingering aftershocks. Today we find a new flirtation with direct realism, albeit a realism of having or "practical engagement" rather than the traditional claim to somehow knowing an object "just as it is" independent of the act of knowing. The question then turns on whether such having is a brute encounter with "independent reality" or the settled product of previously reflective consequences. Hilary Putnam leans toward the former; Dewey insists it's the latter: what is "immediately present," he reminds us, "has meaning because of prior mediation which it would not otherwise have had" (MW 13: 52). Naïve realism? Indeed – but a "cultured naiveté," not the "transparent perception" of direct realism.

Milestone 4: the fact–value relation

In Dewey's day, as in our own, the legitimacy of values was much in doubt. Following the model of the physical sciences, the positivists recognized only two forms of meaningful statements: analytic assertions most useful in mathematics and logic, and synthetic statements about empirical facts subject to strict verification. Since values are not analytic claims, they must be reducible to facts. Thus they are either expressions of emotional preference, descriptions of behavior, or exhortations (prescriptions) to act in certain ways.

Far from a mere theoretical quibble among philosophers, Dewey saw the rehabilitation of value as the most urgent and "deepest problem of modern life" (LW 4: 204). The traditional defenders of values – clergy, teachers, parents – found themselves embattled, their authority increasingly diminished. As Nietzsche had predicted, science had become the new God, or at least God's shadow. But in the growing gap between social and scientific institutions Dewey perceived an impending catastrophe – a technological whirligig unchecked by moral constraint.

Dewey initiates his assessment of value in partial agreement with contemporary positivists. Basic impulses, when obstructed, give rise to acknowledged needs and desires whose fulfillment are, indeed, factual likings or preferences. Dewey calls these "prizings," the de facto possession of such preferences. But this is only the beginning, not the end, of a constructive analysis of conduct. Only a child, or perhaps a positivist, would regard "I want it, I want it," as an ultimate expression of worth (LW 4: 208). But even though such preferences are not values, they are value candidates – potential values whose worth is estimable through a process Dewey calls appraisal or valuation (LW 13: 216–218).

Valuation is the intelligent evaluation of a factual preference within the context of a total situation, whose aim is to convert a value candidate, as a hypothesis, into a genuine value. It confirms that what is liked is truly likeable, what is preferred is preferable, what is desired is desirable (LW 4: 207). It projects, and empirically verifies, the long-term consequences of acting upon preferences both in terms of the welfare of the individual and that of the greater community. In the spirit of Aristotle, valuation seeks to establish not just a list of prescribed values, but a genuine disposition to evaluate desires in terms of long-range goods (LW 2: 88, 4: 204).

That fact is intrinsically connected to value, indeed a literal means to value, erases both the fact–value dualism and the attempted reduction of values to facts. Socially, it helps close the perilous rift between moral and scientific institutions. Moral institutions must become more "scientific" – flexible, anti-dogmatic, willing to sacrifice old traditions for beneficial new approaches. Scientific institutions must become more moral – facts have consequences that affect ourselves, our communities, our world. The union of facts and values subsumes technological growth to a view that is far-reaching and ecologically responsible.

Milestone 5: transaction

Though hardly uncontestable, the pragmatic milestones of inquiry, truth, primary experience, and fact–value seem significant enough to have won a permanent place in American thought. Why, then, did pragmatism fall so far so fast? We've heard the familiar excuses: the "linguistic turn," the lure of formalism, the fashionability of existentialism and deconstruction. In honesty, however, Dewey was also hounded by an internal demon. A massed chorus of critics – Russell, Santayana, Cohen, Lovejoy, Rogers, Murphy, Kahn – stridently insisted Dewey had left the basic relationship between experience and existence unresolved, and thus had not settled the debate as to whether he was "really" an idealist or a realist. In 1961 Richard Bernstein labeled this the "deep crack" in Dewey's metaphysics – a divide between a "phenomenological" strain where experience looms large, and a "metaphysical" strain affirming an impersonal universe largely oblivious to human affairs (Bernstein 1961: 5–6). To Sholom Kahn's pointed question: "what is the relationship between experience and existence in Dewey's naturalistic universe?"[14] Bernstein replies that Dewey had no consistent answer:

> Dewey claimed so much for experience that it became increasingly difficult to see what was not experience, what, if anything, controlled and limited experience. It looked as if Dewey, who had so many harsh words to say about idealism, was serving it up in another form.
>
> (Bernstein 1961: 9).

Dewey's conciliatory attempts only made things worse, apparently conceding with one hand what he withdrew with the other. He would affirm, for example, a level of meaningless natural events, but then note that "meaningless event" itself inscribes "a character or nature and hence a meaning" (LW 4: 84, 88). By 1930 Dewey seemed ready to throw in the towel, confessing to being "chameleon-like, yielding one after another to many diverse and even incompatible influences" (LW 5: 9).

But Dewey was not at his best when looking back or defending his tracks. He was an avatar of advance, and he blazed his last frontier, transaction, in the span of a fifteen-year collaboration with ex-newspaperman Arthur F. Bentley. The problem, Bentley surmised, is that Dewey "hedged" when attacked as an idealist for placing existence within experience. But "hedging has brought no fruit," advised Bentley. "I am against any more of it (Ratner and Altman 1964: 205)."

Dewey and Bentley realized that "no more hedging" commits the "extreme heresy" of undercutting the very notion of a primary relation between experience and nature, organism and environment, knower and known. What he once called "experience," Dewey explains, was an attempt to cover "the whole range of transactions within which the needed distinctions have to be made" (Ratner and Altman 1964: 331, emphasis added). Freed from all "mentalistic" overtones, "experience" is recast as "cosmos of fact" (LW 16: 263).[15] A cosmos of fact encompasses "nature as known and in the process of being known – ourselves and our knowings included. ... We do not introduce, either by hypothesis or by dogma, knowers and knowns as prerequisite to fact" (LW 16: 58).

This is not the "chameleon" Dewey of 1930, but a Dewey who, thanks to his working partnership with Bentley, could report a decade later to "have moved fairly steadily in one direction" since his turn to pragmatism (LW 14: 6).[16] The last milestone Dewey erects along this highway is "transaction," "the right to see together" what other philosophies have separated into knower and known, subject and object, mind and world (LW 16: 67). In *Knowing and the Known*, Dewey and Bentley flex remarkably agile muscles in extricating transaction from outmoded self-actional and interactional views. Self-action, the notion of inherent powers and essences, has long departed every discipline save psychology and philosophy. Interaction, where "thing is balanced against thing in causal interaction" (LW 16: 101), has given way to a transactional "field" in physics, yet still dominates most areas of inquiry. Indeed, even Dewey's earlier claims must be rephrased: though "you always 'see' existence transactionally," advises Bentley, you do not always "get it safely so used" (Ratner and Altman 1964: 483). Dewey agrees, and regrets having stressed "organism–environment interaction." "Interaction is dangerous," he admits, "as it is easily taken to imply two or more prior existences" (Ratner and Altman 1964: 105, see also 206). Bentley suggests that just as pragmatism's knowing-through-doing eclipsed the "spectator theory" of knowledge, its "further development" yields the transactional, where the "range of existence" is coextensive with the "range of namings" (Ratner and Altman 1964: 288).

I think Bentley has missed something here. Ontology must be broader than "namings" alone. As we've seen, the objectives (objects) of cognitive namings return to and enrich primary experience, and in thus undercutting the subject–object dichotomy having justly deserved its ontological priority. Nor should we underestimate the shock or interruption – Peirce's "existence" or "secondness" – that marks the transition from having to problem solving activity.

As coextensive not just with namings, but with the entire functional circle of inquiry, the "extreme heresy" of the transactional view of existence is manifest. The "deep crack" between existence and experience is closed by an unflinching assault upon what Dewey and Bentley call the "putative" existential – the "in-itself reality" that would creep in – where? – through the "shock of secondness" perhaps?, and thus exert its surreptitious control upon the known (Ratner and Altman 1964: 184). Dewey once said there is an indefinite "beyond of" experience, but nothing intrinsically beyond the reach of experience: the more we know the more we realize there is to know, including countless things we may never actually know.[17] But these are not "putative existentials," philosophical denizens that lurk "outside of experience." That model, the "philosophical fallacy" of converting attained objectives of inquiry into autonomous antecedent existences, is replaced by the integral reciprocality of the knower–known relation. For a "real world" that has no knower to know it, has, so far as human inquiry is concerned … just about the same "reality" that has the palace that in Xanadu Kubla Kahn decreed. … A knower without anything to know has perhaps even less claim to reality than that.

(LW 16: 129)

Milestones: new and renewed

Twenty years of close hard work have vindicated Rorty's claim that pragmatism stood at the end of the road traveled by logical empiricism. We are not just recovering the past in restoring these milestones, but literally renewing philosophy. It is both natural, and welcome, that pragmatists disagree about the route. But if I might play a pragmatic Horace Greeley for a moment, here are three promising passes through the Great Divide: first, get right with primary experience – it dissolves the intractable problems of philosophy and calibrates the compass of pragmatism. Second, with Dewey and Bentley, complete the evolutionary leap from interaction to transaction: had I a nickel for each time I've encountered "transaction" used synonymously with "interaction," or read "transaction between" or "with," I'd treat these deserving authors to copies of *Knowing and the Known*. Finally, promote the good work of doing pragmatism. Perhaps someday I'll outgrow my fixation with methodological pulchritude, and thus join those forging vital connections between pragmatism and issues in technology, education, social relations, biology, the environment, and economics. My friends at the American Institute of Economic Research exemplify the transactional approach in concrete action – widely cast nets of data and conjecture are subsequently pared to sound advice in critical discourse, then tested and revised in the wake of unfolding events.

Given the quality of the original craftsmanship and the extent of the damage and neglect, I'm not surprised we're still just excavating the milestones of pragmatism. Hopefully, however, the day is not too distant when we'll not only finish resurfacing the road between these markers, but break ground beyond the current barrier. Recently new surveying instruments have been spotted at the end of the road. I, for one, can't wait to peek through these telescopes.

Notes

1 Hereafter references to the *Collected Papers* (CP) will appear by volume and paragraph number in the text.
2 If you are uncertain about this, ask yourself the following question: were you consciously regarding the rectangular shape of this page qua "rectangular" a moment ago?
3 In the cognitive grasp of, e.g., a red thing, the quality assumes an indexical function that either points to some facet of a problem or its solution – for example, a red light on a panel flashing a warning. Even seemingly trivial occasions of simply "noticing" or "apprehending" indicate some (perhaps slight) maladjustment or

anomaly in the "fit" between a habituated background and a present context of circumstances; in such circumstances, of course, neither sustained cognitive attention nor remedial action is usually necessary.

4 We might wonder how such cases of feeling, of sheer particularity (or "firstness") are nonetheless "shot through" with generality (or "thirdness"). In insisting that "feelings are all alike and require no explanation, since they contain only what is universal," (5.290) Peirce integrates what traditional empiricism regards as polar opposites. For a more detailed account of the crucial notion of "thirdness into firstness," see Ryan 2003: 321–350.

5 Also see 5.266, where Peirce claims "we can admit no statement concerning what passes within us except as a hypothesis necessary to explain what takes place in what we commonly call the external world" – "commonly called" the external world inasmuch as "everything which is present to us is a phenomenal manifestation of ourselves" interpreting reality.

6 Hereafter the *Early Works (EW), Middle Works (MW)* and *Later Works (LW)* of the Boydston edition will be abbreviated and cited in the text. For Dewey's "classic" formulation of the pattern of inquiry, see "Logic: The Theory of Inquiry", LW 12: 105–122.

7 In "The Problem of Truth," for example, Dewey challenges the correspondence to "how things really are" with the rejoinder: "how are they really?"; in other words, how is it that "the mind can get out of itself to know a world beyond, or how the world out there can creep into 'consciousness?' " See *MW* 6: 34, 18.

8 This implies, of course, that some currently accepted truths will undoubtedly be declared "absolutely false" by future generations. Because we currently lack such a perspective, however, we have no warrant to question the veracity of presently accepted truths (see James 2001: 133).

9 James's unhelpful reply is that reality is just more "conceptual or perceptual experiences with which a given present experience may find itself in point of fact mixed up" (James 1984: 267–268, 279–280).

10 Dewey consistently uses "thing" in the broadest possible sense. As late as *Knowing and the Known* (1948) "thing" means "anything named," whose merit is in its "very looseness of application." (*LW* 16: 271)

11 For Dewey, "appearance" versus "reality" is but one more pernicious dualism. His alternative is to regard all experiences as equally real, but note that the consequences of acting upon such suppositions determine their worth. Thus, for example, I would suffer direct negative consequences should I attempt to spend the presumed bonus. Dewey claims truth and falsity are disclosed as a result of acting upon assumptions, not by an antecedent distinction of "appearance" versus "reality" (see *MW* 3: 163).

12 We should note that no waking experience is wholly cognitive or noncognitive. As Dewey explains in "Experience and Nature", consciousness is a foreground – sometimes a steady light, more often a mere "flicker," set against a "fringe" of peripheral attention and a "background" that denotes "mind" – the noncognitive "whole system of meanings as they are embodied in organic life" (*LW* 1: 229, see also 233–237).

13 That the experience itself is "just what it is" does not mean that a reflective account of such an experience (such as the one offered here) is similarly inviolable. As such, my claim that the postulate of immediate empiricism is a "starting point" for philosophical inquiry is not based on an appeal to something "incorrigible," "self-evident," or "necessarily true." Because it is a reflective account of a nonreflective state, the acceptability of the postulate itself depends upon its ability to explain the phenomenon of experience.

14 Sholom Kahn, "Experience and Existence in Dewey's Naturalistic Metaphysics." Reprinted in *LW* 16: 456.

15　It is interesting that in this period Dewey also redefined "experience" as "culture," (see *LW* 1: 361) which realistic interpreters have taken as a hopeful step toward recasting experience/culture within nature. But "culture" enjoys the same definition as the original "experience" and the contemporaneous "cosmos of fact": "the vast range of things experienced in an indefinite variety of ways," including scientific facts (1: 362). Clearly, then, Dewey has expanded the meaning of "culture" rather than constricted that of "experience."

16　Quite late in life, Dewey puts his entire relationship with Bentley into perspective for Grace De Laguna: "Largely due to him, I've finally got the nerve inside of me to do what I should have done years ago" (*LW* 16: 489).

17　As Dewey later writes to Bentley, the world as cosmos of fact functionally names "all that is, or can be inquired into ..., knowledge of it when reached is not knowledge of something else, but is increased knowledge and improved or extended [by] what is known at any previous date and place" (Ratner and Altman 1964: 216).

Bibliography

Bernstein R. (1961) "John Dewey's metaphysics of experience," *Journal of Philosophy*, 58: 5–13.

Chandler, K. (1977) "Dewey's phenomenology of knowledge," *Philosophy Today*, 21: 43–55.

Dewey, J. (1976) *The Middle Works: 1899–1924*, ed. Jo Ann Boydston, vol. 2: 1902–1903, Carbondale and Edwardsville: Southern Illinois University Press.

—— (1981) *The Later Works: 1925–1953*, ed. Jo Ann Boydston, Carbondale and Edwardsville: Southern Illinois University Press.

James, W. (1981) *Pragmatism* (ed. B. Kuklick), Indianapolis: Hackett Publishing Co.

—— (1984) "Humanism and truth," reprinted in B.W. Wilshire (ed.) *William James, The Essential Writings*, Albany: State University of New York Press.

—— (2001) "The Pragmatic notion of truth," reprinted in L.J. Pojman (ed.) *Classics in Philosophy, Volume III: The Twentieth-Century*, New York and Oxford: Oxford University Press.

Peirce, C.S. (1868) "Some consequences of four incapacities", *The Journal of Speculative Philosophy*, 2: 155; reprinted in C. Hartshorne and P. Weiss (eds) *Collected Papers of Charles Sanders Peirce*, Cambridge: The Belknap Press of Harvard University Press, 1931–1935, vol. V, §313.

Quine, W.V. (1953) "Two Dogmas of Empiricism," in *From a Logical Point of View*, Cambridge: Harvard University Press.

—— (1981) *Theories and Things*, Cambridge: Harvard University Press.

Ratner, S. and Altman, J. (eds) (1964) *John Dewey and Arthur F. Bentley: A Philosophical Correspondence: 1932–1951*, New Brunswick: Rutgers University Press.

Ryan, F.X. (2003) "Scholastic realism as contextual pragmatism," in J.R. Shook (ed.) *Pragmatic Naturalism and Realism*, Amherst, NY: Prometheus Books.

2 John Dewey and the pragmatic century

Richard J. Bernstein

There are many ways of telling the story of the vicissitudes of pragmatism in the United States. I want to begin with a brief account of what may be considered the standard story, because I intend to challenge it. The standard story goes something like this: pragmatism was popularized primarily through the lecturing and writing of William James at the beginning of the twentieth century. We can even date the explicit introduction of the term "pragmatism" by James in his 1898 address delivered at the University of California, Berkeley: "Philosophical Conceptions and Practical Results." In that address, James generously acknowledged his debt to Peirce, "one of the most original contemporary thinkers" and refers to "the principle of practicalism – or pragmatism as he called it when I first heard him enunciate it at Cambridge in the early, '70s. James."

James initially gives a rather metaphorical description of "Peirce's principle": "the soul and meaning of thought, he says, can never be made to direct itself towards anything but the production of belief, belief being the demicadence which closes a musical phrase in the symphony of our intellectual life." Furthermore, "beliefs, in short are really rules of action; and the whole function of thinking is but one step in the production of habits of action" (James 1967: 348). In 1898, Peirce was barely known as a philosopher (except to a small group of admirers such as James). As James' popular version of pragmatism spread, Peirce was so appalled and outraged that he renamed his own doctrine of meaning " 'pragmaticism,' which is ugly enough to be safe from kidnappers" (Peirce 1931–1935: 5.414). There is the famous quip that pragmatism is the movement that was founded on James' misunderstanding of Peirce.

In the 1890s, the young John Dewey was in active communication with James, and was working on his Studies in Logical Theory. Earlier, when Dewey was a graduate student at Johns Hopkins, he had studied logic with Peirce. At the time, Dewey was much more influenced by the Hegelian, G.S. Morris. Dewey originally characterized his own philosophic orientation as "instrumentalism" or "experimentalism," but as Dewey's reputation and renown grew during the early decades of the twentieth century, "pragmatism" is the name that took hold as the name identifying the style of thinking exemplified by Peirce, James, Dewey, and Dewey's close associate at Michigan and Chicago, George Herbert Mead. With the passing decades of the twentieth century, pragmatism began to fade from the philosophic scene. During the 1950s, a quiet but dramatic revolution was taking place in American philosophy departments. Positivism, logical empiricism, the philosophy of science, and the new logic inspired by the legacy of Frege and Russell captured the imagination of young philosophers. These currents, together with the varieties of conceptual analysis and ordinary language philosophy practiced at Oxford, reshaped most of the prestigious philosophy departments in the United States. It is to this period that we can date the infamous Anglo-American analytic/continental split in philosophy with its ugly ideological resonances.

Furthermore, the philosophies of Peirce, James, Dewey, and Mead were almost completely marginalized. To the extent that their contribution was even acknowledged (and this was rare indeed), a patronizing attitude was prevalent. The pragmatists might have had their hearts in the right place, but they lacked the rigor, clarity and argumentative finesse required for "serious" philosophizing. Furthermore, the original pragmatic thinkers had not made the "linguistic turn." The sad truth is that, from that time until today, the overwhelming majority of PhD's in America have never really studied – and probably have never even read – the classic American pragmatic thinkers. By the 1950s and 1960s interest in pragmatism reached an absolute nadir. The pragmatic movement seemed quite moribund – except for a few courageous persons who tried to keep the tradition alive.

It was primarily due to the provocative intervention of a single individual that the interest in pragmatism began to change. Richard Rorty, a philosopher from Princeton who had made his reputation as a bright analytic philosopher, began to question the foundations and pretensions of analytic philosophy. He shocked many of his colleagues when he declared that Wittgenstein, Heidegger, and Dewey were the three most important philosophers of the twentieth century. Analytic philosophers might concur with his judgment about Wittgenstein, just as continental philosophers might endorse Rorty's judgment about the significance of Heidegger. But virtually no one (except a few dedicated followers) would have even dared to claim that Dewey was one of the most important philosophers of the twentieth century. Since the publication of *Philosophy and the Mirror of Nature* in 1979, Rorty has identified himself (and his controversial views) with the pragmatic tradition. There is now a virtual industry of scholarship showing how Rorty misunderstands, distorts, and betrays the pragmatic tradition. Nevertheless many thinkers (who probably have never even read a word of the classic pragmatic thinkers) have come to identify pragmatism or neopragmatism with Rorty's idiosyncratic philosophic outlook. Although Rorty still remains a key player, today there are many thinkers from diverse disciplines – religious thinkers, political and social theorists, literary critics and lawyers who think of themselves as pragmatists. It is becoming increasingly common to speak about the "resurgence" or the "revival" of pragmatism.

Now, although some variation of the above account is generally accepted as an accurate narrative, it is – so I want to argue – superficial and misleading. It misses what is most important, vital, and philosophically significant about the pragmatic tradition. If I may steal a phrase from Heidegger, it is correct (richtig), it just isn't true (wahr). The thesis I intend to sketch is that the classic American pragmatists introduced a number of interrelated themes that have been explored and elaborated in novel ways throughout the twentieth century. Sometimes this has happened because of direct influence, but more frequently we can detect independent lines of inquiry that exemplify a pragmatic way of thinking, and reinforce pragmatic insights in novel ways. I fully endorse Hilary Putnam's claim that pragmatism is a "way of thinking" that involves "a certain group of theses, theses which can and indeed were argued very differently by different philosophers with different concerns." He summarizes some of these key theses as

> (1) antiskepticism; pragmatists hold that doubt requires justification just as much as belief …; (2) fallibilism: pragmatists hold that there is never a metaphysical guarantee to be had that such and such a belief will never need revision (that one can be fallibilistic and antiskeptical is perhaps the unique insight of American pragmatism); (3) the thesis that there is no fundamental dichotomy between "facts" and "values"; and the thesis that, in a certain sense, practice is primary in philosophy.
>
> (Putnam 1994: 152)

I think this list might be supplemented with a few other closely related theses, although I do agree that the classical pragmatists would endorse Putnam's claims – even if they interpret them in divergent ways. It is only now at the end of the twentieth century that we can appreciate how much of the best philosophic thinking of our century can be understood as variations on pragmatic themes. This is my warrant for calling the twentieth century the pragmatic century. Let me be explicit and blunt. I not only think that pragmatic themes have had a strong influence on the range of cultural and social disciplines, but that we can detect the centrality of pragmatic concerns in continental philosophy. I sometimes like to speculate that future historians of philosophy will look back on the so-called analytic-continental split as a minor ideological ripple that holds little philosophic interest when compared with the common pragmatic themes of our time. But that is part of a larger narrative. Today, I want to limit myself to beginning my counter narrative to the standard one.

Let me start by going back to what Rorty himself identified as the central chapter of *Philosophy and the Mirror of Nature*, the chapter entitled "Privileged Representations." This is the chapter in which Rorty deals with Quine's critique of the language–fact distinction, and Sellars' critique of the "myth of the given." The reason why Quine and Sellars are so important for Rorty's overall argument is that he claims that modern epistemology and analytic philosophy rest on the "Kantian picture of concepts and intuitions getting together to produce knowledge." For Rorty this turns out to be the equivalent to

> saying that if we do not have the distinction between what is "given" and what is "added by the mind" or between the contingent (because influenced by what is given) and the "necessary" (because entirely "within" the mind and under its control), then we will not know what would count as a "rational reconstruction" of our knowledge.
>
> (Rorty 1979: 169)

According to Rorty, Quine renounces the language–fact distinction (along with the conceptual–empirical and analytic–synthetic distinctions) while Sellars questions the given–postulated distinction. But without at least one of these Kantian distinctions "analytic philosophy could not be written." It is by pressing (some would say distorting) Sellars' and Quine's critiques that Rorty arrives at his own distinctive version of pragmatism – one that abandons both of these Kantian distinctions and repudiates epistemological foundationalism.

I want to return to the article of Sellars that so influenced Rorty: "Empiricism and the Philosophy of Mind." It is here that we find Sellars' famous critique of the myth of the given. What is so striking about this 1956 monograph is the way in which it reads like a commentary on a famous series of papers that Peirce published in 1868–1869 ("Questions Concerning Certain Faculties Claimed for Man," "Some Consequences of Four Incapacities," and "Grounds of Validity of the Laws of Logic: Further Consequences of Four Incapacities" (Peirce 1931–1935: vol. 5)). I think that the real beginning of American pragmatism dates from the publication of these articles rather than the more popular articles that Peirce published a decade later. The language and concerns of Peirce and Sellars reflect the differences of their philosophic contexts, but there is a remarkable similarity between the arguments advanced. Sellars, like Peirce, claims that the epistemological doctrine of immediacy or direct intuitive knowledge lies at the heart of much of modern (Cartesian) epistemology. I do not think that there is an argument presented by Sellars that is not anticipated by Peirce. Both reject the very idea of epistemological foundationalism, both reject the idea of "self-authenticating epistemic episodes." Both claim that we can give an adequate account of the intentionality of mental states and our privileged first person access of our own thoughts without any appeal to immediate introspection. There are also profound similarities in the alternative conception of language, knowledge, and inquiry that they develop. Sellars' linguistic turn is anticipated in Peirce's more comprehensive theory of signs. Both agree there is an irreducible intersubjectivity – or more accurately, sociality – involved in the acquisition of conceptual capacities and the mastery of language. Sellars is clearly drawing on the insights of the later Wittgenstein, especially in his characterization of what he calls the "logical space of reasons," which are embedded in normative discursive practices. But in so doing, he is calling attention to the pragmatic motifs that recur throughout the *Investigations*. Both Peirce and Sellars argue that an adequate account of concepts and language presupposes the acknowledgment of norms implicit in practices. Sellars gives an eloquent expression of Peirce's antiskeptical fallibilism when he asserts that "empirical knowledge, like its sophisticated extension science, is rational, not because it has a foundation, but because it is a self-correcting enterprise which can put any claim into jeopardy, though not all at once." This is a principle that all pragmatists would endorse.

It is not surprising that there should be so much agreement between Peirce and Sellars. I do not think that this is to be explained by direct influence (although Sellars is clearly familiar with Peirce's work). Both of these philosophers came to their insights by way of a pragmatic reading of Kant. By this I mean that they both appreciate Kant's insights about the character of experience and empirical knowledge insofar as it already involves conceptual capacities, but nevertheless voice a certain caution about Kant's transcendental machinery. Both are arguing for a more pragmatically open appropriation of Kant – one that also reflects some of the Hegelian criticisms of Kant – and is compatible with the fallibilistic spirit of modern science and the social character of linguistic practices.

Here, Rorty (who I am not going to discuss today) has done a serious injustice to a robust understanding of the pragmatic tradition. Kant is Rorty's bête noire. Rorty frequently writes as if Kant is the source of everything that is misguided about modern epistemology, and that his "rigid" dichotomies are the basis for much of analytic philosophy. Indeed, in "Pragmatism, Relativism and Irrationality," Rorty's presidential address to the APA, he virtually excludes Peirce from the pragmatic tradition because he remained the most Kantian of thinkers. Rorty dismisses Peirce when he remarks that Peirce's contribution to pragmatism was merely to have given it a name, and to have stimulated James.

But we do a great injustice to the pragmatic legacy if we downplay the Kantian (and the Kantian–Hegelian) influence. It was reflection on Kant's categories that led Peirce to his pragmatism. Even Dewey wrote his dissertation on Kant, although he was reading Kant through the spectacles of neo-Hegelianism. Furthermore, we can see both the continuity and the fertility of this legacy by turning to the recent work of Hilary Putnam, John McDowell, and Robert Brandom. Each of these thinkers illustrates my general thesis that the resurgence and development of pragmatism is not exclusively due to the influence of the classic American pragmatic thinkers, but is the result of the dialectical thinking through of issues which are at the cutting edge of philosophic discussion. From the time that I first started working on the classic pragmatic thinkers in the 1950s I have always felt that, contrary to the myth of the pragmatists being passé, they were actually ahead of their times. And it is only now at the end of the twentieth century that philosophy is catching up. This is what Hegel might have called the "cunning of Reason" (*List der Vernunft*).

Let me begin to show this by turning to the philosophic development of Hilary Putnam. Putnam received his graduate education at UCLA at a time when Hans Reichenbach taught there. The young Putnam was the very exemplar of the "tough-minded" analytic philosopher who possessed a sophisticated understanding of mathematical logic and recent developments in quantum physics. His early heroes were Reichenbach, Carnap, and Quine. He thought of himself as a philosopher of science working in the tradition of logical empiricism, even though he was critical of many aspects of this tradition. He moved in that inner circle of analytic philosophy – UCLA, Princeton, MIT, Harvard. Many of the "positions" that he advocated, including "functionalism," "scientific realism," and "metaphysical realism" became the "hot" topics debated by analytic philosophers. This is not the occasion to follow in detail his philosophic development, but what is most manifest and exciting is the explicit pragmatic turn that his thinking has taken – especially during the past two decades. Putnam is extremely knowledgeable about Peirce, James, and Dewey, and has made significant contributions to the scholarship of these three pragmatists. In the best tradition of pragmatism, he has not been hesitant to press his criticisms of them. Putnam's distinctive philosophic orientation integrates Peircian, Jamesian, and Deweyan motifs. Temperamentally, and by training, Putnam is closest to Peirce who also came to philosophy trained as a logician and a natural scientist. But Putnam argues that Peirce's "convergence thesis" – the thesis that at the ideal "end of inquiry" there will be a convergence of our knowledge of reality – is mistaken. It is a thesis that is no longer compatible, so Putnam argues, with a more contemporary scientific outlook. Indeed, Putnam argues that the convergence thesis betrays the deeper pragmatic insight about irreducible pluralism. One might think that James' graceful metaphorical style of philoso-phizing might offend the "tough-minded" proclivities of Putnam – as Peirce had been offended. But Putnam is a great fan of James and thinks that philosophers have failed to appreciate James' argumentative finesse. What Putnam finds especially attractive about James is his "direct realism" – what James called "natural realism" – the thesis that we have direct perceptual contact with a real world of common sense objects. Like James, Putnam rejects the idea that we are in immediate contact with our own "sense data," which are then taken to "represent" external real objects. But Putnam's interest in this aspect of James' thought goes beyond a technical interest in a proper theory of perception. Rather, it is an essential aspect of his pragmatic vision of "realism with a human face." Like all the classical pragmatists, Putnam takes the contributions of natural science seriously. But he rejects all versions of reductionism, eliminativism, and what John McDowell has called "bald naturalism." The everyday world in which we live our lives – our *Lebenswelt* (the word that Putnam uses) – is just as real as what we learn from science. In this respect, Putnam now rejects all forms of scientific realism and metaphysical realism that do not do justice to the human position – the human world of everyday objects and persons that we confront as agents. Like

Dewey, Putnam thinks that a good deal of traditional philosophy has been motivated by a "quest for certainty" – or to use his own term – a "craving for absolutes." Putnam even thinks that, despite claims to the contrary, much of analytic philosophy has been motivated by the same craving – a craving that needs to be exposed and exorcized. Putnam also appropriates Dewey's multi-faceted critique of the fact–value dichotomy. Without values there would not even be a world of facts. Furthermore, values are objective and can be rationally debated.

Objectivity – including moral objectivity – is not incompatible with moral disagreement. In Dewey, Putnam finds a political ideal that he himself endorses – the ideal of human flourishing in a democratic community. He defends and endorses the Deweyan thesis that "democracy is not just a form of social life among other workable forms of social life; it is the precondition for the full application of intelligence to the solution of social problems" (Putnam 1991: 217).

Hilary Putnam started his philosophic career as the very model of a "tough-minded" analytic philosopher. Some of his "hard core" analytic colleagues think that he has gone soft and fuzzy. But let me remind you that when William James sought to characterize the distinctive pragmatic esprit, he employed what I think is still one of the best philosophical distinctions ever invented – the distinction between the "tough-minded" and the "tender-minded." And he argued that pragmatism combines the virtues of both of these attitudes, but avoids their excesses. This is Putnam's way of making a similar point:

> I would agree with Myles Burnyeat who once said that philosophy needs vision and argument. Burnyeat's point was that there is something disappointing about a philosophic work that contains arguments, however good, which are not inspired by some genuine vision, and something disappointing about a philosophic work that contains a vision, however inspiring, which is unsupported by arguments. ... I take [vision] to mean vision as to how to live our lives, and how to order our societies. Philosophers have a double task: to integrate our various views of our world and ourselves ... and to help us find a meaningful orientation.
>
> (Putnam, in Pyle 1999: 44).

Putnam cites Myles Burnyeat, but he might have cited William James, who said much the same thing in *A Pluralistic Universe*. As Putnam has shown, James had a healthy respect for arguments – and invented a number of ingenious arguments, but it was James who said "a man's vision is the great fact about him." He also declared: "where there is no vision the people perish." When philosophers have a genuine vision, then one can read them over and over again "and each time bring away a fresh sense of reality" (James 1977: 14, 77). The philosophic humane pragmatic vision that has emerged in Putnam's development during the past half century beautifully illustrates the way in which the pragmatic themes that we find in Peirce, James and Dewey have been appropriated, criticized, refined and transformed in novel ways.

In turning to John McDowell and Robert Brandom (sometimes referred to as "the Pittsburgh neo-Hegelians,") or as I prefer to say, "the Pittsburgh pragmatic neo-Hegelians," I must be much more brief. Not because their thought deserves less attention, but because of the constraints of space. McDowell's philosophic credentials as an analytic philosopher are impeccable. Trained at Oxford, he has been philosophically engaged with the works of the most important analytic philosophers of our time. He has a strong background in classical philosophy and has written illuminating articles on both Aristotle and Wittgenstein. There is little evidence that McDowell has more than a superficial acquaintance with the classical American pragmatists. But in his thought-provoking book, *Mind and World*, and his recent John Dewey lectures delivered at Columbia University indicate, he shows how deeply he has been influenced by the pragmatic reading of Kant, Hegel, Wittgenstein and Sellars. One can begin to wonder what is happening to the analytic–continental split when a philosopher with McDowell's background and analytic credentials announces in his preface "that one way that I would like to conceive this work is a prolegomenon to a reading of [Hegel's] Phenomenology" (McDowell 1996: ix). The pragmatic themes that I find in McDowell's work are due to his own appropriation of Sellars' critique of the myth of the given. McDowell is a good example of a philosopher who, following his own independent line of inquiry, has evolved an orientation that echoes (and reinforces) pragmatic themes. In *Mind and World*, McDowell seeks to show that there is a way of dismounting from the oscillating seesaw between the myth of the given and coherentism. This was also the basic project of the pragmatists, and is especially evident in Peirce's work. Peirce declared that

> the truth is that pragmaticism is closely allied to Hegelian absolute idealism, from which, however it is sundered by its vigorous denial that the third category ... suffices to make the world, or is even so much as self-sufficient. Had Hegel, instead of regarding the first two stages with his smile of contempt, held on to them as independent or distinct elements of the triune Reality, pragmaticists might have looked upon him as the great vindicator of their truth.
>
> (Peirce 1931–1935: 5.436)

Peirce is here referring to his elaboration of the categories of Firstness, Secondness, and Thirdness. The point that Peirce emphasizes in distinguishing Secondness and Thirdness anticipates that crucial point that McDowell makes when he insists that there are rational constraints on our thinking that come "from outside thinking, but not outside what is thinkable" (McDowell 1996: 28). Peirce would certainly agree with McDowell when he goes on to say: "When we trace justifications back, the last thing we come to is still a thinkable content; not something more ultimate than that, a bare pointing to a bit of the Given" (McDowell 1996: 27). Like Peirce, and the other pragmatists, McDowell doesn't think that spontaneity – the source of our conceptual capacities – can be naturalized, if "naturalized" is taken to mean reduced to bald or disenchanted nature. Like the pragmatists, McDowell seeks to develop a richer and thicker conception of nature in which we can find a place for the second nature characteristic of human beings. McDowell appeals to Aristotle to justify his conception of nature. But he might just as well have appealed to John Dewey who argued for the continuity of human experience and nature. It is not surprising that Putnam, who is much more explicitly indebted to, and influenced by, the classical pragmatists, should find so much in common with McDowell. He thoroughly endorses McDowell's claim that what Kant calls spontaneity and what Sellars calls the "logical space of reasons" is essentially and intrinsically normative. Furthermore, Putnam praises McDowell for independently showing the truth of direct realism – the type of realism that Putnam finds in James. McDowell tells us "there is no ontological gap between the sort of thing one can mean, or generally the sort of thing one can think, and the sort of thing that can be the case. When one thinks truly, what one thinks is what is the case" (McDowell 1996: 28).

Here I think it is appropriate to acknowledge the relevance of the later Wittgenstein for a pragmatic way of thinking. I certainly do not want to suggest that Wittgenstein was a pragmatist. If there ever was a thinker who wasn't any kind of "ist" it must surely be Wittgenstein. But I don't think that it is an accident that many contemporary thinkers who identify themselves with the pragmatic tradition are drawn to the later Wittgenstein. Earlier, I cited Putnam's remark that for the pragmatic way of thinking "practice is primary." Wittgenstein, more than any other twentieth century philosopher has brought out the nuances and the variety of human practices – especially linguistic practices. I can indicate the significance of Wittgenstein's reflections concerning practices by turning to the work of McDowell's colleague, Robert Brandom.

At a time when the journal article has become the favored form of philosophic writing, Brandom has written a closely argued book of 741 pages. To round out this phase of my discussion of pragmatic themes, I want to focus on a single, but central theme of Making It Explicit. The title of his opening chapter is "Toward a Normative Pragmatics" (Brandom 1994). In this chapter Brandom tells a story whose main characters are Kant, Frege, and Wittgenstein. Brandom argues that it was Kant who initially brought out the normative character of concepts and rationality. Building on Kant, Frege makes a sharp distinction between justification – where assessments of correctness of propositional contents are involved and causation. It is Wittgenstein, however, who shows that norms are embedded in practices. They are implicit in social practices. Indeed the explicit formulation of rules itself presupposes norms implicit in practices. We make these norms explicit. Brandom's larger aim is to clarify what it means to be a rational creature. In a manner that echoes the classical pragmatists, Brandom tells us: "Being rational is being bound or constrained by norms." Brandom too is influenced by the Kantian pragmatic themes in Sellars and Wittgenstein. Wittgenstein shows us why, unless we acknowledge the role of implicit norms in linguistic practices, we cannot adequately account for our capacity to follow rules. In a recent paper "Pragmatics and Pragmatism," Brandom succinctly states his primary thesis: "Some norms are implicit in practices – in what practioners actually do – rather than explicit in the form of rules that say what the norm is" (Brandom, forthcoming). The power of Brandom's book is that he seeks to justify this general thesis in exhaustive detail – to show precisely how norms are implicit in social practices, and how they shape what we say and do. He seeks to show how his normative pragmatics leads to, and is compatible with, an inferential semantics. Although Brandom does not include Peirce in his narrative of the emergence of normative pragmatics, I would argue that Peirce not only plays a vital role in this narrative, but anticipates the main thesis about norms being implicit in practices. We even find the anticipations of an inferential semantics in Peirce in his reflections on "leading principles."

I feel that, as I am coming to the end of this chapter, I am only just beginning. This is only a fragment of what I want to say. That is why I hope to write a book in which I can fully develop and justify the thesis that the twentieth century is the pragmatic century. So, by way of conclusion, let me outline what I would like to show in detail. Today, I have focused on a series of thinkers, Sellars, Putnam, McDowell and Brandom, who are frequently identified as "analytic philosophers" in order to show how they exemplify a pragmatic way of thinking. In my larger project, I also want to focus on some developments in contemporary continental philosophy – especially German philosophy – where we find a similar dialectic at work. I am referring to the work of Karl-Otto Apel, who is largely responsible for the introduction of Peirce into Germany, and who has developed his own version of a transcendental pragmatics. Jürgen Habermas has appropriated Peircian, Meadean, and Deweyan themes into his own creative synthesis. His understanding of deliberative democracy bears a strong affinity with John Dewey's ideal of democracy. There is also Hans Joas, the German sociologist who has not only written one of the best studies of George Herbert Mead, but who has one of the finest understandings of the creative fertility of the American pragmatic tradition. The renewed interest in Mead, and especially the way in which Mead's understanding of the genesis of intersubjectivity and sociality has influenced contemporary discussions of communicative rationality and intersubjectivity deserves special attention. I would also like to explore some of the striking affinities (as well as some of the differences) between the pragmatists' rejection of all forms of epistemological and metaphysical foundationalism and the critique of the "metaphysics of presence" in Derrida. There are even important similarities in the way in which Derrida has recently discussed what he calls the "democracy to come" and Dewey's ideal of creative democracy.

But it is not just that the pragmatic way of thinking cuts across the so-called analytic–continental divide, it is also essential to see how the pragmatic esprit and the pragmatic way of thinking have influenced other domains of culture, including our understanding of religious experience. The classic American thinkers were never antireligious. Indeed, they sought to recover the integrity of religious experience from dogmatism and fundamentalism. Let me remind you that in the very essay in which James introduced pragmatism, he sought to apply the pragmatic approach to help to clarify and test the religious hypothesis by showing its relevance to our concrete practical experience. And finally, I would also like to discuss the work of those thinkers who, at a time when the classic pragmatic thinkers were neglected and marginalized, sought to keep this tradition alive – philosophers such as John E. Smith, John McDermott, and Max Fisch.

In 1954, when I was a graduate student at Yale, I had the good fortune to participate in a reading group of Dewey's Experience and Nature that was organized by a young assistant professor, John E. Smith. It was that experience that opened my eyes to the vitality and fertility of the pragmatic tradition, and inspired me to write my dissertation, "John Dewey's Metaphysics of Experience." Yale was also the institution where Paul Weiss, the co-editor of the Collected Papers of Peirce taught. And many graduate students had a serious interest in Peirce. Mt first book, a collection of articles by Dewey entitled "John Dewey: On Experience, Nature and Freedom" was published in 1960. In the Introduction to that book I wrote:

> There is a felt need for reunion in philosophy, for new perspective and vision that is informed by the lessons of careful analysis. In this search for new directions, there is much to be learned from John Dewey, who sought to unite speculative imagination with a sensitive concern for the variety of human experience and the specific "problems of men."

During the decade of the 1950s, when pragmatism had reached its low point among professional philosophers, I felt that the day would come when philosophy would catch up with the pragmatists. Now, almost half a century later I feel vindicated. Pragmatism originally burst upon the philosophic scene at the turn of the twentieth century. As we look forward to fresh philosophic developments in the current century, we are witnessing an exciting and lively flourishing of pragmatic themes.

References

Brandom, R. (1994) *Making It Explicit*, Cambridge, MA: Harvard University Press.
—— (forthcoming) "Pragmatics and Pragmatism."
James, W. (1967) "Philosophical conceptions and practical results," in J. McDermott (ed.) *The Writings of William James*, Chicago: University of Chicago Press.
—— (1977) *A Pluralistic Universe*, Cambridge, MA: Harvard University Press.
McDowell, J. (1996) *Mind and World*, Cambridge, MA: Harvard University Press.

Peirce, C.S. (1931–1935) *Collected Papers of Charles Sanders Peirce*, ed. Charles Hartshorne and Paul Weiss, Cambridge, MA: Harvard University Press.

Putnam, H. (1991) "A reconsideration of Deweyean democracy," in M. Brint and W. Weaver (eds) *Pragmatism in Law and Society*, Boulder, CO: Westview Press.

—— (1994) *Words and Life*, ed. James Conant, Cambridge, MA: Harvard University Press.

Pyle, A. (ed.) (1999) *Key Philosophers in Conversation: The Cogito Interviews*, New York: Routledge.

Rorty, R. (1979) *Philosophy and the Mirror of Nature*, Princeton: Princeton University Press.

Putnam and Rorty on their pragmatist heritage

Re-reading James and Dewey

Sami Pihlström

Introduction: Putnam and Rorty – rival neopragmatists

As soon as Richard Rorty started to wave the flag of pragmatism in the late 1970s and early 1980s and saw his own work as a continuation of William James's and John Dewey's philosophy (as well as Kierkegaard's, Heidegger's, and Wittgenstein's, not to mention that of his more recent heroes like Sellars, Quine, and especially Davidson), he began to receive critical comments from dedicated James and Dewey scholars who wanted to show that he had got these classics of pragmatism completely wrong. Admittedly, Rorty writes about the pragmatist tradition "in the way original thinkers write about the views of their predecessors" (Brodsky 1982: 321). Even so, his critics may be right in claiming that his readings of the classical pragmatists are problematic at best and seriously distorting at worst.

Arguably, neither James nor Dewey abandoned the traditional picture of philosophy as a systematic and normative enterprise as totally as Rorty wishes to see them having done. For example, James, despite his life-long effort to reconstruct philosophy in a pragmatic spirit avoiding ossified scholastic systems and technicalities, respected genuine philosophical – even metaphysical – problems related to knowledge, truth, and even "being." He would, presumably, never have regarded Rortyan "edifying" or "conversational" philosophy as a significant cultural achievement.[1] Nor would Dewey have rejected all normative questions concerning the relevance and legitimation of various social practices in the way Rorty seems to do; thus, Dewey would hardly have followed Rorty into his postphilosophical utopia in which there is nothing constructive for philosophy to do any longer as an inquiry into the nature and conditions of human experience.[2] It has also been suggested that in a truly Deweyan pragmatism science should be taken much more seriously than Rorty (for whom science is just one manner of talking among others, not distinguished or privileged in any way) is willing to take it (see Nielsen 1991: ch. 8). Rorty has faced these criticisms by admitting that, instead of offering a historically faithful picture of the classical pragmatists, he attempts to construct a hypothetical Dewey – a kind of Rortyan Dewey, a picture of the philosopher that Dewey should have been, by Rorty's lights, in order to have proceeded all the way to the Rortyan position which was open to him but which he didn't quite reach.[3] The real historical Dewey was in several ways entangled with traditional metaphysical questions (e.g., questions concerning the notion of experience); the thoroughly pragmatist, naturalist, historicist, postmetaphysical and antiepistemological Dewey that Rorty postulates is not. Rorty thus wishes to "adapt pragmatism to a changed intellectual environment by emphasizing the differences rather than the similarities with the philosophical tradition" (Rorty 1985: 47).

Rorty's Deweyan or quasi-Deweyan position is by now so well known that it would be futile even to summarize it here. I shall, instead, focus on his debates with Hilary Putnam, another famous neopragmatist. Incidentally, it may be interesting to note that Putnam's readings of James and Dewey have not been met with as strong critiques as Rorty's, even though Putnam's way of situating his own work within the pragmatist tradition is no less explicitly pronounced than Rorty's.[4] Of course, Putnam's pragmatist position has been extensively attacked on other grounds, and these two philosophers have attacked each other's views perhaps more profoundly than anyone else.[5] Thus, it is an interesting task to illuminate their similarities and differences by examining how they employ the pragmatist tradition in trying to explain, both to themselves and to each other, what those similarities and differences are.

For Putnam, James is clearly the central classical pragmatist (although Dewey is highly important for him, too, and Peirce should not be forgotten, either),[6] whereas for Rorty Dewey is number one and Peirce is relatively unimportant, simply the one who gave the tradition its name and made the further developments of the tradition possible by stimulating James.[7] Now, one may of course have a purely historical interest in the development of the pragmatist tradition, but one may also try to assess James's and Dewey's relevance in the contemporary philosophical scene by taking a look at how major neopragmatists such as Putnam and Rorty employ their ideas. One of the problems with which I am preoccupied in this chapter is this: as both Putnam and Rorty reject Peircean pragmati(ci)sm (which, they seem to agree, amounts to metaphysical realism in the end)[8] and turn to James and Dewey instead, we may ask whether there is any stable middle position (such as, possibly, Putnam's own) between metaphysical realism and radical relativism or antirealism, or whether we just have to choose between the (allegedly) Peircean strongly realistic pragmatism that embraces correspondence truth and the idea that there is a way the world is independent of our perspectives on it, on the one hand, and Rortyan ethnocentrist conversationalism which carries no such implications but must give up objectivity and rationality altogether, on the other (as a number of recent critics and interpreters of pragmatism have argued). In short, we should try to answer the following question: are there just "two pragmatisms" (i.e., Peirce's original pragmatism and its distortions, beginning with James and ending with Rorty and his followers),[9] or is the pragmatist tradition more complex and heterogeneous?

Several critics of Putnam have argued that his pragmatism, unless supported by a more realistic account of the world with which we (in a Deweyan sense) are said to interact, and of the causal regularities enabling such interaction or transaction, becomes in the end practically indistinguishable from the Rortyan antirealistic type of pragmatism that Putnam (rightly) opposes.[10] Yet, I am tempted to defend the idea that there are many different kinds of pragmatism, without any single defining, essentialistic feature combining them all, and that Putnam's conceptions of truth, reality, rationality, etc., constitute one of the most promising candidates for a moderate, reasonably realistic but not dangerously metaphysical "middle path" position – even though his views do have their severe problems, too. I am, in any event, willing to classify both Putnam and Rorty as pragmatists, although some scholars may adopt a more exclusive policy in their use of the word "pragmatism." While a full defense of a Putnamean variety of neopragmatism is obviously impossible here, I shall try to say something about the resources Putnam might have in distinguishing his views from Rorty's. I am not saying that Putnam himself, or anyone else, has up to now coherently employed those resources.

I shall proceed by studying Putnam's and Rorty's use of James's and Dewey's pragmatism – not in any comprehensive manner (since there would be too much material to be discussed in a single chapter), but by focusing on how they refer to James and Dewey when they are criticizing each other's views. I hope this relatively selective method of reading the two great neopragmatists' readings of their two great predecessors teaches us something about their relation to each other with regard to their attitudes to the classics they find themselves to be following.[11]

My findings will perhaps be somewhat surprising. It turns out that Putnam does not usually refer to Rorty when he discusses classical pragmatism; his references to Rorty are almost exclusively situated within his discussions of recent postanalytical philosophy of mind and language and the realism issue (e.g., the work of philosophers such as Quine and Davidson).[12] And the same seems to be true vice versa: there is little in Rorty's critique of Putnam that directly questions his (Putnam's) readings of the classical pragmatists. This may be considered odd, given the importance of pragmatism for both thinkers, and given the importance (again, for both of them) of their mutual attacks on each other. Still, the few references that the two philosophers make to each other's views in relation to their discussions of the pragmatist tradition offer us a handy selection of material that can, hopefully, lead us to the heart of their disputes.

Truth and the problem of normativity

One of the central questions that has continuously been taken up in the Rorty vs. Putnam debate concerns the notion of truth. While both thinkers give up the kind of correspondence theory of truth associated with metaphysical realism, they disagree deeply over the correct interpretation of the notion – or, more precisely, over the question of whether truth should be philosophically interpreted at all. Since his rejection of the correspondence theory in *Reason, Truth and History* (1981: especially ch. 3), Putnam has argued that while we cannot make sense of a nonepistemic, metaphysically privileged correspondence relation between linguistic expressions and the items of the nonlinguistic world that those expressions are supposed to be about, we nonetheless need standards and ideals of truth and rationality that transcend the limits of our own cultural or historical context(s) – even though, of course, this practical need is something that belongs to our life within this particular context or practice in which we live.

What this ineliminability of truth (and related notions, such as rationality and epistemic justification) means is that we cannot give up our commitment to normative standards of rational acceptability, standards that extend transculturally and transhistorically over particular forms of life and periods of time, even if they are never universally given for all forms of life and all periods of time. Putnam says he finds "shocking" the idea that "truth" is "an empty notion" – an idea shared by thinkers as diverse as Rorty and Quine (Putnam 1994: 331). Instead, we need a "substantial" conception of truth as a normative property of our statements and world-views. Even though we cannot even meaningfully speak about truth in a metaphysically heavy correspondence sense, there is no reason to deny the prephilosophical, commonsensical notion of truth as representation of nonlinguistic (though not "ready-made" or precategorized) reality:

> I agree with Rorty that we have no access to "unconceptualized reality."
> … But it doesn't follow that language and thought do not describe something outside themselves, even if that something can only be described by describing it (that is by employing language and thought); and, as Rorty ought to have seen, the belief that they do plays an essential role within language and thought themselves and, more importantly, within our lives.
> (Putnam 1994: 297.)

A model of the kind of non-metaphysically realist concept of truth that we need is, according to Putnam, given to us in James's reflections on the "pragmatist theory of truth" (which, admittedly, is problematic in many ways).[13] James can teach us that truth is inextricably entangled with our practices of rational assessment of beliefs in the various problematic situations we encounter in our lives. Truth may outrun what is "warrantedly assertible" in any given situation, but it is not to be separated from the practice (or, to prefer a Peircean term, habit)[14] of evaluation in which the notion of warrant plays a crucial role.[15] This insight has sometimes led Putnam to characterize truth as an idealization of such epistemic, normative notions as warrant, assertibility, acceptability, or justification, notions that we habitually employ in our practices of assessing the legitimacy of our statements about the world. Although Putnam has now given up the particular formulations of the epistemic "idealization" theory of truth he defended in the early 1980s, it is not entirely clear what kind of picture he has adopted instead. I believe it is still accurate to speak about Putnam as favoring an epistemic and normative construal of truth – or at least as opposing the metaphysical realist's nonepistemic one.[16]

In any case, we should be careful in our claim that correspondence truth is not to be had. The fact that metaphysical realism is unintelligible or incoherent (and not simply false) deprives, Putnam argues, intelligibility from the Rortyan view that we "cannot" describe the world as it is in itself, independently of our cultural or ethnocentric perspectives. There is, in a sense, nothing (not any queer "something") that we cannot do from our perspectival and practice-laden points of view; we do not "fail" in any meaningful sense by failing to describe the world as it is in itself, independently of our practices.[17] Rorty, in Putnam's view, has in effect embraced a "linguistic idealism" through his critique of metaphysical realism and correspondence truth.[18] The implicit suggestion seems to be that no such idealism is necessary if one follows the teachings of the classical pragmatists. Contra Rorty's and his followers' reconstrual of pragmatism as a form of "antirealism," the classical pragmatists can be interpreted in an essentially realistic fashion (Putnam 1994: 37ff).

It is here that we ought to turn to Rorty's and Putnam's more specific references to James and Dewey in the context of their assessments of each other's views. As has already been mentioned, such references are relatively few; yet, they sometimes occur in most illuminating contexts.

Occasionally, the two neopragmatists warmly express sympathy to each other's ways of employing the classics of their tradition. For example, when discussing James's theory of perception, Putnam notes that "Rorty is right" to the extent that "James is not going to give an answer to skepticism that is deeper than the perspective of shared human experience" (Putnam 1990: 247).[19] Accordingly, it is obvious that neither James, Dewey, Putnam nor Rorty attempts to offer a "traditional" answer to the skeptic in epistemological affairs; in pragmatism, skeptical doubts about the existence of the external world are simply non-starters, because all human (trans)actions, which pragmatists take for granted, always already take place in the world, a habitually interpreted practice-laden world whose existence must be assumed for any specific doubts to arise. Skepticism cannot be demonstratively refuted, of course, but it is pragmatically idle in our inquiries and, indeed, in practices of any kind (except perhaps the practice of philosophical sophistry, which is itself pragmatically idle). As Peirce already insisted in his well-known anti-Cartesian papers,[20] we should not pretend to doubt as philosophers what we do not doubt as human beings. And as Dewey reminded us, it is only the "quest for certainty," for absolute knowledge about "Being," a quest typical of our epistemological tradition, as well as the resulting "depreciation of practice," that makes skepticism seem philosophically interesting (see Dewey 1960 [1929]).

So, antiskepticism is a common point of departure which unites Putnam's and Rorty's and virtually all other pragmatists' views. Another point of agreement is related to the pragmatist theory of truth, as opposed to the traditional correspondence theory: Putnam classifies Rorty as one of the philosophers who (rightly)

> take very seriously just the point that James insisted on, that our grasp of the notion of truth must not be represented as simply a mystery mental act by which we relate ourselves to a relation called "correspondence" totally independent of the practices by which we decide what is and is not true.
>
> (Putnam 1995: 11)

Similarly, Rorty (1998b) says approvingly that "Dewey and Putnam agree that the aim of inquiry is what Putnam calls 'human flourishing' " (instead of truth as accurate representation of a mind- and inquiry-independent world). Both thus seem to respect each other's admiration of the Jamesian and Deweyan idea that truth and value are fundamentally tied to each other in human affairs – that truth is, in a Jamesian slogan, a species of the good, closely related to our normative, value-laden practices of evaluation (and thus to the epistemic vocabulary in which our notions of warrant, assertibility, etc., are operative). Rorty also explicitly gives credit to Putnam's (and Davidson's) Jamesian refusal to assume any contrast between the world itself and the world as known by us (Rorty 1991: 12).[21] It is, as is well known, this contrast between reality and appearance that makes the problem of skepticism seem inevitable; it is by giving up the metaphysically realistic background assumption of skeptical puzzles that Putnam and Rorty join the classical pragmatists' antiskeptical camp. Both seem to subscribe to the Deweyan maxim that the reality we seek to know through our inquiries, "reality-to-be-known," is a reality possessing a "practical character," a "reality-of-use-and-in-use" (Dewey 1931: 41). Any humanly possible truth about such a reality is something much weaker and more dynamic than the correspondence theorist's stable, nonepistemic truth.

Nevertheless, while Rorty and Putnam agree, among other things, on the artificiality of Cartesian skeptical scenarios, and agree that the classical pragmatists considered skepticism equally artificial, Putnam (unlike Rorty) finds a philosophical use both for what James called "truth" and for what Dewey called "warranted assertibility." Thus, he does not seem to share Rorty's purely negative conviction that epistemology is over as soon as we have realized that the problem of skepticism and the foundationalist project that grounds it (a project itself based on the notion of truth as correspondence or accurate representation of a mind- and language-independent reality) should be given up. Putnam's theses concerning warrant – which he develops with an explicit (albeit unspecified) reference to Dewey – are genuinely epistemological theses, very far from the Rortyan "now philosophy is over" tone of voice. Against Rorty, Putnam argues

1 that "[i]n ordinary circumstances, there is usually a fact of the matter as to whether the statements people make are warranted or not";

2 that whether or not a statement is warranted "is independent of whether the majority of one's cultural peers would say it is warranted or unwarranted"; even though

3 our norms governing warrant are "historical products" and evolve in time;

4 that those norms and standards "always reflect our interests and values" in the sense that our "picture of intellectual flourishing is part of, and only makes sense as part of, our picture of human flourishing in general"; and

5 that any norm or standard is capable of reform, for there are "better and worse" norms and standards.

(Putnam 1990: 21)[22]

He adds that these principles have, since Peirce's earliest writings, been endorsed by pragmatists (Putnam 1990: 22). Thus, he at least implicitly challenges Rorty's – who, Putnam claims, rejects most of these principles (especially 1, 2, and 5), or is bound to reject them because of his other pronouncements – entitlement to the term "pragmatism." In Rorty's so-called pragmatism, there is room only for a historicist conception of norms as evolving products rooted in particular circumstances or vocabularies; there is no room for the idea that norms, either epistemic or ethical ones, could be genuinely better or worse, or capable of reform (or deterioration) as distinguished from mere change.

Another interesting passage is the following, in which Putnam attacks Rorty's entitlement to Deweyanism in particular:

[Rorty] does retain strong traces of his physicalist past. Certain passages in his Philosophy and the Mirror of Nature seem to assume that mind talk can just be replaced by brain talk when science becomes sufficiently advanced. And in spite of Rorty's frequently expressed admiration for Dewey, he seems not to have noticed Dewey's wonderful remark that the old soul/body or mind/body dualism still survives in a scientific age as a dualism between "the brain and the rest of the body."[23] In any case, Rorty's response[24] to the statement I just made (the statement that our mental abilities cannot be described in language which does not avail itself of intentional and normative notions) is to say that while it is true, understood simply as a claim about the non-reducibility of one "vocabulary" to another, nothing about reality follows from non-reducibility – an odd move indeed for some one who claims the very vocabulary/reality distinction has to be given up.

(Putnam 1994: 305–306)[25]

Thus, Putnam appears to be accusing Rorty of a highly unpragmatic reliance on dichotomies that pragmatists ought to give up, e.g., the one between our "vocabularies" and the reality those vocabularies are about. Elsewhere, Putnam tells us that, even though Rorty likes to call himself a pragmatist, "his habit of dichotomizing human thought into speech within 'criterion governed language games' and speech 'outside' language games" is unpragmatistic (and equally un-Wittgensteinian, Rorty's adherence to Wittgenstein notwithstanding) (Putnam 1995: 64).[26]

The final charge comes, toward the end of Putnam's Pragmatism (1995: 74), in the claim that Rorty, because of his view (in which he again claims to follow James and Dewey) that our talk of "truth" is "merely emotive," a "compliment" we sometimes pay to some beliefs or statements, assumes that "we are connected to the world 'causally but not semantically' " and is thus "in the grip of the picture that the Eliminative Materialism is true of the Noumenal World." No such picture, according to Putnam, was assumed in classical pragmatism. In Peirce, James and Dewey, there is equally little room for "postmodern antimetaphysics" as there is for traditional metaphysics (or its more recent scientistic and physicalistic variants).[27] What is needed, instead of fruitless metaphysical speculations and their equally fruitless negations, is democratic, self-correcting inquiry into how we humans conceptualize the experiential world we live in, an on-going inquiry that critically revises its own standards of rationality. If Putnam's account of pragmatism and his reading of Rorty are on the right track, the possibility of such normative revision which is so central in the pragmatist tradition is given up in Rorty's neopragmatism.

Rorty, of course, refuses to take seriously such appeals to normativity and rationality. Reminding Putnam and others that there is no reason to give up "normative stories" about truth in the disquotationalist and behaviorist setting which he favors (and reads James and Dewey as favoring), he remarks:

> Putnam, I think, still takes a "philosophical account of X" to be a synoptic vision which will somehow synthesize every other possible view, will somehow bring the outside and the inside points of view together.
>
> It seems to me precisely the virtue of James and of Dewey to insist that we cannot have such a synoptic vision – that we cannot back up our norms by "grounding" them in a metaphysical or scientific account of the world.
>
> (Rorty 1991: 141)

Rorty sees Putnam (and Davidson) as continuing Dewey's effort to liberate us from "representationalism," and thus judges "Putnam's continuing insistence on using the term 'representation' " as a mistake that in a way betrays his otherwise healthy Deweyan pragmatism (Rorty 1998a: 48). There are, Rorty tells us, two principal strategies that the pragmatist can adopt with respect to the notion of truth. Faced with the choice between these strategies, Putnam and Rorty stand in opposite camps:

Some [pragmatists], like Peirce, James and Putnam, have said that we can retain an absolute sense of "true" by identifying it with "justification in the ideal situation" – the situation which Peirce called "the end of inquiry." Others, like Dewey (and, I have argued, Davidson), have suggested that there is little to be said about truth, and that philosophers should explicitly and self-consciously confine themselves to justification, to what Dewey called "warranted assertibility."

I prefer the latter strategy. Despite the efforts of Putnam and Habermas to clarify the notion of "ideal epistemic situation," that notion seems to me no more useful than that of "correspondence to reality," or any of the other notions which philosophers have used to provide an interesting gloss on the word "true."

(Rorty 1999: 32)

On the basis of the material I have cited, we seem to arrive at the following general picture. Putnam revives the classical pragmatists', as well as Wittgenstein's, emphasis on irreducible normativity, on our need to critically investigate the practices, vocabularies, or language-games we find ourselves engaging in (a need inherent in those practices themselves), without forgetting the importance of a moderately realistically interpreted concept of truth, which cannot be entirely disentangled from the idea of representation – even though the metaphysical realist's conception of representation is to be given up.[28] Rorty, however, simply emphasizes our Darwinistically describable need to "cope" with our natural, causally explainable environment by inventing new ways of speaking and by freeing ourselves from unnecessary philosophical problems concerning our relation to that environment, such as the problem of realism vs. idealism, the mind–body problem, or the problem of how to respond to the skeptic. In a way, from Putnam's point of view, Rorty, by recognizing only practice-internal, "conversational" criteria for the justification of statements and beliefs and by restricting the audience of justification to a culturally and historically particularized ethnos, just gives up the task of normative reflection which has always been part and parcel of the pragmatist tradition and which Dewey, Rorty's greatest hero, also respected, despite his historicism and thoroughgoing naturalism. From Rorty's point of view, on the other hand, Putnam, like so many other critics, seeks some mysterious, practice-transcendent connection between human beings and the world. His appeal to normativity, to an irreducibly normative and "substantial" notion of truth, and to other such notions, is pragmatically empty, Rorty seems to be saying – as empty as the skeptical challenges which traditional philosophers' substantial (correspondence) notions of truth were meant to meet in the first place.

The argumentation between the two neopragmatists appears to end up with a blind alley precisely at this point. Rorty refuses to find anything meaningful in Putnam's defense of truth, rationality, and normativity. He says he stays with James and Dewey (or the hypothetical James and Dewey he has invented for his own pragmatic purposes); Putnam denies this and claims that his, not Rorty's, picture of pragmatism is more faithful to the classics.

The following diagnosis of this dialectical situation suggests itself. Putnam never forgets, while Rorty deliberately does, the Kantian heritage of pragmatism.[29] James was, arguably, in certain ways more Kantian than Dewey, but one can perhaps find something like transcendental arguments even in Dewey: the Deweyan naturalist, defining philosophy as "the critical method for developing methods of criticism" (Dewey 1989 [1925]: 354) engages in a critical self-reflection on the experimental methods of inquiry she or he already employs, in a manner resembling the Kantian self-reflection of human reason.[30] In developing his pragmatism, Putnam has taken seriously – much more seriously than Dewey – what we may describe as the crucial Kantian issue of modern philosophy, namely the problem of realism vs. idealism. Indeed, his "internal" or "pragmatic" realism can quite naturally be construed as a modern variant of Kantian empirical realism. Rorty, on the contrary, has tried to trivialize this issue by his (in Putnam's view) one-sided reading of pragmatism and of figures like Wittgenstein and Heidegger. On the other hand, we should not fail to note that there are some Kantian assumptions at work even in Rorty's own project: the rejection of the picture of human knowledge (or the mind, or language) as a "mirror of nature" is, of course, a most Kantian theme, since Kant surely abandoned what Dewey called the "spectator theory of knowledge," insisting that the world about which we can know something is in a sense our own construction, a product of human practices rather than anything ready-made and practice-independent that we could merely spectate. Indeed, Kant can and perhaps should be treated as an ally rather than an enemy in Deweyan pragmatism.[31]

Presumably, both James and Putnam, and perhaps even Dewey, can be interpreted not only as empirical realists in a Kantian sense, but also as transcendental idealists (contra their own statements that they do not subscribe to this Kantian doctrine). A full defense of this suggestion is beyond the scope of this chapter. Let me just re-emphasize the fact that all three of them, James, Dewey and Putnam, in their various ways treat the empirical world as a construction based on human activities, on our practices of inquiry, of moral deliberation, of social engagement, etc., through which we shape the world into a meaningful pattern enabling future transactions and interactions. On the most general level, our human practice or form of life itself, the very engagement we cannot disentangle ourselves from, is analogous to the Kantian transcendental subject of knowledge, although the notion of "practice" is a notion of something that is more dynamic and processual, historically contingent and developing than Kant's "I." The practices we engage in can be regarded as the necessary presuppositions of the possibility of cognition, and (in a Kantian style) of the objects of cognition. None of these pragmatists claims that we humans create the world *ex nihilo*; nor did Kant himself claim that. What they claim is something much more modest, i.e., that the world as a world for us inevitably reflects our practice-embedded interests, habits, and purposes. Even Rorty, despite his avowed antitranscendentalism, seems to ascribe a quasi-transcendental role to human "vocabularies" as constitutive of reality.[32] Natural objects such as atoms appear to be, for him, socio-linguistic, conversational constructions, and there is no discourse-independent truth "out there" about them – unless we read some of his statements as expressions of austere scientistic physicalism, according to which the world just is fundamentally physical and all nonphysical ways of talking about it are simply that, ways of talking, moves within fictitious language-games.

The kind of transcendental idealism we may see Putnam and even Rorty as holding is, it should be clear by now, a view close to James's, for whom pragmatism (or humanism, as he also called it, following F.C.S. Schiller) was, in addition to being a theory of meaning and truth, a form of ontological constructivism.[33] It is also close to Dewey's position, since Dewey held that knowing alters its object, thus embracing a form of idealism (cf. Shook 2000). Putnam and Rorty may have offered some good reasons for not classifying their views as idealistic, but certainly neither of them has taken us beyond the realism vs. idealism dispute. Putnam has not claimed to take us beyond it, but Rorty has. In this sense, Putnam's self-understanding of his place in the pragmatist tradition is more nuanced than Rorty's. It is even more nuanced than James's or Dewey's, but this results from the fact that Putnam has had the privilege of standing on these giants' shoulders. He can see their pragmatism, as well as his own, as a continuation of Kant's transcendental philosophy more clearly than they themselves did. Even so, Putnam himself may need help from other pragmatists in situating his thought more firmly in the Kantian tradition than he has been able to do so far.

Different naturalisms, different (post)modernisms

Another, perhaps related difference between Rorty and most other major figures of the pragmatist tradition, including Putnam, is this. Pragmatists are usually naturalists but highly antireductionist ones: Dewey's, and perhaps also Putnam's, basic position might plausibly be described as a form of emergent naturalism; even James can be seen as a nonreductive naturalist insisting on "novelty" in experience and on the need to take seriously whatever belongs to our "human nature."[34] Rorty, however, appears to be a nonreductionist only nominally. His bottom-line metaphysics, as some of Putnam's above-cited criticisms lucidly bring to the fore, is an eliminative physicalism which reduces the experienceable world to a blind causal interaction of microphysically describable particles – while reminding us, astonishingly, that scientific descriptions are not privileged in relation to other descriptions of the world, since all descriptions are, in the end, just manners of speaking. It is, in fact, not easy to decide whether Rorty is ultimately a physicalist, or an idealist for whom the physical world is a human construction based on our ways of speaking. Both interpretations can be supported by textual evidence. Both of these extremes may, however, be resisted in a more sophisticated – Jamesian and/or Deweyan – pragmatism which maintains an empirical realism and naturalism within a more comprehensive, meta-level transcendental commitment to the constitutive role of human practices in the determination of the reality our vocabularies are about.[35]

Several pragmatists' somewhat anti-Kantian prejudices notwithstanding, we may be able to find, from James, Dewey, and Putnam, a fruitful route to what might be called naturalistic (though not reductively naturalized) Kantianism, in which universal, immutable transcendental conditions for the possibility of cognitive experience are replaced by dynamically evolving conditions rooted in our historically situated habitual actions and practices themselves.[36] Rorty, however, tries to block this particular road of inquiry, offering us a flat and reductive picture of the historical contingency of any concept or vocabulary we may find useful to work on. There is no consistent way to read Rorty as a transcendental pragmatist. In Putnam's case such a reading may be possible, although I am sure that Putnam himself would resist this terminology as fiercely as James and Dewey would have done.

As related to the tension between transcendentalism and naturalism, a short note on two different construals of pragmatist moral philosophy is in order. Putnam's pragmatic (Jamesian and Deweyan) moral realism[37] can, it seems to me, be reinterpreted as a "Wittgensteinian" insistence on the personal seriousness of moral problems, to be compared to the work of such important ethical thinkers as Iris Murdoch, Peter Winch, and Raimond Gaita, whereas Rorty's Deweyan conception of ethics and politics is, unsurprisingly, much more naturalized and down-to-earth. Morality, for Rorty, is simply a matter of redescribing human life through the invention of new interesting vocabularies, each of which is as contingent, ethnocentric and "optional" as any other. There is nothing over and above the ways in which we happen to talk to each other about human life and its problems. If we all suddenly started to think and talk like the Nazis did, then, presumably, Rorty would have to say that there is nothing wrong in Nazism. Even though it is natural for a pragmatist to emphasize our linguistic practices in relation to metaethics, such a conclusion need not be drawn on any pragmatist principles. The idea that we cannot simply make bad things good by beginning to speak about them differently is, again, built into the very practices we engage in.

One may ask, then, whether there is any room left in Rorty's position for the kind of moral seriousness we find in James, Putnam, and the "Wittgensteinians."[38] Rorty may, in brief, be unable to account for the fact that we do – within our practice of moral deliberation – experience moral problems as genuine problems, not to be settled by mere redescription or insightful new uses of words. He has, then, nothing to say about our genuine need to do the right thing in our lives, or about the practices based upon this need. His notoriously sharp dichotomy between private and public concerns is unable to deal with the requirement that ethical issues, if genuine, are typically both personal and "absolute," i.e., about what is the right thing to do for some particular person (me) in a given situation. Rorty's ideals of liberty and the toleration of private conceptions of the good life are not connected with any normative account of the criteria by means of which conflicting ideals or principles of toleration can be assessed. Moreover, Putnam – like Kant and the classical pragmatists (James in particular) – seems to let our ethical needs influence our metaphysical commitments. For instance, the fact that we cannot, from the point of view of our actual life practices, simply view ethics as a "second-grade" subject in comparison to natural science leads us to give up scientistic conceptions of the physical world as "absolute." Ethical statements are not merely emotive or factually erroneous, as reductive naturalists have claimed; in our ethical deliberations we are genuinely in touch with the world, though not with the metaphysical realists' world *an sich* but rather with a world that we, through our practices, help to constitute. From Rorty's perspective, such a step from ethics to metaphysics should presumably just be deconstructed.

Rorty's failure to recognize moral seriousness and the fact that ethical orientation may not be metaphysically neutral is, apparently, parallel to his previously discussed inability to account for the pursuit of objective truth, or for our need to commit ourselves to a normative framework in which such a pursuit is seen as valuable. An analogue can also be found in the philosophy of religion: Putnam is prepared to reflect on religious themes in a Wittgensteinian manner, attacking scientistic critiques of religion which misconstrue people's expressions of religious faith as hypotheses requiring "evidence," but Rorty's attitude to religion is almost completely hostile.[39] Here, again, Putnam seems to be more faithful to the spirit of classical pragmatism than Rorty, who resembles a scientistic physicalist more than a pragmatist when it comes to religious issues. For Rorty, the human importance of religion seems to have disappeared through the secularization of culture – that is, through the invention of new, irreligious, ways of speaking about the world and about human life. But one of the defining characteristics of contemporary debates in the philosophy of religion seems to be the persistence of religious problems, or ways of experiencing life problematic in a religious sense, even within a secularized culture. Putnam, unlike Rorty, has been able to contribute to this debate – although, again, his contributions must be considered far from unproblematic.[40]

This brings me to my final point. I want to conclude with a few words on Putnam's and Rorty's (and, by extension, James's and Dewey's) relation to modernism and postmodernism. We should not use these notions as easy catch-words; rather, we should try to specify what we mean by them in relevant contexts. Yet, we may end up with a summarizing interpretation of Putnam's and Rorty's versions of neopragmatism that can be expressed by means of this vocabulary. The preceding discussion of their differences regarding truth, naturalism and normativity is a necessary background for such an interpretation.[41]

Rorty's neopragmatism is, we might say, self-consciously postmodernistic. Putnam, while also being a "postanalytic" philosopher, is much closer to the modernist heritage of the Enlightenment, which the pragmatist tradition largely shares, too. As a modernist thinker, Putnam, as we have seen, is not willing to give up the normative task of the rational legitimation of human practices (including the practices of scientific inquiry and of moral deliberation) in the way Rorty is, even though Putnam, too, insists that such a legitimation cannot be handed to us from any imaginary point of view lying outside those practices themselves. Thus, Putnam still has some use for the modernist notions of reason, truth, reality, and self, not only in science but especially in relation to ethical and religious concerns,[42] while for Rorty these notions have become almost entirely obsolete – perhaps primarily because Rorty is more prepared than Putnam to follow, with the Dewey he constructs, the naturalistic spirit of pragmatism. Putnam, unlike Rorty, is precisely for this reason able to resist certain excessive tendencies of modernism, such as scientistic naturalism. We might perhaps say that Putnam's pragmatism, like Dewey's, is a form of "post-postmodernism" rather than simply modernism or postmodernism.[43]

Even so, Putnam's own position is constantly in danger of sliding into Rortyan antirepresentationalism because of his increasing insistence on our ordinary, "naive" and "prephilosophical" notions of perception, conception, truth, reality, and representation. Putnam, it seems to me, can hardly save philosophical innocence by this allegedly Wittgensteinian maneuver.[44] Nor can he step outside powerful philosophical critique by subscribing to religious mysticism at the end of the day, as he appears to do in some of his recent writings on the philosophy of religion. Our pragmatic commitments to a quite ordinary world, to quite ordinary truth about it, to what James and Putnam call "natural realism," or to the view that there is still something to be found in the premodern notion of God that is significant for us moderns or postmoderns, are philosophical commitments – not simply commitments that are made by the man on the street entirely independently of philosophical traditions and worries. This has, I am convinced, never really been denied in the pragmatist movement, even though the pragmatists have always, with good reason, resisted philosophers' typical over-intellectualizations and artificial theorizations of the notions of world, truth, reason, or God.

In philosophy, whether modernist or postmodernist, naturalist or antinaturalist, there can, then, be no overcoming of the "philosophical." Nor can we philosophers escape our duty to examine philosophically what we take to be "philosophical" in the views we formulate, interpret, or criticize. While my description of Putnam's pragmatism in the preceding pages has been largely sympathetic, I am afraid that Putnam has not taken up this task as seriously as he should have done.

Conclusion

Originally, I did not plan to give the final word to Rorty, because (as should be obvious by now) I find, with Putnam, many of his ethnocentrist, post-philosophical statements antirealistic, too radically pragmatistic and irresponsibly relativistic to be incorporated in a solid pragmatism, but I do think that his most recent criticism of Putnam is on the right track:

> Putnam's recent alliance with Stanley Cavell, Cora Diamond, and James Conant – his emphasis on the Ordinary and on the need to avoid putting forward theses in philosophy – seems to me an unfortunate throwback to pre-Hegelian attempts to find something ahistorical to which philosophers may pledge allegiance. The Ordinary strikes me as just the latest disguise of the *ontos on.*
>
> (Rorty 2000b: 90.)

This statement by Rorty is, indeed, a striking example of the use of the pragmatic method which, as Peirce and James insisted in their various ways, encourages us to seek the meaning of our conceptions in the practical outcome that their use may bring into our future actions. Putnam's (and other Wittgensteinian philosophers') frequent use of the word "ordinary" can and ought to be subjected to such an examination. We cannot, I think, avoid our ordinary linguistic practices – or, to put it in more Rortyan terms, the vocabularies we naturally use in our attempts to cope with our natural environment – being conceptualized and interpreted, when we begin to philosophize about them, in a philosophical manner, either premodern, modern, post-modern, or post-postmodern (whatever these words are taken to mean in specific cases). The philosophical practice of using the word "ordinary" is itself something quite unordinary and in need of further philosophical scrutiny, preferably on a pragmatist basis.

Continuing the practice of philosophizing is, then, something that neither Putnam nor Rorty can (or should even try to) successfully avoid. Had they learned their pragmatistic lessons well enough, they would neither ascribe any "overcoming philosophy" tendency to any of the classical pragmatists nor manifest such a tendency in their own work. "Philosophy always buries its undertakers."[45]

Notes

1   See Seigfried 1990: 294, 417. One of the best critiques of Rorty's interpretation of James's theory of truth is Ben-Menahim 1995. According to Ben-Menahim, James (unlike Rorty) leaves our ordinary practices of speaking about truth and falsity untouched.

2   Cf., e.g., Bernstein 1980: 768; Tiles 1988: 4; Smith 1992: 9–13. More detailed expositions of Rorty's misreadings (and "misuses") of Dewey in particular (and classical pragmatism in general) include Brodsky 1982; Sleeper 1985; Edel 1985; Stuhr 1992; Gouinlock 1995 (see also, however, Rorty's response to Gouinlock in

Saatkamp 1995); and Kloppenberg 1998. A somewhat different critique has been presented by Kulp (1992), who argues that both Dewey and Rorty are overhasty in rejecting the "spectator theory of knowledge." Wilshire (1997), in turn, has pointed out that Rorty ignores the classical pragmatists' essentially phenomenological orientation to experience. For related criticisms, see also several contributions to this volume, e.g., Sandra Rosenthal's and David Hildebrand's chapters. (I received a copy of Hildebrand's highly relevant book, *Beyond Realism and Anti-Realism: John Dewey and the Neopragmatists* (2003), only when I was in the final stages of revising this chapter for publication; it includes a detailed critical discussion of Rorty's – and Putnam's – problematic relation to Deweyan pragmatism.)

3 See Rorty 1995. Hall (1994: 71, 89) perceptively notes that Rorty prefers the "Jamesian," or "literary," Dewey to the "Peircean," "scientific" one.

4 See, however, Hildebrand 2000. Hildebrand's essay is a useful critical discussion of Putnam's recent interest in Dewey and of the ways in which Putnam's pragmatism might be further developed through a more careful consideration of certain Deweyan themes. (See also Hildebrand 2003.) Putnam's interpretation of Dewey's views on democracy as a precondition of inquiry is discussed in Westbrook 1998. On pragmatist themes in Putnam's philosophy, see also Richard Bernstein's contribution to this collection.

5 Extensive references to Putnam's and Rorty's controversy and to their discussions of earlier pragmatists can be found, e.g., in Pihlström 1996, 1998. This chapter is partly an attempt to continue the critique of Rorty's pragmatism already presented in these works of mine. Important new material by and on Rorty can be found in Brandom 2000.

6 See Putnam's essays on James, Peirce, and Dewey in Putnam 1990: chs 16–18; 1992a.

7 See the notorious remark to this effect in Rorty's 1980 paper, "Pragmatism, Relativism, and Irrationalism," in Rorty 1982: 161. One sometimes gets the feeling that the adjective "Peircean" is almost a pejorative term not only for Rorty but even (at least occasionally) for Putnam, referring to the questionable ideas of truth as the final opinion of the scientific community, the limit of inquiry, the absolute (scientific) conception of the world, etc. On the other hand, even Rorty once in a while makes rhetorical appeals to Peirce: he says, for instance, that "we pragmatists" are "impressed by Peirce's criticisms of Descartes" and reject both skepticism and foundationalism in epistemology (see Rorty 2000a: 5). For a reconsideration of Putnam's relation to Peirce, and for an argument to the effect that it is not necessary to read Peirce as being committed to the metaphysically realist "absolute conception of the world" that Putnam repudiates, see Hookway 2000.

8 Both Putnam and Rorty reject what Putnam has called "metaphysical realism," i.e., the view that the world possesses its own precategorized ontological structure which can, in principle, be described by means of a single true theory that corresponds to the way the world mind- and discourse-independently is. For a standard formulation and critique of this position, see Putnam 1981; for Putnam's more recent reflections, see Putnam 1994. In his comments on Peirce's 1898 Cambridge Conferences Lectures on pragmatism, Putnam (1992b) finds Peirce's strong scholastic realism a species of metaphysical realism and, hence, unacceptable. We need not determine here whether Putnam's and Rorty's rejection of Peirce's pragmatism as a form of metaphysical realism is correct or not (see also Hookway 2000).

9 This picture of the "two pragmatisms" has been defended in different ways at least in Mounce 1997; Haack 1998; and Rescher 2000. Haack, in particular, has been concerned with showing how Rorty thoroughly misrepresents Peirce and thus hides the scientifically responsible and realistic origin of the pragmatist tradition.

10 For a relatively recent review making this basic point, see Farrell 1998. (This paper, like many others on Putnam and other pragmatists, can also be found through the "Pragmatism Cybrary" website, http://www.pragmatism.org) See also the works cited in the previous note.

11 I am omitting Peirce both because James and Dewey are more important than Peirce for both Putnam and Rorty and because Peirce's inclusion in this brief chapter would complicate matters enormously. This does not mean that Peirce would be unimportant in the assessment of neopragmatism. On the contrary, the differences between Putnam and Rorty might be usefully compared to the differences between Peirce and James, as Richard Bernstein (1995: 58) suggests. For a comparison, inspired by James, of Putnam's and Rorty's different "philosophical temperaments," see also Goodman 1995: 10.

12 An exception to this is Putnam 1995, a book to which we will return. Putnam does discuss his dissatisfaction with Rorty's reading of Wittgenstein, but that would be a topic for another paper. (Sometimes Wittgensteinian and pragmatist issues converge, of course.)

13 I cannot here dwell on the intricacies of Putnam's interpretation of James (let alone James's own views). See Putnam's discussions of James in Putnam 1995; 1998. James's theory is formulated in his classical works, *Pragmatism: A New Name for Some Old Ways of Thinking* (1907) and *The Meaning of Truth: A Sequel to Pragmatism* (1909), conveniently reissued in a single edition (James 1978).

14 For the central importance of the notion of habit in the pragmatist tradition, see, e.g., Kilpinen 2000.

15 Dewey's notion of warranted assertibility is developed, e.g., in Dewey's article, "Propositions, Warranted Assertibility, and Truth," reprinted in Dewey 1946: 331–353.

16 See my discussion of Putnam's conception(s) of truth, as compared to the correspondence theory, in Pihlström 1998: ch. 3.

17 See also Putnam 1995: 39–41. Rorty's reply here is that instead of talking about the incoherence of metaphysical realism (or of "nonpragmatic positions" in general), it would be better to talk merely about their "lack of convenience." See Rorty's paper, "Is Truth a Goal of Inquiry? Donald Davidson versus Crispin Wright" (1995), in Rorty 1998a: especially 42, n. 63.

18 Putnam notes that while he has himself become an "increasingly realist" philosopher, Rorty has "moved from his physicalism to an extreme linguistic idealism that teeters on the edge of solipsism" (Putnam 1994: 306). For the accusation that Rorty's position becomes indistinguishable from solipsism (or from a solipsism "with a 'we' instead of an 'I' "), see also Putnam 2000.

19 Cf. Putnam's favorable reference to both James and Rorty in connection with the idea that "any given event can be traced to a multitude of different causes" (Putnam 1994: 285); see also Putnam 1998.

20 These writings from 1868–1869, originally published in the *Journal of Speculative Philosophy*, can be found in Peirce (1992).

21 In fact, Rorty quite often refers to Putnam as a pragmatist (see, e.g., Rorty 1991: 86, n. 7). He mentions Putnam and Davidson as the philosophers who "linguistify" Deweyan pragmatism (Rorty 1998a: 211) and even describes Putnam as "the most important contemporary philosopher to call himself a pragmatist" (1998a: 213) and as "the leading contemporary pragmatist" (Rorty 1999: xxvii; see also 1999: 24–25). In Rorty 1998b, a piece which is problematic as an encyclopedia entry because it describes Rorty's own interpretation of pragmatism as Darwinian antirepresentationalism rather than offering any neutral survey of the pragmatist tradition, Putnam is again referred to as "the best-known contemporary philosopher to identify himself as a pragmatist."

22 See also Putnam 2002, where Putnam puts the matter succinctly: "Commonsense realism about the views of my cultural peers coupled with anti-realism about everything else makes no sense" (2002: 16, emphasis omitted). We may note in passing that a pragmatist theory of norms, perhaps more fully developed than Putnam's but equally opposed to Rorty's flatly non-normative account, can be found in Will 1997.

23 Putnam here refers to Dewey 1916: 336.

24 Here Putnam's reference is to Rorty's paper, "Putnam and the Relativist Menace" (1993), reprinted as chapter 2 of Rorty 1998a.

25 Putnam's more recent reflections on why and how we should avoid traditional dualisms in the philosophy of mind – dualisms that survive even in our allegedly scientific era of physicalism and reductionism – are collected in Putnam 1999.

26 Cf. here especially the distinction between "normal" and "abnormal" discourse in Rorty 1979.

27 One might argue, however, that Putnam has not drawn due attention to the ways in which certain traditional metaphysical (e.g., Kantian and Hegelian) themes continue to dominate the classical pragmatists' thought.

28 Putnam's recent use of late-Wittgensteinian ideas, as well as his endorsement of John McDowell's defense of ordinary, nonmetaphysical objectivity, would also be relevant in this respect but must be neglected here (see Putnam 1994: chs 12–15; and especially his more recent treatment of Wittgensteinian themes in Putnam 2001). For McDowell's views, essentially accepted by Putnam, see McDowell 1994; for some critical reflections and comparisons, see Pihlström (2003: ch. 4). For the ways in which Putnam's critique of Rorty is connected with his Wittgensteinianism and his indebtedness to McDowell, see Conant's (1994) most illuminating introduction to *Words and Life*. (It is worth noting that Putnam's attachment to Wittgenstein adds little to his interpretations of the pragmatist tradition, although it does encourage the reading of Wittgenstein as a kind of a pragmatist.)

29 The question of how both James and Wittgenstein are "Kantians" is a major topic in Putnam 1995.

30 Burke (1994: 83, 107–108) has described Dewey as a naturalized Kantian. Cf. the discussion of James and Dewey as quasi-transcendental philosophers in Pihlström 1998: chs 4–5; see further my attempt to reinterpret pragmatism as a naturalized and historicized form of transcendental inquiry in Pihlström 2003.

31 See McDowell 2000. McDowell perceptively argues that Rorty's "phobia of objectivity" and his refusal to acknowledge any non-human, external authority over our thought in relation to the world are unpragmatic and "unDeweyan" (2000: 120).

32 Cf. Robert Brandom's own contribution, "Vocabularies of Pragmatism: Synthesizing Naturalism and Historicism," in Brandom 2000: 156–183.

33 I discuss the constructivist dimension of pragmatism in Pihlström 1996: chs 3.3 and 4.4; 1998: ch. 1.

34 Such a non-reductive naturalism is important even when we are discussing topics where a kind of supernaturalism may, according to James, in the end be desirable, as in the philosophy of religion; cf. again Pihlström 1998: ch. 6. Pragmatism is, unfortunately, seldom even mentioned in contemporary discussions of the concept of emergence. See, however, El-Hani and Pihlström 2002.

35 Cf. here Joseph Margolis's recent discussions of the pragmatist tradition (both in his contribution to this volume and earlier, e.g. in Margolis 1999). Rorty should, according to Margolis, be seen as one of the recent "naturalizers" of philosophy (along with Quine, Davidson, and physicalist philosophers of mind), but such a project of "naturalizing" is incompatible with the non-reductive form of natu-ralism we find in the pragmatist tradition (Margolis 1999: 225 ff) – indeed,

according to Margolis, "pragmatism's true center of gravity lies … in the dialectical contest with naturalizing" (1999: 228). Putnam (whose view does have its difficulties) is closer to the original project of pragmatism, which is a form of "naturalism" but never forgets normative and legitimative ("second-order") questions. Thus, Putnam is in many ways closer to both James and Dewey (and to Margolis himself) than Rorty is. Margolis admits that we would not have a "revival" of pragmatism at all, had Rorty and Putnam not identified themselves as pragmatists (1999: 222), but remarks that "Putnam and Rorty are bound to fade" and that they "have nearly completed their appointed roles" (1999: 223). For example, "Putnam has hardly settled on a viable realism of his own" (1999: 235). We should agree with Margolis when he reminds us that pragmatism will have to concede, pace recent "naturalizers," "second-order epistemological explanations or legitimations that are not expressible in (that is, not restricted to) causal terms" (1999: 236). We should also follow him to the rejection of traditional dualisms between, say, subject and object, epistemology and metaphysics, and idealism and realism (1999: 237). But I am not sure whether we should follow him to the rejection of the position he finds in Putnam. On the contrary, Margolis appears to agree with Putnam on many things, including the possibility of developing a moderate form of realism within a pragmatist framework. See also Margolis 2002a; 2002b.

36 I have tried to develop this idea in Pihlström 2003.

37 For Putnam's defense of the objectivity (or "objectivity humanly speaking") of ethics and of the fact-value entanglement, see Putnam 1981: chs 6 and 9; 1990: chs 11–12; 1995). See also my treatment of Putnam's argument in Pihlström 2003: ch. 7.

38 Cf. here Conant's (2000) critical discussion of Rorty's reading of Orwell's Nineteen Eighty-Four (1949). A convincing recent pragmatist critique of Rorty's ethical thought has been presented by Misak (2000). (One need not agree either with Conant or with Misak on everything they say in order to find their critiques of Rorty impressive.)

39 This hostility does not prevent him from speaking metaphorically of pragmatism as "romantic polytheism," as a celebration of a plurality of values as opposed to a "monotheistically" conceived unified system. See Rorty 1998c.

40 See, e.g., Putnam 1997a; 1997b; 1997c. I analyze Putnam's problems in the philosophy of religion in Pihlström 1999.

41 On pragmatism as a response to the "crisis of modernity," see Diggins 1994.

42 We may say that Putnam also maintains an important premodern source of insight, religion, which he believes can still illuminate the problems people face in their lives. Even such a modernist thinker as Dewey did not entirely reject religious attitudes and experiences: see Dewey 1962 [1934]. Putnam's philosophy of religion is, in any event, much more crucially indebted to James (and to Wittgenstein) than to Dewey, whose conception of "the religious" is thoroughly naturalized, as distinguished from the supernaturalist assumptions inherent in all actual religions.

43 See Larry Hickman's discussion of Dewey as a "post-postmodernist" in this volume.

44 I have criticized Putnam's approach in Pihlström 1996: chs 5.3 and 6. For a brief comparison between Putnam's commonsense philosophy and Peirce's "critical commonsensism," see Hookway 2000.

45 I am indebted to David Hildebrand for his valuable comments on my chapter at the AIER Dewey Symposium in Great Barrington, MA, on 20 July 2001. In his comment, Hildebrand took up large and important questions concerning, among other things, the need to interpret pragmatism as a form of transcendental philosophy. (Cf. also Hildebrand 2003.) No adequate responses to his worries can be

found in the present chapter; here I can only refer back to some of my other writings on this topic mentioned in the notes. I am also grateful to many other participants of the symposium, especially Richard Bernstein and Joseph Margolis, for stimulating comments, and to Elias L. Khalil for inviting this chapter. Furthermore, I wish to thank my Finnish colleagues Erkki Kilpinen and Mats Bergman, as well as other participants of the meeting of the "Metaphysical Club" at the University of Helsinki on 20 February 2001, where some of this material was first discussed. For the continuing exchange of ideas related to Putnam's and Rorty's work, I am, finally, grateful to Thomas Wallgren and Ken Westphal.

Bibliography

Ben-Menahim, Y. (1995) "Pragmatism and Revisionism: James's Conception of Truth," *International Journal of Philosophical Studies*, 3: 270–289.

Bernstein, R.J. (1980) "Philosophy in the Conversation of Mankind," *The Review of Metaphysics*, 33: 745–775.

—— (1995) "American Pragmatism: The Conflict of Narratives," in H.J. Saatkamp, Jr (ed.), *Rorty and Pragmatism: The Philosopher Responds to His Critics*, Nashville, TN and London: Vanderbilt University Press.

Brandom, R.B. (ed.) (2000) *Rorty and His Critics*, Malden, MA and Oxford: Blackwell.

Brodsky, G. (1982) "Rorty's Interpretation of Pragmatism," *Transactions of the Charles S. Peirce Society*, 18: 311–337.

Burke, T. (1994) *Dewey's New Logic: A Reply to Russell*, Chicago: Chicago University Press.

Conant, J. (1994) "Introduction," in H. Putnam, *Words and Life*, ed. J. Conant, Cambridge, MA and London: Harvard University Press.

—— (2000) "Freedom, Cruelty, and Truth: Rorty versus Orwell," in R.B. Brandom (ed.), *Rorty and His Critics*, Malden, MA and Oxford: Blackwell.

Dewey, J. (1916) *Democracy and Education*, New York: Macmillan.

—— (1931) *Philosophy and Civilization*, New York: Milton, Balch & Company.

—— (1946) *Problems of Men*, New York: Philosophical Library.

—— (1960 [1929]) *The Quest for Certainty: A Study on the Relation of Knowledge and Action*, New York: G.P. Putnam's Sons.

—— (1962 [1934]) *A Common Faith*, New Haven, CT and London: Yale University Press.

—— (1989 [1925, 2nd edn 1929]) *Experience and Nature*, La Salle, IL: Open Court.

Dickstein, M. (ed.) (1998) *The Revival of Pragmatism: New Essays on Social Thought, Law, and Culture*, Durham, NC and London: Duke University Press.

Diggins, J.P. (1994) *The Promise of Pragmatism: Modernism and the Crisis of Knowledge and Authority*, Chicago and London: University of Chicago Press.

Edel, A. (1985) "A Missing Dimension in Rorty's Use of Pragmatism," *Transactions of the Charles S. Peirce Society*, 21: 21–37.

El-Hani, C.N. and Pihlström, S. (2002) "Emergence Theories and Pragmatic Realism," *Essays in Philosophy*, 3 (2). Online at: http://www.humboldt.edu/~essays (accessed April 2003).

Farrell, F.B. (1998) "Review of Hilary Putnam, Pragmatism: An Open Question," *Style*, Spring. Online at: http://www.findarticles.com/cf_0/m2342/1_32/54019330/print.jhtml (accessed June 2001).

Goodman, R.B. (1995) "Introduction," in Goodman (ed.), *Pragmatism: A Contemporary Reader*, New York and London: Routledge.

Gouinlock, J. (1995) "What Is the Legacy of Instrumentalism? Rorty's Interpretation of Dewey," in H.J. Saatkamp, Jr (ed.), *Rorty and Pragmatism: The Philosopher Responds to His Critics*, Nashville, TN and London: Vanderbilt University Press.

Haack, S. (1998) *Manifesto of a Passionate Moderate: Unfashionable Essays*, Chicago and London: University of Chicago Press.

Hall, D.L. (1994) *Richard Rorty: Prophet and Poet of the New Pragmatism*, Albany, NY: SUNY Press.

Hildebrand, D.L. (2000) "Putnam, Pragmatism, and Dewey," *Transactions of the Charles S. Peirce Society*, 36: 109–132.

—— (2003) *Beyond Realism and Anti-Realism: John Dewey and the Neopragmatists*, Nashville, TN: Vanderbilt University Press.

Hookway, C. (2000) "Truth and Reality: Putnam and the Pragmatist Conception of Truth," paper presented at the Münster conference on Putnam's philosophy, June 2000. Online at: http://www.shef.ac.uk/uni/academic/N-Q/phil/department/staff/ho.../truth_and_reality.html (accessed June 2001).

James, W. (1978 [1907–1909]) *Pragmatism and the Meaning of Truth*, ed. F.H. Burkhardt, F. Bowers and I.K. Skrupskelis, Cambridge, MA and London: Harvard University Press.

Kilpinen, E. (2000) *The Enormous Fly-Wheel of Society: Pragmatism's Habitual Conception of Rationality and Social Theory*, Helsinki: University of Helsinki, Department of Sociology, *Research Reports* 235.

Kloppenberg, J.T. (1998) "Pragmatism: An Old Name for Some New Ways of Thinking?" in M. Dickstein (ed.), *The Revival of Pragmatism: New Essays on Social Thought, Law, and Culture*, Durham, NC and London: Duke University Press.

Kulp, C.B. (1992) *The End of Epistemology: Dewey and His Current Allies on the Spectator Theory of Knowledge*, Westport, CT and London: Greenwood Press.

McDowell, J. (1994; 2nd edn 1996), *Mind and World*, Cambridge, MA and London: Harvard University Press.

—— (2000) "Towards Rehabilitating Objectivity," in R.B. Brandom (ed.), *Rorty and His Critics*, Malden, MA and Oxford: Blackwell.

Margolis, J. (1999) "Reconstruction in Pragmatism," *The Journal of Speculative Philosophy*, 13: 221–239.

—— (2002a) "Dewey's and Rorty's Opposed Pragmatisms," *Transactions of the Charles S. Peirce Society*, 38: 117–135

—— (2002b) *Reinventing American Pragmatism: American Philosophy at the End of the Twentieth Century*, Ithaca, NY: Cornell University Press.

Misak, C. (2000) *Truth, Politics, Morality: Pragmatism and Deliberation*, London and New York: Routledge.

Mounce, H.O. (1997) *The Two Pragmatisms: From Peirce to Rorty*, London and New York: Routledge.

Nielsen, K. (1991) *After the Demise of the Tradition: Rorty, Critical Theory, and the Fate of Philosophy*, Boulder, CO: Westview Press.

Peirce, Charles S. (1992) *The Essential Peirce, vol. 1*, The Peirce Edition Project, Bloomington: Indiana University Press.

Pihlström, S. (1996) *Structuring the World: The Issue of Realism and the Nature of Ontological Problems in Classical and Contemporary Pragmatism*, Helsinki: Acta Philosophica Fennica 59.

—— (1998) *Pragmatism and Philosophical Anthropology: Understanding Our Human Life in a Human World*, New York: Peter Lang.

—— (1999) "Hilary Putnam as a Religious Thinker," *Journal of Interdisciplinary Studies*, 11: 39–60.

—— (2003) *Naturalizing the Transcendental: A Pragmatic View*, Amherst, NY: Prometheus/Humanity Books.

Putnam, H. (1981) *Reason, Truth and History*, Cambridge: Cambridge University Press.

—— (1990) *Realism with a Human Face*, ed. J. Conant, Cambridge, MA and London: Harvard University Press.

—— (1992a) *Renewing Philosophy*, Cambridge, MA and London: Harvard University Press.

—— (1992b) "Comments on the Lectures," in C.S. Peirce, *Reasoning and the Logic of Things: The Cambridge Conferences Lectures of 1898*, ed. K.L. Ketner, Cambridge, MA and London: Harvard University Press.

—— (1994) *Words and Life*, ed. J. Conant, Cambridge, MA and London: Harvard University Press.

—— (1995) *Pragmatism: An Open Question*, Oxford and Cambridge, MA: Blackwell.

—— (1997a) "God and the Philosophers," in P.A. French et al. (eds), *Philosophy of Religion*, Midwest Studies in Philosophy 21, Minneapolis, MN: University of Minnesota Press.

—— (1997b) "On Negative Theology," *Faith and Philosophy*, 14: 407–422.

—— (1997c) "Thoughts Addressed to an Analytical Thomist," *The Monist*, 80: 487–499.

—— (1998) "Pragmatism and Realism," in M. Dickstein (ed.), *The Revival of Pragmatism: New Essays on Social Thought, Law, and Culture*, Durham, NC and London: Duke University Press.

—— (1999) *The Threefold Cord: Mind, Body, and World*, New York: Columbia University Press.

—— (2000) "Richard Rorty on Reality and Justification," in R.B. Brandom (ed.), *Rorty and His Critics*, Malden, MA and Oxford: Blackwell.

—— (2001) "Was Wittgenstein Really an Anti-Realist about Mathematics?" in T. McCarthy and S.C. Stidd (eds), *Wittgenstein in America*, Oxford: Clarendon Press.

—— (2002) "Pragmatism and Nonscientific Knowledge," in J. Conant and U.M. Zeglen (eds), *Hilary Putnam: Pragmatism and Realism*, London and New York: Routledge.

Rescher, N. (2000) *Realistic Pragmatism: An Introduction to Pragmatic Philosophy*, Albany, NY: SUNY Press.

Rorty, R. (1979) *Philosophy and the Mirror of Nature*, Princeton, NJ: Princeton University Press.

—— (1982) *Consequences of Pragmatism*, Brighton: The Harvester Press.

—— (1985) "Comments on Sleeper and Edel," *Transactions of the Charles S. Peirce Society*, 21: 39–48.

—— (1991) *Objectivity, Relativism, and Truth*, Cambridge: Cambridge University Press.

—— (1995) "Dewey between Hegel and Darwin," in H.J. Saatkamp, Jr (ed.), *Rorty and Pragmatism: The Philosopher Responds to His Critics*, Nashville, TN and London: Vanderbilt University Press.

—— (1998a) *Truth and Progress*, Cambridge: Cambridge University Press.

—— (1998b) "Pragmatism," in E. Craig (ed.), *Routledge Encyclopedia of Philosophy*, London and New York: Routledge, CD-ROM Version 1.0.

—— (1998c) "Pragmatism as Romantic Polytheism," in M. Dickstein (ed.), *The Revival of Pragmatism: New Essays on Social Thought, Law, and Culture*, Durham, NC and London: Duke University Press.

—— (1999) *Philosophy and Social Hope*, Harmondsworth: Penguin Books.

—— (2000a) "Universality and Truth," in R.B. Brandom (ed.), *Rorty and His Critics*, Malden, MA and Oxford: Blackwell.

—— (2000b) "Response to Hilary Putnam," in R.B. Brandom (ed.), *Rorty and His Critics*, Malden, MA and Oxford: Blackwell.

Saatkamp, H.J., Jr (ed.) (1995) *Rorty and Pragmatism: The Philosopher Responds to His Critics*, Nashville, TN and London: Vanderbilt University Press.

Seigfried, C.H. (1990) *William James's Radical Reconstruction of Philosophy*, Albany, NY: SUNY Press.

Shook, J.R. (2000) *Dewey's Empirical Theory of Knowledge and Reality*, Albany, NY: SUNY Press.

Sleeper, R.W. (1985) "Rorty's Pragmatism: Afloat in Neurath's Boat, But Why Adrift?" *Transactions of the Charles S. Peirce Society*, 21: 9–20.

Smith, J.E. (1992) *America's Philosophical Vision*, Chicago and London: University of Chicago Press.

Stuhr, J.J. (1992) "Dewey's Reconstruction of Metaphysics," *Transactions of the Charles S. Peirce Society*, 28: 161–176.

Tiles, J.E. (1988) *Dewey*, London and New York: Routledge.

Westbrook, R.B. (1998) "Pragmatism and Democracy: Reconstructing the Logic of John Dewey's Faith," in M. Dickstein (ed.), *The Revival of Pragmatism: New Essays on Social Thought, Law, and Culture*, Durham, NC and London: Duke University Press.

Will, F.L. (1997) *Pragmatism and Realism*, ed. K.R. Westphal, Totowa, NJ: Rowman and Littlefield.

Wilshire, B. (1997) "Pragmatism, Neopragmatism, and Phenomenology: The Richard Rorty Phenomenon," *Human Studies*, 20: 95–108.

4 Dewey and/or Rorty

Joseph Margolis

Robert Brandom, following Michael Dummett's lead (I would say), with an eye to explaining the novelty of his own self-styled pragmatism, offers a curious summary of the difference between the youthful Gottlob Frege (the Frege of the Begriffsschrift of 1879) and the Frege of the 1890s, the "mature" Frege, the Frege of the Grundgesetze – of which Dummett (1972: 432) unceremoniously remarks (Brandom (2000: 50–51) concurring): "Frege's new approach to logic was retrograde."

Brandom favors the youthful Frege over the "mature" Frege, because, more or less as Dummett (1972: 432) observes, Frege came to characterize the role of truth, in logic, "not merely [as] the goal, but [as] the object of study. The traditional answer [Dummett explains] to the question what is the subject-matter of logic is, however, that it is, not truth, but inference, or, more properly, the relation of logical consequence." Brandom (2000: 50, 51) draws from this the verdict that "the young Frege had not yet made the false step," the one just mentioned. That Frege, he says, "starts his semantic investigations not with the idea of reference but with that of inference. His seminal first work, the *Begriffsschrift* of 1879, takes as its aim the explication of 'conceptual content' (*begriffliche Inhalt*), [where] that is, the qualification 'conceptual' is explicitly construed in inferential terms."

I'm sure you hear the slippage in the use of the term "inference" from "the relation of logical consequence" to that of "nondeductive consequence" and in the implied double question – in flagging the mistake of making the analysis of "truth" the object of the analysis of deductive inference – as if the first confirmed that it was also a mistake to treat the analysis of truth as an essential part of the analysis of nondeductive inference. That is a serious mistake in its own right, also a fatal one as far as recruiting Frege for pragmatist uses is concerned. The opponents of classic pragmatism – Brandom, now, as well as Richard Rorty (1986) and (on Rorty's say-so) Donald Davidson (1986) – have, famously, masqueraded as pragmatism's new champions by reversing the main thrust of James's and Dewey's conception of truth.

The very example Brandom features – the familiar one about the matched active- and passive-voice sentences regarding the Greek defeat of the Persians at Plataea – has, however, now come to signify the restriction of conceptual content to what Frege thought justified his attack on psychologism in deductive contexts and, more generally, his attack on idealism (see, e.g., Coffa 1991: 64–65). The *Begriffschrift* (Frege 1960) itself tells us nothing (beyond his formal treatment of logic and arithmetic) about the epistemological or metaphysical or psychological or generally philosophical import of Frege's having isolated the predicative role of "conceptual content" from any "referential" (or "representational" or, in effect, metaphysical) function or his having distinguished between "assertion" and "proposition" or "thought." Frege's work has no philosophical bearing on pragmatism, unless it is to oppose it hands down. Indeed, the point of the Begriffschrift was to demonstrate that arithmetic was entirely analytic and did not depend on nonlogical "content" at all. Just compare Dewey's *Logic* (1938)! The idea of Frege's kind of disjunction is the contradictory of Peirce's and Dewey's views.

There seems to be nothing here that bears in the remotest way on what Brandom marks as Frege's "pragmatist" leanings. Frege's intention was to segregate arithmetic reasoning from both the empiricist (Millian) alternative and the Kantian version of the rationalist alternative, without ever grounding the use of propositions in the natural contexts of ordinary human life. Does Brandom mean that pragmatism should now, or actually does, follow Frege in this regard? If he does, he can only have meant to follow Dummett's judgment (1967: vol. 3, 225), which follows Frege's: namely, that "it is evident that some branches of philosophy are logically prior to others" (metaphysics to "natural theology," philosophy of mind to ethics, semantics or "logic" (in Frege's sense) to metaphysics).[1] No pragmatism, plausibly viewed as building on the work of either Peirce or Dewey, could have followed Frege or Dummett in this regard.

I take this to be the symptom of a profound mistake, classificatory at least but surely philosophical as well. For all of Brandom's distinctions regarding his own "linguistic pragmatism," which he claims to share (as a recognizable version of pragmatism) with the continuous tradition that includes Frege, Wilfrid Sellars, W.V. Quine, Davidson, and Rorty, depends on a fatal and completely unobserved equivocation on such terms as "inference," "semantic content," "proposition," "truth," "logic," and "rationality" that runs through the whole of his recent book *Articulating Reasons* (Brandom 2000) – which is itself intended as a compendium of the up-to-date pragmatism of his first book Making It Explicit (Brandom 1994). What Brandom confuses by his would-be history, Rorty endorses by something approaching ukase. But we have three errors here already: one, that pragmatists would disjoin proposition and assertion within natural-language contexts (per Brandom); two, that they would concede a hierarchy of cognitive powers (per Dummett); and, three, that they would acknowledge some non-natural domain of inquiry or conceptual resource (per Frege).

My objection to Brandom is not narrowly directed against Brandom himself but, through Brandom, against all claimants who

1   never bother to confirm a proper linkage between a well-established movement (pragmatism) and their own rationales for the various extensions they propose; and

2   never admit or follow through on the need to answer pertinent objections to such a linkage and such a rationale. In Rorty's hands, the complaint is blithely turned aside in the "postmodernist" or "postphilosophical" manner by sheer definitional opportunism;[2] in Brandom's hands, the same postphilosophical liberty is now tamed to serve the interests of a version of analytic philosophy as much opposed to pragmatism as one can imagine. Frege supplies the knockdown evidence. But, closer to home, so do Sellars and Davidson.

I am indeed speaking about the relationship between John Dewey's and Richard Rorty's pragmatisms, though, understandably, you might not have thought so. The missing connection would have added that Brandom (2000: 6, 11, 51) regards himself as a pragmatist, a "linguistic pragmatist"; regards the young Frege as committed to a "fundamental pragmatic principle" (the one implicit in what I have cited from Brandom); and that the theme of linguistic pragmatism helps to define the sense in which a startling number of philosophers who you might not have thought were rightly called pragmatists turn out to have spearheaded a movement that links (if you can believe it) Hegel and Frege and Sellars and Dummett and Rorty and Brandom in a continuous endeavor that, however much it owes to the classic pragmatists, has a very different source and turns itself in an entirely new direction, if not on its head. It transpires, for instance, that "James and Dewey were pragmatists [all right] in the sense [that] they try to understand conceptual content in terms of practices of using concepts. But, in line with their generally assimilationist approach to concept use, they were not specifically linguistic pragmatists." The sense is that they should rightly be superseded. A related weakness is attributed (Brandom 2000: 14) to Wittgenstein's (1953) primitive language games (the game of "Slab" for instance).

What Brandom refers to as "practices of using concepts" has, you realize, nothing to do in any straightforward way with what Frege had in mind by the logical function of "conceptual content": whatever Brandom or Quine or Rorty or Dewey or Wittgenstein had in mind as the practice of using concepts would have counted (for Frege) as sheer psychologism, incapable therefore of reclaiming logic or arithmetic, although the argument was not yet developed by the young Frege. I press the point in order to provide a perfectly clear example of a distinctly alien takeover of a well-marked category for largely promotional reasons. What Brandom (2000: 12) calls "linguistic pragmatism" or "inferentialism," developed chiefly from certain of Wilfrid Sellars's notions (ultimately disconnected from both Frege's and Dewey's), maintains – under Rorty's endorsement, in terms of applying the "linguistic turn" to pragmatism – that "the fundamental form of the conceptual is the propositional, and the core of concept use is applying concepts in propositionally contentful assertions, beliefs, and thoughts." The qualification is meant to be a stricture applied at once in Frege's and Sellars's way, which is itself decidedly problematic.

"Pragmatic force" is best served, apparently, by acknowledging (Brandom 2000: 3) the "priority of the propositional" (which is what entitles Frege to count as a pragmatist). That's all! Ditto Sellars (Brandom 2000: 4), except that Sellars defines the pragmatist mode of linguistic functioning in natural-language contexts, in terms of asking for, and providing, reasons for belief and action: that is, in terms of "knowing how (being able) to do something" (see Sellars 2000).

The effective downgrading of Dewey and Wittgenstein (also Heidegger) – all "mentors" of Rorty, by the way – attests to the purely rhetorical advantage Brandom has in mind. Which, applied to Rorty, must count as something of an irony. In any case, the "propositional" cannot, for Dewey (as the paradig-matic pragmatist), take precedence over the "experiential," with regard to conception and cognition: because, of course, Dewey would (as a Darwinian) admit conceptual structures in "experience" and would assign a cognitive function to the "experiential." In fact, it cannot really take precedence in Sellars's (1963a) "forensic" (or fictionalized) treatment of persons and their thoughts and assertions, since his eliminativism makes the question entirely moot (a fact Brandom and Rorty conveniently ignore). Sellars (1963b: 123, 126) is absolutely clear that, in his view, "[scientific] theories explain laws by explaining why the objects of [any] domain in question obey the laws that they do to the extent that they do"; and that, "[a]ccording to the view I [that is, Sellars] am proposing, correspondence rules would appear in the material mode as statements to the effect that the objects of the observational frame-work do not really exist – there really are no such things."[3] If you see the point of Frege's and Sellars's separate projects, you cannot fail to see that, in coopting both at once, Rorty and Brandom have embraced two of the most strategically placed anti-pragmatists one can imagine as the new totems of pragmatism's latest and best extension. Extraordinary!

In his Introduction (Rorty 2000a: 4, 7) to the reprinting of Sellars's "Empiricism and the philosophy of mind" (1963c) as a separate volume, Rorty straightforwardly affirms that Sellars "may have been the first philoso-pher to insist that we see 'mind' as a sort of hypostatization of language. He argued that the intentionality of beliefs is a reflection of the intentionality of sentences rather than conversely." He adds – an impossible concession for a classic pragmatist – that Sellars "identified the possession of a concept with the mastery of the use of a word. So for him, mastery of a language is a prerequisite of conscious experience." This is the gist of section 29 of Sellars's essay, on which Brandom also relies.

Of course, the remark must be read (with whatever paradoxical results) within the terms of Sellars's eliminativism: which, first, is the upshot of Sellars's "linguistic" interpretation of the self, consciousness, and belief – a view that is unconditionally irreconcilable with any classic pragmatist account of language, experience, concept, or consciousness; and, second, properly construed, is not a defense of anything like Rorty's (1967) "linguistic turn" but rather a complete subversion of it – along the lines of rejecting not only empiricism (Sellars's target) but all folk experience as well. Rorty appears content with the linguistic treatment of selves or persons (borrowed, for his own purposes, from Sellars); but, already in his excellent Introduction (Rorty 1967), it is clear that the idea of replacing the analysis of "experience" (let us say) by the analysis of "language" is (without reference to pragmatism) bound to fail "methodologically." My sense of what Rorty patiently explains is that the Fregean "priorities" (which Dummet favors) – that is, prioritizing the analysis of language over the analysis of experience (or the world) – have no chance of ever being compelling.

I agree entirely. But, then, Rorty cannot, as a pragmatist himself, in any reasonably extended sense that avoids perverse uses of the term, be satisfied with Sellars's standing as a pragmatist: How can the fictionalizing of persons be reconciled with Dewey's robust conception of human agents? How can the linguistic displace the experiential? – unless (in accord with Sellars's "psychological nominalism") we mean to prefer eliminativism to pragmatism? (see Rorty 1998: vol. 3, 126).

Rorty (1998: vol. 3, 127) explicitly says: "I read Sellars and Brandom as pragmatists, because I treat psychological nominalism as a version of the pragmatist doctrine that truth is a matter of the utility of a belief rather than of a relation between pieces of the world and pieces of language." Bear in mind that Rorty (1998: vol. 3, 122) had already urged: "Brandom can be read as carrying through on 'the linguistic turn' by restating pragmatism in a form that makes James's and Dewey's talk of experience entirely obsolete." Yes, of course, if you read Dewey as an empiricist in the sense in which, in Sellars's (1963c) account of the "Myth of the Given," the empiricists failed utterly; though that is surely not the sense in which Dewey holds to "experience." Yes, if you treat selves as linguistic fictions; but that too is not the sense in which any of the pragmatists talk of human persons. Yes, again, if you suppose that there is a certain precision we lose if we don't accommodate the rigors of linguistic philosophy; but that also is not the sense in which Dewey clings to experience (within which, alone, the analysis of language makes sense). Yes, if truth is a "matter of the utility of a belief" rather than a matter of objective knowledge; but that disjunction is not the sense in which Dewey would allow the formula – and Rorty knows it! You begin to see how dismantling Brandom's pragmatism counts in favor of dismantling Rorty's as well.

This is not a muddle but a deliberate leap over a conceptual puddle. It holds a key, I believe, to what we should understand by the classic forms of pragmatism (if, that is, pragmatism reaches its fullest form in Dewey's mature views – which is by no means uncontroversial, relegating as it does both Peirce and James to lesser standing) and to what we should understand by pragmatism's "second" life primarily due to Rorty's exertions, however complicated by his perceived relationship to Hilary Putnam, Davidson, Quine,

Sellars, Wittgenstein, Martin Heidegger, and of course Dewey and Brandom, all of whom, at one time or another, Rorty has regarded as bona fide pragmatists. Brandom supports the same list (with supplementary qualifications) and expressly remarks that he is carrying out a line of analysis (a pragmatist analysis) that owes most to Sellars (on Rorty's say-so); hence, involves a "transition from a kantian to a hegelian approach to thought and action" (Sellars's own formulation) – ultimately yielding, as we may guess, the benefits of what Brandom (Brandom 2000: 23, 32–33) calls linguistic pragmatism. You may not see the full argument as yet, but you begin to see its drift.

I shall continue a little longer with Brandom's intervention, because, along the lines of speculation I've been sketching, Brandom (2000: 23) pointedly speaks of "my teacher Richard Rorty," who, as is well known, favors the recovery of Sellars as a strong pragmatist, and because the distinction of Rorty's own version of pragmatism owes so much to his interpretation of Sellars's work – particularly "Empiricism and the philosophy of mind" (Sellars 1963c). So much, in fact, that, beginning with that, we gain a march on the question of how, finally, Rorty's and Dewey's pragmatisms differ and are related, and how they compare in interest and power and philosophical relevance.

If I may put the matter this way, Rorty is right to treat the explication of Dewey's pragmatism as requiring a union of some sort between Hegelian and Darwinian themes: that same line of thought should help to explain what linguistic pragmatism comes to, that is, the meaning of the "linguistic turn" applied to pragmatism's original energies. But it also shows that there are two very different ways of reading the conjunction – in effect, what Dewey might have said but obviously could not, and what Brandom does say, allegedly drawing on Rorty, though Rorty says and means something altogether different. Here, the puddle may actually have become a muddle. Pragmatism has become extraordinarily complicated.

Two pertinent distinctions, drawn from a comparison between Sellars and Dewey and retrieved partly from Brandom and partly from Rorty, should set us on the right path to a useful comparison between Dewey and Rorty. Both distinctions distantly involve Hegel and Darwin, though they are not pointedly invoked by either Brandom or Rorty where they are introduced. Let me tip my hand's strategy here, for clarity of argument. I mean to indicate why, via Brandom and Rorty, Sellars and Dewey can't be pragmatists in the same or in any reasonably shared extended sense; also why Rorty finally opposes Brandom's project, though in a way that distances his own project from Dewey's.[4] (Brandom really sides, of course, with the distinctly anti-pragmatist side of Sellars, in spite of his intention – which recalls what is uncongenial in Frege.)

I'll add a gratuitous conjecture here, to intrigue you – one for which I haven't the slightest evidence, apart from the gathering effect of reading Rorty with care! Rorty, I suggest, may have deliberately launched Brandom as something of a trial balloon for his own eventual return, under altered circumstances, to defend a recuperated philosophy that might even tolerate metaphysics and epistemology again. If so, then the reckoning between Dewey and Rorty may require another inning, one perhaps already partly bruited in Rorty's recent objections to the views of both Brandom and Davidson. (I admit I find the conjecture plausible.)

The essential consideration concerns

> the relative priority accorded ... the continuities and discontinuities between discursive and nondiscursive creatures: the similarities and differences between the judgments and actions of concept users, on the one hand, and the uptake of environmental information and instrumental interventions of non-concept-using organisms and artifacts, on the other.
>
> (Brandom 2000, pp. 2–3)

Here, Brandom says very clearly:

> Theories that assimilate conceptually structured activity to the nonconceptual activity out of which it arises (in evolutionary, historical, and individual-developmental terms) are in danger of failing to make enough of the difference. Theories that adopt the converse strategy, addressing themselves at the outset to what is distinctive of or exceptional about the conceptual, court the danger of not doing justice to generic similarities.
>
> (Brandom 2000, p. 3)

I take this to be profoundly (however obscurely) anti-pragmatist – in being profoundly anti-Darwinian.

It is indeed Brandom's intention, in *Articulating Reasons* (2000: 2–3), hence also in *Making It Explicit* (1994), to favor the "second" strategy, which, he realizes, sets his view against the broadly Darwinian concessions made by figures such as (Fred) Dretske, (Jerry) Fodor, and (Ruth) Millikan, hardly pragmatists themselves, though Darwinians all – but why not count them pragmatists as well if Frege and Sellars fall within the pale and Dewey and James and Wittgenstein (and Heidegger) must cool their heels at a distinct remove? This is not a matter of mere philosophical taste among pragmatist cousins; it signifies, rather, a fundamental (but unobserved) division about how realism (or any suitable replacement for realism) could be recovered in, say, Dewey and Brandom (or Rorty) – as a way of assessing one's pragmatist credentials.

Dewey (1958) certainly holds that the enlanguaged and encultured form of cognition that distinguishes humans from other creatures is existentially grounded – for Darwinian and realist reasons – in the noncognitive and nonlinguistic powers of pre-human animal life. The sense of Dewey's argument is simply that there is no ground for denying concepts to advanced animals or prelinguistic children; nor, a fortiori, is there a reason to refuse to analyze animal intelligence in accord with a propositional model of judgment, despite their lacking language. There, at one stroke, you have the complete eclipse of the doctrine Sellars, Brandom, and Rorty favor – which, as I say, is profoundly anti-Darwinian, profoundly anti-pragmatist, and profoundly arbitrary in the light of familiar studies in sublinguistic and prelinguistic intelligence. My own solution of the puzzle is simply to acknowledge that the enlanguaged (reportorial) forms of cognition count as the paradigm of knowledge and thought (that is, as a model for making acceptable analogies), though not as marking the sine qua non of cognition as such: hence, that conceptual and cognizing abilities are understandably (perhaps ineluctably, if behaviorism fails) modeled – faute de mieux, at least heuristically – on the linguistic paradigm.

The point is this. The "assimilationist" line is Dewey's and is ineliminable in Dewey as it is in Peirce. It is the nerve of Dewey's best-known and most important Darwinian theme, that of a "problematic [or indeterminate] situation," on which Dewey's ingenious realism and account of science and practical intelligence are developed. It is the master theme of Dewey (1958, 1938, 1929). It is the pivot of Dewey's countermove against the whole of the philosophical tradition that moves between Descartes and Kant – and would, for Dewey, undoubtedly have included (as targets) figures such as Frege, Sellars, Davidson, and Brandom, whom Rorty is willing to treat as pragmatists, possibly pragmatists of a superior strain.

Dewey was also very strongly attracted to Hegel's philosophical vision and wrote (in 1897) a long unpublished (and still unexamined) analysis of Hegel that suggests detailed affinities between Hegel and Dewey along classic pragmatist and Darwinian lines.[5] Now, Brandom (2000: 34) characterizes Hegel's "pragmatism" (otherwise unexamined) as a "rationalist pragmatism," as opposed to the pragmatisms of Dewey, Heidegger, and Wittgenstein. As he explains, Hegel's pragmatism, true to the "Romantic expressionist tradition Hegel inherited" can be counted on to do "real semantic work" (unusual charge, you must admit, since it means that Dewey's and Wittgenstein's alternative strategies probably cannot be)! Hegel is said to employ a "representational semantic paradigm" (though an "expressive" one, one that fits the Sellarsian version of linguistic pragmatism) – that could profitably be supplemented, Brandom suggests, by (say) a model-theoretic account of representationalism, a possible-worlds semantics, or "an account of the distinctive function of logical vocabulary" (sic). Classic pragmatists need not apply! This is, admittedly, a little hard to believe: Hegel's *Phenomenology*, for example, is plainly centered on the analysis of experience.

Rorty, in a recent, sustained criticism of Brandom's epistemology (Rorty 2000b: 188–189), notes that both he and Brandom admire Romanticism, by which both mean Herder and Humboldt (as linguistically oriented critics of Kant), who influenced Hegel and their own Sellarsian loyalties (which is something of a leap). In Rorty's hands, the remark conveys an impression of Brandom's inconsistency on truth and realism (remember Frege), possibly also an inconsistency on inferentialism and linguistic pragmatism (which Rorty does not expressly address).

I cannot see any explanation for Brandom's gymnastic contrasts among Hegel and Frege and Sellars and Dewey and Wittgenstein as pragmatists, except: (a) to reconcile at all costs the emerging "pragmatism" Brandom professes to share with Rorty (and Davidson) in such a way as to make the case that the most blatant anti-pragmatists are really the best exemplars of what pragmatism now means; (b) in pressing that advantage, to persuade Rorty to come along, to give up his so-called postmodernist or "postphilosophical" pragmatism, which (Rorty's view) vows that all canonical epistemology and metaphysics and philosophical semantics are at an end; and (c) to coopt, as opportunistically as need be, all the pivotal figures his would-be new canon regards as useful to the success of his own adventure – notably, Hegel, Frege, and Sellars at the moment.

In all of this, Rorty and Brandom seem complicitous, except (arguably) for the decisive opposition between them regarding the recovery of an up-to-date version of conventional philosophy. Rorty, you remember, quite openly proclaimed (1999: 24) that, on his own reading, "the paradigmatic pragmatists are John Dewey and Donald Davidson," though, of course, Davidson (Davidson 2000) is unconditionally opposed to James's (and Dewey's) pragmatist account of truth. Actually, one of Rorty's most important papers (Rorty 1986), presses Davidson's "naturalizing" account of truth and knowledge even more zealously and in a more extreme form than does Davidson (1986; 2000), which may have encouraged Brandom, as a loyal Rortyan (though willing enough to strike out in an original way), to have wondered whether Rorty might not finally countenance a refurbished epistemology.

The point is this: the Darwinian (the "assimilationist") reading of the continuity between language-using and nonlanguage-using creatures is absolutely ineliminable in the classic versions of pragmatism that both Dewey and Peirce advance (in their very different ways). In Dewey especially, that continuity (or "similarity," in Brandom's idiom) is precisely what enables Dewey to formulate his original resolution of the paradoxes of Cartesian realism, the very necessity of which, judging from Putnam's and Davidson's and John McDowell's more recent efforts, still cripples our philosophical inventions even as we move into the twenty-first century (see Putnam 1994; Davidson 1986; McDowell 1996).

Nevertheless, Dewey's solution is as good and as robust as any realism the analytic tradition has ever supplied. So when Brandom indicates that he means to marginalize the Darwinian commitment (more or less as Dewey defines it) in order to bring figures like Frege and Sellars under the tent, even if doing so displaces the classic pragmatists themselves and those Rorty regards as their next of kin, one must ask, not for the details of the new classification, but for its rationale.

I do not find a definite rationale in Brandom; that is, I do not see any palpable advantage offered in marginalizing classic pragmatism, or in favoring Hegel but opposing Dewey, or in preferring "linguistic" pragmatism (Sellars, say) over "experiential" pragmatism (Dewey), though I do see the beginnings of a new brotherhood. I also see that some aspects of inferentialism could be easily reconciled with pragmatism's classic themes. But assuredly not all, not if inferentialism must also (as it means to do) embrace Sellars's scientism as its intended home. For, failure to accommodate Dewey's Darwinian themes ("assimilationism," in Brandom's idiom) entails a failure to accommodate Dewey's Hegelian themes as well. What Dewey grasped – it is the spine of his philosophy – was simply that the continuity of the precognitive and prelinguistic sources of human intelligence (the lesson of the notion of a "problematic situation") could, under broadly historical conditions, redeem a viable realism freed of Cartesian paradox and transcendental privilege. Rorty doesn't believe it, but never says why it can't succeed; and Brandom is unwilling to give up semantics and epistemology in the analytic sense, but sees no reason to feature the classic pragmatists or their nearest kin in his own theory, except as footnotes to Frege and Sellars.

Notes

1   This is also the essential thesis of Dummett 1991.
2   I offer a selection of pertinent examples in Margolis 2000.
3   Compare Sellars 1963a: 39–40. It is true that, in Sellars 1968, which is meant to flesh out the issues raised in Sellars 1963d, in effect, explicating Sellars's John Locke Lectures, the eliminativist issue of "Scientific Realism" is rendered more tentative (see Preface), though the issue is never really addressed again.
4   For further considerations regarding the gap between Frege and recent analytic philosophy, see Diamond 1984; Carruthers 1984; Noonan 1984; Hale 1984. I claim no special competence in deciding the right interpretation of Frege. On the contrary, I am impressed with the unusual difficulty, even today, of getting clear about Frege's precise views.
5   The typescript, somewhat more than a hundred pages, titled "Hegel's Philosophy of Spirit: Lectures by John Dewey" (University of Chicago, 1897), belongs to Southern Illinois University, Morris Library, Special Collection, John Dewey Papers, Collection 102. I was alerted to the essay by James Allan Good and a reading of his dissertation (Good 2001).

Bibliography

Brandom, R.B. (1994) *Making It Explicit*, Cambridge, MA: Harvard University Press.
—— (2000) *Articulating Reasons*, Cambridge, MA: Harvard University Press.
Carruthers, P. (1984) "Formal thoughts," in C. Wright (ed.), *Frege: Tradition and Influence*, Oxford: Basil Blackwell.
Coffa, J. A. (1991) *The Semantic Tradition from Kant to Carnap: To the Vienna Station*, Cambridge: Cambridge University Press.
Davidson, D. (1986) "A coherence theory of truth and knowledge," in E. Lepore (ed.), *Truth and Interpretation: Perspectives on the Philosophy of Donald Davidson*, Oxford: Basil Blackwell.
—— (2000), "Truth rehabilitated," in R.B. Brandom (ed.), *Rorty and His Critics*, Oxford: Blackwell.
Dewey, J. (1929) *The Quest for Certainty*, New York: Minton, Balch.
—— (1938) *Logic: The Theory of Inquiry*, New York: Henry Holt.

—— (1958) *Experience and Nature*, 2nd edn, New York: Dover.

Diamond, C. (1984) "What does a concept script do?" in C. Wright (ed.), *Frege: Tradition and Influence*, Oxford: Basil Blackwell.

Dummett, M. (1967) "Frege, Gottlob," in *The Encyclopedia of Philosophy*, ed. P. Edwards, 8 vols, New York: Macmillan.

—— (1973) *Frege; Philosophy of Language*, New York: Harper & Row.

—— (1991) *The Logical Basis of Metaphysics*, Cambridge, MA: Harvard University Press.

Frege, B. (1960) "Begriffschrift (Chapter 1)," trans. P.T. Geach, in P. Geach and M. Black (eds), *Translations from the Philosophical Writings of Gottlob Frege*, Oxford: Basil Blackwell.

Good, J.A. (2001) *A Search for Unity in Diversity: The "Permanent Hegelian Deposit" in the Philosophy of John Dewey*, Houston: Rice University, PhD dissertation.

Hale, B. (1984), "Frege's platonism," in C. Wright (ed.), *Frege: Tradition and Influence*, Oxford: Basil Blackwell.

Margolis, J. (2000) "Richard Rorty: philosophy by other means," *Metaphilosophy*, 31: 329–346.

McDowell, J. (1994, 1996), *Mind and World*. Cambridge: Harvard University Press.

Noonan, H. (1984) "Fregean thoughts," in C. Wright (ed.), *Frege: Tradition & Influence*., Oxford: Basil Blackwell.

Putnam, H. (1994), "Sense, nonsense, and the senses: an inquiry into the powers of the human mind," *Journal of Philosophy*, 91.

Rorty, R. (1967) *The Linguistic Turn: Recent Essays in Philosophical Method*, Chicago: University of Chicago Press.

—— (1986), "Pragmatism, Davidson and truth," in E. Lepore (ed.), *Truth and Interpretation: Perspectives on the Philosophy of Donald Davidson*, Oxford: Basil Blackwell.

—— (1998) "Robert Brandom on social practices and representations," *Philosophical Papers*, vol. 3, Cambridge: Cambridge University Press.

—— (1999) "Truth without correspondence to reality," *Philosophy and Social Hope*, Harmondsworth: Penguin.

—— (ed.) (2000a) "Introduction," in W. Sellars, *Empiricism and the Philosophy of Mind*, Cambridge, MA: Harvard University Press.

—— (2000b) "Response to Robert Brandom," in R.B. Brandom (ed.), *Rorty and His Critics*, Oxford: Blackwell.

Sellars, W. (1963a), "The language of theories," *Science, Perception and Reality*, London: Routledge and Kegan Paul.

—— (1963b), "Philosophy and the scientific image of man," *Science, Perception and Reality*, London: Routledge and Kegan Paul.

—— (1963c) "Empiricism and the philosophy of mind," *Science, Perception and Reality*, London: Routledge and Kegan Paul.

—— (1963d) *Science, Perception and Reality*, London: Routledge and Kegan Paul.

—— (1968) *Science and Metaphysics: Variation on Kantian Themes*. London: Routledge and Kegan Paul.

—— (1997) *Experience and the Philosophy of the Mind*, Cambridge: Harvard University Press.

—— (2000), *Empiricism and the Philosophy of Mind*, Cambridge, MA: Harvard University Press.

Wittgenstein, L. (1953) *Philosophical Investigations*, trans. G. E. M. Anscombe. Oxford: Basil Blackwell.

5 Avoiding wrong turns
A philippic against the linguistification of pragmatism

David L. Hildebrand

There is a general consensus that pragmatism's twenty-year renaissance produced two readily identifiable versions. One is typically called "classic" pragmatism, while the other goes by several names: "neopragmatism," "post-modern pragmatism," and the name I will use in this chapter, "linguistic pragmatism." To assess this newer form of pragmatism I pose and reply to three questions. First, how did linguistic pragmatism "update" classical pragmatism? Second, why does linguistic pragmatism reject "experience" as a useful philosophical notion? Finally, why is linguistic pragmatism wrong about "experience"? My general conclusion is this: because it is methodologically inseparable from pragmatism, experience is integral to pragmatism's vitality, to its ability to evolve with and make a difference in the world. It is this openness – not pragmatism's recent and fashionable association with postmodernism – that best explains a renewed and widespread enthusiasm for it. Thus, linguistic pragmatism may neglect or extirpate experience from pragmatism only at the terrible cost of rendering it philosophically impotent and practically unpopular.

Linguistic pragmatism

The development of linguistic pragmatism may be principally, if not exhaustively, attributed to Richard Rorty. In 1995 Rorty wrote,

> I linguisticize as many pre-linguistic-turn philosophers as I can, in order to read them as prophets of the utopia in which all metaphysical problems have been dissolved, and religion and science have yielded their place to poetry.
>
> (Rorty 1995: 35)

Rorty's influence upon intellectual life has been enormous, and for many outside the American philosophical community Rortyan pragmatism has become virtually synonymous with pragmatism itself. Given this fact, and the limits of this chapter, I shall treat Rorty's formulation of linguistic pragmatism as a type rather than a token.[1] The linguistic philosopher attempts to transform classical pragmatism with three basic steps. First, one applauds pragmatism for repudiating a variety of methods and goals in traditional philosophy. Second, one renounces classical pragmatism's attempt to reconstruct what should not be reconstructed. Finally, once these steps are completed – and one gets comfortable with the idea that only language can furnish philosophy's materiel – one creates freely, perhaps even poetically, with language that serves whatever ends seem best.

Since classical pragmatism's critiques of the tradition are well-known, I will not rehearse them. Consider instead the second part of linguistification, its renunciations. Classical pragmatism went awry, the story goes, by reconstructing such traditional ideas as "experience," "reality" and "inquiry" – and the very philosophical projects it sought to debunk. Had these pragmatists let such sterile projects rest in peace, they could have made a more persuasive and enduring case against the tradition.

Rorty's now-familiar fix of classical pragmatism split Dewey into two halves, good and bad. Good Dewey comprised Dewey's criticisms of the tradition – his attack on certainty, his antifoundationalism, his opposition to hosts of dualisms. Bad Dewey was the backsliding Dewey, the guy who couldn't resist concocting positive metaphysical notions. This Dewey, Rorty writes,

> thought it essential to say "Inquiry is the controlled or directed transformation of an indeterminate situation," where "an indeterminate situation" did not mean simply "one in which it is not clear what language to use for describing what is going on" but something stronger, something metaphysically distinctive.
>
> (Rorty 1985: 42–43)

Even more destructive to Dewey's momentum, Rorty claims, was his reconstruction of experience.

> [Dewey] was never to escape the notion that what he himself said about experience described what experience itself looked like, whereas what others said of experience was a confusion between the data and the products of their analyses. Others might be transcendentalizing metaphysicians, but he was a "humble psychologist." Other philosophers produced dualisms, he was to insist throughout his life, because they "erected the results of an analysis into real entities." But a nondualistic account of experience, of the sort Dewey himself proposed, was to be a true return to *die Sache selbst*.
>
> (Rorty 1982: 79–80)

I defend Dewey against this charge in the next section. What is important for Rorty's linguistic pragmatism is his claim that these essentializing moves (typical of several classical pragmatists) could have been avoided by utilizing the "linguistic turn." Rorty writes:

[A]nalytic philosophy, thanks to its concentration on language, was able to defend certain crucial pragmatist theses better than James and Dewey themselves. … By focusing our attention on the relation between language and the rest of the world rather than between experience and nature, post-positivistic analytic philosophy was able to make a more radical break with the philosophical tradition.

(Rorty 1985: 40)

Taking the linguistic turn would have enabled Dewey to avoid the fruitless task of determining the "methodological" differences between inquiries in different fields and, mistakenly, formulating philosophical portraits of the best method. He would have been able to see that scientific progress is not the result of improved "method" (itself a dubious notion) but rather one of the "development of particular vocabularies" (Rorty 1985: 41). As I understand it, Rorty's solution to the problem of incommensurable philosophical vocabularies is the adoption of a linguistic vocabulary which may serve as a metaphilosophical lingua franca. Somehow this vocabulary would be devoid of any metaphysical baggage of its own. Rorty writes:

"Language" is a more suitable notion than "experience" for saying the holistic and anti-foundational things which James and Dewey had wanted to say. This … [is] simply because the malleability of language is a less paradoxical notion than the malleability of nature or of "objects." By taking … "the linguistic turn" and emphasizing that no language is more intrinsically related to nature than any other, analytic philosophers such as Goodman and Putnam have been able to make the anti-realist arguments common to Dewey and Green more plausible than either of the latter made them.

(Rorty 1985: 40)

Linguistic pragmatism, then, eschews philosophical terms that refer to non-linguistic entities or effects; instead, it asks how we can "reweave beliefs" by using new and better "vocabularies." For example, "[a]ll talk about doing things to objects must, in a pragmatic account of inquiry 'into' objects, be paraphrasable as talk about reweaving beliefs. Nothing but efficiency will be lost in such translation" (Rorty 1991: 98). This interpolation by a linguistic vocabulary would simplify matters by insisting that referents be expressed in the same vocabulary. The effectiveness of language is measured with more language – not by dividing the world into "things" and "contexts," or into "hard lumps and squishy texts" (Rorty 1991: 98). "Reweaving a web of beliefs," Rorty says, "is … all anybody can do" (Rorty 1991: 101).

Assessment of linguistic pragmatism

Linguistic pragmatism clearly has an allure. It promises to strip philosophy of heavily freighted terms, facilitate communication and dissolve old conundrums.

It also promises to be completely adequate to new experience – since everything is characterized in language, language must be adequate to experience.[2] In addition, by promising to trim away philosophical jargon, it may eliminate barriers between philosophers and thinkers in other disciplines who share concerns about the same issues.

While I believe that the best defense one can make for the role of experience in pragmatism is a positive one (which I offer later in this chapter) I will conclude this exposition of linguistic pragmatism by indicating its shortcomings. First, there is the move from linguistic pragmatism's understandable skepticism about ever finding an ultimate ground for warrant to the more dubious postulate that language is ubiquitous. In Consequences of Pragmatism Rorty cites Derrida, Wilfrid Sellars, Gadamer, Foucault, and Heidegger and interprets them as all agreeing "that attempts to get back behind language to something which 'grounds' it, or which it 'expresses,' or to which it might hope to be 'adequate,' have not worked" (Rorty 1982: xx). But then Rorty immediately makes the following claim:

> The ubiquity of language is a matter of language moving into the vacancies left by the failure of all the various candidates for the position of "natural starting-points" of thought, starting-points which are prior to and independent of the way some culture speaks or spoke.
>
> (Rorty 1982: xx)

In one hurried leap, Rorty has taken us from the empirical observation that no one has achieved a God-like standpoint for comparing our language and the world to the metaphysical assertion that language (or "a web of belief") is ubiquitous, in other words, that "it is contexts all the way down" and that one "can only inquire after things under a description" (Rorty 1991: 99–100).[3] This inference is unwarranted. As Hilary Putnam observed,

> if we agree that it is unintelligible to say, "We sometimes succeed in comparing our language and thought with reality as it is in itself," then we must realize that it is also unintelligible to say, "It is impossible to stand outside and compare our thought and language with the world. ... Failing to inquire into the character of the unintelligibility which vitiates metaphysical realism, Rorty remains blind to the way in which his own rejection of metaphysical realism partakes of the same unintelligibility.
>
> (Putnam 1994: 299, 300)

Whether Rorty's move is "unintelligible" is a difficult question. What is of greater concern for a Deweyan is that the starting point of Rorty's claims (which form the pillars of linguistic pragmatism) is theoretical and not practical. By "theoretical" I mean this: all of Rorty's declarations – that language is ubiquitous, that everything is contexts, that nothing extra-linguistic can be appealed to in philosophical arguments – fail to follow as empirical generalizations from experience. Instead, their plausibility relies on their presumption in advance of inquiry. Rorty rightly calls traditional starting points "failures" but his view that language can now move "into the vacancies" reveals tacit acceptance of a traditional, theoretical approach. In my view, the adoption of that approach, in lieu of a practical one, is the fundamental error of linguistic pragmatism.[4] And it all begins with the extirpation of experience from Deweyan pragmatism.

Why linguistic pragmatism rejects "experience"

Before defending Dewey's reconstruction of experience, it is worth remembering two reasons it was rejected by linguistic pragmatists and others. First, it was incomprehensible to those with starkly different worldviews; second, it was mistaken for a traditional metaphysical notion meant to authorize a systematic and absolute description of reality. Rorty holds the latter view, arguing that experience was Dewey's theoretical way of dissolving intractable philosophical dualisms. Rorty writes:

> [Dewey's] resolution of the [rationalism–empiricism] conflict amounted to saying: there must be a standpoint from which experience can be seen in terms of some "generic traits" which, once recognized, will make it impossible for us to describe it in these misleading ways which generate the subject–object and mind–matter dualisms. … This viewpoint … would resemble traditional metaphysics in providing a permanent neutral matrix for future inquiry. Such a naturalistic metaphysics would say, "here is what experience is really like, before dualistic analysis has done its fell work."
>
> (Rorty 1982: 80, my emphasis)

On Rorty's skeptical reading, experience was a substitute for the hopeless notion of substance, and Dewey "should have dropped the term experience rather than redefining it [looking] … elsewhere for continuity between us and the brutes" ("Dewey Between Hegel and Darwin," Rorty 1995: 7). That he did not was unfortunate, Rorty believes, because his effort diverted crucial momentum netted by his criticisms of the tradition. Taking the linguistic turn would have helped Dewey refrain from anchoring justification in experience and allowed him to recognize that, as Rorty puts it, "we can eliminate epistemological problems by eliminating the assumption that justification must repose on something other than social practices and human needs" (Rorty 1982: 82). All pragmatist inquiry would need to aim for, then, is "the attainment of an appropriate mixture of unforced agreement with tolerant disagreement" (Rorty 1991: 41). In Rortyan shorthand, we may replace Objectivity (guaranteed by experience) with Solidarity (formed through community).

Why "experience" is indispensable to pragmatism

Having discussed some of linguistic pragmatism's methods and motivations, I shall now defend experience as an integral and coherent part of a fertile pragmatism. Dewey's writings on experience were extensive and revolutionary. He pushed philosophers toward recognizing the somatic (or non-discursive) dimension of experience;[5] he broadened aesthetics and ethics by directing philosophical discussion away from static values and toward the ongoing function of valuations. When judging the viability of linguistic pragmatism, "experience" is a crucial term because of its contributions to philosophical method.

A defense of experience may begin by noting that it is phenomenologically earnest. The intended meaning is quite ordinary. Pace Rorty, "experience" is not intended as "a permanent neutral matrix for future inquiry," nor as any other theoretical intermediary between appearance and reality; rather "experience" is to be synonymous with everyday things and events. Dewey writes,

> The plain man, for a surety, does not regard noises heard, lights seen, etc., as mental existences; but neither does he regard them as things known. That they are just things is good enough for him. ... [H]is attitude to these things as things involves their not being in relation to mind or a knower.
>
> (*MW* 6: 108)

To update the point, we might substitute "language" for "mind" and say that the average person doesn't regard noises, lights, or cars as "bits of language" or "moves in a language game." As they are had, they just are as they are experienced. As Ralph Sleeper put it, "it is not experience that is experienced, but things and events, an environing context that we can 'cope' with ... through transactional inquiry" (Sleeper 1985: 14–15). "Experience" is radically empirical by not being radical at all. It points to what Ortega y Gassett called "my life," a continuum of things, events, relations, and transactions. My life is havings, sayings, doings, and knowings, and while I can refer to my life (as in the melancholy rumination "So this is my life"), I cannot stand behind or above it while I do.

This method of pointing constitutes another way experience is earnest: it recommends a method that neither offers nor authorizes wholesale accounts that permanently abstract concepts from their practical contexts – e.g., "color" into "vibrations," "pain" into "brain states," or "talk about objects" into "talk about beliefs." As method, experience guides philosophical energies away from spectatorial definitions toward an engaged and conscientious denotation of what is concretely present. Dewey writes:

> The value ... of the notion of experience for philosophy is that it asserts the finality and comprehensiveness of the method of pointing, finding, showing, and the necessity of seeing what is pointed to and accepting what is found in good faith and without discount.
>
> (*LW* 1: 372)

One of the observations Dewey makes "in good faith and without discount" is that experiencing occurs in ways both "had" (or "undergone") and "known."

> [I]n the process of living both absorption in a present situation and a response that takes account of its effect upon … later experiences are equally necessary for maintenance of life. … [S]ituations are immediate in their direct occurrence, and mediating and mediated in the temporal continuum constituting life-experience.
>
> (*LW* 14: 30)

Now, these two crucial ideas – that philosophy should start with denotation rather than theoretical supposition and that observation indicates a persistent and generic difference between reflective and non-reflective experiencing – are both anathematic to linguistic pragmatism. But both have been widely misunderstood.

Some saw Dewey's repeated insistence that philosophy use the denotative method as simplistic – how, they objected, can reality just be pointed to? Dewey elaborated that denotation "is not so simple and direct an affair as pointing a finger – or tapping on a table" but is rather "having such ideas as point and lead by use as methods to some directly experienced situation" (*LW* 3: 82–83).

A second and more tenacious objection (from both realists and linguistic pragmatists) is that "experience" is a foundationalist notion. This misapprehension develops out of the conviction that any attempt to describe "had" or non-discursive experience requires a privileged (i.e., extra-experiential) standpoint. But such a standpoint would violate Dewey's naturalism, putting it in what Douglas Browning calls "the phenomenological paradox." The paradox, Browning writes, is as follows:

> how can [Dewey] adequately describe our immediately lived, pre-reflective experiences without assuming a stance for surveying them which, being reflective and retrospective, cannot help but disclose them, not as they were experienced in the intimacy of our living through them, but as "objects" which we are viewing externally?[6]

Being itself a reflective (linguistic) act, description must color any pre-reflective subject matter it describes; since philosophy – pragmatism included – comments only by means of reflective symbols it cannot illuminate this level of experience (if it can even be shown to exist). Insofar as Dewey did this anyway, he was in bad faith. This accusation strikes at the core of Dewey's pragmatism and may be the most important issue to clarify and defend.

Dewey might begin his defense by citing a lesson from "The Postulate of Immediate Empiricism." Here, he argues that a thing's reality is not solely a matter of what it is known to be; other modes of experiencing are no less important in the constitution of reality. (Revulsion, while it is an experience that resists precise characterization, is no less real than a theory of rights.) Once a critic acknowledges Dewey's point (the equal reality of non-rational modes of experiencing), they must then admit that Dewey need not choose between offering either a precise and final anatomy of the non-discursive or none at all. Under the postulate of immediate empiricism, the vague is reinstated and can remain vague.[7] In this connection, it is also relevant that since experience has duration, the penumbra and foci of one's experiences are fluid – what is now peripheral may later move front and center and could be neatly encapsulated. A vague fear-of-flying, for example, later serves as a focal point for autobiographical inquiries. Dewey writes that

> [I]n any object of primary experience there are always potentialities which are not explicit; any object that is overt is charged with possible consequences that are hidden; the most overt act has factors which are not explicit. Strain thought as far as we may and not all consequences can be foreseen or made an express or known part of reflection and decision.
>
> (*LW* 1: 28)

Dewey's point is that while much of "had" experience is peripheral to conscious attention, it is not for that reason, thin. Nevertheless, he is not saying that the qualitative uniqueness of an experienced moment can be captured by language. Characterization of such experiences may proceed empirically: observe, propose, test, and revise. It is given, Dewey believes, that we never pin down primary experiences – their fullness passes with their moment – but we may approximate them, conscious of the fact that approximations stand or fall based upon their instrumentality to a particular inquiry.

In sum, pragmatism gives no axiomatic answer to the metaphysical question, "What is primary experience?" but responds to it with inquiry. Dewey, Sleeper reminds us, was not attempting to ground inquiry by first working out a metaphysics of experience. Rather, "[h]e was trying to work out a metaphysics of existence on the basis of the successes of inquiry already in practice" (Sleeper 1985: 17). All inquiries begin in media res; a pragmatist metaphysics can serve as a ground map of criticism "only after the territory has been explored, and only after you have made [the map] can it serve as a guide to further explorations" (Sleeper 1992: 184). And of course, a map's cartographic assertions will be warranted by the historical context, needs and purposes that make up the practical matrix.

If this connection between inquiry and metaphysics is taken to heart, it becomes clear that experience is not the keystone to Dewey's secret foundationalism; it is not what Sellars called a "self-authenticating nonverbal episode," a basis for certainty. For Dewey, epistemological warrant doesn't rest or repose on experience, it draws from and submits to it for experimental verification. Moreover, a proposition is warranted if it "agrees" with its issue, but linguistic pragmatists must remember that this is warrant-through-action not warrant-though-intersubjective-discourse. The "agreement," Dewey writes, "is agreement in activities, not intellectual acceptance of the same set of propositions. ... A proposition does not gain validity because of the number of persons who accept it" (*LW* 12: 484, emphasis mine). While Dewey does not draw a categorical distinction between language and action (language is clearly a species of action for Dewey), he leaves little room for the linguistic pragmatists' restricted notion of warrant-as-intersubjective-agreement-within-an-ethnos. While norms of warrant are shaped by cultural and historical circumstances, experienced situations are their ultimate measure, and such situations always overflow present formulas. When something works, it works, and when it fits, it fits.[8]

The ineffability of experience

The arguments just trotted out will not convince linguistic pragmatists to endorse extra-linguistic experience unless they make a fundamental, methodological shift: they must inhabit a practical standpoint. Contemplation of Dewey's position isn't sufficient – they must be invited to try it out and see how it plays out. The romantic suitor quickly discovers that he cannot argue the beloved into marriage; rather, the beloved must be invited to imagine what it would be like. Likewise must Deweyans court other philosophers to see that

> all intellectual knowing is but a method for conducting an experiment, and that arguments and objections are but stimuli to induce somebody to try a certain experiment – to have recourse, that is, to a non-logical non-intellectual affair. ... The importance attached to the word "experience" ... is to be understood as an invitation to employ thought and discriminative knowledge as a means of plunging into something which no argument and no term can express; The word "experience" is, I repeat, a notation of an inexpressible as that which decides the ultimate status of all which is expressed; inexpressible not because it is so remote and transcendent, but because it is so immediately engrossing and matter of course.
>
> (Dewey MW 10: 325, fn. 1)

The fact that experience has varieties – aesthetic, moral, discursive, non-discursive – is neither unnatural nor exclusively the product of linguistic practice. But because habits of description and categorization are so deeply ingrained, the linguistic pragmatist chafes at the idea that language is constrained by a description-defying world, and perhaps even doubts that world altogether. This predicament – the incommunicability of the non-linguistic – Dewey says, is inherent, according to genuine empiricism, in the derived relationship of discourse to primary experience. Any one who refuses to go outside the universe of discourse ... has of course shut himself off from understanding what a "situation," as directly experienced subject-matter, is.

(*LW* 14: 30–31)

The danger of pragmatism's adoption of a linguistic starting point is that one eventually shuns the practical arena where intellectual terms must ultimately sink or swim. Skirting such verification is unpragmatic as it blocks the road of inquiry.

Experience: a directive for philosophical method

Let me conclude my defense of the term experience by saying a word about its fallible and ethical dimensions. Life, as we live it, is largely beyond our control. It foists upon us the good, the bad, the beautiful, and the ugly. Since we have significantly greater control over theories than over experience, we develop a penchant to have them to limn our wishes. To balance this, Dewey believes, we need

a cautionary and directive word, like experience, to remind us that the world which is lived, suffered and enjoyed as well as logically thought of, has the last word in all human inquiries and surmises. This is a doctrine of humility; but it is also a doctrine of direction. For it tells us to open the eyes and ears of the mind, to be sensitive to all the varied phases of life and history.

(*LW* 1: 372–373)

As a doctrine for pragmatist method, experience commits pragmatism to radical fallibility; it defies totalizing appraisals declaring "it's contexts all the way down" or "all experience is a linguistic affair" or "reweaving a web of beliefs is ... all anybody can do." It forbids neither realism nor legitimation, but insists that they be advocated, as Joseph Margolis puts it, "in a relativistic, historicized, anti-universalistic spirit" (Margolis 1992: 38).

Such methodological cautions are also ethical enhancements since they help sustain our sensitivity to the world as it is fully present. As an integral part of philosophical method, experience links pragmatism and social progress. When experience serves as the starting point for inquiry, the resulting philosophy can, as Dewey put it, provide "criticism of the influential beliefs that underlie culture; a criticism which traces the beliefs to their generating conditions as far as may be, [and] which tracks them to their results" ("Context and Thought," *LW* 6: 19). If one subscribes to the philosopher-as-gadfly ideal, it follows that she can only fulfill that obligation if she is not tangled in endless scholastic disputes. A gadfly must be free, in other words, to follow the horse. Experience as method encourages this ideal by keeping alive in philosophy the recurring admonition to address social and political issues, and to ensure that, in Dewey's words,

> the distinctive office, problems and subject matter of philosophy grow out of stresses and strains in the community life ... and that ... its specific problems vary with the changes in human life that are always going on and that at times constitute a crisis and a turning point in human history.
>
> (*MW* 12: 256)

Conclusion

There is little need to radically reconstruct Deweyan pragmatism. While pragmatism must accommodate contemporary circumstances, such accommodations are enhanced and not hindered by the notion of experience. Pragmatists can root theory in experience without being foundationalists; the choice is not "be anchored or be adrift." They can dodge the totalizing thrust of linguistic pragmatism by remembering that there is a continuity of language and action.

> [T]he sound, gesture, or written mark which is involved in language is a particular existence. But as such it is not a word, and it does not become a word by declaring a mental existence; it becomes a word by gaining meaning; and it gains meaning when its use establishes a genuine community of action.
>
> (*LW* 1: 145)

This connection to action remains the ethical pivot on which pragmatism turns. One embraces experience as integral to pragmatist philosophy because it relates, it transacts – it keeps us doing philosophy, rather than just reading and writing about it.

To the extent that the elimination of experience (i.e., the elimination of a practical starting point) underwrites linguistic pragmatism, I believe it is in serious error.[9] It results in a pragmatism with an all-language metaphysics that divides word from world; more important, it philosophizes from a theoretical standpoint that reemploys, under the name "pragmatism," a spectator theory of knowledge.

Finally, it perhaps behooves me to explain why, in the end, anyone should care about this issue. What difference does it make if one believes one version of pragmatism or another? One practical reason is that the spectatorial stance embodied in linguistic pragmatism poses a serious threat to classical pragmatism's long-term viability. Many outside American philosophy are excited about pragmatism because they perceive it to be applicable to contemporary problems while remaining honest about its own fallibilities. The more the perception grows that pragmatism is spectatorial in approach (as, I have argued, linguistic pragmatism is), the more it will seem like just another theory. That perception would overshadow pragmatism's enduring appeal as equipment for living.

Notes

1   For a fuller discussion of Rorty and linguistic pragmatism (sometimes called "neopragmatism") see my *Beyond Realism and Antirealism: John Dewey and the Neopragmatists* (Hildebrand 2003).

2   Despite the fact Rorty is suspicious of the concept "experience," he is nevertheless willing to assign language the task of enriching it. In "Response to Hartshorne" Rorty says,

> Hartshorne defines a necessary truth as one "with which any conceivable experience is at least compatible." My objection is that we do not yet have any idea what is and what is not a conceivable experience. Because I think of the enrichment of language as the only way to enrich experience, and because I think that language has no transcendental limits, I think of experience as potentially infinitely enrichable.
>
> (Rorty 1995: 36, my emphasis)

3   The claim that language adequately captures experience is shared by others such as Wilfrid Sellars ("all awareness is a linguistic affair"), Hans-Georg Gadamer (who emphasizes "the essential linguisticality of all human experience of the world"), and Jacques Derrida (there cannot be a "hors-texte," "a reality ... whose content could take place, could have taken place outside of language.") See Sellars 1963: 60; Gadamer 1976: 19; Derrida 1976: 158. These passages are quoted in Shusterman 1999: 210.

4   Thus linguistic pragmatism shares territory with the epistemologies Dewey had set himself against. "Modern epistemology," Dewey wrote, "leads to the view that realities must themselves have a theoretic and intellectual complexion – not a practical one" (*MW* 4:127). This and future citations of Dewey's works are based on the critical edition and abbreviated as follows: *John Dewey: The Middle Works*, 14 vols (Carbondale: Southern Illinois University Press, 1976–1988) is abbreviated to *MW*; *John Dewey: The Later Works*, 17 vols (Carbondale: Southern Illinois University Press, 1981–1991) is abbreviated to *LW*.

5   See, for example, Wilshire 1993: 266; see also Shusterman 1999.

6   Browning, forthcoming.

7   "It is important for philosophic theory to be aware that the distinct and evident are prized and why they are. But it is equally important to note that the dark and twilight abound. For in any object of primary experience there are always potentialities which are not explicit; any object that is overt is charged with possible consequences that are hidden; the most overt act has factors which are not explicit" (*LW* 1: 28).

8   It is valuable to remember what Dewey pointed out in *Logic: The Theory of Inquiry* about the intermediate phase occupied by theory in the process of inquiry.

> Understanding or interpretation is a matter of the ordering of those materials that are ascertained to be facts; that is, determination of their relations. In any given subject-matter there exist many relations of many kinds. That particular set of relations which is relevant to the problem in hand has to be determined. Relevant theoretical conceptions come into play only as the problem in hand is clear and definite; that is, theory alone cannot decide what set of relations is to be instituted, or how a given body of facts is to be understood. A mechanic, for example, understands the various parts of a machine, say an automobile, when and only when he knows how the parts work together. ... The conception of "working together" involves the conception of consequences: the significance of things resides in the conse-

quences they produce when they interact with other specified things. The heart of the experimental method is determination of the significance of observed things by means of deliberate institution of modes of interaction.

(*LW* 12: 504)

9   It should be understood that I am advocating a course correction and not an abolition of linguistic pragmatism (unless they come to the same thing). What Dewey wrote about logical standpoints (on experience) applies equally well to linguistic ones:

> There is, then, nothing final about a logical [linguistic] rendering of experience. Its value is not contained in itself; its significance is that of standpoint, outlook, method. It intervenes between the more casual, tentative, and round-about experiences of the past, and more controlled and orderly experiences of the future. It gives past experience in that net form which renders it most available and most significant, most fecund for future experience. The abstractions, generalizations, and classifications which it introduces all have prospective meaning.
>
> (*MW* 2: 285)

Bibliography

Browning, D. (forthcoming) "Introduction," in reissue of *John Dewey, The Influence of Darwin on Philosophy*, Southern Illinois University Press, manuscript page 29.

Derrida, J. (1976) *Of Grammatology*, Baltimore: Johns Hopkins University Press.

Dewey, J. (1981–91) *The Later Works*, 17 vols, Carbondale: Southern Illinois University Press.

—— (1976–88) *The Middle Works*, 14 vols, Carbondale: Southern Illinois University Press.

Gadamer, H. (1976) *Philosophical Hermeneutics*, Berkeley: University of California Press.

Hildebrand, D. (2003) *Beyond Realism and Antirealism: John Dewey and the Neopragmatists*, Nashville: Vanderbilt University Press.

Margolis, J. (1992) "A Convergence of Pragmatisms," in Robert W. Burch and Herman J. Saatkamp, Jr (eds), *Frontiers of American Philosophy*, vol. 1, College Station: Texas A&M University Press.

Putnam, H. (1994) in J. Conant (ed.), *Words and Life*, Cambridge, MA: Harvard University Press.

Rorty, R. (1982) *Consequences of Pragmatism: Essays: 1972–1980*, Minneapolis: University of Minnesota Press.

—— (1985) "Comments on Sleeper and Edel," *Transactions of the Charles S. Peirce Society*, 21: 39–48.

—— (1991) "Objectivity, Relativism, and Truth," *Philosophical Papers*, vol. 1, Cambridge: Cambridge University Press.

—— (1995) "Response to Hartshorne," in H. Saatkamp (ed.), *Rorty and Pragmatism: The Philosopher Responds to His Critics*, Nashville: Vanderbilt University Press.

Sellars, W. (1963) *Science, Perception, and Reality*, London: Routledge and Kegan Paul.

Shusterman, R. (1999) "Dewey on Experience: Foundation or Reconstruction?" in Haskins and Seiple (eds), *Dewey Reconfigured: Essays on Deweyan Pragmatism*, New York: SUNY Press.

Sleeper, R. (1985) "Rorty's Pragmatism: Afloat in Neurath's Boat, But Why Adrift?" *Transactions of the Charles S. Peirce Society*, 21: 9–20.

—— (1992) "What is Metaphysics?" *Transactions of the Charles S. Peirce Society*, 28: 177–187.

Wilshire, B. (1993) "Body–Mind and Subconsciousness," in J. Stuhr (ed.), *Philosophy and the Reconstruction of Culture*, Albany: SUNY Press, pp. 257–272.

6 Pragmatism as post-postmodernism[1]

Larry A. Hickman

I take as my point of departure the now famous remark by Richard Rorty, that when certain of the postmodernists reach the end of the road they are traveling they will find Dewey there waiting for them. The precise text I have in mind is from the introduction to *The Consequences of Pragmatism*. It goes like this: "On my view," Rorty writes, "James and Dewey were not only waiting at the end of the dialectical road which analytic philosophy traveled, but are waiting at the end of the road which, for example, Foucault and Deleuze are currently traveling" (1982: xvii).

Now I freely admit that when Rorty wrote this sentence he probably had something different in mind than what I intend to suggest in this chapter. That much is clear from his remarks on Foucault and Dewey several hundred pages later. He tells us there that the burden of his argument:

> is that we should see Dewey as having already gone the route Foucault is traveling, and as having arrived at the point Foucault is still trying to reach – the point at which we can make philosophical and historical ("genealogical") reflection useful to those, in Foucault's phrase, "whose fight is located in the fine meshes of the webs of power."
>
> (Rorty 1982: 207)

Rorty fleshes this point out in an admirable manner when he writes that although Foucault's philosophy of language and his analysis of power relations seem new, Dewey anticipated both. Even further, he suggests that Foucault's "structures of power" are not much different from what Dewey described as "structures of culture."

But these remarks, taken as they stand, allow us only to conclude that Dewey is on the same road and has reached the same point that the others have traveled. In what sense is he, as Rorty has put it, "waiting at the end of the road?" Rorty thinks that this is a matter of Dewey's superior vocabulary, which "allows room for unjustifiable hope and an ungroundable but vital sense of human solidarity" (1982: 208).

In what follows I want to indicate some of the ways in which Dewey's version of pragmatism can be viewed as having advanced beyond the positions held by some of the authors commonly identified as postmodern. In other words, I will suggest that Dewey's pragmatism can and should be viewed as a form of "post-postmodernism." Of course I do not intend to argue that there is any sort of "linear" progress in philosophy, or that Dewey has somehow leapfrogged postmodernism. There are in fact several important senses in which Dewey is a postmodern thinker. Kwame Anthony Appiah (1992) and James Livingston, among others, have called attention to elements of postmodernism in Dewey's thought, and Livingston has even identified some of those elements as already well formed during the first decades of the twentieth century (1994: 214ff). What I intend to do instead is to identify some of the problems that I believe postmodernism leaves unresolved, and then indicate how I think Dewey had already dealt with them early in the twentieth century. It is in this sense that I am terming his variety of pragmatism "post-postmodernism." Or to put matters another way, it is postmodernism without some of its problems. To put this in some sort of perspective, however, it would probably be good to say something about how I understand the term "postmodernism."[2]

What, precisely, is postmodernism?

What precisely is it that is postmodern about postmodernism? Precision is difficult here, since the term is notoriously slippery. Elizabeth Deeds Ermarth, who has written an admirable book on the subject (1992), has even gone as far as to suggest that the word may not function so much as a term of reference as a way to "hold open a space for that which exceeds expression" (Ermarth 1998). Stated negatively, however, I believe that it is fair to say that postmodernism rejects some of the key assumptions, methods, and conclusions of the period from Descartes to Hegel and beyond. In so doing, of course, it also rejects many of the assumptions, methods, and conclusions of the philosophical tradition going all the way back to Plato and Aristotle. In Appiah's book, this involves the rejection of foundationalism and other forms of epistemological exclusivism, the rejection of metaphysical realism and other forms of ontological exclusivism, and the celebration of such figures as Nietzsche and Dewey (1992: 143).

Ermarth has provided us with what is probably one of the best summary statements of the movement, if indeed that is what we wish to call it. She suggests that postmodernism can be recognized by two key assumptions:

> First, the assumption that there is no common denominator – in "nature" or "God" or "the future" – that guarantees either the One-ness of the world or the possibility of neutral or objective thought. Second, the assumption that all human systems operate like language, being self-reflexive rather than referential systems – systems of differential function

which are powerful but finite, and which construct and maintain meaning and value.

(Ermarth 1998)

I find it extremely helpful that she is keen to differentiate postmodernism from its near relative, deconstruction. The latter, she argues, often gets caught up in its own circularity because of its preoccupation with what a text is not, rather than what it is. On the other hand, postmodernism is characterized by its positive efforts to construct meaning in the absence of transcendent value and to find ways of acting in the absence of Absolute truth. Despite the fact that some may find this view controversial, I hope that I will be allowed just to stipulate it and move on (Ermarth 1998).

It is instructive to move back and forth between Ermarth's tight characterization of what the varieties of postmodernism have in common and Appiah's similarly precise characterization of how they differ by discipline. In technical philosophy, as I have already indicated, Appiah thinks that postmodernism involves the rejection of foundationalism and other forms of epistemological exclusivism, the rejection of metaphysical realism and other forms of ontological exclusivism, and the celebration of such figures as Nietzsche and Dewey. A discussion of this claim and its implications is, of course, the main subject of this chapter.

In architecture, postmodernism rejects the exclusivism of function, and thus the styles of Le Corbusier and Mies, in favor of a taste for playfulness and pastiche. This means, I suppose, that postmodernist architects would include the great Antonio Gaudi of Catalonia, as well as the less accomplished but equally playful designers of those taco restaurants of the American southwest that resemble giant sombreros. And then of course there is the incomparable postmodernist architecture of Las Vegas.

A third type of postmodernism is encountered in literature. In this form, Appiah tells us, it is a reaction against the "high seriousness" of authors such as Proust, Eliot, and Woolf. This, I suppose, implies a turn toward the self-reflexive playfulness of authors such as James Joyce and Donald Barthelme. In addition, given the preoccupation of some French and American philosophers with the permutations of the trope, it may well be that their work would fit this category better than the first, that is, postmodernism in philosophy. It is also significant in this regard that postmodernist Richard Rorty, trained as a philosopher and widely regarded as one of its most important practitioners, has most recently occupied a position as professor of comparative literature.

Appiah finds a fourth type of postmodernism exhibited in political theory. In this case it rejects the tendencies of "Big-M" Marxism and other monolithic enterprises, turning instead to a celebration of pluralism and perspectivism. Appiah's characterization of this last variety of postmodernism appears to be supported by the evolution of the Frankfurt School, to take just one example. First generation critical theorists, such as Adorno, tended to regard techno-science in block fashion as reified ideology, operating apart from and opposed to the activities of the lifeworld. Second generation critical theorists, such as Habermas, tended to focus on the problems of constitutionality and consensus by means of communicative action. And their third generation heirs, such as Andrew Feenberg and Axel Honneth, tend to regard technoscience as embedded in the social matrix and thus to concentrate on problems of globalization, pluralism, and multi-culturalism.

What all of this boils down to for Appiah is space: postmodernism is in his view "a new way of understanding the multiplication of distinctions that flows from the need to clear oneself a space; the need that drives the underlying dynamic of cultural modernity." "Modernism," he writes, "saw the economization of the world as the triumph of reason; postmodernism rejects that claim, allowing in the realm of theory the same multiplication of distinctions we see in the cultures it seeks to understand" (1992: 145). For Appiah, who is an up-close observer of modernism as it has been expressed in the form of colonialism, postmodernism is culturally liberating. In its function as a system of communication, postmodernism is more or less the phenomenon that Marshall McLuhan[3] described in great detail during the 1960s, that is, an opening to the celebration of individual and group differences under an overarching communications superstructure that eventually replaces the function of the nation state. In its commercial, and even its educational manifestations, it may well turn out to be what some entrepreneurs are now calling "mass customization" – the mass production of objects tailored to individual wants and needs.

At this point it seems appropriate to recall one of the best known statements of postmodernism, the one that occurs in the work of Jean-François Lyotard. A crucial feature of what Lyotard calls "the postmodern condition" is the end of what he terms "the master narrative." What does this mean? Even more to the point of my title, what does it mean in terms of how we should understand Dewey's work?

Postmodernism without some of its problems

(1) If the end of the master narrative means recognition of the futility of attempts to build metaphysical systems such as those constructed by Hegel and Marx, systems that attempt to encompass everything, then Dewey was already a card-carrying postmodernist more than a century ago. In a letter to James Rowland Angell, dated 10 May 1893, for example, he wrote that "Metaphysics has had its day, and if the truths which Hegel saw cannot be stated as direct, practical truths, they are not true" (Dewey 1997: 1893.05.10).

An indication of Dewey's disdain for systematic metaphysics, metaphysics-as-usual, can be found even in familiar remarks addressed to his wife Alice. In 1891, two years before his "metaphysics has had its day" remark to Angell, Dewey had written to Alice that he had been approached by a speculator at the Chicago Board of Trade, a certain Mr Van Ostrand, who had been working on a philosophical "scheme." Van Ostrand had offered Dewey $100 to serve as a kind of philosophical consultant. (This was, by the way, no mean sum. We know, for example, that just 18 months earlier Dewey's contract had called for an annual salary of $2,200.) "[F]or the first time on record," he told Alice, "in our experience at least, metaphysics made the connexion [sic] with the objective world – If there are many men like him in Chicago," he joked, "I'll resign & go out there & hang up a sign 'Dr. Dewey, Metaphysical healer' " (Dewey 1997: 1891.05.31).

In short, if Lyotard's remark about master narratives means that meta-physics-as-system-that-accounts-for-everything[4] is defunct, then Dewey was already a postmodernist almost a century before Lyotard's famous dictum was published in French in 1979.

(2) There is a second possible interpretation of Lyotard's remark. The end of the master narrative might be taken to mean that metaphysics in any form is impossible because it claims too much as a privileged position, that the varieties of human experience are deep down at their most fundamental levels ungrounded and incommensurable. On this reading, the best that we can do is to "cope" with that fact, to construct whatever solidarity that we can in our roles as what Rorty terms "ironists," that is, as people who know that our brave front and our best efforts may be futile. As Rorty puts it:

> liberals have come to expect philosophy to do a certain job – namely, answering questions like "Why not be cruel?" and "Why be kind?" – and they feel that any philosophy which refuses this assignment must be heartless. But that expectation is a result of a metaphysical upbringing. If we could get rid of the expectation, liberals would not ask ironist philosophy to do a job which it cannot do, and which it defines itself as unable to do.
>
> (1989: 94)

So this second possibility seems to reflect Rorty's own version of the postmodernist distaste for metaphysics. If we accept this alternative, then Dewey was not a postmodernist, I would argue, but in fact laid out a position that is much richer and goes well beyond that feckless view of matters. In other words, Dewey was a post-postmodernist. (Of course there is an irony here that Rorty may not have fully appreciated. The positivism that he dislikes and the forms of postmodernism that he appears to like share an interesting trait: they both hold some form of the position that philosophy is not capable of addressing ethical issues such as the ones that Rorty raised in the passage just quoted. In the case of positivism it is because such issues are consigned to the jam-packed realm of everything that is non-cognitive. In the case of Rortian postmodernism, it is because there is no adequate common denominator for human experience.)

Bruno Latour is among the few thinkers who have noted this remarkable situation. In a 1993 interview, for example, he charged "much of postmodernism" with being scientistic:

they are not indignant at the ahuman dimension of technology – again they leave indignation to the moderns – no, they like it. They relish its completely naked, sleek, ahuman aspect. In other words, they accept the disenchantment argument, but they just take it as a positive feature instead of a negative one.

(Crawford 1993: 254)[5]

How did Dewey go beyond postmodernism in this context? How did he resolve some of its core difficulties? Put simply, he argued that there is a commonality of human experience that can ultimately trump the compartmentalizing, hyper-relativistic tendencies latent in most forms of postmodernism. This view, which is a part of his evolutionary naturalism, is grounded in the empirical observations and experimental work of anthropologists and evolutionary biologists, and its fruition comes in what he regards as the natural activity of communication, which for human beings includes inquiry as an essential component and which is able to construct pluralistic links across the various cultures and disciplines that would otherwise be isolated. As humans we share certain common features. And one of the most important of those common features, Dewey contends, is our ability to do the type of cognitive, reconstructive work with respect to our environing conditions, including our environing social conditions, that allows us to think in terms of those common features.

This general cultural point is sharpened and called upon to do a prodigious amount of philosophical work in Dewey's famous remark about the role of philosophy as "liaison officer." In *Experience and Nature*, he writes: "Thus philosophy as a critical organ becomes in effect a messenger, a liaison officer, making reciprocally intelligible voices speaking provincial tongues, and thereby enlarging as well as rectifying the meanings with which they are charged" (1981: 306). This metaphor, by the way, has distinct advantages over some of its alternatives. It is more positive than getting flies out of fly bottles, it is more active than philosophy as platzhalter, and it is less imperious than philosophy as platzfinder. The first of these alternative metaphors, of course, we owe to Wittgenstein. The latter two we owe to Habermas, who accepts the first and rejects the second.

Dewey is thus a postmodernist in the sense that he rejects the notion that there is some foundation of certainty on which we can stand. He made that much clear early on, and put the matter to rest fairly well in his important little book *The Quest for Certainty*. But he is post-postmodernist in the sense that he reconstructed and put to work what the postmodernists had just dismissed: he argued that there is a set of organic functions or activities that are natural to human beings as a group, that reveal their common evolution, and that can be employed as a part of the process of testing and securing desired ends. He argued, for example, that human communication, within which inquiry is embedded, is as natural an activity as is chewing or walking.

If we fast-forward some thirty-two years past Dewey's "metaphysics is dead" remark to Angell, to take the measure of the three dozen or so times Dewey employs the term "metaphysics" in *Experience and Nature*, then we find him taking a position that is critical of both modernist and postmodernist conceptions of metaphysics. Whereas he had washed his hands of metaphysics-as-system earlier in his career, he now rejects the view that metaphysics should be abandoned altogether. His naturalism compels him to attempt to reconstruct the term, as well as the enterprise for which it stands. He wants to break new ground. Of course there is still a postmodernist component to his efforts: he has jettisoned what philosophers from Plato to Hegel and beyond had held dear, namely an "antecedent metaphysics of existence" (1981: 49). This is without a doubt one of the features of his thought that has led Appiah to include him among postmodernists, or at least as having inspired postmodernists.

Put another way, if we take Ermarth's suggestion, that for postmodernism "there is no common denominator – in 'nature' or 'God' or 'the future' – that guarantees either the One-ness of the world or the possibility of neutral or objective thought," then Dewey's naturalistic metaphysics has already gone beyond that skeptical point – beyond the postmodernist idea that there is no common denominator – to the more mature position that I am calling post-postmodernism. A key feature of this post-postmodernism is his argument that there are, after all, common features of human experience, and that those common features are accessible by means of (what I am calling) a post-postmodernist metaphysics as "the generic traits of existence." As for the matter of objectivity, Dewey's treatment is similar to the one since advanced by Bruno Latour: objectivity means that something can be experimentally objected to, and this within a community of inquiry – perhaps even one that is very broad indeed.

So we must read Dewey with care. To those who are attentive to his remarks, it is clear that he is not interested in merely exhuming the corpse of Enlightenment reason and giving it a new set of clothes. That critics as different as Bertrand Russell and Max Horkheimer accused him of doing something like this is a comment not about his work but about their careless reading of it. For all of his praise of Bacon's experimentalism, Dewey is doing something much more interesting than merely restating, or even reinstating, modernism. He seems to be saying that once the reactions to the extremes of Enlightenment rationality expend their fits of energy, once cultural criticism has reached the point in its trajectory at which essentialism has given way to forms of relativism that prove to be irrelevant (or worse, divisive), or to preoccupation with irony-as-our-only-hope hand-wringing, or to an emphasis on self-reflexivity to the extent that referentiality goes into total eclipse, then it will be time for a renewed attention to what he terms "the denotative method," namely, method that focuses experimental attention on the pushes and pulls of existential affairs. Philosophy, having abandoned observation and experiment in favor of arcane stylistic felicities, will once again have to become more public, more vigorous. Philosophy will once again have to attempt to regain its footing by addressing some of the core problems of postmodernism.

Philosophy can remain relevant, indeed vigorous, as it employs what Dewey called "the denotative method." This denotation is, of course, not one of simple correspondence. It is rather experimental, reconstructive, and dialogical. The experiential or denotative method, Dewey writes,

> tells us that we must go behind the refinements and elaborations of reflective experience to the gross and compulsory things of our doings, enjoyments and sufferings – to the things that force us to labor, that satisfy needs, that surprise us with beauty, that compel obedience under penalty. A common divisor is a convenience, and a greatest common divisor has the greatest degree of convenience. But there is no reason for supposing that its intrinsic "reality" or truth is greater than that of the numbers it divides. The objects of intellectual experience are the greatest common divisor of the things of other modes; they have that remarkable value, but to convert them into exclusive reality is the sure road to arbitrary divisions and insoluble problems.
>
> (1981: 375–6)

Dewey's post-postmodernist assessment of the human situation will, I suggest, turn out to provide the advantage of objectivity without the twin disadvantages of the inflexibility of modernist attempts at foundationalism, at one extreme, and the disconnectedness of deracinated postmodernist topologies, at the other.

In order to see what is at stake, it may be helpful to understand this dialectic between modernism and postmodernism as reflecting the ancient struggle between classicism and romanticism. The classical position of the modernists – with its emphasis on foundationalism, essentialism, and realism – demands narrow discipline and thus forecloses many of our options. The space it provides now seems closed and cramped. But the romanticism of the postmodernists – with its emphasis on uprootedness, narrativity, and nominalism – tends to be short on discipline and thus seems to promise what it cannot deliver. The space it provides is so open that it is able to provide little in the way of resistance. It is within the arena where these two positions come into conflict that we find some of Dewey's most fertile insights.

Dewey expands these ideas when he contrasts what I have termed his post-postmodernist metaphysics to the modernist metaphysics of fixity and certainty only forty-seven pages into *Experience and Nature*. A careful reader can also ascertain a response to those postmodernists who argue that metaphysics ueberhaupt, including metaphysics as the study of the generic traits of existence, is now defunct.

We live in a world which is an impressive and irresistible mixture of suffi-
ciencies, tight completenesses, order, recurrences which make possible
prediction and control, and singularities, ambiguities, uncertain possibilities, processes going on to consequences as yet indeterminate. They are
mixed not mechanically but vitally like the wheat and tares of the
parable. We may recognize them separately but we cannot divide them,
for unlike wheat and tares they grow from the same root. Qualities have
defects as necessary conditions of their excellencies; the instrumentalities
of truth are the causes of error; change gives meaning to permanence and
recurrence makes novelty possible. A world that was wholly risky would
be a world in which adventure is impossible, and only a living world can
include death. Such facts have been celebrated by thinkers like
Heracleitus and Lao-tze; they have been greeted by theologians as
furnishing occasions for exercise of divine grace; they have been elaborately formulated by various schools under a principle of relativity, so
defined as to become itself final and absolute. They have rarely been
frankly recognized as fundamentally significant for the formation of a
naturalistic metaphysics.

(Dewey 1981: 47)

Dewey then clarifies what he means by a naturalistic metaphysics, returning to
the theme of communication, and thus inquiry, as natural functions of the
human organism.

A naturalistic metaphysics is bound to consider reflection as itself a natural
event occurring within nature because of traits of the latter. It is bound to
inference from the empirical traits of thinking in precisely the same way as
the sciences make inferences from the happening of suns, radio-activity,
thunder-storms or any other natural event. Traits of reflection are as truly
indicative or evidential of the traits of other things as are the traits of these
events (Dewey 1981: 62).

In short, we live in a world that is both precarious and stable. Ours is a
world in which a certain amount of knowledge is necessary if we are to avoid
disaster, and in which even more knowledge is required if we are to flourish.
Common sense knowledge based on observation, and scientific knowledge
based on experimentation, are key ingredients in this mix, but they are not
enough. The problem is that inquiry has proceeded over the centuries in ways
that have left vestigial structures, cul-de-sacs, detritus, and other impediments
to clear thinking. Once valuable materials, now turned toxic, separate mind
from body, subject from object, human beings from nature, the individual
from society. Infelicitous remnants of dualistic metaphysical expeditionary
adventures continue to block the road to inquiry. In short, there is a lot of
junk that has been just left rusting on the philosophical landscape, and some
of it is corrosive of thought.

One of the ways to clean up this littered landscape is to develop a sound
philosophical ecology. Against the modernists, Dewey therefore proposes that

we cease our attempts to attain certain knowledge of Being in general, and proceed instead with an investigation of "the generic traits of existence." Against the position now occupied by postmodernists, he argues that these traits are empirically available, that they are assumed by science, and that they include such items as "structure and process, substance and accident, matter and energy," to name a few (1981: 67). Traits of inference are also a part of his naturalistic metaphysics.

This, then, is the "special service" that Dewey thinks the study of philosophy renders. At its most basic level, philosophy employs a set of discipline-specific tools in its attempt to come to terms with life experience. But this enterprise often runs into difficulties. Our experiences are already "overlaid and saturated with the products of the reflection of past generations and by-gone ages." We encounter the many interpretations, classifications, and abstractions that Dewey terms "prejudices" (he uses this term in its neutral sense). It is not possible to go back and see how all these prejudices became established, but we can utilize philosophical tools to criticize them and sort them out. As Dewey puts it:

> These incorporated results of past reflection, welded into the genuine materials of first-hand experience, may become organs of enrichment if they are detected and reflected upon. If they are not detected, they often obfuscate and distort. Clarification and emancipation follow when they are detected and cast out; and one great object of philosophy is to accomplish this task.
>
> (1981: 40)

The prejudices that lie strewn all about us can either cause us to stumble, endangering ourselves and others, or we can seek them out, haul them in, melt them down, and recycle them as materials for fabricating something more useful. The one thing we shouldn't do, however, is to declare that metaphysics is at an end and retire to the cocktail party or the library. The wreckage of modernist metaphysics cannot be dismissed with a wave of the hand any more than can the wreckage of past industrial excess. This is because there are still people attempting to negotiate a terrain that is littered with religious and philosophical junk. As long as it is accepted that the mind and the body are ontologically distinct, for example, then insurance companies will be able to claim rational grounds for insuring the health of the body while ignoring the health of the organism as a whole. And as long as it is accepted that human beings are bodies in which there dwells a literal, immortal soul, then many men and women will be tempted to neglect the pressing needs of the here and now even while attending to the putative prospects of the hereafter.[6]

It is in this connection that Dewey characterizes metaphysics as a ground map of the province of criticism. On one interpretation this means that we need a map to find our way through potentially dangerous metaphysical entities so that we won't injure ourselves. But we also need the map to find out what such things are covering up, what they conceal, and thereby to get a better picture of the landscape. In a passage that is now quite famous, Dewey writes that:

> [q]ualitative individuality and constant relations, contingency and need, movement and arrest are common traits of all existence. This fact is source both of values and of their precariousness; both of immediate possession which is casual and of reflection which is a precondition of secure attainment and appropriation. Any theory that detects and defines these traits is therefore but a ground-map of the province of criticism, establishing base lines to be employed in more intricate triangulations.
>
> (1981: 308–309)

What I am calling Dewey's post-postmodernist metaphysics, then, constitutes an attempt to reconstruct that enterprise along naturalistic lines. In Experience and Nature he works out what he had tentatively advanced ten years earlier, in 1915, in his essay "The Subject Matter of Metaphysical Inquiry." He continues to eschew speculation about first and last things, he continues his attempt to undercut reliance on unwarranted hypostatized entities, and he treats inquiry into Being qua Being as a historical curiosity.

He also denies the claims of those who argue that there is no longer any place for metaphysics. He attempts to take account of the fact that the generic traits of existence are too complex to be the subject of common sense observation and too general to be the subject of scientific experimentation. He expands on his claim that the generic traits are assumed by science. He locates his reconstructed metaphysics in the context of the live creature transacting business with its environing conditions.

Dewey's attack on modernist metaphysics thus provides an alternative to the claim of some postmodernists that metaphysics is at an end, as well as an alternative to the claim that philosophy no longer has anything interesting to say about cruelty or kindness, for example,[7] and an alternative to the claim that there is "no common denominator – in 'nature' ... – that guarantees the One-ness of the world or the possibility of neutral or objective thought" (Ermarth 1998). Dewey's post-postmodernism calls each of these positions to account.

There are no doubt those who will object that at the end of his life Dewey had a change of heart regarding the possibility of a naturalistic metaphysics. In an essay published in 1949, as he was approaching his 90th birthday, Dewey announced that his attempts to reconstruct the term had failed. He promised never to use the word again in connection with his own position.

But that is not the full story. It is clear that Dewey gave up the word, but not the enterprise. As for the enterprise, or what he had accomplished in terms of reconstructing the traditional discipline of metaphysics, he happily stood by that. And why? Simply because the point of recognizing generic traits, as he put it, "lies in their application in the conduct of life: that is, in their moral bearing provided moral be taken in its basic broad human sense" (1989: 389). In other words, his reconstructed metaphysics – whatever it might come to be called – has a connection to the existential, which is to say objective, world that features certain generic traits.

(3) Returning now to Lyotard's famous remark, there is a third possible interpretation of his "end of the master narrative" remark. If the first possibility has to do with the end of abstract metaphysical systems, and the second with the end of metaphysics generally, then the third might be understood to mean the end of the idea that the physical sciences are the models and measures for all other types of experience. In this sense it would signal the end of the positivist program advanced by philosophers such as Carnap and Reichenbach from the 1930s to the 1950s. In its most extreme form, proponents of this view held that, as one of the professors for whom I worked as a graduate student was still moved to tell his freshmen as late as 1965, "all philosophy can be reduced either to the physical sciences or to lexicography." But of course Dewey was postmodernist in this special sense as well. He was an ardent opponent of the positivists, rejecting their protocol sentences, their view of the nature of truth, and their various forms of reductionism and foundationalism.

Of the logical positivists Dewey wrote to Arthur F. Bentley, in a letter dated 5 March 1939, that "the profession seems to absolve them from responsibility for examining their own basic postulates – or finding out what they are" (1997: 1939.03.05). On 10 July 1940, Max Otto wrote to Dewey that he had talked to several students who had taken courses in Positivism. They wanted to know how they should react to the positivist claim that much of philosophy was meaningless. He asked Dewey how he should respond (Dewey 1997: 1940.07.10).

Eight days later, on 18 July, Dewey responded.

> It seems to be at least hopeful that the students reacted to Logical Positivism they [sic] way they did – of course there are a number always who like manipulating symbols, but who haven't had the energy or opportunity or skill to learn to do it in mathematics where at least it is something with a background & foreground. Im [sic] about convinced that most of this logistics is just pseudo-mathematics.
>
> (1997: 1940.07.18)

In his revised introduction to *Experience and Nature*, written in 1949, Dewey's assessment of the positivists was even more ascerbic. They assume, he wrote,

> that science as a total enterprise is inherently non-self-supportive, that it is necessarily incapable of supplying itself with whatever "foundations" it

may need and hence it is the task of the new type of rigoristic philosophers and their Logic to do for science what science cannot do for itself.

In view of the fly-blown condition of most of what passes as "logic" today there is something outright comical, rather than merely ironical, in the assumption that Logic is the author of and authority for the required foundations. This claim of competence is supposedly based on the fact that the new Logic is formulated in esoteric symbols which simulate, at least in form, the symbolism of mathematics. But the "foundations" of mathematics have undergone a radical, indeed, a revolutionary change. The old view that mathematical subject-matter is deduced from an ultimate set of self-evident or axiomatic truths has been supplanted by the view that the ultimates, the "foundations" of the mathematical enterprise are deliberately designed postulates. The method of postulation puts mathematical subject-matter beyond the need of any "foundation" supplied from without. The old view produced Kant. The ultra-moderns are, unwittingly, neo-Kantians of a very special and very peculiar sort.

(Dewey 1981: 350)

These texts should provide sufficient evidence that Dewey viewed the brief reign of the logical positivists as one of modernism's final gasps, since new ways of thinking had already rendered their versions of foundationalism untenable. It was, of course, highly ironic that the positivists' criticism of traditional metaphysics tended to be buttressed by stripped down metaphysical positions of their own.

Nevertheless, Dewey refused to respond to the outsized claims of modernism as have some postmodernists. Take the claim by Ermarth, for example, that "all human systems operate like language, being self-reflexive rather than referential systems – systems of differential function which are powerful but finite, and which construct and maintain meaning and value." If not taken cautiously, this remark would be understood to disallow even the minimal referentiality that is required to account for the successes of common sense inquiries, to say nothing of the experiments mounted by the natural sciences. In Dewey's post-postmodernism, scientific results are constructed, to be sure. But they are neither arbitrary, nor are they constructed out of nothing.

If Dewey was postmodernist in his disdain for the modernist program of the positivists, as well as in developing his own version of constructivism, then he was anything but postmodernist in terms of his interest in logic and his commitment to working out a theory of living inquiry, of which his treatment of metaphysics was an integral part. I have trolled the works of Delueze and Guattari, Derrida, Barthes, and even the master postmodernist Lyotard, in search of a comprehensive and coherent theory of inquiry. Nothing I have found approaches the treatment that Dewey gave the subject in his logics of 1903, 1916, and 1938, and the numerous published essays that served as sketches for, and clarifications of, those works.

Dewey developed his own moderate form of constructivism, then, and this is one of the senses in which he was a postmodernist. From a pragmatist perspective, however, what seems to be missing in postmodernism, and what Dewey provides as a corrective, is a theory of experimental inquiry that takes its point of departure from real, felt existential affairs. And this analysis of the "generic traits of existence" is one of the areas in which Dewey's work shines brightly as what I have termed post-postmodernism.

Notes

1   I am grateful to my conference respondent, Elise Springer, for the meticulous care with which she read this chapter and her numerous helpful suggestions for its improvement.
2   Elise Springer has reminded me that Dewey did not subscribe to linear models of thinking, let alone linear models of progress, and that it is therefore important to emphasize that my characterization of his work as post-postmodern does not require any metaphor of this sort. My claim is a more modest one, namely that he anticipated and resolved some of the very problems now faced by "post-modernist" writers.
3   See, for example, McLuhan 1964.
4   Metaphysics as system, of course, takes many forms. One interesting interpretation of what this might mean can be found in the essay on the subject by Walsh (1967). According to Walsh, there are "three main features in the projected science of metaphysics. It claims to tell us what really exists of what the real nature of things is, it claims to be fundamental and comprehensive in a way in which no individual science is, and it claims to reach conclusions which are intellectually impregnable and thus possess a unique kind of certainty."
5   Crawford 1993.
6   I am grateful to Stanley Fish for suggestions regarding this paragraph. He reminded me that there are in fact individuals who are temperamentally disposed to belief in a literal soul – one that can either be saved or lost for eternity – as a part of their pressing need to come to terms with the events of this world. This is of course a point that William James also made.
7   If liberals expect that philosophy should have anything to say about cruelty and kindness, then that "expectation is a result of a metaphysical upbringing. If we could get rid of the expectation, liberals would not ask ironist philosophy to do a job which it cannot do, and which it defines itself as unable to do" (Rorty 1982: 94).

Bibliography

Appiah, K.A. (1992) *In My Father's House: Africa in the Philosophy of Culture*, Oxford: Oxford University Press.

Crawford, T.H. (1993) "An Interview with Bruno Latour," *Configurations*, Baltimore: Johns Hopkins University Press. Available online at: http://muse.jhu.edu/demo/configurations/1.2crawford.html

Dewey, J. (1981) "The Collected Works of John Dewey", ed. J.A. Boydston, *The Later Works*, vol. 1, Carbondale: Southern Illinois University Press.

—— (1989) "The Collected Works of John Dewey", ed. J.A. Boydston, *The Later Works*, vol. 16, Carbondale: Southern Illinois University Press.

—— (1997) *The Correspondence of John Dewey, 1871–1952*, vol. 1, 1871–1918, ed. L.A. Hickman, Charlottesville, Virginia: Intelex.

Ermarth, E.D. (1992) *Sequel to History: Postmodernism and the Crisis of Representational Time*, Princeton: Princeton University Press.

—— (1998) "Postmodernism," *Routledge Encyclopedia of Philosophy*, London and New York: Routledge.

Livingston, J. (1994) *Pragmatism and the Political Economy of Cultural Revolution, 1850–1940*, Chapel Hill: University of North Carolina Press.

McLuhan, M. (1964) *Understanding Media*, New York: McGraw-Hill Book Company.

Rorty, R. (1982) *Consequences of Pragmatism*, Minneapolis: University of Minnesota Press.

—— (1989) *Contingency, Irony, and Solidarity*, Cambridge: Cambridge University Press.

Walsh, W.H. (1967) "Metaphysics," *Encyclopedia of Philosophy*, vol. 5, ed. Paul Edwards, New York: Macmillan, p. 302.

7 Toward a truly pragmatic theory of signs

Reading Peirce's semeiotic in light of Dewey's gloss

Vincent Colapietro

Introduction

In "Pragmatism, Relativism, and Irrationalism" Richard Rorty contends that: "For all his genius ... Peirce never made up his mind what he wanted a general theory of signs for, nor what it might look like. ... His contribution to pragmatism was merely to have given it a name, and to have stimulated James" (1982: 161).[1] But is it likely that a pragmatic thinker such as Peirce did not design his semeiotic for a purpose or that such an architectonic philosopher had no inkling about the shape of this theory? Part of my task is to suggest just how unlikely this is.

John Dewey is helpful for discerning the function, if not the form, of Charles Peirce's theory of signs. His *Knowing and the Known* is of a piece with other writings from roughly this time, most notably, his reviews of Peirce's *Collected Papers* (of volume 1 in 1932; of volume 5 in 1935; and of volumes 1–6 in 1937), "Peirce's theory of quality" (1935), "The vanishing subject in the psychology of William James" (1940), "Ethical subject-matter and language" (1945), and "Peirce's theory of linguistic signs, thought, and meaning" (1946). In these writings, Dewey stresses the points Rorty apparently misses or dismisses as irrelevant to the questions at hand (What use could there be for a general theory of signs? What would be its appropriate form?). Put positively, Dewey aids us in seeing how to read in Peirce the movement toward a truly pragmatic theory of signs.

The thesis of my chapter is that Peirce's doctrine of pragmatism is formally semeiotic while his theory of signs is thoroughly pragmatic. The purpose of this chapter is simply to propose, rather than prove, this thesis, though in the process of doing so I hope to render this point plausible. Many of Peirce's series of articles have the structure of abduction, deduction, and induction, where the first moment is the formulation of a hypothesis, the second is the deduction of consequences whereby the hypothesis might be tested, and the third commences the process of testing the hypothesis. This chapter can be conceived as the first in such a potential series. The implications of my thesis would have to be formulated more fully and, then, tested more systematically than I can accomplish within the compass of this chapter. There is, nonetheless, value in pressing this hypothesis, especially since taking this guess seriously will help us plumb the depths of both Peirce's pragmatic commitments and Dewey's hermeneutic insights.

In Dewey's judgment, Peirce was more of a pragmatist than James (*LW* 11: 479–484): he transcended his Kantian youth and attained a pragmatic perspective of continuing relevance. In Rorty's judgment, however, Peirce's kinship to Kant marks his distance from James and Dewey. In effect, it disqualifies him as a pragmatist. He perhaps coined the word and undoubtedly inspired James (cf. Menand 2001: 204),[2] but his own architectonic aspiration allegedly betrays a philosophical temperament at odds with a truly pragmatic sensibility. This temperament is evident in Peirce's supposedly persistent efforts to secure an immutable foundation for human inquiry:

> Peirce himself remained the most Kantian of thinkers – the most convinced that philosophy gave us an all-embracing ahistoric framework to which every other species of discourse could be assigned its proper place and rank. It was just this Kantian assumption that there was such a context … against which James and Dewey reacted.
>
> (Rorty 1982: 161)

There are unquestionably texts in Peirce that lend support to Rorty's interpretation of Peirce's project. One of these was placed by Charles Hartshorne and Paul Weiss as the opening paragraph of volume 1 of the *Collected Papers* (Peirce 1931, hereafter abbreviated as *CP*): "To erect a philosophical edifice that shall outlast the vicissitudes of time, my care has been, not so much to set each brick with nicest accuracy, as to lay the foundations deep and passive" (*CP* 1.1).[3] But the aspiration to erect such an edifice is acknowledged, in the same paragraph (as it were, in the same breath), to outstrip any possibility of realization. Peirce's hope is to construct "a philosophy like that of Aristotle, that is to say, to outline a theory so comprehensive that, for a long time to come, the entire work of human reason … shall appear as the filling up of its details" (*CP* 1.1, emphasis added).[4]

The first step toward such a comprehensive framework is the critical elaboration of a categorial scheme comparable to Aristotle's or Kant's doctrine of categories (*CP* 1.1).[5] But the use of such a framework is principally heuristic. For this framework is deliberately designed to guide and goad inquiry. Its purpose is not to offer transcendental grounds for our historical practices; rather it presupposes that these evolving practices alone provide the grounds for all of our theoretical endeavors, including whatever categorial framework or comprehensive systematization of human discourses we are able to devise.

Peirce's categories are, thus, heuristic. This is nowhere better seen than in Peirce's investigation of signs in their myriad forms and intertwined functions (Savan 1987–1988; Shapiro 1983). In turn, the use of such a theory of signs, in the immediate foreground of Peirce's most characteristic presentations, is to offer a normative theory of objective inquiry. Beyond this, a general theory of signs ought to provide conceptual and rhetorical resources for investigating the entire range of semiosis (or sign-action), not just the work of inquirers aiming at truth.[6] It should, for example, contribute as much to the interpretation of literary texts or other cultural artifacts as to the investigation of natural phenomena (cf. Weinsheimer 1983; Short 1998).

Pragmatism, modernism, and postmodernism

Given one theme in this volume, I feel obliged to address, albeit very briefly, pragmatism vis-à-vis both modernism and postmodernism. Pragmatism grants primacy to our practices. It does not reduce theory to practice but envisions theory itself as a mode of practice (see, e.g., Dewey's *Knowing and the Known*, *LW* 16: 250–251). Pragmatism also drives toward recognition of the irreducible plurality of human practices. An appreciation of this plurality makes clear the need for an ongoing, cooperative, and indeed inclusive exchange among representatives of quite divergent perspectives.

As we shall see, Peirce's theory of signs is pragmatic precisely because it accords primacy to our practices of investigation, interpretation, communication, and countless other analogous activities. Because it does so, this theory opens a field of inquiry too vast for any single inquirer and too protean for any one intellectual tradition. Dewey's reading of Peirce's theory brings these dimensions sharply into focus. He discerns in Peirce's writings on signs a movement toward an expressly pragmatic account.

Since this marks a movement away from mentalistic conceptions of signs, language, and meaning as well as a movement toward a thoroughly semeiotic conception of consciousness, mind, and subjectivity, it arguably points beyond modernism.[7] More than this, Peirce's investigation of signs drives toward an explicitly situated, social, somatic, and semiotic understanding of human agents and their historical practices. In so doing, it should foster an appreciation of how Anthony Giddens, Clifford Geertz, Gianni Vattimo, Paul Ricoeur, Maurice Merleau-Ponty, Michel Foucault, Jacques Lacan, Jacques Derrida, Pierre Bourdieu, Michel de Certeau, and countless others might be enlisted as co-inquirers rather than attacked as enemies. Such appreciation would push beyond postmodernism in its more fashionable forms (also pragmatism in its more contentious, less pluralistic forms). Let me illustrate this point by reference to one of these figures.

In his contribution to *Deconstruction and Pragmatism*, a book based on a symposium held at the Collège International de Philosophie in Paris on 29 May 1993, Derrida emphasizes that deconstruction "shares much … with certain motifs of pragmatism" (1996: 78). But he is quick to point out he "obviously cannot accept the public/private distinction in the way he [Rorty] uses it in relation to my work" (1996: 78). Derrida readily acknowledges, however, that his notion of the trace is "connected with a certain notion of labour, of doing"; and, thus, it shares much with a central motif of classical pragmatism. Moreover, "all the attention given [by him] to the performative dimension … is also one of the places of affinity between deconstruction and pragmatism."

Derrida's attention to this dimension has, in his judgment, been used as a basis for a defamation of deconstructionists ("I am reproached – deconstructionists are reproached – with not arguing or not liking argumentation, etc. This is obviously a defamation"). This defamation "derives from the fact that there is argumentation and argumentation"; that is, strategies of argumentation must always be assessed in terms of the contexts in which and the topoi about which we are struggling to articulate our disagreements and ascertain the stakes in our differences – or perhaps to repress all of this and much more. Thus, I do not take Derrida to be in the least disingenuous when he announces that: "I think that the question of argumentation is here central, discussion is here central, and I think that the accusations often made against deconstruction derive from the fact that its raising the stakes of argumentation is not taken into account." At this point in his defense of deconstruction, Derrida takes a pragmatic turn, insisting "it is always a question of reconsidering the protocols and the contexts of argumentation, the questions of competence, the language of discussion, etc."[8] In other words, we must conscientiously attend to what we are actually doing when we are engaging in argumentation with these others, in this context and about these topics: we must become clearer about what we are doing with words, especially when used as weapons. Should pragmatists not especially welcome the insights of a thinker so finely attentive to the performative dimension of our argumentative exchanges?

By means of this example, I simply wish to counteract the impulse to treat potentially helpful co-inquirers as opponents to be annihilated rather than allies to be joined. Even though I will have recourse to a number of such locutions, -isms are all too often banners under which warring tribes mount fierce charges against one another. They also function as the identification of targets at which to shoot. In philosophical warfare no less than in other human frenzies of mutual annihilation, however, each side ordinarily knows very little about the other: an almost total blindness in human beings contributes to the ease with which they dismiss, disfigure, defame, and destroy one another (James 1977). We are able to destroy others with such clear consciences because we have such utterly abstract, hence effectively emptied, conceptions of who they are and what they hold.[9]

Though often himself personally irascible, Peirce denounced "the inhumanity of a polemical spirit" (*Writings of Charles S. Pierce* (Peirce 1982; hereafter abbreviated as *W*) 1: 5). To many people today, he must sound naïve in advising that hatred ought not to be met with hatred, nor violence countered with violence, but rather love has the capacity to recognize "germs of loveliness [even] in the hateful." In our suspicious if not cynical time, Peirce must sound naïve or worse when, beyond this, he claims love has the capacity to warm such germs into life and thereby to transfigure the hateful into the admirable ("Evolutionary Love," *CP* 6.289; also in *The Essential Peirce* (Peirce 1992, 1998; hereafter abbreviated as *EP*) 1: 354).

Ideals are, however, operative even in a hermeneutic of suspicion, though such a hermeneutic often makes it difficult to acknowledge them, much less give a convincing account of their actual operation (Bernstein 1992a: 162, 165, 191). In contrast, Peirce explicitly supposed that ideals have the power to move us in accord with our rational agency.[10] Their power to do so means that human conduct can be the result of rational suasion, not just brute force or blind necessity. There is, at the heart of Peirce's pragmatism, a robust affirmation of the capacity of rational agents to be moved by the lure of ideals and, thus, to be moved in accord with their own integrity (cf. Colapietro 1989; Bernstein 1991: 29–43). It is also at least implicit in the most obviously pragmatic part of his tripartite semeiotic, its third branch. For Peirce's theory of signs culminates in a branch of inquiry he identifies most usually as rhetoric (qualifying it as pure or speculative rhetoric), for it concerns the effects and power of signs to move and even shape discourses, practices, and institutions.[11] In certain respects, Dewey's *Logic* of 1938 is a contribution to this branch of semeiotic. But in complementary respects, Ricoeur, Foucault, Derrida, de Certeau, Giddens, Geertz, Vattimo, etc. provide invaluable resources for articulating a sufficiently thick account of discursive authority, competency, protocols, and contexts. In order to formulate a truly pragmatic theory of signs, then, we cannot limit ourselves to a narrowly circumscribed group of authors. Those of us who work out of the pragmatic tradition betray that tradition when we pit ourselves, might and main, against allegedly or even actually rival traditions, movements, or positions. We honor that tradition when we abandon myths of originary purity and forge alliances, cutting across diverse boundaries (ideological, disciplinary, linguistic, cultural, and national), for the sake of advancing inquiry and enhancing interpretation.

While Rorty admirably exhibits this spirit, he seems to miss what Dewey discerns – the pragmatic thrust of Peircean semeiotic. The trajectory of Peirce's theory of signs itself, thus, prompts us to move in diverse directions and to draw upon various resources, not the least of these resources being an incredibly heterogeneous group of contemporary authors all too glibly grouped together under the rubric postmodernists.

But at this point I will turn from where this trajectory might land us and focus eventually on this theory itself, as envisioned by Peirce and illuminated by Dewey, but immediately on the context in which it must be situated in order to be understood. This context is of course Peirce's philosophy, one Dewey insightfully identifies as "Critical Common-sensism" (*LW* 11: 480). Of Peirce, Dewey noted in his review of volume 1 of the Collected Papers that: "There is [in his own writings] no adequate presentation of his thought as a well developed whole" (*LW* 6: 274). For both attaining an interior understanding of Peirce's philosophical project and reorienting philosophy in the present, however, Dewey claims: "There is one aspect of Peirce's thought which comes out most clearly ... in his conception of philosophy itself, a conception which in my judgment is likely to be revived in the future and to dominate thought for a period at least" (*LW* 6: 276).

This conception comes into view when our attention fastens upon the fact that, for Peirce, "philosophy is that kind of common sense which has become critically aware of itself. It is based on observations which are within the range of every man's normal experience" (*LW* 6: 276). This view is all the more impressive because it is put forth by "a man who was so devoted to the sciences and learned in them." Its potential fecundity resides, above all else, in taking "the starting point and ultimate test" of philosophical reflection to be nothing other than "gross or macroscopic experience." Philosophical problems are human problems writ large, at least large enough to be legible to critically animated intelligence. They are only incidentally technical questions; when properly approached, they are irreducibly human problems. Accordingly, philosophy draws from science not its subject matter but its fallibilistic sensibility (*LW* 6: 276). It draws its subject matter from lived experience. There is more to Peirce's philosophy than commonsensism tempered and tutored by fallibilism; and Dewey takes note of what else there is. Yet he rightly stresses this conjunction.

Commonsensism and Fallibilism

Dewey saw his own work in logic as an extension of Peirce's efforts in this field. He tried to rescue the study of signs, conceived as an integrated, pragmatic undertaking, from Charles Morris's act of kidnapping. Arguably, Dewey allowed his co-author Bentley to allow Morris to kidnap the field as well as the name, conceding Peirce's word and perhaps much else to Morris's usurpation. Early in their critique of Morris's theory of signs ("A Confused 'Semiotic' "), we are informed that:

> From this point on I shall use the word semiotic to name, and to name only, the contents of the book before us [Charles Morris's *Signs, Language, and Behavior* (1946)]. I shall use the word semiosis to name, and to name only, those ranges of sign-process which semiotic identifies and portrays. It is evident that, so proceeding, the word 'semiocian' will name Professor Morris in his characteristic activity in person, and nothing else.
>
> (*Knowing and the Known*, *LW* 16: 211–212)

But Dewey took pains to show that Peirce's integrated, pragmatic theory of signs was fundamentally at odds with Morris's fragmented, behavioristic theory. Finally, it is illuminating to recall that, in Dewey's judgment, "Peirce was much more of a pragmatist [than James] in the literal sense in which the word expresses action or practice" (*LW* 11: 483), for Peirce was concerned more with practice in its irreducible generality than experience in its utter singularity. Dewey appreciated what many Deweyans appear strenuously to suppress or deny – Peirce was a pragmatist. He eventually felt a philosophical kinship to the intimidating instructor at Johns Hopkins University toward whom he initially felt little affinity. In particular, Peirce's evolutionism, fallibilism, commonsensism, synechism, and indeed pragmatism were the doctrines prompting Dewey's eventual sense of intellectual kinship.

So too was Peirce's antipathy toward Cartesianism – toward (at least) subjectivism, dualism, intuitionism, and wholesale rejection of intellectual traditions. A central but neglected feature of this antipathy concerns Peirce's valorization of traditions and institutions.

> Descartes marks the period when Philosophy put off childish things and began to be a conceited young man. By the time the young man has grown to be an old [at least an older] man, he will have learned that traditions are precious treasures, while iconoclastic inventions are always cheap and often nasty.
>
> (*CP* 4.71)

John Herman Randall, Jr, learned from Dewey what many of his other associates and students seem to have overlooked altogether: "What I have learned from them [my teachers] is presumably not what they intended to teach. Doubtless John Dewey did not set out to impress me with the overwhelming importance of tradition" (Randall 1958: 2). That is, however, what Dewey most forcefully taught Randall, in Randall's own judgment.

This valorization of traditions is as much a part of Dewey's as it is of Peirce's robust affirmation of our humanizing inheritances.[12] He fully appreciates that "knowledge is a function of association and communication; [that] it depends upon tradition, upon tools socially transmitted, developed and sanctioned" (LW 2: 334). He contends that "no one would deny that personal mental growth is furthered in any branch of human undertaking by contact with the accumulated and sifted experience of others in that line" (*LW* 2: 56). Furthermore, he identifies tradition with "the customs, methods and working standards" of a calling such as carpentry or chemistry, plumbing or philosophy. Dewey stresses that initiation "into the tradition is the means by which the powers of learners are released and directed" (*LW* 2: 56). As we shall see, the appeal to practice is almost always an appeal to a tradition, since human practices are the experientially funded and sifted results of intergenerational undertakings. In brief, human practices are almost always traditional ones. Take, as an example, our linguistic practices. Words mean what they have come to mean over countless generations and what they might otherwise come to mean in an unknown future. The simplest use of a linguistic sign implicates us in a complex, extended history, though in countless circumstances linguistic competence and wholesale ignorance of this authorizing history are found together. But our natural languages are unquestionably intergenerational practices.

We are, from the outset, innovative in the very appropriation of our inheritance. But the range, character, and possibilities of our innovations point not simply to our individual ingenuity (cf. Vico). They disclose the riches inherent in our inheritance. Shakespeare and English are, for instance, in such immense debt to one another that the innovator greatly owes his status to his inheritance, while the language deeply owes its riches to this originator of words, phrases, and tropes. To realize this, we need but ask: Where would Shakespeare be without English or, in turn, English without Shakespeare?

The abuses of authority, especially enshrined, sanctified authority, always need to be weighed against the dangers of anarchy. In his general stance toward such questions, Dewey stands between James and Peirce. Of the three, James inclines most dramatically toward anarchism, being deeply suspicious of instituted authorities and especially large institutions,[13] also being habitually sympathetic to the outsider or even the outlaw. He tends to stress that "most human institutions, by the purely technical and professorial manner in which they come to be administered, end by being obstacles to the very purposes which their founders had in view" (McDermott 1977: 516).

In contrast, Peirce was extremely attentive to the abiding need for acknowledged authorities (cf. Certeau 1997).[14] In concrete circumstances, there is often little or no possibility of drawing a sharp or even a very clear distinction between the authoritative and the authoritarian acceptable to everyone. But it is better to preserve the instituted authorities charged with overseeing our traditional institutions than to allow dread of authoritarianism to erase the effective exercise of appropriate authority. He was as opposed to what might be called cultural Cartesianism as he was to its philosophical form. Alexis de Tocqueville: "So, of all the countries in the world, America is the one in which the precepts of Descartes are least studied and best followed" (1969: 430). This is nowhere more evident than in the unhesitant claim of insular minds to omnicompetent expertise: "So each man narrowly shut up in himself, and from that basis, makes the pretension to judge the world" (Tocqueville 1969: 430). "The belief in the right to a private opinion[,] which is the essence of protestantism, is carried to a ridiculous excess in our community" (*W* 2: 356–357). The example Peirce uses to make this point concerns the authority of physicists being discounted by the general population and popular press (*W* 2: 357). Of course, there are frequently grounds for contesting the authority of scientists – indeed, the life of science is a process of contestation – but the manner, basis, and arrogance involved in this instance helped to convince Peirce that appropriate intellectual authority was a precarious cultural achievement. Like James, he was sensitive to the ways scientist ideologues have been inclined, in the name of Science, to browbeat ordinary persons out of their religious convictions; yet, unlike James, he was not sanguine about the uncontrolled clash of untutored impulses, intellectual and otherwise, usually leading to felicitous outcomes. It is likely that he would hear contemporary charges of paternalism as largely misguided attacks on authority, symptomatic of a culture in which the exercise of the authoritative, however legitimate, carries the sting of the authoritarian.

"To view institutions as enemies of freedom, and all conventions as slaveries, is," in Dewey's judgment, "to deny the only means by which positive freedom in action can be secured" (MW 14: 115). "Convention and custom are necessary to carrying forward impulse to any happy conclusion. A romantic return to nature and a freedom sought within the individual without regard to the existing environment finds its terminus in chaos" (*MW* 14: 115). "Not convention but stupid and rigid convention is the foe." The same may be said of tradition, institution, and authority.

Against the most popular reading of R.W. Emerson's transcendentalism, wherein the individual is unqualifiedly primordial and institutions are derivative, Dewey and to a greater degree Peirce stress the dependency of individual humans upon historical institutions or, more accurately, upon human communities in their historical embodiments (these concrete embodiments being intergenerational or traditional institutions, the historically instituted and sustained ways of framing and pursuing humanly recognizable ends and ideals). The individual is never truly in the position to take a stand within himself and, from the haven of interiority, to judge competently anything, let alone everything. The dialogical subject is, in contrast, an agent self-consciously implicated in historical practices and responsive at least to other human beings. Thus, the dialogical subject of classical pragmatism ought never to be confused with the monological self of American individualism. To be true to themselves such subjects must be responsive to the alterity of their own histories (cf. Mazzotta 1997, on Vico),[15] but also to the criticisms, objections, and viewpoints of other humans.

Such subjects are always already caught up in activities and processes antedating their appearance and largely exceeding their control. In the course of initiating their own endeavors, ones sustained as well as frustrated by currents and forces for the most part too vast or too subtle to comprehend or to direct, they ineluctably discover their limits and liability to make mistakes.

In his reviews of the Collected Papers, Dewey highlighted Peirce's fallibilism and commonsensism. A central feature of common sense is an appreciation of fallibility as well as an awareness of finitude. The adage that "To err is human" is, after all, a commonsensical one. But the prior question of what the expression "common sense" means begs answering. Dewey brings into sharp focus the Peircean understanding of this protean term when he suggests that common sense consists, for Peirce, "not so much of a body of beliefs that are widely held as of the ideas that are forced upon us in the processes of living by the very nature of the world in which we live" (*LW* 11: 480). Dewey notes that Peirce attached great importance to our innate dispositions – our instinctual drives – "not as forms of knowledge but as the ways of acting out of which knowledge grows" (*LW* 11: 480).

The Peircean advocacy of common sense is an explicitly critical, thus a consciously self-critical, advocacy, wherein one part of our cultural inheritance is frequently turned against another. The uncritical appeal to common sense is philosophical treason as much as uncommon nonsense. "Uncriticized common sense is both too vague to serve as a dependable guide to action in new conditions and too fixed to allow the free play of inquiry – which always begins in doubt" (*LW* 11: 480). Critical energies reduce excessive vagueness and liquify constraining fixities. Dewey reminds us that, for Peirce, the first rule of reason is to avoid blocking the road of inquiry.[16] "Uncriticized common sense is often the great block to inquiry."

Critical commonsensism is common sense tempered and tutored – thereby transformed – by a contrite fallibilism[17] best exemplified in the actual practice of experimental inquirers. In Peircean no less than Deweyan pragmatism, the transcendental question (What warrants and indeed grounds critique? What undergirds the possibility of criticism?) receives a commonsensical answer: our actual practices in their historical heterogeneity and complex intersections. There is no need or possibility of jumping outside the histories of these practices in order to comport ourselves more intelligently. For these histories contain within themselves resources sufficient unto the day. The critical commonsensist thus abandons the desperate search for an ahistoric framework for commensurating our intellectual disputes and cultural differences; s/he turns rather to the ongoing reconstruction of thick histories, narrated by multiple voices and thus framed by diverse perspectives. In showing the bearing of these points on Peirce's theory of signs, I will have taken significant steps toward also showing his semeiotic to be a truly pragmatic theory.

Dewey's gloss on Peirce's Semeiotic

Even today Peirce's pragmatism is known primarily through its earliest formulations, above all, "The fixation of belief" (1877) and "How to make our ideas clear" (1878). In his review of volume 5 of the Collected Papers ("Pragmatism and Pragmaticism"), however, Dewey noted in 1935 that Peirce's 1903 lectures on pragmatism are, "with the articles in the Monist dating from 1905 … the most mature expression of his pragmaticist philosophy – as he finally called it to distinguish it from the pragmatism of James and the humanism of Schiller" (*LW* 11: 421–422).[18] If we interpret Peirce's pragmaticism in the light of these later writings, and in turn interpret his theory of signs in light of his pragmaticist philosophy, it is likely that we will have attained an interior understanding of Peircean semeiotic. Such, at least, is the advice of Dewey.

As we have already noted, Dewey saw his own work in logic as a development of Peirce's efforts in the field. The principal task of logical theory is neither the construction of an ideal language nor the formalization of inferential patterns. It is rather to provide a theory of inquiry designed to facilitate the practice of inquiry. Dewey concludes his essay "Peirce's theory of linguistic signs, thought, and meaning" (1946) by suggesting that, given the present state of logical theory, "Peirce has a great deal to say that is of value" (*LW* 15: 152). Much of what Peirce has to say in this context concerns signs and symbols, linguistic and otherwise. Dewey immediately adds that: "There is potential advance contained in the present concern with language and 'symbols' " (*LW* 15: 152).

This advance is, however, likely to be sidetracked, because "language," "symbol" and a host of other words are used in accord with the epistemological obsessions of traditional philosophy. Such epistemological dichotomies as thought and language, immaterial minds and perceptible symbols, invariably lead investigation away from fruitful fields. Indeed, the tendency to treat signs and symbols as merely the external, accidental clothing of thought denigrates semiosis and mystifies thought. As Dewey points out, however, Peirce not only frequently uses the word "thought" (*LW* 15: 149) but also does so in a way seemingly enmeshed in the very tendencies he is struggling to eradicate (mentalism, subjectivism, and dualism). His theory of signs, nonetheless, points the way toward offering a truly semeiotic account of consciousness, mind, and psyche, rather than lapsing into the sterile position of trying to provide a mentalistic account of signs, symbols, and meaning. Signs are not made intelligible by referring them to the inaccessible acts of an occult power (cf. Wittgenstein); rather minds become intelligible by tracing their origin and development to publicly observable processes involving intersubjectively shared signs. Meaning is an irreducibly situated, social, somatic, and semeiotic affair (cf. Colapietro 1989; Halton 1986). It is inherent in the life of signs, as this life is itself manifest in communicative and indeed even perceptual processes.

When Dewey in 1946 called attention to the potential for advance in focusing on language and symbols (*LW* 15: 152), he did so guardedly. His wariness was warranted. For, historically, the linguistic turn was a crucial phase in a process of turning away from the positions of classical pragmatism. In more recent years, however, those who were caught up in this movement have come to recognize that, in fundamental respects and surprising ways, Peirce, James, Dewey, and Mead anticipated the positions to which Quine, Putnam, Davidson, Rorty, McDowell, and others have been led by what has been arguably the immanent dialectic of analytic philosophy (i.e., Anglo-American academic philosophy after the linguistic turn) (cf. Bernstein 1992b: 813–840). Of course, at least since *Philosophy and the Mirror of Nature* (1979), Richard Rorty has accorded Dewey a status comparable to Wittgenstein and Heidegger ("the three most important philosophers of our century" (Rorty 1979: 5)).

The linguistic turn might mark a path of regression, in turning inquiry back in the direction of mentalism. Further, it might identify a circumvention, in diverting critical attention away from critical issues of human concern. But it might also mark the way forward, by opening new approaches to mind, meaning, and logic. For Dewey no less than for Peirce, however, it is more appropriate to speak of a semiotic turn rather than the linguistic turn, a turn toward signs in all of their variety and not just toward that form of symbolization so prominent in our lives. This is nowhere more clearly stated than in "Context and Thought":

> If language is identified with speech, there is undoubtedly thought without speech. But if "language" is used to signify all kinds of signs and symbols, then assuredly there is no thought without language; while signs

and symbols depend for their meaning upon the contextual situation in which they appear and are used.

(*LW* 6: 4).

In sum, all thought is (as Peirce noted in some of his earliest publications) in signs, though not all thought is in language in its more restricted senses.

In Dewey no less than Peirce, the pragmatic turn encompasses the linguistic turn, since a turn toward the full range of human practices of course includes our linguistic practices, our historically instituted ways of speaking and writing. Moreover, the pragmatic turn is at once an experiential and a semiotic turn. For it is decisively a turn toward experience and also toward the manner in which our encounters are semiotically and technologically mediated (cf. *LW* 1: 75f, 101–2, 105, 134). But this way of stating the matter is likely to be misleading, for it appears to imply that language and more generally signs and tools constitute a tertium quid (*LW* 15: 152). The need for a tertium quid to bring together the outward domain of physical things and events, on the one hand, and the inward domain of psychical states and processes, on the other, only arises on the dualistic supposition of there being two separable realms.[19] There is one world in which functional, contextual, and thus variable distinctions between self and other, organism and environment, thought and thing, language and reality, are replete. There is not a world divided into two by an absolute, ontological, and hence invariant distinction between mind and matter, or thought and thing. Language is not a bridge over an ontological chasm, but an empirical reality caught up with other such realities in complex, functional ways. In this world, there are organisms inseparably intertwined with their environments, though in many instances not confined to any specific region of their biological niche.[20] The boundaries between organisms and their environments are inherently vague. For certain purposes (e.g., the diagnosis and treatment of a disease), clear distinctions can be drawn. But our ability to institute clear and even precise distinctions depends upon abstracting, for a narrowly focused purpose, certain salient features of an incredibly complex and subtly integrated network of organic and environmental factors.

Part of the function of Peirce's synechism (or doctrine of continuity) was to orient inquiry toward connections and relationships, thus away from the chimerical quest for the ultimate units of theoretical analysis. His synechism was of a piece with his commonsensism for "we must begin with things in their complex entanglements rather than with simplifications made for the purpose of effective judgment and action" (*LW* 1: 387).[21] It "is needful that we return to the mixed and entangled things expressed by the term experience" (*LW* 1: 388), the commonsensical world of macroscopic experience, in all its messiness, rather than the refined worlds of our theoretical reductions in all their elegance and simplicity.

Peirce's synechism was, as Dewey pointed out, also of a piece with his pragmatism. For he "was peculiarly, and with intellectual conscientiousness, concerned with working out the implications of the idea of continuity" (*LW* 11: 423). Perhaps the best way to see this connection is to take the upshot of synechism to be, with reference to inquiry, the rejection of any notion that "the consequences, the practical effects ... are so many independent particular items" (LW 11: 423). These consequences must be just the opposite:

> they are the establishment of habits of ever increasing generality, of what he [Peirce] terms "concrete reasonableness" – a reasonableness that is concrete because it does not consist in reasoning merely, but in ways of acting – that have an ever widening scope and ever deepening richness of meaning.
>
> (*LW* 11: 423)

Though Dewey does not make the following two points explicitly, his gloss on Peirce's writings helps us to do so. First, Pragmatism is formally semeiotic: pragmatism concerns how to make our ideas clear, i.e., how to make certain signs in a distinct range of human engagements clearer than tacit familiarity or even abstract definitions ever can. Second, semeiotic is thoroughly pragmatic, that is, semeiotic concerns the purposes of investigators and arguably also interpreters. Its function is not to ground but to guide and goad inquiry; hence, it is not a foundational but a normative discourse, wherein the ultimate appeals are only provisionally ultimate. What grounds semeiotic are our practices of inquiry and interpretation, and what underlies these practices are processes continuous with processes observable throughout the biosphere. But what grounds these practices themselves is nothing other than their own histories in the actuality of their own self-transformations. The theory of signs is a form of semiosis dependent upon more rudimentary, pervasive forms of this process. This theory is rooted in these processes; they are not grounded in it.

In "Pragmatism, language, and categories," Rorty argues for an affinity between Peirce and the later Wittgenstein bearing upon the primacy and irreducibility of our practices. In his judgment, these two philosophers replace the appeal to intuitions with the appeal to practice (see, e.g., Rorty 1961: 222). In this they exhibit their opposition to Cartesianism. Cartesianism is a form of intuitionism, for it ultimately appeals to intuitions, to self-warranting cognitions, in order to escape the snares of skepticism. Its intuitionism is thereby linked to its foundationalism: incorrigible cognitions alone can provide for the Cartesian an adequate (because unshakable) foundation for the edifice of human knowledge. Thus, the Cartesian hopes to arrest the infinite regress of conceivable doubts, by providing an unshakable foundation of cognitive certainty.

Peirce and Wittgenstein however accept "the regress of rules, habits, and signs standing behind rules, habits, and signs" (Rorty 1961: 222–223). This regress is not vicious. The fact that there is nothing underlying our rules, habits, and signs other than more of the same does not condemn us to skepticism, since inherent in them are the resources for self-criticism and self-correction. The pragmatic spirals constitutive of human practices make it manifest that the metaphor of being imprisoned in our practices is utterly inappropriate. Our practices are modes not of enclosure or confinement but of access and availability: they make available to us the world in which we move and breathe and have our being. The appeal to our self-corrective practices is sufficient, that to supposedly self-warranting cognitions is unnecessary. Because they are self-corrective, these practices are self-transformative.

Human agents are divided, implicated beings. One of the divisions constitutive of their being is that between the ideals with which they identify and whatever in them thwarts their efforts to realize these ideals (Plato, Aristotle, Saint Paul, Freud, Ricoeur). Another is that between their conscious selves and the darker regions of the human psyche not readily accessible to their conscious selves. Moreover, human agents are implicated in historical practices extending far back into an ancestral past and, thereby, implicating these mortal beings in a historical world of unimaginable scope (cf. Dewey's *A Common Faith*; also *Human Nature and Conduct*).

In turn, human practices are fatefully diremptive, intricately intertwined processes caught up in a natural world not of their own making but also not accessible apart from these processes. The limits of our world are defined by the limits of our action; and the limits of our action are defined by the range of our somatic involvements and their symbolic extensions. This makes our world somatically bounded yet symbolically boundless (Dewey, LW 4: 121).[22]

Formal rationality versus concrete reasonableness

Because of its apparent kinship with the infinite and the eternal, and also its alleged capacity to transcend entirely the local and the temporal (cf. Diggins 1994: 439–440), our reason was characterized by Plato as the spark of divinity within us. But is it possible, especially in the wake of Darwin (cf. Knowing and the Known, LW 16: 184), to account for this capacity by referring to nothing other than natural processes, historical practices, individual habituation, ingenuity, and perseverance as well as the technological innovations this complex background makes possible? In brief, is it reasonable to hope that we can offer a thoroughly naturalistic and historicist, but experientially compelling, account of human reason? Arguably, such hope underlies James's conception of intelligent intelligence,[23] Dewey's notion of creative intelligence, and Peirce's vision of concrete reasonableness, though Dewey was more consistently naturalistic and historicist than either James or Peirce.

Even given its imperfections, science is not only the embodiment of reasonableness but also the product of an embodied, social, semiotic, and evolving reason. This is as true of the science of signs as it is of any other science. But the interpretations of Karl-Otto Apel, James Liszka, and others so stress the allegedly transcendental or formal character of Peircean semeiotic that they obscure from view the extent to which Peirce was, in his own words, "a convinced Pragmaticist in Semeiotic." Peirce's theory of signs is not a monument to formal rationality, but an instrument of concrete reasonableness. His characterization of semeiotic as the formal doctrine of signs (*CP* 2.227; cf. Liszka 1996: 1–3) needs to be read in light of alternative characterizations and complementary emphases, the very ones to which Dewey is so finely attuned. When this is done, the seemingly lifeless forms of formal rationality are transfigured into the living forms of concrete reasonableness.

At the heart of Peirce's semeiotic is the conviction that "every symbol is a living thing, in a very strict sense ..." (*CP* 2.222). This conviction is fully expressed in an unpublished manuscript when he suggests a symbol "may have a rudimentary life, so that it can have a history, and gradually undergo a great change, while preserving a certain self-identity" (MS 290 [1905], quoted in Shapiro 1983: 92; cf. *CP* 2.302). Whereas formal rationality tends to kill what it tries to hold, forever in its grip, concrete reasonableness approaches ideas the way a solicitous gardener approaches flowers: "It is not by dealing out cold justice to the circle of my ideas that I can make them grow, but by cherishing and tending them as I would the flowers in my garden" ("Evolutionary love," *CP* 6.289; also in *EP* 1: 354). In so doing, concrete reasonableness takes these ideas – these signs – to have a life of their own with which we have somehow become entrusted.

Peirce was of course aware that, to modern ears, this must sound like "stark madness, or mysticism, or something equally devoid of reason and good sense" (MS 290: 58, quoted in Colapietro 1989: 113).[24] But he took this harsh judgment to be symptomatic of the systematic blindness of the deracinated consciousness of Western modernity. An awareness more firmly and deeply rooted in nature and history would see this as an invaluable part of our ancestral wisdom. Anyone infused with such awareness would take the pronouncement of late modernity to be an aberration, the conviction of ancestral wisdom to be a gift. This is a truly gracious gift, for it allows us to be open to the reception of what nature and history themselves have to give.

In the background of Peirce's philosophy, then, there is what might be called a mystical naturalism (or naturalistic mysticism),[25] for his investigations were informed and animated by a sense of deep kinship (though not a thoroughgoing one) with the natural world.[26] I must turn, however, from this background to what is in the foreground of his theory of signs. My contention is that, in the foreground of Peirce's investigation into signs, we can glimpse a nuanced phenomological sense of signs in their myriad forms, though this sense is quickly eclipsed in many of his writings by his efforts to formulate a truly comprehensive definition of sign or, better, semiosis (sign-acivity).[27] This definition cannot but be abstract.

Precisely because semeiotic is "the quasi-necessary, or formal, doctrine of signs," it must begin with the manifest facts of macroscopic experience (*CP* 2.227); that is, it must begin commonsensically, calling our attention to what is observable by any normal human being during virtually every hour s/he is awake. We begin by observing "such signs as we know" and, on the basis of this familiarity, abstract what seem to us to be their necessary features. In addition, we test our abstract definitions and putative necessities against the direct disclosures of our everyday experience. The starting points and ultimate tests of our semeiotic investigations, then, are our shared experience (in a sense, our common sense, what the course of our lives has forced us as agents to acknowledge).[28]

In other words, signs have the status of pragma,[29] being integral to the business at hand (whatever it might be), the affairs in which we are caught up, the matters with which we are forced to deal in our endeavors, or these endeavors or affairs themselves (these being among the most prominent meanings of πρᾶγμα).[30] Despite the prominence in Peirce's own writings of abstract definitions and also the emphasis of some commentators on the formal character of his semeiotic inquiries, Peirce begins his study of signs with the tacit familiarity and collateral experience of any competent sign-user (cf. Deledalle 2000: 18–20). His formal attempts at abstract definition are self-consciously efforts to clarify what is implicit in the processes and practices in which he, as a sign-user, is ineluctably caught up. In addition, the conceptual clarification achieved by means of abstract definition is, for Peirce the pragmatist, inadequate: one must move beyond abstraction definition to pragmatic clarification. When this is done, signs are defined ultimately in terms of tendencies, processes, and practices culminating in habits, skills, and even artifacts such as books or computers. Most of the definitions of sign and semiosis upon which Peirce's commentators have focused are at the second level of clarity (they are unmistakably abstract definitions). But these presuppose a prior, tacit acquaintance with sign-processes and practices. In addition, these abstract definitions are themselves formulated for the purpose of carrying our inquiry into signs toward a higher level of conceptual clarification, the one attained by the conscientious application of the pragmatic maxim. Peirce was a pragmaticist in semeiotic. In part, this means that the investigator of signs cannot rest content with abstract definitions, but must translate even the most ethereal abstractions into, at least, imaginable lines of conceivable conduct.

There is no question that Peirce indulged in the play of ideas for its own sake, becoming utterly fascinated by the intricate fabrications of his own theoretical imagination. But part of his motivation here was the conviction that the work of reason is carried forward by the play of ideas (cf. chapter 6 ("The Play of Ideas") of *The Quest for Certainty*, *LW* 4: 112ff). As a pragmatist he appreciated the value of not only humor[31] but also playfulness. The only work worthy of rational agents is some open-ended form of playful endeavor, in which the undertaking is not externally imposed upon but voluntarily espoused by these agents themselves, moreover, one in which intrinsic delight is taken even in the more arduous phases of this ongoing activity.

In addition, the only play worthy of us is a process in which not every move counts as competent or legitimate. It is not a process of pure firstness, devoid of challenging opponents or forceful opposition, but one in which self-imposed rules make possible an ongoing self-transformation. Play opens possibilities for confrontation with otherness and, in doing so, it generates possibilities of struggle, frustration, and in some respects defeat. Umberto Eco has proposed as a definition of sign anything that might be used to lie (1976: 7). In contrast, I have suggested elsewhere that error rather than deception might be the key to understanding semiosis. Signs make mistakes possible: they are our humanly fallible takes so often revealed by experience to be mistakes.

If we return to the text in which Peirce defines semeiotic itself as a "quasi-necessary, or formal, doctrine," we see that such a conception of sign is clearly implicit even here. For in this passage Peirce identifies his focus as "what must be the characters of all signs used by a 'scientific' intelligence, that is to say, an intelligence capable of learning by experience" (*CP* 2. 227). But to learn by experience is, first and foremost, to learn from our errors, from the shocks and surprises involved in discovering, often painfully, that things run counter to our expectations (*CP* 5.51; cf. Dewey, *LW* 11: 423).

We have circled back to two important conclusions drawn in the previous section. First, pragmatism is a semeiotic doctrine since it concerns our use of signs. Second, semeiotic is a pragmatic affair since it is concerned, in the first instance, with pragmata and, in its crucial role in the complex economy of Peirce's philosophical investigations, with the continuous growth of concrete reasonableness. Its purpose is facilitating a finer and fuller attunement between the habits of human sign-users and those of the beings with which such agents conduct business.

Hence, pragmatism immediately concerns the intelligent use of signs and semeiotic ultimately regards the deliberate crafting of the means requisite for the growth of concrete reasonableness. Pragmatism in its dissatisfaction with abstract definitions and semeiotic in its culmination in speculative rhetoric are, in effect, contributions to a critique of reason, being integral parts of a truly pragmatic critique of abstract rationality.

Concrete reasonableness obviously encompasses more than abstract ratio-nality. Part of its concreteness resides in its willingness to acknowledge its status as a tradition and thus its historicity; another part resides in its drive toward fuller embodiment. Concrete reasonableness overlaps with what Dewey means by embodied intelligence. "The level of action fixed by embodied intelligence is," as he stresses, "always the important thing" (*LW* 2: 366). Intelligence in Dewey's sense or reasonableness in Peirce's is embodied principally in habits and artifacts.

The distinction between abstract rationality and concrete reasonableness overlaps with a number of other distinctions, including that between Verstand and Vernunft,[32] pure reason and narrative (or historical) reason (Ortega 1984: 118), formal and living reason. Since the distinction between formal and living reason has been articulated by a thinker deeply rooted in the tradition of pragmatism, it is especially pertinent to the one that is the focus of this section. Let us, accordingly, enlist the aid of John E. Smith in our efforts to mark a crucial difference.

Smith stresses that, regarding "the nature of reason, we must distinguish between, first, formal reason ... and, second, living reason or reason as the quest on the part of the concrete self for [maximal] intelligibility" (1995: 111). "Formal reason ... is inadequate for disciplines [and practices] more intimately related to historical events and to the direct, felt experience of selves" (1995: 112). It is, however, ideally suited to those sciences, such as mathematics and logic, "in which it is not only unnecessary but detrimental to introduce the concerns of the individual thinking self into the situation" (1995: 111–112). But such abstract disciplines purchase their certainty and precision precisely by virtue of their formal abstractions from concrete affairs. Intelligent involvement in the historical affairs in and through which human lives, individually and communally, assume their actual form by virtue of participation, not abstraction. Living reason thus "needs to be recovered, for it is the form of reason required for all the concrete rational pursuits in which men [and women] are engaged – art, morality, politics, and religion" (1995: 112).

The question arises, however, whether philosophy is, for Peirce, to be counted among these "concrete rational pursuits." In opposition to F.C.S. Schiller's humanism, envisioned as "a philosophy not purely intellectual because every department of man's nature must be voiced in it," Peirce was emphatic: "For my part, I beg to be excused from having any dealings with such a philosophy" (*CP* 5.537). His reason bears directly on our question: "I wish philosophy to be a strict science, passionless and severely fair." Schiller's judgment of such an endeavor is unequivocal: philosophers "have rendered philosophy like unto themselves, abstruse, arid, abstract, and abhorrent" (*Humanism: Philosophical Essays* (1903), quoted by Peirce, *CP* 5.537). But Peirce's response to this judgment is equally pointed: "some branches of science are not in a healthy state if they are not abstruse, arid, and abstract." The context makes it clear that Peirce counted philosophy among these branches of science. Hence, it seems clear that, from Peirce's perspective, philosophy is not a concrete rational pursuit, but an abstract formal inquiry.

The matter is, however, not nearly so straightforward as this. There is little question that, in Peirce's writings, philosophy as *scientia* largely eclipses philosophy as *sapientia*. But, at the center of Peirce's philosophy, there is an *askesis*, a self-imposed discipline. But there is also a confidence that the insights derived from this discipline will contribute to wisdom. "The soul's deeper parts can only be reached through its surface" (*CP* 1.648). In this way, the insights obtained from "mathematics and philosophy and the other sciences ... will by slow percolation gradually reach the very core of one's being; and will come to influence our lives." Impersonal inquiry, where personal concerns are sacrificed for the overarching ideals of a communal undertaking (where one comes to identify oneself with the success of what transcends oneself), is a moral achievement of personal agents. An adequate understanding of human inquiry must do justice to both the possibility of impersonal inquiry and the nature of such a remarkable accomplishment.

Insofar as there is an imperative need to take historical account of the passionate engagements of fallible agents, the work of attaining such understanding falls to living, rather than formal, reason.

"Whatever the true definition of Pragmatism may be, I find it very hard to say; but it is a sort of instinctive attraction for living facts" (*CP* 5.64). Is it unreasonable to suggest that Peirce's own fascination with signs, with the life of signs in its myriad forms, displays just this "instinctive attraction for living facts"? Is it naïve to suppose that Peirce's self-depiction ("a convinced Pragmaticist in Semeiotic") is a compensatory self-deception rather than a more or less accurate self-description? Further, do the general drift and most consistent emphases in Peirce's writings on signs warrant the view that "he never made up his mind what he wanted a general theory of signs for, nor what it might look like"?

Conclusion

The concluding sentences of Dewey's review of volume 1 of Peirce's *Collected Papers* can serve to bring this chapter to its conclusion:

> What professional philosophy most needs at the present time is new and fresh imagination. Only new imagination is capable of getting away from traditional positions and schools – realism, idealism, pragmatism, empiricism and the rest of them. Nothing much will happen in philosophy as long as the main object is defense of some formulated historic position. I do not know of any other thinker more calculated [better positioned] than Peirce to give emancipation from the intellectual fortification of the past and to arouse fresh imagination.[33]
>
> (*LW* 6: 227)

The emancipatory power of Peirce's philosophical imagination is nowhere more evident than in his pragmatic theory of signs.[34] Hence, one of the more seemingly arcane parts of Peirce's philosophy is, when properly understood, one of the most truly pragmatic and intellectually liberating. Here, as in many other instances, one figure in our history enables us to appreciate the value and ascertain the character of another's contribution. If it is true that the "invention of discovery of symbols is doubtless by far the single greatest event in the history of man" (*LW* 4: 121), arguably the event by which our ancestors attained the status of humanity, then the investigation of symbols and other species of signs is crucial for the cultivation of critical self-consciousness. At this stage in our history, the actual growth of concrete reasonableness virtually enforces such consciousness, though often in a disfigured or ineffective form. Herein lies the ultimate purpose of Peircean semeiotic. Its most proximate purpose is to help us differentiate the map from the terrain as well as immunize us from the paper doubts of philosophical skepticism. For veridical signs, reliable maps, and even veracious utterances abound, as do unwitting errors and deliberate deceptions.[35] These pragma provide investigators of signs with both their starting points and ultimate tests. Consequently, the coenoscopic science[36] of semeiotic as a distinct branch of philosophy is best understood as every other branch of philosophy should be – "that kind of common sense which has become critically aware of itself" (Dewey, *LW* 6: 276). What could be more pragmatic than common sense infused with critical awareness?

Notes

1   Rorty's recovery of pragmatism has been from at least this time a circumvention of Peirce. But, in one of his earliest publications, "Pragmatism, categories, and language" (1961), an essay from which I will draw a crucial distinction, he explored an affinity between Peirce and Wittgenstein. Dewey has however become for Rorty the paradigmatic pragmatist, whereas Peirce's differences from Wittgenstein and also from Dewey have prompted Rorty to see Peirce at best as a very problematic pragmatist. Even so, the distinction drawn by Rorty in "Pragmatism, categories, and language" between the intuitionist appeal to self-warranting cognitions and the pragmatist appeal to self-corrective practices helps us capture a crucial feature of Peirce's pragmatism.

2   After quoting a famous letter from William to Henry James, one in which the elder brother advises the younger how to deal with Peirce ("grasp firmly, push hard, make fun of him, and he is as pleasant as anyone"), Menand suggests James treated "Peirce the way Emerson treated other people's books: he skimmed them, in effect, for insight and stimulation, and abandoned the effort at complete comprehension" (Menand 2001: 204).

3   In his review of volume 1 of the *Collected Papers*, Dewey calls attention to the fact that:

> In one of his fragments, printed as a preface, he [Peirce] confesses to the ambition of setting forth a philosophy as deep and massive in its foundations as that of Aristotle. He wanted to outline, in terms of modern knowledge, a theory so comprehensive that the findings of thought in all fields, for a long time, would be used only as illustrative detail. The scheme was too grandiose to be carried out; it agreed neither with Peirce's own habits nor with his relations to other thinkers, to universities or publishers.
>
> (*LW* 6: 273–4)

In one of his other reviews, Dewey proposes that Peirce united "a disciplined mind and an undisciplined personality" (*LW* 11: 479).

4   It is significant that Dewey focuses on the more modest formulation of this architectonic aspiration ("for a long time to come" (*LW* 11: 274)).

5   In *Process and Reality*, A.N. Whitehead (1978) defends a position very close to Peirce's own:

> Philosophy will not regain its proper status until the gradual elaboration of categorial schemes, definitely stated at each stage of progress, is recognized as its proper objective. There may be rival schemes, inconsistent among themselves; each with its own merits and its own failures. It will then be the purpose of research to conciliate the differences. Metaphysical categories are

not dogmatic statements of the obvious; they are tentative formulations of the ultimate generalities.

(Whitehead 1978: 8)

"Metaphysics is nothing but the description of the generalities which apply to all the details of practice" (1978: 13). "The ultimate test is always widespread, recurrent experience" (1978: 17).

6 Peirce supposed that "by the True is meant that at which inquiry aims" (*CP* 5.557). Truth is a thoroughly practical notion, being defined as the desired outcome of a human practice.

7 The global characterization of a specific epoch, such as that of modernity or postmodernity (alternately, modernism or postmodernism), is pragmatically problematic. It is accordingly imperative to inquire into the motives and purposes animating us to devise formulae or slogans that would allegedly enable one to hold securely a vast stretch of historical time.

8 Such pragmatic turns are in fact quite commonplace in Derridean texts. For example, he responds in an interview to a question posed by Julia Kristeva regarding the concept of structure by asserting:

The case of the concept of structure ... is certainly more ambiguous [than even that of communication]. Everything depends upon how one sets it to work. Like the concept of the sign – and therefore of semiology – it can simultaneously confirm and shake logocentric and ethnocentric assuredness. It is not a question of junking these concepts, nor do we have the means of doing so. Doubtless it is more necessary, from within semiology, to transform concepts, to displace them, to turn them against their presuppositions, to reinscribe them in new chains, and little by little modify the terrain of our work and thereby produce new configurations.

(Derrida 1981 [1972]: 240)

9 William James makes just this point in reference to an invasion of the Philippines: "It is obvious that for our rulers in Washington the Filipinos have not existed as psychological quantities at all. ... We have treated [them] as if they were a painted picture, an amount of mere matter in our way. They are too remote from us ever to be realized as they exist in their inwardness" (Perry 1935: vol. II, 311). Of this invasion, he also wrote: "We are now openly engaged in crushing out the scaredest thing in this great human world – the attempt of a people long enslaved to attain to the possession of itself, to organize its laws and government, to be free to follow its internal destinies according to its own ideals. Why, then, do we go on? First, the war fever; and then the pride which always refuses to back down when under fire" (Perry: vol. II, 310).

10 In "The social value of the college bred," James proposed: "The ceaseless whisper of the more permanent ideals, the steady tug of truth and justice, give them but time, must warp the world in their direction" (1987 [1907]).

11 Peirce identified the first branch of semeiotic as pure or speculative grammar, since it deals with the most basic elements (cf. Fisch 1986: 373–390). But even here we can see the rhetorical dimension of Peirce's sign theory, for signs are conceived in reference to their capacity to generate interpretants, i.e., to produce effects. For seeing this more clearly and, indeed, for much else regarding Peirce's semeiotic, I owe a debt to Tom Short (in this instance, not a published essay but private correspondence).

12 This is true because Dewey was nearly as pious as Peirce toward aspects of his inheritances, pious in the classical sense of this ambiguous word. George Santayana captures this sense when he writes: "Piety … may be said to mean man's reverent attachment to the sources of his being and the steadying of his life by that attachment" (1962: 125). It is significant that, in the context of the US invasion of the Philippines in 1899, James exhibits a sentiment closely allied with this: "As if anything could be of value anywhere that had no native historic roots" (Perry 1935: vol. II, 311). In a different context (while abroad giving the Gifford lectures), he wrote: "I long to steep myself in America again and let the broken rootlets make new adhesions to the native soil. A man coquetting with too many countries is as bad as a bigamist, and loses his soul altogether" (Perry 1935: vol. II, 316).

13 His sentiment is forcefully expressed when he states: "Damn great Empires! Including that of the Absolute. … Give me individuals and their spheres of activity" (Perry 1935: vol. II, 315).

> I am against bigness and greatness in all their forms, and with the invisible molecular moral forces that work from individual to individual, stealing in through the crannies of the world like so many soft rootlets, or like the capillary oozing of water, and yet rending the hardest monuments of man's pride, if you give them time. The bigger the unit you deal with, the hollower, the more brutal, the more mendacious is the life displayed. So I am against big organizations as such, national ones first and foremost.
>
> (Perry 1935: vol. II, 315)

14 *In The Metaphysical Club*, Louis Menand points out that: "Since the defining characteristic of modern life is social change – not onward or upward, but forward, and toward a future always in the making – the problem of legitimacy continually arises" (2001: 431). Peirce was aware of this already in his own time. This indeed prompts his concern for conserving, or recovering, bases of legitimacy.

15 The present is other than the past and thus must be discerned as such. But the present is, in crucial respects, also other than itself, for there are unresolved contradictions constitutive of any historical time. By the alterity of their histories, hence, I mean both the present as other than the past and the present as other than itself.

16 Susan Haack (1997) has rightly called attention to a widespread misreading of the Peircean text to which Dewey is most likely referring in this review: "Upon this one, and in one sense this sole, rule of reason, that in order to learn you must desire to learn, and in so desiring not be satisfied with what you already incline to think, there follows one corollary. … Do not block the way of inquiry" (*CP* 1.135). The first "rule" of reason then is the desire to learn, its corollary the frequently quoted maxim.

17 Peirce insists that, "out of contrite fallibilism, combined with a high faith in the reality of knowledge, and an intense desire to find things out, all my philosophy has always seemed to me to grow" (*CP* 1.14). In his review of the volume in which this text is found, Dewey suggests that "the peculiarity of Peirce is that in his thought the idea [of fallibility] is not connected with skepticism, and proneness to error is itself taken to be a reliable indication of the state of the universe, instead of being a merely human trait. Peirce is not a skeptic, for he has an intense faith in the possibility of finding out, of learning – if only we will inquire and observe. The assertion of certainty is harmful precisely because it blocks the road to the inquiry by which things are found out" (*LW* 6: 275).

18 There are numerous unpublished manuscripts from this same period that also need to be consulted, but for the general student of pragmatism (in contrast to the specialist in Peircean pragmaticism) one cannot do better than follow Dewey's advice.

19 In *Knowing and the Known*, Bentley recalls that:

> Peirce very early in life [here Dewey adds in a footnote a reference to Peirce's "Questions Concerning Certain Faculties Claimed for Man" (1868)] came to the conclusion that all thought was in signs and required a time. He was under the influence of the then fresh Darwinian discoveries and was striving to see the intellectual processes of men as taking place in this new natural field. His pragmaticism, his theory of signs, and his search for a functional logic all lay in this line of growth. Peirce introduced the word "interpretant," not in order to maintain the old mentalistic view of thought, but for quite the opposite purpose, as device, in organization with other terminological devices, to show how "thought" or "ideas" as subjects of inquiry were not to be viewed as psychic substances or as psychically substantial, but were actually processes under way in human living. In contrast, semiotic [i.e., Morris] uses Peirce's term in accordance with its own notions as an aid to bring back sub rosa, the very thing that Peirce – and James and Dewey as well – spent a good part of their lives trying to get rid of.
>
> (*LW* 16: 238–239)

20 At the conclusion of chapter 1 ("Vagueness in Logic") of *Knowing and the Known*, Bentley stresses that "the man who talks and thinks and knows belongs to the world in which he has been evolved in all his talkings, thinkings and knowings; while at the same time this world in which he has been evolved is the world of his knowing" (LW 16: 45). Earlier in *The Quest for Certainty* (1929) Dewey had made an analogous point when he emphasized:

> we do not have to go to knowledge to obtain an exclusive hold on reality. The world as we experience it is a real world. But it is not in its primary phases a world that is known, a world that is understood, and is intellectually coherent and secure. Knowing consists of operations that give experienced objects a form in which the relations, upon which the outward course of events depends, are securely experienced. It marks a transitional redirection and rearrangement of the real. It is intermediate and instrumental; it comes between a relatively casual and accidental experience of existence and one relatively settled and defined. The knower is within the world of existence; his knowing, as experimental, marks an interaction of one existence with other existences.
>
> (*LW* 4: 235–236)

21 Though Dewey is here presenting his own position, not Peirce's, the view being put forth is one Peirce shared with Dewey.

22 In "The Poet" R.W. Emerson asserted that: "The symbol has a certain power of emancipation and exhilaration for all men" not merely poets (Emerson 1982: 276).

23 James defines intelligent intelligence as that form of consciousness that not only judges what is going on but also judges its own processes, criteria, and ideals of judgment: "It seems both to supply the means and the standard by which they are measured. It not only serves a final purpose, but brings a final purpose – posits, declares it" (Wilshire 1971: 22).

24 "Most of us, such is the depravity of the human heart, look askance at the notion that ideas have any power; although that some power they have we cannot but admit. The present work, on the other hand, will maintain the extreme position that every general idea has more or less power of working itself out into fact; some more so, some less so" (*CP* 2.149). Ideas, or signs, are neither inert nor lifeless, but dynamic and alive – dynamic because they are in a sense alive.

25 This is different from the ecstatic naturalism Robert Corrington (1993) attributes to Peirce.

26 "There is a reason, an interpretation, a logic, in the course of scientific advance, and this indisputably proves to him who has perceptions of rational or significant relations, that man's mind must have been attuned to the truth of things in order to discover what he has discovered. It is the very bedrock of logical truth" (*CP* 6.476). "It is somehow more than a mere figure of speech to say that nature fecundates the mind of man with ideas which, when those ideas grow up, will resemble their father, Nature" (*CP* 5.591; cf. *CP* 7.39, 7.46). But this naturalism is not thoroughgoing since for Peirce it points toward a more or less traditional form of theism. Our kinship with nature is, in his thought, linked to the kinship between nature and divinity, where the divine is envisioned to be "vaguely like a man" (cf. chapter 11 of Potter 1996).

27 "The fundamental distinction is," as Max H. Fisch notes, "not between things that are signs and things that are not, but between triadic or sign-action and dyadic or dynamical action (5.473). So the fundamental conception of semeiotic is not that of sign but that of semeiosis; and semeiotic should be defined in terms of semeiosis rather than of sign, unless sign has antecedently been defined in terms of semeiosis" (1986: 330). Joseph Ransdell (1976) and T.L. Short (1998) also stress this crucial point.

28 "Philosophers have exhibited proper ingenuity in pointing out holes in the beliefs of common sense, but they have also displayed improper ingenuity in ignoring the empirical things that every one has; the things that so denote themselves [that so force themselves upon our attention and lives] that they have to be dealt with" (Dewey, *LW* 1: 374).

29 "Commonsense knowing has to do with the concerns of living; and nowadays living in an environment pervaded by the activities and consequences of scientific knowing involves a wide-ranging, diversified network of communications. Articulate speech, written and printed words, indeed everything that happens may become a sign speaking to us as evidence of something else where scientific inquiry has taken it out of its specific, commonsense spatial-temporal setting" (Dewey, *LW*: 344–345).

30 "The English unpacking [of this term] … is the deed, action, behavior, affair, pursuit, occupation, business, going concern. The Greek formula has several advantages over the Latin. The Latin factum emphasizes the completed actuality, the pastness, of the deed. The Greek πραγμα covers also an action still in course or not yet begun; and even a line of conduct that would be adopted under circumstances that may never arise. The Latin is retrospective; the Greek is, or may be, prospective" (Fisch 1986: 223–224).

31 In his 1903 lectures on Pragmatism, Peirce claims "a bit of fun helps thought and tends to keep it pragmatical" (*CP* 71).

32 Emerson maintained that there is a whole philosophy implicit in the fundamental distinction between *Verstand* and *Vernunft*, or understanding and reason. One way to read his transcendentalism is as an attempt to draw out fully the implications of this distinction.

33 This is consonant with a plea issued at the conclusion of "Philosophy and civilization" (1927b), "a plea for the casting off of that intellectual timidity which
hampers the wings of imagination, a plea for speculative audacity, for more faith in
ideas, sloughing off a cowardly reliance upon those partial ideas to which we are
wont to give the name of facts" (*LW* 3: 10).

34 A sign of this is the fact that Peirce's writings on signs have had the widest influence. In particular, his trichotomy of icon, index, and symbol is encountered in
numerous discourses.

35 James supposed that "the strongest force in politics is human scheming, and the
schemers will capture every machinery that is set up against them" (Perry 1935:
vol. II, 298).

36 Peirce adopted the terminology of Jeremy Bentham for his own purposes: whereas
the idioscopic sciences depend upon special observations, the coenscopic do not.
The astronomer needs telescopes and other instruments, the anthropologist
depends upon travel to sites often far distant, whereas philosophical reflection is
limited to the everyday experience of normal human beings.

Bibliography

Bernstein, R.J. (1991) "The lure of the ideal," in R. Kevelson (ed.), *Peirce and Law:
Issues in Pragmatism, Legal Realism, and Semiotics*, New York: Peter Lang.

—— (1992a) *The New Constellation: The Ethical-Political Horizons of Modernity/Post-
modernity*, Cambridge, MA: MIT Press.

—— (1992b) "The resurgence of pragmatism," *Social Research*, 59b: 813–840.

Certeau, M. (1997) *Culture in the Plural*, trans. T. Conley, Minneapolis: University of
Minnesota Press.

Christensen, C.B. (1994) "Peirce's transformation of Kant," *Review of Metaphysics*, 48:
91–120.

Colapietro, V. (1989) *Peirce's Approach to the Self: A Semiotic Perspective on Human Subjectivity*, Albany, NY: SUNY Press.

—— (1997a) "Tradition: first steps toward a pragmaticist clarification," in R.E. Hart
and D.R. Anderson (eds), *Philosophy in Experience: American Philosophy in Transition*,
New York: Fordham University Press.

—— (1997b) "The dynamical object and the deliberative subject," in J. Brunning and
P. Forster (eds), *The Rule of Reason: The Philosophy of Charles Sanders Peirce*, Toronto:
University of Toronto Press.

—— (1998) "American evasions of Foucault," *The Southern Journal of Philosophy*, 3(36):
329–351.

—— (2000) "Robust realism and real externality: the complex commitments of a
convinced pragmaticist," *Semiotica*, 130(3/4): 301–372.

Corrington, R. (1993) *An Introduction to C.S. Peirce: Philosopher, Semiotician, and Ecstatic
Naturalist*, Lanham, MD: Rowman & Littlefield.

Deledalle, G. (2000) *Charles Peirce's Philosophy of Signs: Essays in Comparative Semiotics*,
Bloomington: Indiana University Press.

Derrida, J. (1981 [1972]) *Positions*, trans. A. Bass, Chicago: University of Chicago Press.

—— (1996) "Remarks on deconstruction and pragmatism," in C. Mouffe (ed.), *Deconstruction and Pragmatism*, London and New York: Routledge.

Dewey, J. (1922) *Human Nature and Conduct*. All references to this work are to *The
Middle Works: 1899–1924*, vol. 14, ed. Jo Ann Boydston, Carbondale: Southern Illinois University Press. Cited as MW 14.

—— (1925) "The development of American pragmatism," *Studies in the History of Ideas* (NY: Columbia University Press), 2: 353–377. Reprinted in *The Later Works: 1925–1953*, vol. 2, ed. Jo Ann Boydston, Carbondale: Southern Illinois University Press, pp. 3–21.

—— (1927a) *The Public and Its Problems.* All references to this book are to *The Later Works: 1925–1953*, vol. 2, ed. Jo Ann Boydston, Carbondale: Southern Illinois University Press. Cited as *LW* 2.

—— (1927b) "Philosophy and civilization," *Philosophical Review*, 36: 1–9. All references to this article are to *The Later Works: 1925–1953*, vol. 3, ed. Jo Ann Boydston, Carbondale: Southern Illinois University Press. Cited as *LW* 3.

—— (1929) *The Quest for Certainty, The Later Works: 1925–1953*, vol. 4, ed. Jo Ann Boydston, Carbondale: Southern Illinois University Press. Cited as *LW* 4.

—— (1932) *Review of Collected Papers, vol. 1*, ed. C. Hartshorne and P. Weiss, New Republic, 68 (6 January): 220–221. Reprinted in *The Later Works: 1925–1953*, vol. 3, ed. Jo Ann Boydston, Carbondale: Southern Illinois University Press, pp. 273–277. Cited as *LW* 6.

—— (1935a) *Review of Collected Papers*, vol. 5, *The New Republic*. Reprinted in *Later Works, vol. 11.* Cited as *LW* 11.

—— (1935b) "Peirce's theory of quality," *Journal of Philosophy*, XXXII: 701–708. Reprinted in *The Later Works: 1925–1953*, vol. 11, ed. Jo Ann Boydston, Carbondale: Southern Illinois University Press.

—— (1937) *Review of Collected Papers*, vols 1–6, *The New Republic*. Reprinted in *The Later Works: 1925–1953*, vol. 11, ed. Jo Ann Boydston, Carbondale: Southern Illinois University Press.

—— (1940) "The vanishing subject in the psychology of William James," *Journal of Philosophy*, 37 (24 October): 589–599. Reprinted in *The Later Works: 1925–1953*, vol. 14, ed. Jo Ann Boydston, Carbondale: Southern Illinois University Press, pp. 155–167.

—— (1945) "Ethical subject-matter and language." Reprinted in *The Later Works: 1925–1953*, vol. 15, ed. Jo Ann Boydston, Carbondale: Southern Illinois University Press, pp. 127–140.

—— (1946a) "Peirce's theory of linguistic signs, thought, and meaning," *Journal of Philosophy*, 43 (14 February): 85–95. Reprinted in *The Later Works: 1925–1953*, vol. 15, ed. Jo Ann Boydston, Carbondale: Southern Illinois University Press.

—— (1946b) "Rejoinder to Charles W. Morris," *Journal of Philosophy*, 43 (9 May): 280. Reprinted in *The Later Works: 1925–1953*, vol. 15, ed. Jo Ann Boydston, Carbondale: Southern Illinois University Press.

—— (1949) *Knowing and the Known*, with Arthur Bentley, Boston: Beacon Press. All references in this paper are to *The Later Works: 1925–1953*, vol. 16, ed. Jo Ann Boydston, Carbondale: Southern Illinois University Press. Cited as LW 16.

Diggins, J.P. (1994) *The Promise of Pragmatism: Modernism and the Crisis of Knowledge and Authority*, Chicago and London: University of Chicago Press.

Eco, U. (1976) *A Theory of Semiotics*, Bloomington: Indiana University Press.

Emerson, R.W. (1971) *Ralph Waldo Emerson: Selected Essays*, ed. Larzer Ziff, New York: Penguin.

Fisch, M.H. (1986) *Peirce, Semeiotic, and Pragmatism*, edited by K.L. Ketner and C. Kloesel (eds), Bloomington: Indiana University Press.

Foucault, M. (1988) *Politics, Philosophy, Culture: Interviews and Other Writings 1977–1984*, edited by L.D. Kritzman, New York and London: Routledge.

Haack, S. (1997) "The first rule of reason," in J. Brunning and P. Forster (eds), *The Rule of Reason: The Philosophy of Charles Sanders Peirce*, Toronto: University of Toronto Press.

Halton, E. [Rochberg-Halton] (1986) *Meaning and Modernity: Social Theory in the Pragmatic Attitude*, Chicago and London: University of Chicago Press.

James, W. (1975) *Pragmatism and the Meaning of Truth*, Cambridge, MA: Harvard University Press.

—— (1977) "On a certain blindness in human beings," *The Writings of William James: A Comprehensive Edition*, ed. John J. McDermott, Chicago: University of Chicago Press, pp. 629-645.

—— (1987 [1907]) *Essays, Comments, and Reviews*, Cambridge, MA: Harvard University Press.

Lentricchia, F. (1988) *Ariel and the Police: Michel Foucault, William James, Wallace Stevens*, Madison: University of Wisconsin Press.

Liszka, J.J. (1996) *A General Introduction to the Semeiotic of Charles Sanders Peirce*, Bloomington: Indiana University Press.

Margolis, J. (1993) *The Flux of History and the Flux of Science*, Berkeley: University of California Press.

Mazzotta, G. (1997) *The New Map of the World: The Poetic Philosophy of Giambattista Vico*, Princeton, NJ: Princeton University Press.

Menand, L. (2001) *The Metaphysical Club: A Story of Ideas in America*, New York: Farrar, Strauss and Giroux.

McDermott, J.J. (ed.) (1977) *The Writings of William James: A Comprehensive Edition*, Chicago and London: University of Chicago Press.

Morris, C.W. (1946) "Reply to Dewey," *Journal of Philosophy*, 43 (28 March): 196. Reprinted in *John Dewey, The Later Works: 1925–1953*, vol. 15, ed. Jo Ann Boydston, Carbondale: Southern Illinois University Press, p. 473.

Nagl, L. (1994) "The ambivalent status of reality in K.O. Apel's 'Transcendental-Pragmatic' reconstruction of Peirce's Semiotic," in E.C. Moore and R.S. Robin (eds), *From Time and Chance to Consciousness: Studies in the Metaphysics of Charles Peirce*, Oxford/Providence: Berg.

Ortega, J.y.G. (1984) *Historical Reason*, trans. P.W. Silver, New York: W.W. Norton & Co.

Peirce, C.S. (1931) *Collected Papers*, vols 1–6 ed. C. Hartshorne and P. Weiss, vols 7 & 8 ed. A.W. Burks, Cambridge, MA: Belknap Press of Harvard University Press.

—— (1977) *Semiotic and Significs: The Correspondence Between Charles S. Peirce and Victoria Lady Welby*, Bloomington: Indiana University Press.

—— (1982) *Writings of Charles S. Peirce: A Chronological Edition*, vol. 1 (1857–1866), ed. the Peirce Edition Project, Bloomington: Indiana University Press. Cited as *W* 1.

—— (1992) *The Essential Peirce: Selected Philosophical Writings*, vol. 1 (1867–1893), ed. N. Houser and C. Kloesel, Bloomington: Indiana University Press.

—— (1998) *The Essential Peirce: Selected Philosophical Writings*, vol. 2 (1893–1913), ed. the Peirce Edition Project, Bloomington: Indiana University Press.

Perry, R.B. (1935) *The Thought and Character of William James*, 2 vols, Boston: Little, Brown, and Co.

Potter, V.G. (1996) *Peirce's Philosophical Perspectives*, ed. V.M. Colapietro, New York: Fordham University Press.

Randall, H.J. Jr (1958) *Nature and Historical Experience*, New York: Columbia University Press.

Ransdell, Joseph (1976) "Another Interpretation of Peirce's Semiotic," *Transactions of Charles S. Peirce Society* XII (2).

Rorty, R. (1961) "Pragmatism, categories, and language," *Philosophical Review*, 70 (April): 197–223.

—— (1979) *Philosophy and the Mirror of Nature*, Princeton, NJ: Princeton University Press.

—— (1982) *Consequences of Pragmatism*, Minneapolis: University of Minnesota Press.

—— (1995) "Untruth of consequences" [Review of Killing Time: The Autobiography of Paul Feyerabend], *The New Republic*, 31 July: 32–36.

Rosenthal, S.B. (1994) *Charles Peirce's Pragmatic Pluralism*, Albany, NY: SUNY Press.

Santayana, G. (1962) *Reason in Religion, The Life of Reason*, vol. 3, New York: Collier.

Savan D. (1987–1988) *An Introduction to C.S. Peirce's Full System of Semeiotic*, Toronto: Toronto Semiotic Circle; Toronto: Victoria College in University of Toronto.

Shapiro, M. (1983) *The Sense of Grammar: Language as Semeiotic*, Bloomington: Indiana University Press.

—— (1991) *The Sense of Change*, Bloomington: Indiana University Press.

Short, T.L. (1998) "What's the use?" *Semiotica*, 122(1/2): 1–68.

Sleeper, R.W. (1986) *The Necessity of Pragmatism: John Dewey's Conception of Philosophy*, New Haven: Yale University Press.

Smith, J.E. (1978) *Purpose and Thought: The Meaning of Pragmatism*, Chicago: University of Chicago Press.

—— (1992) *America's Philosophical Vision*, Chicago: University of Chicago Press.

—— (1995) *Experience and God*, New York: Fordham University Press.

Stuhr, J.J. (1997) *Genealogical Pragmatism: Philosophy, Experience, and Community*, Albany, NY: SUNY Press.

Tocqueville, A. de (1969) *Democracy in America*, trans. G. Lawrence, ed. J.P. Mayer, Garden City, NY: Doubleday.

Weinsheimer, J. (1983) "The realism of C.S. Peirce; or how Homer and nature can be the same," *American Journal of Semiotics*, 2(1–2): 225–263.

Whitehead, A.N. (1971) *Process and Reality* [Corrected Edition], ed. David Ray Griffin and Donald W. Sherburne, New York: Free Press.

Wilshire, Bruce (ed.) (1978) *William James: The Essential Writings*, New York: Harper and Row.

Wittgenstein, L. (1970) *Zettel*, ed. G.E.M. Anscombe and G.H. von Wright, trans. G.E.M. Anscombe, Berkeley: University of California Press.

Part II

Inquiry, language and nature

8 Dewey on inquiry and language

After Bentley

John E. Smith

More than half a century has passed since the publication of *Knowing and the Known*, the volume resulting from the remarkable collaboration between John Dewey and Arthur F. Bentley (1949). I confess that I did not take much notice of the book when it appeared in 1949. I was not familiar with the name of Bentley nor was I aware of the extensive correspondence he had carried on with Dewey for more than twenty years. I was, moreover, puzzled by the title, or rather by what seemed to be Dewey's focusing at such a late date on the theory of knowledge after he had so long attacked what he called the "epistemology industry." I recall asking myself, in biblical mode, is Dewey now also among the epistemologists?[1]

I later discovered, both from the book itself and from the published letters that my suspicions were misguided (Dewey and Bentley 1964). Dewey drew the clearest distinction between his approach to knowing and the approach called "epistemology." In a letter to Bentley (26 March 1944; Dewey and Bentley 1964: 234), he wrote: "Our inquiry to attain knowlege of knowledge is [thus] radically marked off from the start from epistemological inquiries purporting to attain the same conclusion."

We must not forget that the central question raised by Locke and Kant was whether a certain kind of knowledge falls beyond our knowing powers. Accordingly, as one can see from the following description of his own approach, he had no intention of carrying on the epistemological discussion:

> we begin with what is accepted as knowledge, at the given space–time period, on the ground of the best existing authorized (that is, tested) methods of inquiry, and undertake to observe and report them as facts by further use of the methods by which the knowledge under study or inquiry was itself arrived at. In short, what is already known is the data for knowledge of knowledge.

This explains why he was not satisfied with a theory of knowledge über-haupt, as he liked to say, but demanded instead a recipe for gaining knowledge which he found in methods of inquiry that had already proved their worth.

Dewey's rejection of epistemology is far more important than has generally been recognized. To begin with, he rightly claimed that the epistemological approach of the empiricists starts with a dualism of subject/object and assumes in advance a conception of knowledge according to which it is an edifice built on a foundation of sense perceptions, or secure data, to which are added generalizations less secure than the foundation on which they rest. As a number of his letters to Bentley show, Dewey was firmly convinced that the term "knowledge" should have no meaning prior to an inquiry into the sort of inquiry from which knowledge results.

The position Dewey opposed is best understood by a brief comparison with that of Russell. Although he sought to dismiss James and Dewey as proponents of what he called "transatlantic truth," Russell's criticisms are nevertheless instructive because they stem from the form of "empiricism" Dewey opposed. Dewey focused on things and events as they figure in controlled inquiry, whereas Russell, in the tradition of Hume and Mill, stressed the priority of data or true propositions which serve as the basis for generalizations that are seen as more precarious. Accordingly, Russell claims that Dewey rejected data in the ordinary empiricist sense as a starting point for knowledge and substituted inquiry instead. It is paradoxical indeed that Russell, the long time champion of a "scientific" philosophy, should have ignored how science actually proceeds and appealed instead to a theory of knowledge derived from Hume. Dewey, by contrast, made inquiry central and saw that whatever knowledge we possess can have come about only as the outcome of a critical process. Russell, following Hume, found the authority for knowledge in a beginning supposed to be certain. The difference is crucial; criticism is always discursive, never immediate, while beginnings and immediacies are complete in themselves and preclude criticism.

For Dewey, epistemological questions such as how to reach the "external world" starting from private perceptions, or how to explain why the penny "appears" as an ellipse when it is "really" round, are not enduring issues. They are instead the abortive result of the non-empirical conception of experience as a veil of subjectivity standing between ourselves and the world. I stress Dewey's objections here chiefly to show that he had a number of reasons for opposing the "empiricist" epistemological enterprise that went far beyond the more obvious objection that it sets out from a subject/object dualism.

Knowing and the Known – a work that may also be seen as an analysis of the behavior called knowing, minus a knower – was the main product of the Dewey/Bentley collaboration. Since they jointly selected and endorsed the contents and the title, the book came to be regarded, and rightly so, as the official summary of their philosophical exchange. It contains a good statement of what Dewey meant by "transaction," the term he settled on as preferable to "interaction" for expressing the working together of distinguishable elements or factors in any ongoing process. The book also includes an important essay by Dewey about common sense and science in which the meaning of a transaction is spelled out in a concrete fashion. As we now know from the published letters, however, they discussed many topics of importance beyond those featured in their book and not least among these are questions concerning inquiry and language. Calling attention to these questions is not, as the phrase goes, "merely historical," since the issues involved are very much alive on the philosophical scene today.

The correspondence between Dewey and Bentley is a formidable exchange; the printed letters amount to 650 pages and cover topics of mutual interest to a philosopher with a foot in the social sciences and an economist with a philosophical bent. The correspondence is intense; in many cases letter and response are three days apart, a silent comment on the mail service as well as the authors. To make the situation at all manageable, I took Aristotle's advice that the intelligent way to confront a multitude is through a principle which in this case was the question, "What impact did Bentley's suggestions, queries, comments have on Dewey's ideas about language and inquiry?"

In response to Bentley's charge that Dewey was reluctant to say that there were differences in their views, Dewey claimed that he saw their respective modes of approach as complementary, but their interests as different. (6 June 1944; Dewey and Bentley 1964: 264). You, he writes to Bentley, are concerned with knowledge as a sociological fact whose nature has to be spelled out so as to provide a sound basis for sociological theory in research. My interest, Dewey continues, is not in the body of knowledge as a fact, "but in its further extension, through use of the existing body (taken for granted), by means of inquiry." Though brief, this is one of the most important statements in the entire correspondence; it signals the focal points that commanded Dewey's attention – the growth of knowledge through the intelligent use of what we already know to gain more knowledge through more inquiry. As I shall point out, in rethinking what is to be meant by knowledge and its necessary relation to inquiry, Dewey became almost obsessed with trying to express accurately how we can speak of knowledge being the outcome of an inquiry that is fallible and incomplete. Put another way, the question is how can we claim to have knowledge as a fixed possession when at the same time we must acknowledge that the outcome of all inquiry is provisional and subject to further inquiry. This problem, to be sure, is not new and it has been a continuing one for pragmatism, which rightly abandoned certainty, but was then beset by critics and skeptics claiming that it values usefulness and success over knowledge and truth.

Before returning to this and related problems about inquiry, it is worthwhile to consider the matter of language and how Bentley's gad-fly like queries, especially about terminology, led Dewey to engage in extensive rethinking of several of his basic contentions. These queries are important because Dewey believed that he had failed in the past to express many of his ideas in the most precise way and, with the prodding of Bentley, he set out to improve the situation. In 1943, after a series of letters about signs, symbols and names, Dewey wrote:

> I am not stuck on anything in the Logic – certainly [not] on its vocabulary. ... I rarely look at what I've written in the past. ... So this

correspondence with you has been the first conscious, serious effort I ever made to get a firm terminology.

(27 December 1943; Dewey and Bentley 1964: 193)

It is true that in the following years Dewey showed a greater concern for appropriate, accurate terms and phrases than ever before. His main aim was to avoid dualisms and other unwarranted separations. Viewing the results in a general way, one might say that he was bent on trying to save the world from dualisms by inserting hyphens wherever he could! One critic described this practice as the introduction of many barbarisms to philosophical discourse. This quest for a firm terminology was not a purely linguistic affair but involved basic conceptions. Bentley clearly tended, as a matter of basic orientation, towards a neo-positivism according to which things are what they are said to be. He insisted, moreover, on behavior as the most fundamental category; he was suspicious of any term that could not be understood as a form of observable behavior. Dewey displayed throughout his writings an uneasiness in the face of such terms as "self," "person," "agent," and, at times, even "individual," largely because he thought these expressions put too much emphasis on one side of the organism/environment relation and fostered subjectivism. Dewey was never quite sure about how to deal with the subject side of the many relations he analyzed and sometimes wrote as though one could get along without the subject. Here Bentley's attitude acted as a stimulus leading Dewey to propose dropping the terms generally used to denote the subject and made a point of saying that the term "agent" should not be used. I think this particular case must have been an overreaction on Dewey's part as he must have been aware of the paradoxical character of a pragmatism without an agent! But he was aware of the problem, as we see in his candid report about a paper sent to him for comment by a sergeant in the army, which contained the following question: "Isn't the existence of an investigator a constant factor in every ethical (or other) investigation. … There is a human being present who is doing the inquiring" (2 October 1945; Dewey and Bentley 1964: 476). Dewey responded, first by warning against misunderstanding due to the currency of the old subject–object and mind–world dualisms, and second, by insisting on the need for the analysis of such words as "agent" to show that they indicate no more than a single factor in a complex transaction. At the end of the letter, Dewey expressed his bias against giving prominence to the person who carries out any project, and did so with a note of frustration. "There ought to be," he wrote, "some way by which this or that investigator could be treated as a deputy or representative or 'agent' of the whole damn business of knowings-knowns." I cannot determine whether Dewey's quite obvious concern to down-play the person was due to his concern to avoid subjectivism and idealism, or to his interest in presenting inquiry and science as both universal and objective and hence independent of what any individual or group of individuals may think. Perhaps we may say, with William James in mind, that when the personal factor was involved Dewey was more concerned to shun error than to follow truth as he saw it.

The change from "interaction" to "transaction," the most important result of Dewey's new concern about terminology, involves the point just discussed. He believed that "transaction" does justice to the distinguishable elements or factors in a complex, while holding them together so that neither appears as a separate element or has precedence over the other. By contrast, "interaction" seemed to him "dualistic" in the sense of bestowing too much emphasis on the elements involved at the expense of the unity and continuity of the process itself. He had used "transaction" in previous writings where the aim was (like his use of "integration" in the *Logic*) to stress system and the full event for which he did not think "interaction" was adequate. This earlier use, as it turns out, foreshadows the later account of transactionism.

In *Knowing and the Known*, Dewey set forth the meaning of "transaction" in close connection to inquiry as represented by a three-stage transformation in the basic concepts used in physics for explaining the world. Dewey was in fact making a strong claim for his conception of inquiry. His aim in examining the changes of viewpoints in physics was to show that his proposed approach to inquiry "has been already developed by the most potent of all existing sciences" and that it is "transactional" in character (Dewey and Bentley 1949: 113). Dewey gave to the three ideas the names of "self-action," "inter-action" and "transaction," and correlated them respectively with the physics of Aristotle, the physics of Newton and modern physics from Maxwell to Einstein. The three ideas involved are: that things act under their own powers, that thing is balanced against thing as in causal connections, and that systems deal with aspects and phases of action without any attribution to "elements" or "entities" supposedly detachable from the system that includes them.

Despite the foregoing claim about the emergence of "transaction" in the course of changes in the basic conceptions of physics, it seems clear that Dewey found examples of transactions in many ordinary situations and experiences. A fine example is found in a note he attached to the chapter, "Common Sense and Science." In consulting the Oxford Dictionary under "Organism," he tells us that he found the following passage: "When an artist has finished a fiddle to give all the notes in the gamut, but not without a hand to play upon it, this is an organism."

One is reminded of the poetic version in which the fiddle is said to play the tune on the fiddler. The cooperation of the two, Dewey says, is "typical of what a transaction is" (Dewey and Bentley 1949: 286, n. 8). Upon further reflection, one sees that we are face to face with what he meant by communication – the essential function of language – which is at the same time the overcoming of isolation through participation and sharing.

In what was to be Dewey's final statement about knowing as a transaction – in a letter written in 1951 (9 April; Dewey and Bentley 1964: 646) – he expressed a hope: "If I ever get the needed strength," he wrote, "I want to write on knowing as the way of behaving in which linguistic artifacts transact business with physical artifacts, tools, implements, apparatus, both kinds being planned for the purpose and rendering *inquiry* of necessity an *experimental transaction.*" This is Dewey's most abstract characterization of knowing; it is akin in this respect to his initial definition of inquiry as the transformation of an indeterminate situation into something determinate. Here knowing – a way of behaving – is identified as a transaction or a "doing business" between what is actually two sets of tools ("language is the tool of tools") made for the purpose. Why inquiry is necessarily "experimental" is not clear from the previous statement, but it does indicate a concern to take into account the tentative or provisional character of the outcome of inquiry.

I have purposely emphasized these examples of his concern for terminology in order to underline my general conclusion that his new effort to find adequate terms is not an indication that he had changed his belief that the function of language is *communication*. The following statement from Experience and Nature is typical and is confirmed time and again by his other works and his letters: "The heart of language … is communication; the establishment of cooperation in an activity in which there are partners and in which the activity of each is modified and regulated by partnership" (Dewey 1925: 138; cf. 137). Dewey's criticism of nominalism furnishes an excellent example. Language, he claimed, is a means of *concerted* action accompanied by a sense of *sharing*. Accordingly, nominalism can only make nonsense of meaning by taking the word, not as a mode of social action, but as the expression of an *individual* sensation which is necessarily particular. This concrete approach to language as the creator and sustainer of a social world is quite different from the later treatment of language by philosophers in terms of syntactics and semantics on one side and of ordinary language analysis on the other. Dewey, in a remark that becomes more striking in retrospect, lamented that while philosophers "have discoursed so fluently about many topics they have discoursed so little about discourse itself" (Dewey 1925: 139). He went on to point out that, by contrast, it is the anthropologists, philologists and psychologists who have had the most to say about saying. The work of these social scientists interested Dewey most because he believed in the importance of their focus on natural languages in their socio-cultural setting. His remark about philosophers, we must remember, dates from 1925; it is, I believe, correct in its description of the situation up to that time, but by 1940 things had changed radically and the linguistic turn was in full swing. For the next fifty years at least no one could accuse philosophers of failing to discourse about discourse!

I do not see, however, that against this background the later Dewey showed any signs of becoming a "linguistic" philosopher or of taking the linguistic turn. Nor does it appear that he ever thought of the world as so encapsulated in language that we are forced to ask whether there is any reality beyond it. I cannot say whether Dewey regarded the turn to language as excessive and believed, as I do, that, regardless of its contribution, it has served along with epistemology to postpone discussion of many first-order philosophical questions. In any case, it seems clear that in view of his rich understanding of language, especially of its crucial role in actualizing the human associations sustaining civilized life, the new linguistic orientation did not attract him.

While I see no fundamental change in Dewey's understanding of language during the period under consideration, the same cannot be said of his reflections on the theory of inquiry. Ten years had passed since the publication of his *Logic*, with its ambitious program of showing how logical forms, including the constants, are derived from the pattern of inquiry. This program does not come up for any extensive discussion in the letters, but there is no indication that Dewey gave it up and we need not consider it here. He was more troubled by his own questions about inquiry and knowledge than by the criticism of others. He was not bothered, for example, by Russell's attack on his initial description of inquiry as the transformation of an indeterminate situation into a determinate one. Russell claimed that this condition is too abstract for the purpose since it is fulfilled by a drill-sergeant turning a group of raw recruits into an organized company or by a mason building a wall with bricks. His main concern about inquiry had to do with uncertainties about its exact connection with "knowledge" and these were prompted by his exchange with Bentley about what they called knowings/knowns. These uncertainties were two-fold: first, the overwhelming ambiguities he found in the use of the term "knowledge" both in ordinary discourse and technical discussions; second, whether it is legitimate to use the term "knowledge" to designate the outcome of inquiry when inquiry is by nature never ending. This is the core of the problem cited earlier about how best to account for the *tentative* character – the "fallibility" factor – of knowledge since it can be acquired only through a process whose outcome can never be called final. The following comment by Dewey (8 February 1944; Dewey and Bentley 1964: 215) expresses this concern, one that became virtually an obsession:

> The kind of factivity [a term in linguistics indicating that the truth of an included sentence is presupposed; as "realize" in "I did not realize that he had left."] marking the particular warranted assertion of a specified inquiry does not have to be named as a case of knowledge – it is a case of what is there, that which is done, made, till there is occasion for further inquiry.

This statement is not without ambiguity: on the one hand, it indicates Dewey's reluctance to call the outcome of a particular inquiry a case of knowledge, but on the other, it suggests that the outcome of further inquiry would merit the name of knowledge. It might appear that this issue could be settled merely by distinguishing between the aim of a theory of inquiry as such and the aim of a specific inquiry. Dewey could then say that knowledge is the aim of inquiry in the generic sense, and appeal to his idea of warranted assertion as a way of expressing the outcome of a specific inquiry. This possibility, however, is not one that Dewey adopted. Among other difficulties, he had to contend with the claim he had often made that the term "knowledge" should have no meaning other than "outcome of inquiry." That is to say, an inquiry into what actual inquiry shows itself to be is the sole route to understanding what knowledge means. This almost tautological connection between knowledge and inquiry was, of course, his way of thwarting the tendency of many philosophers to come to a discussion about knowledge with a ready-made conception of its nature derived from epistemological theory. It might seem unlikely that Dewey would go on to question the validity of the basic thesis in the Logic that the aim of inquiry is knowledge, as he put it, "knowledge is related to inquiry as a product to the operations by which it is produced" (Dewey 1938: 118). Nevertheless, he did question his thesis, chiefly, I believe, because he could not reconcile the aspect that knowledge reveals of itself when it comes as a possession, a definite outcome of a particular inquiry, with the fact that inquiry can never come to an end. But I run ahead of the record.

Bentley precipitated the issue for Dewey when he reminded him (31 May 1947; Dewey and Bentley 1964: 584) that in the Logic he "officially" made knowledge the end or outcome of inquiry, but that "in some recent letter" he said directly "knowledge is inquiry." Bentley's response was, "This made a considerable impression on me – one that is growing," and he went on to explain that it gives knowledge a "localized meaning" it never had before since inquiry finds its place in active human organisms. As a rule, Dewey took responses of this sort from Bentley very seriously and, while his answer in the next letter is rather oblique, he devoted much thought to the hope that identifying knowledge with inquiry could overcome the difficulties that troubled him.

Although we do not have the letter Bentley referred to, Dewey's reply makes it clear that he had written "knowledge is inquiry" (5 June 1947; Dewey and Bentley 1964: 585), and he added, "inquiry as knowing … 'intrigues' me … I'll have to give the whole matter considerable thought, before I'll be able to see just where it takes me."

Subsequent exchanges make it clear that Dewey's uneasiness over his original straightforward thesis that "knowledge is the aim of inquiry" stemmed, as I have suggested above, from the sense that there is an incompatibility between calling the outcome of any inquiry by the name of "knowledge" when further inquiry is always necessary. His hope that knowing could somehow be understood as an ingredient within inquiry – a muting of the original thesis – is expressed in a letter a few months later (11 September 1947; Dewey and Bentley 1964: 586) in connection with the preparation of copy for their book. "The insertion," Dewey wrote, "of knowing as 'goal within inquiry' is all to the good and should be employed systematically till it gets recognition." It may have been that the idea of "goal within inquiry" attracted him as a middle way between knowledge as the end of inquiry and knowledge as inquiry itself. There is no final resolution of the matter either in *Knowing and the Known* or in the remaining letters.

I wish now to offer some reflections on the Dewey who revealed himself in what we may call the Bentley era. To begin with, he seems to have lost that sense of proportion Peirce had in mind when he said that if adding up some figures in one's head as distinct from using pencil and paper were taken to be a difference in practice, pragmatism would be exploded. Further, Peirce insisted that the degree of precision required in any situation depends on the purpose at hand. For example, it is perfectly sensible for the clerk to use a yardstick in measuring four yards of cloth instead of using a measuring device appropriate only for the laboratory. Dewey's protracted quest for ever more precise terminology displays an uncharacteristic absolutism that was without any sense of proportion. And, as we have seen, he carried his uneasiness about the term "knowledge" to an extreme by denying that the warranted outcome of inquiry is knowledge because further inquiry might be needed.

He became, I believe, excessively critical of his previous views; the best example is his identifying knowledge with inquiry. He should have seen that this would not work simply because in his accounts of scientific development he always assumed a distinction between the putting of questions in research and the procedures needed to answer these questions. The questions that initiate and guide inquiry, although they obviously presuppose some knowledge or information about the matter under investigation sufficient for framing relevant questions, must certainly be distinct from the aim of inquiry. That aim would seem to be finding the answers to these questions and it is the answers that would seem to merit the name of knowledge. To say that inquiry itself is knowledge, however, is to say that the means is also the end. I do not see that he could have meant to identify inquiry and knowing in this sense.

If Dewey possessed the metaphysical instinct that Peirce showed so well in, for example, his analysis of hypothesis formation, he might have considered that every purposeful process has what we may call interim realizations of the aim that defines the process. It is interesting that both Hegel and Whitehead considered this factor, each in his own way. Hegel said that in becoming unless there are definite results from time to time – "something has become" – we are left with sheer becoming and no progress. In the same vein Whitehead saw that without a principle of limitation making possible definite outcomes there is only process. Dewey could have availed himself of such an idea in order to deal with the problem that troubled him most – calling a tentative and incomplete result of an inquiry by the name of "knowledge." Accordingly, he could have said that the outcomes of particular inquiries represent the aim of inquiry itself – knowledge – even though further inquiry is still called for.

The problem of growth in knowledge, of how to, in James's words, marry new fact to old truth with a maximum of continuity and a minimum of jolt, has been the subject of extensive discussion during the past half century. If I read the record accurately, current thinking about the matter is much in agreement with the idea that James proposed. Dewey's account of inquiry in his Logic echoes a similar note, and takes into account the sort of growth in knowledge that takes place in every active field of research. I believe the brief illustration I am about to offer – borrowed from Michael Polanyi – expresses the coming together of change and continuity in knowing which I take to be one of the hallmarks of the pragmatic outlook.

The focus here is on the response of scientists to the discovery of some serious anomalies in the Periodic Table of the elements. To begin with, the Table that arranges the elements in groups and according to their atomic numbers represents the results of a vast cooperative endeavor by many inquirers in a number of fields and stretching over many decades. The discovery that some elements, though sharing an identical atomic number, proved to have different atomic weights presented a major problem, in Dewey's terms the difficulty or obstacle demanding inquiry. An immediate, but unreflective, response might have been a proposal to set the Table aside. This response, Polanyi pointed out, would have been most unwise, especially in view of the fact that the huge body of evidence on which the Table is based cannot simply be ignored and, in addition, it exceeds in scope the evidence on which the source of the anomalies was based. The wiser course, the one in fact adopted, was to conjecture that other, as yet unknown, factors are at work and inquire further in the hope of modifying what is already known in a coherent way. As is now well known, the problem was resolved through the discovery of what were called "isotopes" or forms of the same element having different atomic weights. Thus the anomalies were resolved by the discovery of a new factor with the sacrifice of as little as possible of what was previously warranted.

Data, information such as that upon which the Table is based deserves to be called knowledge, despite the appearance of anomalies and the consequent need for further inquiry. Dewey's chief problem in his period of rethinking was that he became too fastidious about use of the term "knowledge" and was uneasy about using it for the tentative and provisional. Curiously enough, however, it belonged to the spirit of pragmatism from the beginning to abandon the quest for certainty but not to give way to skepticism. In short, the pragmatists recognized that knowledge develops, that at any time we have what is incomplete and subject to revision, and that it is folly to deny the status of knowledge to the outcome of reliable inquiry. I do not see that there is anything in Dewey's main legacy that basically runs counter to this outlook. Perhaps in the end it is not the better part of wisdom for aging philosophers to entertain too many doubts about their insights, especially when others have found them profound and trustworthy.

Notes

1   This question was made even more relevant by a talk I heard Dewey give at Columbia (about 1948) in which he chastised philosophers for *postponing* important philosophical issues because they were devoting almost all of their attention to questions about the nature of knowledge first posed by the British Empiricists and continued in a similar vein by the logical positivists.

Bibliography

Dewey, J. (1925) *Experience and Nature*, Chicago: Open Court Publishing.
—— (1938) *Logic: The Theory of Inquiry*, New York: Henry Holt and Co.
Dewey, J. and Bentley, A.F. (1949) *Knowing and the Known*, Boston: Beacon Press.
—— (1964) *A Philosophical Correspondence, 1932–1951*, ed. Sidney Ratner and Jules Altman, New Brunswick: Rutgers University Press.

9   Dewey, analytic epistemology, and biology

Peter H. Hare

Of late there has been much exploration of the convergences and divergences between recent epistemology and classical pragmatism and naturalism. In an earlier essay I discussed some of those relations between analytic philosophy and the American tradition, and commented on the relevance of recent empirical science (Hare 1998; see also Hare 2003). Here I wish to continue that effort; on this occasion I shall give more attention to Deweyan epistemology than hitherto. Contrary to the advice of Richard Rorty, Hilary Putnam and other influential commentators, I shall contend that what is needed is more metaphysics and more science. Cooperative inquiry, I shall also strongly urge, is called for.

Usually, in discussing Dewey's theory of knowledge, little attention is given to the book he wrote very late in life with Arthur Bentley, Knowing and the Known (Dewey 1991) (see Shook 2000 for an otherwise excellent account of Dewey's theory of knowledge). Among the many reasons for this neglect surely one of the more important is that the book's character is thought to reflect to a considerable degree the distinctive views of Bentley, views considered unfortunate by many. Thelma Lavine is one of the distinguished philosophers who have taken a dim view of some aspects of the book. Consider her comment toward the end of her otherwise excellent introduction to the Carbondale edition:

> Knowing and the Known emerges as a rigorous scientific transactionalism, mirroring (despite differences) the logical positivism it opposes, offering its own formal language, maintaining the exclusive legitimacy of science as mode of knowledge and as frame of reference, denying cognitive significance to metaphysics and ethics, and denying connection between science and common sense. The scientific transactionalism of Knowing and the Known leaves the philosophical constructions of Dewey hopelessly undermined. ... Hopelessly undermined also is the austerely magnificent Bentley tellurian-sidereal floating cosmology.
> (Dewey 1991)

And in response to Frank Ryan's recent defense of the Deweyan character of the book (Ryan 1997) she has reaffirmed her estimate in no uncertain terms (Lavine 1997). I share Ryan's attitude. Indeed, in some respects that I will explain below, even Ryan does not seem to appreciate fully the book's merits.

To be sure, the book has a focus in some respects quite specialized. Dewey did not intend to repeat even in outline what he had labored to expound in *Experience and Nature*. Nor did Bentley intend to repeat even in brief his "tellurian-sidereal floating cosmology." Omitting in this collaborative effort those aspects of their respective philosophies made good strategic sense. In those areas they had serious disagreements. What could be more natural than for them to focus on those areas where their views were shared? Each man knew that his published views on other topics were readily available to interested readers.

Nor did it make sense for them to go over all the ground that Dewey had covered in *Logic: The Theory of Inquiry*. Dewey and Bentley made it abundantly clear that their readers should read their book in conjunction with Dewey's Logic. References to that book abound. Moreover, by the time Dewey and Bentley began their collaboration "the linguistic turn" had happened. Logical positivism had been largely discredited, but respect for mathematical logic and precision in language was much more pervasive in American philosophy than it had been during the brief period in which logical positivism had scandalized the profession while winning few converts. *Knowing and the Known* was a valiant effort by Dewey and Bentley to present their epistemological views in a format and style that would be "user friendly" to their contemporaries in academic philosophy. It is no accident that much of the book reads as a series of technical polemics against recent publications. That was the style of the journal articles that had come to dominate discussion of issues in epistemology. If Dewey's Logic had been enthusiastically received and understood by philosophers steeped in formal logic and analytic epistemology, Dewey probably would not have fallen into collaboration with Bentley. But among logicians and other analytic philosophers his Logic was as "stillborn" in 1938 as Hume complained his Treatise was on its publication in the eighteenth century.

Regrettably, *Knowing and the Known* had as little impact on its target audience as the Logic had had. I wish to suggest that this neglect was partly due to the fact that the book was many decades ahead of its time in analytic epistemology and philosophy of mind, not to mention cognitive science. It was even ahead of what logician/pragmatist W.V. Quine famously did in the 1960s, 1970s and 1980s to develop "epistemology naturalized." To the end, Quine's epistemology was committed to a version of Carnap's semantics. This radical anticipation can perhaps be seen most clearly in Oxford logician/epistemologist Timothy Williamson's work (though he notes that McDowell and others have presented similar ideas). Consider this introductory summary Williamson offers of the view he defends in impressive technical detail in his recent book:

Recent developments in the philosophy of mind have called the meta-physics of internalism into question by indicating ways in which the content of a mental state can constitutively depend on the environment. … Some internalists conclude that not even belief as attributed in ordinary language is simply a function of mind, and try in theory to isolate a core of purely mental states. Such attempts have not succeeded. Rather, we may conceive mind and external world as dependent variables, and reject the metaphysics that led us to expect analysis into purely internal and purely external components. On this view, belief as attributed in ordinary language is a genuine mental state constitutively dependent on the external world.

If the content of a mental state can depend on the external world, so can the attitude to that content. Knowledge is one such attitude.

(Williamson 2000: 5–6)

The parallels with *Knowing and the Known* are striking. Dewey and Bentley famously delivered a polemic against any epistemology that supposes that there is an "intervening realm of names as a new and third kind of fact lying between man as speaker and things as spoken" (Dewey 1991: 49), and Williamson similarly insists that the environment is constitutive of the mental state of knowing.

Many have been dumbfounded by Dewey and Bentley's "procedure … that knowings are observable facts in exactly the same sense as are the subject-matters that are known" (Dewey 1991: 48), but Williamson argues that knowledge is conceptually prior to belief, evidence and justification. Moreover, Dewey and Bentley's attention to language was not merely a methodological concession to an audience which had taken the linguistic turn. They "selected namings as the species of knowings most directly open to observation, and thus as our best entry to inquiry" (Dewey 1991: 77). This is species of empiricism radically different from that of the logical positivists and also very different from Quine's. Though Quine rejected some "dogmas of empiricism," he did not reject traditional empiricism's internalist theory of mind.

Perhaps as many readers of *Knowing and the Known* have been put off by its attention to language use as by what Lavine perceives as its logical positivism. But its attention to language was drastically different from the attention to language in the ordinary language philosophy of such philosophers as J.L. Austin and Norman Malcolm. Sadly, the book managed to antagonize simultaneously the enemies and the friends of linguistic analysis, for different reasons.

Some recent discussions of truth in analytic epistemology are also striking from a Deweyan perspective. In "Deflating Truth: Pragmatism vs. Minimalism" Cheryl Misak has ably treated these discussions from what she takes to be the perspective of the pragmatism of Peirce. She starts by rejecting

Horwich's view which takes "the disquotational or equivalence schema ... 'p' is T if and only if p ... to completely capture the content of the predicate 'is true'" (Misak 1998: 407). She goes on to attempt to show that, with the help of Peirce, she can improve on Crispin Wright's effort to develop "a conception of truth ... which is non-metaphysical but which goes beyond the triviality expressed by the disquotational schema" (Misak 1998: 407). She thinks that by looking to "the practice of assertion and to the commitments incurred in it ... we can say something further – something about what truth is" (Misak 1998: 407).

> But the pragmatist thinks that something more comes on the heels of the thought that truth is bound up with assertion. What we know about a concept, our only access to it, is the role that it plays in our cognitive lives. And what we know about truth is that we take truth to be our aim when we assert, inquire, and deliberate.
>
> (Misak 1998: 410)

She does an excellent job of showing how a Peircean account squares the principle of bivalence with the notion that truth is conceptually linked with evidence by proposing that bivalence be taken as a regulative assumption of inquiry.

How could a philosopher who famously equated truth with "warranted assertability" do anything but applaud Misak's account of the concept of truth in terms of the practice of assertion? I concede that a Deweyan should be delighted by Misak's focus on the practice of assertion – as far as she goes. What troubles me is that in her account she is so eager to avoid the "metaphysical" that she lacks the resources to relate the concept of truth to the problems of internalism and externalism in epistemology and philosophy of mind, problems rightly considered serious by Dewey and Williamson, as I have suggested earlier.

Mark Migotti, though he does not discuss this particular essay of Misak's, appreciates this weakness. He attributes to Peirce a "double-aspect theory of truth":

> The truth, for Peirce, is by nature both independent of us and yet accessible to us. ... The theory is double-aspect in attributing to truth each of two properties that have (like matter and mind, or causation and justification) often been assumed to be immiscible; namely, essential independence and equally essential accessibility. ... [But he adds that] the independence and the accessibility share the same root, namely the fact that experience forces itself on us ... we thus form the notion that certain things are as they are independently of how we take them to be because we are the subjects of a mode of consciousness, experience, in which things are thrust upon us willy-nilly.
>
> (Migotti 1999: 76, 93)

In short, insofar as Misak's inquiry into the practice of assertion does not capture the role of the idea of independence in the concept of truth she has left out one of two aspects Migotti finds in the concept. Migotti does not, however, offer an account of how such feelings of compulsion are related to the independent world. Many philosophers would insist that any such account would inevitably lapse into just the sort of "metaphysics" of truth that analytic philosophers, as well as classical pragmatists, have been laboring to avoid. I'm not convinced. While recognizing the risk of lapsing into the type of metaphysics that analytic philosophers and pragmatists rightly abhor, I suggest that we should explore the prospect of developing what might be called a metaphysics of semantic relations, albeit a minimalist metaphysics.

Before trying to explain what I have in mind by such a metaphysics (see Myers, forthcoming for a general defense of pragmatist metaphysics), let me comment on Crispin Wright's treatment of the concept of truth. In an essay found in the same volume, *Pragmatism*, edited by Misak, which includes Migotti's article discussed above, Wright suggests that we compile a list of "platitudes" about truth which includes the Correspondence Platitude. He comments:

> There's much to be said about this general approach, and many hard and interesting questions arise, not least, of course, about the epistemological provenance of the platitudes. But such questions arise on any conception of philosophical analysis, which must always take for granted our ability to recognize truths holding a priori of concepts in which we are interested.
>
> Let us call an analysis based on the accumulation and theoretical organization of a set of platitudes concerning a particular concept an analytical theory of the concept in question. Then the provision of an analytical theory of truth in particular opens up possibilities for a principled pluralism in the following specific way: that in different regions of thought and discourse the theory may hold good, a priori, of – may be satisfied by – different concepts. ... In brief: the unity in the concept of truth will be supplied by the analytical theory; and the pluralism will be underwritten by the fact that the principles composing the theory admit of collective variable realization.
>
> (Wright 1999: 61)

It must first be said that there is much in this theory that Dewey and Bentley would accept. *Knowing and the Known* can be plausibly understood – whatever else it may be – as a piece of conceptual analysis, and Dewey and Bentley in their long-standing commitment to contextualism would welcome "variable realization." But Dewey and Bentley would stress that serious inquiry into the nature of a concept is as fully empirical as any legitimate inquiry. It would seem to them impossible to isolate conceptual analysis in the way that Wright supposes is possible. The impossibility of such isolation is one of the major themes of Dewey's Logic. "Logical forms" cannot be understood in isolation from empirical processes.

Perhaps the fundamental problem with Wright's analysis can best be illustrated by noting what he says about the Correspondence Principle: "As a platitude it thus carries no commitment to a real ontology of facts … 'sentence-shaped' worldly truth-conferrers … nor to any seriously representational construal of 'correspondence'" (Wright 1999: 67). In other words, in his analytical theory Wright is so anxious to avoid "metaphysical" theories of truth and representation that he eschews any attempt to explain semantic relations. As I have noted elsewhere, Kenneth Westphal has used the work of Frederick Will (whose work was, in turn, influenced by Dewey) to make the point that pragmatism explodes the traditional account of the semantic relations between thoughts and things (Hare 1998: 61–62).

Robert Brandom in *Making it Explicit* has elaborated what he takes to be a pragmatist semantics. Consider how Deweyan the following sounds:

> Discursive practices incorporate actual things. They are solid … as one might say, corporeal: they involve actual bodies, including both our own and the others (animate and inanimate) we have practical and empirical dealings with. … According to such a construal of practices, it is wrong to contrast discursive practice with a world of facts and things outside it. … It is wrong to think of facts and the objects they involve as constraining linguistic practice from the outside … not because they do not constrain it but because of the mistaken picture of facts and objects as outside them. … The way the world is, constrains properties of inferential, doxastic and practical commitment in a straightforward way from within those practices.
>
> (Brandom 1994: 332)

This surely is one way of formulating the metaphysical claim that object and thought are not to be found in separate ontological realms, the same claim made repeatedly by Dewey and Bentley in *Knowing and the Known*. And there is as much stress put on social practices by Brandom as by Dewey and Bentley. Though Dewey and Bentley would doubtless challenge some of Brandom's specific points, they would also, I submit, admire the subtlety and care of his harnessing of the technical machinery of analytic philosophy in defense of a theory of knowledge not fundamentally different from theirs.

If Dewey and Bentley are correct in supposing that philosophy is an empirical inquiry continuous with the empirical inquiry of the sciences, we must suppose that more is needed than Brandom's philosophical analysis. A conscientious Deweyan surveying the current world of intellectual achievement would ask what light the biological sciences and empirical linguistics can throw on the nature of knowing and the known. No philosopher can be said to think more in a framework of Darwinian biology than Dewey.

The biologist Terrence W. Deacon has steeped himself in the relevant empirical literature and sketched an alternative to Chomsky's Universal Grammar:

> They [Chomsky and his followers] assert that the source of prior support for language acquisition must originate from inside the brain, on the unstated assumption that there is no other possible source. But there is another alternative: that the extra support for language learning is vested neither in the brain of the child nor in the brains of parents or teachers, but outside brains, in language itself. ... Over countless generations languages should have become better and better adapted to people so that people need to make minimal adjustments to adapt to them. ... Languages don't just change, they evolve. ... Languages are under powerful selective pressure to fit children's likely guesses, because children are the vehicles by which language gets reproduced. ... In some ways it is helpful to imagine language as an independent life form that colonizes or parasitizes human brains, using them to reproduce. ... [There is] a co-evolutionary dynamic between language and its host. ... Of course languages are entirely dependent on humans and are not separate physical organs, replete with their own metabolic processes and reproductive systems. ... They might better be compared to viruses. Viruses are not quite alive, and yet are intimately a part of the web of living processes. ... The parasitic model is almost certainly too extreme, for the relation between language and people is symbiotic. ... Similar analyses have been suggested as a way to describe the dynamic between many biological and social evolutionary processes. ... This is more than just a metaphor. There is an important sense in which artifacts and social practices evolve in parallel with their living hosts, and are not just epiphenomena.
>
>   (Deacon 1997: 105, 107, 109, 111, 112, 114)

As Deacon amply illustrates, the neuropsychological and neurobiological details are fearsomely complex and in many respects unknown. Only in recent decades, after all, have scientists acquired the means of observing a significant number of the processes that go on in the brain. Our knowledge of the architecture of the brain is partial. Deacon does not hesitate to make educated guesses. I suggest, however, that quite enough is known of those processes and that architecture to show that Deacon's co-evolution theory is – at least in its broad outlines – highly plausible. And in its broad outlines Deacon's theory is altogether Deweyan in its semantics, that is, in its account of how language and mental states are related to the independently existing world. The findings of recent biological inquiry undermine the metaphysics of internalism just as devastatingly as the analytic epistemologies of such philosophers as Williamson and Brandom. The chief claims made in *Knowing and the Known* are as strongly supported by biology as by analytic epistemology.

If Dewey and Bentley were alive today and committed to the project of bringing *Knowing and the Known* up to date, they would steep themselves in the neurobiological literature and in the literature of analytic epistemology and philosophy of mind. Mastering this technical literature is a hellishly difficult job, though a number of people have made interesting attempts (Heft 2001, 2002; Horgan 2001; Lynch 1998, 2001; Tye 1995). I doubt that any one philosopher, no matter how well trained, intellectually gifted, energetic and well funded, is capable of articulating a full-blown philosophical theory of knowing that takes adequate account of these scientific and philosophical literatures. Cooperative inquiry is needed on a scale that has never been seen among philosophers. In the natural and social sciences it has long been taken for granted that many of the most important projects demand the highly organized cooperation of many investigators at many institutions in many parts of the world. In numerous areas of scientific research an application for funds (e.g. to NSF) that does not integrally involve scientists at several universities will not receive serious consideration. Sadly, philosophers stubbornly resist organized cooperation. This, I suppose, is not surprising among philosophers who see philosophy as fundamentally different in method from the empirical sciences. But it is ironic that Deweyan philosophers, philosophical naturalists who conceive philosophical inquiry as continuous with, yet distinct from, scientific inquiry, should resist engaging in research as cooperative as that found in the sciences. And, needless to say, the cooperative nature of inquiry is one of the chief tenets of classical pragmatism, as famously found in Peirce as in Dewey.

Bibliography

Brandom, R. (1994) *Making it Explicit: Reasoning, Representing and Discursive Commitment*, Cambridge, MA: Harvard University Press.

Deacon, T.W. (1997) *The Symbolic Species: The Co-Evolution of Language and the Brain*, New York: W.W. Norton & Company.

Dewey, J. (1991) *The Later Works*, Volume 16, 1949–1952, ed. Jo Ann Boydston, Carbondale: Southern Illinois University Press.

Hare, P.H. (1998) "Classical pragmatism, recent naturalistic theories of representation and pragmatic realism," in P. Weingartner et al. (eds), *The Role of Pragmatics in Contemporary Philosophy*, Vienna: Holder-Pinchler-Tempsky.

—— (2003) "Problems and prospects in the ethics of belief," in John R. Shook (ed.), *Pragmatic Naturalism and Realism*, Amherst, NY: Prometheus Books.

Heft, H. (2001) *Ecological Psychology in Context: James Gibson, Roger Barker, and the Legacy of William James's Radical Empiricism*, Mahwah, NJ: Lawrence Erlbaum Associates.

—— (2002) "Restoring naturalism to James's epistemology: a belated reply to Miller and Bode," *Transactions of the C.S. Peirce Society*, 38: 559–580

Horgan, T. (2001) "Contextual semantics and metaphysical realism: truth as indirect correspondence," in Michael P. Lynch (ed.), *The Nature of Truth: Classic and Contemporary Perspectives*, Cambridge, MA: MIT Press.

Lavine, T.Z. (1997)) "Reply to Ryan," *Transactions of the C.S. Peirce Society*, 33: 1025–1028.

Lynch, M.P. (1998) *Truth in Context: An Essay on Pluralism and Objectivity*, Cambridge, MA: MIT Press.

—— (2001) "A functionalist theory of truth," in M.P. Lynch (ed.), *The Nature of Truth: Classical and Contemporary Perspectives*, Cambridge: MIT Press.

Migotti, M. (1999) "Peirce's double-aspect theory of truth," *Pragmatism, Canadian Journal of Philosophy*, Supplementary 24: 75–108.

Misak, C. (1998) "Deflating truth: pragmatism vs. minimalism," *The Monist*, 81: 407–425.

Myers, W. (forthcoming) "Pragmatist metaphysics: a defense," *Transactions of the C.S. Peirce Society*.

Ryan, F. (1997) "The 'extreme heresy' of John Dewey and Arthur F. Bentley I and II," 33: 775–794, 1003–1023.

Shook, J.R. (2000) *Dewey's Empirical Theory of Knowledge and Reality*, Nashville: Vanderbilt University Press.

Tye, M. (1995) *Ten Problems of Consciousness: A Representational Theory of Phenomenal Mind*, Cambridge, MA: MIT Press.

Williamson, T. (2000) *Knowledge and Its Limits*, Oxford: Oxford University Press.

Wright, C. (1999) "Truth: a traditional debate reviewed," *Pragmatism, Canadian Journal of Philosophy*, Supplementary 24: 31–74.

10 Pragmatic naturalism, knowing the world, and the issue of foundations

Beyond the modernist–postmodernist alternative

Sandra B. Rosenthal

One of the major contributions of the Dewey–Bentley book, *Knowing and the Known* (Dewey and Bentley 1989), written near the end of Dewey's career, is its understanding of the transactional nature of science. And, two key dimensions of Dewey's view of science as transactional, which he reaffirmed until the end of his career, are its continuity with the transactional nature of human experience in general and its transactional interrelatedness with the rich existential context within which science emerges as an abstraction and to which it is ultimately responsible, as opposed to the view of a fundamental discontinuity between science and ordinary experience. The ensuing discussion will turn to Dewey's focus on scientific method to draw out its systematic implications in his undercutting of the modernist–postmodernist debate.

Dewey's focus on scientific method, in drawing from developments such as evolutionary theory and Heisenberg's principle of indeterminacy, shows continually that it embodies the key features of human experience in its concrete richness and cannot be understood apart from this. As he examines scientific methodology by focusing on the lived experience of scientists rather than on the objectivities they put forth as their findings or the type of content which tends to occupy their interest, on the history of modern science rather than its assertions, and on the formation of scientific meanings rather than on a formalized deductive model, he clarifies, first, that the beginning phase of scientific method exemplifies noetic creativity. The creation of scientific meanings requires a noetic creativity that goes beyond what is directly observed. Without such meaning structures there is no scientific world and there are no scientific objects. The creativity of science implies a radical rejection of the passive spectator view of knowledge and an introduction of the active, creative agent who through meanings helps structure the objects of knowledge and who thus cannot be separated from the world known. A focus on such creativity reveals several essential features of scientific method which permeate the structure of his distinctively pragmatic world vision.

First, such scientific creativity arises out of the matrix of ordinary experience and in turn refers back to this everyday ordinary "lived" experience. The objects of systematic scientific creativity gain their fullness of meaning from, and in turn fuse their own meaning into, the matrix of ordinary experience. Though the contents of an abstract scientific theory may be far removed from the qualitative aspects of primary experience, such contents are not the found structures of some "ultimate reality" but rather are creative abstractions, the very possibility of which require and are founded upon the lived qualitative experience of the scientist (Dewey 1981: 37). However, the return to the context of everyday or "lived" experience is never a brute returning, for as Dewey observes, "We cannot achieve recovery of primitive naivete, but there is attainable a cultivated naivete of eye, ear, and thought, one that can be acquired only through the discipline of severe thought" (Dewey 1981: 40). Such a return to everyday or primary experience is approached through the systematic categories of scientific thought by which the richness of experience is fused with new meaning.

Thus, the technical knowing of second level reflective experience and the "having" of perceptual experience each gain in meaning through the other. As the later Dewey stresses, "unless the materials (of science) involved can be traced back to the material of common sense concerns there is nothing whatever for scientific concern to be concerned with," while

> the liberative outcome of the abstraction that is supremely manifested in scientific activity is the transformation of the affairs of common sense concern which has come about though the vast return wave of the methods and conclusions of scientific concern into the uses and enjoyments (and sufferings) of everyday affairs; together with an accompanying transformation of judgment and of the emotional affections, preferences, and aversions of everyday human beings.
>
> (Dewey and Bentley 1989: 52–253)

Dewey summarizes the noetic creativity of science in discussing the significance of Heisenberg's principle of indeterminacy. As he states, "What is known is seen to be a product in which the act of observation plays a necessary role. Knowing is seen to be a participant in what is finally known" (Dewey 1929: 163). Further, either the position or the velocity of the electron may be fixed, depending upon the context of meaning structures in terms of which of the interactions of what exists are grasped (Dewey 1929: 165). Thus both perception and the meaningful backdrop within which it occurs are shot through with the intentional unity between knower and known, and how the electron situation is seen depends upon the goal driven purposive activity of the scientist who utilizes one frame of reference rather than the other. Using this characteristic of the model of scientific methodology in understanding everyday experience, Dewey can observe, "What, then, is awareness found to be? The following answer ... represents a general trend of scientific inquiry. ... Awareness, even in its most perplexed and confused state, that of maximum doubt and precariousness of subject-matter, means things entering, via the particular thing known as organism, into a peculiar condition of differential –

or additive – change" (Dewey 1907–1909: 137–138). At all levels, the meanings and beliefs emerging through the transactional unity of knower and known are embodied in the directed or purposive activity of the organism and the test of truth is their workability in yielding anticipated consequences. Dewey, in focusing on scientific methodology, is providing an experientially based description of the lived through activity of scientists which yields the emergence of their objects. In so doing, he is focusing on the explicit, "enlarged" version of the conditions by which any object of awareness can emerge within experience, from the most rudimentary contents of awareness within lived experience to the most sophisticated objects of scientific knowledge. In providing a description of the lived experience within which the objects of science emerge, he is uncovering the essential aspects of the emergence of any objects of awareness.

There is a generic form of human behavior which is continuous with and emergent from the generic form of behavior of lower animals. There is an ongoing problem solving behavior, a coping with the environment by which we attempt to stay in dynamic equilibrium with it. This generic form of behavior, which embodies the dynamics of experimental inquiry, manifests itself in all areas of human endeavor, from the problematic situations of abstract science to the problematic situations of primal concrete experience. We form creative hypotheses which direct our purposive activity and the truth of which is tested by the occurrence within experience of the anticipated consequences.

There is a two-fold philosophical sense of purposive biological activity running throughout Dewey's position, one ontological, the other epistemic, both of which undercut the level of the biological in terms of the contents of scientific analysis. The dependence of the organism on the environment from which it and its habits have emerged is causal or ontological, but this has nothing whatsoever to do with a causal or reductionist or "naturalized" theory of perception, with causality as expressed in scientific categories, or with a related reductionistic ontology. Rather, it concerns the fact that there is an independent "hardness" or "bruteness" to that which is "there" that will either frustrate or allow to progress the purposive activities of the organism. In this sense one may speak of the adequacy of meanings in terms of the objective categories of the ongoing conduct of the biological organism immersed in a natural world.

The dependence of the perceived environment on the organism is, however, also noetic or epistemic. Such noetic/epistemic dependence involves neither the above excluded features nor objective categories, but rather is an intentional mind–object relationship that can be epistemically studied from within. In this second sense one speaks of the adequacy of meanings in terms of the appearance of what is meant. The significance of biological habits, not as ontological categories, but as epistemic categories, is that such ontologically rooted dispositions, habits or tendencies are immediately experienced, and pervade the very tone and structure of immediately grasped content. Thus the focus on scientific method itself for Dewey points toward the richness of concrete experience as well as our ontological-epistemic embeddedness in a reality not exclusively of our making. This is to be expected, for in uncovering, through his focus on scientific method, the essential aspects of the emergence of any objects of awareness, Dewey is at the same time revealing the essential dimensions of the everyday level of experience as foundational for science.

There is an inseparable relationship between the human biological organism bound to a natural environment, and the human knower who through meanings constitutes a world. From the context of organism–environment interaction, there emerge irreducible meanings which allow objects to come to conscious awareness. Such meanings are irreducible to physical causal conditions or to psychological acts and processes; yet they emerge from the biological, when the biological is properly understood, for the content of human perception is inseparable from the structure of human behavior within its natural setting.

The interrelatedness of the content of human perception and the structure of human behavior in its natural environment is well evinced in Dewey's dual expressions of meaning in everyday experience. A prereflective mode of experience "as far as it has meaning is neither mere doing nor mere undergoing, but is an acknowledgement of the connection between something done and something undergone in consequence of the doing" (Dewey 1929: 142). Or, translated from the language of purposive or experimental activity into the language of description of the emergence of objects of awareness:

> An experience is a knowledge, if in its quale there is an experienced distinction and connection of two elements of the following sort: one means or intends the presence of the other in the same fashion in which itself is already present, while the other is that which, while not present in the same fashion, must become so present if the meaning or intention of its companion or yoke-fellow is to be fulfilled through the operation it sets up.
>
> (Dewey 1977: 114–115)

Thus, the irreducibly meaningful behavior of organism–environment transaction is the very foundation of the intentional unity of knower and known. The focus on biological organism does not lead to causal analyses of human awareness and human knowledge in opposition to an irreducible field of meanings, but to a structure of behavior which, as purposive, provides the experimental activity out of which consciousness of meanings emerges. As such, this biological rootedness pervades and is a necessary basis for epistemic activity at all levels, from common sense to the most abstract science and logic. Dewey's pragmatic naturalism is far removed from the popular naturalizing which separates the content of human awareness from the causal forces which give rise to it.

The objects of everyday experience, like the objects of second-level reflection, are the results of meaning organizations used to turn a potentially problematic or indeterminate situation into a resolved or meaningfully experienced one. If, at the level of science, "the object" is an abstraction or meaningful focus marked off within the larger context of the richness of concrete experience, then such a situation can be anticipated at the level of perceptual experience as well. At neither level can "the object" be hypostatized as absolute independently of the meaning structures through which it emerges in experience. Nor can such meaning structures be understood apart from modes of response to a potentially problematic situation. As Dewey elucidates this point, relating it to James as well:

> The table is precisely the constancy among the serial "thises" of whatever serves as an instrument for a single end. ... In the degree in which reactions are inchoate and unformed, "this" tends to be the buzzing, blooming confusion of which James wrote. ... The object is an abstraction, but unless it is hypostatized it is not a vicious abstraction.
>
> (Dewey 1929: 189–190)

Just as the second-level object gives added significance to the level of everyday experience, so the object of everyday experience can be expected to give added significance to the more concrete immediacies of experience. Meaningfully constituted objects at all levels emerge from the indeterminately rich backdrop of experience and cannot be hypostatized as absolute independently of the meaning structures through which they emerge. Dewey's comments are again concisely instructive when he notes that

> the abstracted object has a consequence in the individualized experience, one that is immediate and not merely instrumental to them. It marks an ordering an organizing of responses in a single focused way in virtue of which the original blur is definitized and rendered significant.
>
> (Dewey 1929: 190)

There is no contradiction between Dewey's focus on process and on objects, for the former is transformed into the latter via the experimental nature of experience. Structure, for Dewey, is "constancy of means, of things used for consequences, not of things taken by themselves absolutely." Structure cannot be isolated from the changes whose stable ordering it is (Dewey 1981: 65).

At all levels of experience such emerging interpretive structures set the direction for purposive activity and are tested by their adequacy in grasping what is there, or in allowing what is there to reveal itself in a significant way, by means of experiential consequences. At all levels of experience, scientific method, as representing a self-corrective rather than a building-block model of knowledge, is the only way of determining the truth of a belief. Our creative meaning organizations, developed through our value driven goals and purposes, must be judged by their ability to turn a potentially problematic or indeterminate situation into a resolved or meaningfully experienced one.

The comparison of scientific method with the dynamics of everyday experience that runs through the above discussion is in no way an attempt to assert that perceptual experience is really a highly intellectual affair. Rather, the opposite is more the case. Scientific objects are highly sophisticated and intellectualized tools for dealing with experience at a "second level," but they are not the product of any isolated intellect. The total biological organism in its behavioral response to the world is involved in the very ordering of any level of awareness, and scientific knowledge partakes of the character of even the most rudimentary aspects of organism–environment interaction.

Further, the scientific purpose of manipulation of the environment, and its use of scientific concepts as an instrument of such manipulative control, are not abstract instrumental maneuvers into which human activity is to be absorbed. Rather, again, the opposite is more the case. All human activity, even at its most rudimentary level, is activity guided by direction and noetically transformative of its environment. As such it is instrumental, and the abstractly manipulative and instrumental purposes attributed to science have their roots at the foundation of the very possibility of human experience in general. Moreover, human activity and the concepts which guide it are permeated by a value laden, value driven dimension, and this dimension pervades the activity of the scientist, just as it pervades all human activity. Dewey's claim here holds of course for all the sciences, and turning to a specific example, he directs one to

> look at the sharp division that is currently accepted as gospel truth between moral subject matters and economic subject matters. The separation is now so thoroughly established as to be regarded as virtually "self-evident." In consequence inquiry, knowing, in both cases is tied down in advance. It is pre-committed to reaching certain conclusions instead of conclusions which result from following freely the leads of inquiry.
>
> (Dewey 1989a: 452)

All experience is experimental, then, not in the sense that it is guided by sophisticated levels of thought, but in the sense that the very structure of human behavior both as a way of knowing and as a way of being embodies the features revealed in the examination of scientific method. It is not that human experience, in any of its facets, is a lower or inferior form of scientific endeavor, but rather that scientific endeavor, as experimental inquiry, is a more explicit embodiment of the dynamics operative at all levels of experience and hence the ingredients are easier to distinguish. The pursuit of scientific knowledge is an endeavor throughout which are "writ large" the essential characters of any knowing, and it partakes of the character of the most primal modes of activity by which humans participate in creatively structuring their world. An examination of scientific method, then, provides the features for understanding the very possibility of its existence as emerging from rudimentary experience. If this interplay is not understood, then there results the paradoxical criticisms which are often leveled against Dewey's position, on the one hand that it is too "intellectualist" because all experience is experimental, and on the other hand that it is too "subjectivist" because of its emphasis on the rudimentary, "felt" aspect of experience.

The above understanding of scientific method indicates that the nature into which the human is placed contains the qualitative fullness of lived experience and that human activity cannot be separated from, and in fact partially constitutes, the nature we experience. It has been seen that humans are understood as natural organisms in interaction with a natural world. And, our ontological-epistemic embeddedness in a reality not of our making in the transactional unity of knower and known is more than a postulate of abstract thought, for it has experiential dimensions. That which intrudes itself inexplicably into experience evinces itself as the over-againstness of a dense world "there" for our activity and as a resistance to our thick organic behavior. Thus Dewey stresses that "Experience reaches down into nature; it has depth." As he elaborates, "Experience is of as well as in nature. … Things interacting in certain ways are experience; they are what is experienced. Linked in certain other ways with another natural object – the human organism – they are how things are experienced as well" (Dewey 1981: 13). Hence, one of the key features of objects is that, as Dewey puts it, they object.

And if experience is such a transactional unity, then the nature of experience reflects both the responses we bring and the pervasive textures of that independent reality or surrounding natural environment. In such an interactional unity both poles are manifest: the reality of the otherness onto which experience opens, and the active organism within whose purposive activity it emerges. Thus the experiential sense at the heart of concrete human existence provides the primal sense of ourselves as active beings immersed in a dense world within which we must successfully proceed. Awareness is awareness of reality as it intrudes within our interpretive field of active engagement with it. The phenomenological features of experience themselves point toward a concrete organism immersed in a natural universe and belie interpretations of the field of awareness as any type of self-enclosed experience, linguistic or otherwise.

There is thus a two-directional openness within the structure of experience. What appears within experience embodies features of both the independently real or the surrounding natural universe and our modes of grasping it, for what appears within experience is a structural unity formed by the interaction of our modes of grasping and that which is there to grasp. The pervasive textures of experience, which are exemplified in every experience, are at the same time indications of the pervasive textures of the independent universe which, in every experience, gives itself for our responses and which provides the touchstone for the workability of our meanings. The being of humans in the natural universe and the knowing by humans of the natural universe are inseparably connected within the structure of experience and its pervasive textures, which include the features of continuity, temporal flow, novelty and vagueness.

In this way, there is an elusive resistance at the basis of meaning selection which must be acknowledged in our creative development of meaning systems and choices among them. Moreover, the very textures of experience indicate that this resistance cannot be understood in terms of discrete, structured realities as the furniture of the universe which we merely find, and the finding of which requires that we in some way escape our interpretations and the structures they provide. Rather, this resisting element provides a general compulsiveness which constrains the way networks of beliefs interrelate, and may at times lead to changes, sometimes radical changes, in our understanding of the world which our beliefs – both perceptual and more reflective – incorporate.

What we experience, what we know, then, is reducible neither to what is antecedently there nor to a social construction. There is no sharp distinction between the natural and the social in the sense that one can situate particular objects exclusively within one or the other. As Dewey puts it in his later writings, organism–environment transaction is an inseparable unity in which "What is called environment is that in which the conditions called physical are enmeshed in cultural conditions and thereby are more than 'physical' in its technical sense" (Dewey and Bentley 1989: 244). In continuing, he points out that "Narrowing this medium is the direct source of all unnecessary impoverishment in human living" (Dewey and Bentley 1989: 244).

The contextualism of Dewey's philosophy is rooted in a naturalism which both gives rise to interpretive activity and is the test of its adequacy. Our interpretive activity emerges within and embodies organic activity and is grounded in a world not exclusively of our own making. As such, human awareness is at once theoretical, practical, and ontologically embedded. This rich epistemic-ontological unity at the heart of experience, rather than any falsely reified interpretive content emerging from it, provides the foundational level for ongoing human activity, both as a way of being and a way of knowing. In this way Dewey can hold at once that reality is perceived and knowable, yet all knowledge is relative to the conceptual networks emergent in organism–environment transactions.

Truth is relative to a context of interpretation, not because truth is relative, but because without an interpretive context the concept of truth is meaningless. Truth is not an absolute grasp, a correspondence with an external reality, but neither is it relative. Truth is perspectival. We create the perspective, but whether or not it allows us to grasp that which enters into experience in workable ways is dependent not on our creativity but on the resistant features of that which enters our perspectival net and provides the touchstone for the workability of our interpretations. Reality answers our questions and determines the workability of our meaning structures, but what answers it gives are partially dependent on what questions we ask, and what meaning structures work are partially dependent upon what structures we bring. Truth as workability is understood in terms of answering, and "answering" is ultimately two directional. True beliefs allow us to engage reality in workable ways.

The purpose of knowledge is not to copy reality but to allow us to live in it in enriching ways by grasping the ways it reveals itself in various types of workable contexts. Dewey holds that we can do more than, as Rorty puts it, "converse about our views of the world," "use persuasion rather than force," "be tolerant of diversity," and "be contritely fallibilist" (Rorty 1991: 67). We can also recognize, via the method of experimental inquiry, that some perspectival nets are more successful than others in rendering intelligible a reality which is not beyond the reach of experience, which may be unknown in many ways, but which is eminently knowable, though always via a perspectival net by which we render intelligible its indeterminate richness. True beliefs, at whatever level of abstraction, are beliefs that can withstand the experimental test of allowing the dense reality with which we are intertwined to reveal itself in experience in workable ways.

For Dewey, reason is not fundamentally abstract and discursive but concrete and imaginative. Imagination is not something separate from or opposed to rationality; rather it is part and parcel of it. Understanding and imagination are unified and transformed into the creative functioning of habit as providing a lived or vital transactional unity of knower and known. Reason is also radically historical, not because it embodies the inculcation of a past, but because it acts in the present through the appropriation of a living tradition which it creatively orients in light of a projected future. And it can do this only if imagination is not capricious but rather seizes upon real possibilities which a dynamic past has embedded in the changing present. Dewey's deepening of reason and imagination is not a liberation from the ontological richness of the past and the possibilities it offers the present, but a liberation from a constrictive access to them. What is involved is not a linguistic/conceptual or culturally self-enclosed relativism, but an ontologically grounded open perspectivalism.

The structure of the mute world of active engagement with the other is one of ongoing interpretive activity such that the possibilities of language are already given in it. Dewey thus explains the origins and function of language by examining its role in the social process. As the later Dewey, in focusing on naming, stresses, "The suitability of meaning as name for the importance of the contribution made by the organic partner – especially with respect to words as names" is questionable and misleading unless it is understood in the "functional service of behavior as inquiry," for in its fundamental sense, "to mean is to intend" (Dewey 1989b: 332). Purposive behavioral activity is, again in the later Dewey's words, "as evident of significance as name for the complementary way of being important" (Dewey 1989b: 332), and the two are existentially and intimately unified in all intelligent activity, inseparable even in imagination (Dewey 1989b: 328). Indeed, our fundamental logical laws of thought are themselves abstractions from the concrete matrix of purposive behavioral interactions.

Language is a type of gesture which is intimately incorporated into concrete experience, is inseparably intertwined with thought and, as lived, incorporates both settled tradition and present creativity. Language cannot be divorced from temporally grounded human praxis in a "dense" universe. For Dewey, language is a tool but, in his words, any tool "is a thing in which a connection, a sequential bond with nature is embodied. It possesses an objective relation as its own defining property. ... A tool denotes a perception and acknowledgment of sequential bonds in nature" (Dewey 1981: 101). Language is a tool for providing a perspectival grasp of the natural world in which we are embedded. Language is a tool born of our primal bond with nature and it mediates our experience in and of nature; it does not cut us off from nature's real properties; it does not stand between us and nature; and, if the tool is well formed, it is not something which distorts nature.

The notion that if language is to relate to reality it must be able to capture a series of independently existing fully structured facts, and if it cannot do so it bears no relation to reality at all, is itself a remnant of the alternatives offered by the spectator theory of knowledge and the atomism of the modern period, with its concomitant representative theory of perception and subject–object split. For Dewey, the compulsiveness of the world enters experience within the interpretive net we have cast upon it for delineating facts, for breaking its continuities, for rendering precise its vagueness. Dewey does not reject the ontic-epistemic linkage of language and the world but rather rethinks the nature of this linkage. He does not reject the idea of reality's constraints on our language structures but rather rethinks the nature of these constraints as one which is not that of correspondence.

Language does not deny the presence of reality within experience, nor does it mirror this reality, but rather it opens us on to reality's presence as mediated by meanings, for language is emergent from and intertwined with ongoing praxis in a "dense" universe. We do not think to a reality to which language or conceptual structures correspond, but rather we live through a reality with which we are intertwined, and the intertwining with which constitutes experience. Our primal interactive embeddedness in the world is something which can never be adequately objectified. In this way Dewey, in denying the foundationalism of modernism, does not yield to the anti-foundationalism of post-modernism. Rather, he rethinks the nature of foundations, standing the tradition on its head, so to speak, reconstructing a tradition of philosophy which, in its search for supposed foundations, lost the illusive but pervasive experiential-ontological foundations of its search by ignoring the fundamental, creative, indefinitely rich epistemic and ontological unity at the heart of lived experience.

Much of contemporary philosophy, operating within the seemingly novel paradigm of language or within other seemingly novel paradigms radically restrictive of the nature and limits of philosophical pursuits, has yet not succeeded in breaking with the alternatives offered by, and hence the possible solutions allowable by, a long philosophical tradition. Though the alternatives and possible solutions may take distinctively new turns and though seemingly new alternatives and new limitations emerge, they can too often be seen as new twists to old paradigmatic offerings. The alternatives, whether expressed in older or newer fashion, of correspondence or coherence, realism or idealism, empiricism or rationalism, foundationalism or anti-foundationalism, realism or anti-realism, objectivism or relativism, subjectivism or objectivism, play or pure presence, conversation or a mirror of nature, all are alternatives which grow out of reflective frameworks which ignore the fundamental, creative, interactive unity – at once epistemic, ontological, and practical – that lies at the heart of lived experience and is central to the spirit of Dewey's philosophy.

To separate the importance of creative diversity from its rootedness in compelling constraints, to reject the epistemic-ontological interactive unity of experience and nature with its resulting openness at the heart of our concrete existence in the world in favor of self-enclosed language, to ignore experimental method as the method of learning perspectival truths about our world, is to lose the spirit of Deweyian pragmatism and the paradigmatic novelty it provides for charting a course into the future which winds its way between the self-defeating alternatives of a long philosophical tradition.

Many of the problems and dilemmas housed in what is generally taken to be the cutting edge of philosophy today themselves underscore the need to avoid the all too easy backslide into the all too treacherous, often all too elusive, terrain structured by false alternatives which ultimately have their roots in the alternative of either the spectator understanding of knowledge or the supposed necessary consequences of its rejection, supposed necessary consequences dictated by the very spectator assumptions being rejected. These supposed necessary consequences then guide the direction of many of the very positions most determined to reject spectator assumptions and conclusions. For this paradoxical situation the paradigmatic novelty of pragmatism offers a powerful remedy.

The point of departure for the divergent paths of pragmatism and post-modernism are to be found in their divergent answers to two interrelated fundamental questions. Are our meanings, concepts, languages, and the content they structure veils which cut us off from reality, or do they open us onto reality in a direct but perspectival grasp of or engagement with it? Are the ingrained habits of thinking – either explicitly or implicitly – in terms of a subject–object split something that can be allowed to linger, or should the last vestiges of this be finally and definitively expunged via a thoroughly novel paradigm? Dewey's pragmatic naturalism is structured throughout by its choice of the latter alternative for each of these questions. A rejection of either of these latter alternatives – either explicitly or implicitly – marks entry into a pathway divergent from, indeed contradictory of, Deweyan pragmatic naturalism, and these divergent pathways color and pervade any and all doctrines contained therein.

Bibliography

Dewey, J. (1977), "The Experimental Theory of Knowledge," *The Middle Works*, vol. 3, ed. J. Boydston, Carbondale and Edwardsville: University of Southern Illinois Press.

Dewey, J. (1907–1909) "Does Reality Possess Practical Character?" *The Middle Works*, vol. 4, ed. J. Boydston , Carbondale and Edwardsville: University of Southern Illinois Press.

Dewey, J. (1929) *The Quest for Certainty, The Later Works*, vol. 4, ed. J. Boydston, Carbondale and Edwardsville: University of Southern Illinois Press.

Dewey, J. (1981) *Experience and Nature, The Later Works*, vol. 1, ed. J. Boydston, Carbondale and Edwardsville: University of Southern Illinois Press.

Dewey, J. (1989a) "How, What, and What For in Social Inquiry," *The Later Works*, vol. 16, ed. J. Boydston, Carbondale and Edwardsville: University of Southern Illinois Press.

Dewey, J. (1989b) "Importance, Significance, and Meaning," *The Later Works*, vol. 16, ed. J. Boydston, Carbondale and Edwardsville: University of Southern Illinois Press.

Dewey, J. and Bentley, A.F. (1989) *Knowing and the Known*, in J. Dewey, *The Later Works*, vol. 16., ed. J. Boydston, Carbondale and Edwardsville: University of Southern Illinois Press

Rorty, R. (1991) "Pragmatism without Method," *Objectivity, Relativism, and Truth*, Papers, I, New York: Cambridge University Press.

Part III

Inquiry and society

11 John Dewey and the intersection of democracy and law

Richard A. Posner[1]

Introduction: the philosopher and the public intellectual

Of the leading pragmatist philosophers, John Dewey probably did the most to try to apply his pragmatic philosophy to the law and to other departments of public policy, consistent with his view that philosophers should play a constructive rather than merely an academic role in society. It is true that Richard Rorty, one of Dewey's most prominent contemporary avatars, has also written extensively about policy issues of one sort or another, including some legal issues. But Rorty's discussion of those issues owes little to his philosophy – or at least is not closely integrated with it, perhaps because Rorty's pragmatism is not so much a philosophy as a rejection of philosophy. (More precisely, it is a rejection of much that passes for philosophy, including the sorts of moral and political philosophy that might be thought to inform commentary on public issues.) In contrast, Dewey's discussion of policy, and especially of law, owes much to his philosophy – or at least appears to.

We must be wary of exaggerating either Dewey's influence on law or the unity of his thought. Regarding his influence on law, Thomas Grey has shown that legal pragmatism stands free of philosophical pragmatism (Grey 1996: 254); and Holmes, the most influential expositor of legal pragmatism, preceded Dewey. Still, Dewey is heavily cited by academic lawyers,[2] though less for his specific statements about law (which will, however, be the focus of this chapter) than for his general philosophical stance[3] – pragmatism, or, his preferred term, "experimentalism" – and his views on democracy and education.[4]

Regarding the unity of Dewey's thought, we must recognize that most of his commentaries on public affairs have no organic relation to his philosophy. I have in mind such things as his support for making war illegal (Dewey 1984c: 349), his criticism of the New Deal as too timid and advocacy of public control of the economy, his isolationism before Pearl Harbor. In retrospect we think poorly of people who thought we could just sit out the Second World War; and many of the New Deal programs are now recognized as excessively dirigiste, especially those based on a belief, naturally fostered by businessmen, that the Depression had been caused by excessive competition. We think that Roosevelt had a much better grasp of the nation's problems both domestically and internationally than Dewey did.[5] And most of Dewey's commentaries on public affairs, right or wrong, are severely dated.

But they are to one side of his philosophy, these commentaries; they belong rather to his career as a "public intellectual,"[6] a career that, as so often is the case with academics, was very much a mixed bag, though on the plus side must be reckoned Dewey's steadfast anticommunism after the briefest of flirtations with the Soviet Union following a visit there in 1928. He has been praised as a model public intellectual – "one of the last of what seems to be a dying breed," "represent[ing] what social philosophy can hope to become," his "sustained philosophical engagement with the social and political issues of his day stand[ing] as an attractive beacon" (Morris and Shapiro 1993: ix, xi). Yet he can equally be viewed as a cautionary example, one of many[7] (Russell, Heidegger, and Sartre come immediately to mind), of the dangers of trying to lever philosophy into commentary on current affairs. Philosophy is not the master key to knowledge. Dewey wrote on too many subjects remote from his discipline; his reach exceeded his grasp.[8] And he was handicapped in discussing concrete issues of policy by lacking, so far as I can see, either a consistent or a realistic understanding of human motivation; he was too much the preacher. In the decades since he wrote, moreover, the increased profes-sionalization of philosophy has carried it ever further away from constructive engagement with concrete social problems; pragmatism itself has become academized. Yet we shall see that what Dewey had to say about law has enduring value.

Democracy – epistemic and political

The master concept that unites Dewey's philosophy with the policy realm is that of "democracy," and the nature and implications of this union, specifically but not only for Dewey's analysis of law, will be the principal focus of this chapter. The word "democracy" has many meanings, but two are particularly important to understanding Dewey's "take" on law and policy: epistemic democracy, which is the idea that inquiry and decision making in general, not just political inquiry and decision making, are democratic in character; and political democracy, which, in its most common modern form, is a system of political governance, the defining feature of which is that the principal officials are selected by popular vote. Dewey's attempt to join these two conceptions is one of the distinctive features of his version of pragmatism.

By "epistemic democracy" is meant a challenge to the tenacious and, when Dewey wrote, the orthodox conception of scientific and other inquiry as essentially an individual search for truth using the tools of logic (in the strict sense exemplified by the syllogism) either to reveal truth directly (as in math-ematics and some versions of moral reasoning) or to generate hypotheses verifiable or refutable by experimental or other exact data. In the case of moral or political reasoning, hypotheses were to be tested if at all by intuition, though in those areas the emphasis fell not on hypothesis testing at all but rather on logical deduction from accepted premises, just as in mathematical reasoning. The search in any case was for truth, the "antecedently real," that which exists independently of human cognition. The world, including mathematical and even moral and political concepts, was regarded as a passive object waiting to be discovered by human beings using the methods of exact reasoning. And the quest for its secrets was seen as a lonely one, conducted by trained experts, or by persons of great insight, operating as individuals.

Dewey, following on Peirce and James, questioned the emphasis both on "truth" and on the "individual." Against the orthodox conception of scientific and other inquiry he set up a conception of it as oriented toward the cooperative acquisition of useful knowledge using whatever tools lay to hand, including imagination, common sense, know how, and intuition, and thus of tacit knowledge as well as knowledge acquired by formal reasoning and systematic empirical methods. He deemphasized the pursuit of "truth" as such, rejecting the possibility of disinterested, "objective," conclusive inquiry and pointing out that there is no way of knowing when one has found the "truth" because one cannot step outside the world and observe the correspondence between one's descriptions and the world as it really is. All that people are capable of and fortunately all they are really interested in is getting better control over their environment, enlarging their horizons, and enriching and improving their lives. The knowledge required for these endeavors is collective in the sense of being both acquired by the cooperative efforts of diverse inquirers – intelligence being distributed throughout the community rather than concentrated in a handful of outstanding experts – and validated by the community's evaluation of its utility; as a practical matter, "truth" is consensus.

This is the positive side of Dewey's epistemology and the negative is skepticism about the claims of the orthodox approach. The more precise term for this skepticism is "fallibilism," the idea that knowledge grows by challenging and superseding existing beliefs without necessarily achieving a resting point called "truth."[9] Hypothesis testing has an important role to play in this process. Indeed, scientific inquiry is the very model of rational inquiry because of its demonstrated capacity to yield useful knowledge. That capacity is rooted in the ethics of scientific inquiry with its insistence on willingness to test belief against evidence and thus to accept – what people not schooled to the scientific ethic find so difficult to do – the possibility that one's belief is false. Science does not bring us to a resting point, as religion claims to do: a point at which ultimate truth is revealed to us.

A critical issue is the process by which the scientist obtains the theories that he seeks to test, the process Peirce called "abduction." The "scientific method" provides no guidance here. Abduction belongs to the domain of imagination, a faculty that the orthodox approach cannot explain, rather than to that of formulaic procedures. The orthodox approach also overlooks the importance of doubt as the essential stimulus of challenges to existing beliefs; habit as reluctance to give up existing beliefs and therefore as obstacle to progress; and diversity and competition as conditions that favor, as in Darwin's theory of natural selection, the creation of new theories by a "blind" process akin to trial and error. Dewey's approach is also Darwinian, I note parenthetically, in its emphasis on human reason as a mode of coping with the environment rather than of establishing a pipeline to the truth – the former being a more plausible description of the emergence of mind as a product of biological evolution.

The value of diversity in inquiry is closely connected to the inability of the scientific method to generate the theories that it tests and explores. Because there is no algorithm for creating new theories, a diversity of approaches is necessary for there to be a good chance of hitting on one that works; we cannot tell in advance which one that will be. It is because we can't know in advance which path is best that progress is a social undertaking and achievement, which in turn implies that intelligence is distributed throughout the community. This has egalitarian implications that interested Dewey and that suggest a third, a social rather than an epistemological or a political concept of democracy: the democratic temperament or ethos so emphasized by Tocqueville.[10]

Dewey's preferred term for his epistemic approach, which I'll call "distributed intelligence" (as in "distributed processing" of data by computers)[11] from now on, was not pragmatism, with its connotations of the utilitarian, but "experimentalism." The word aptly describes the tenor of his thought. He repeatedly commends the experimental temper, which is impatient with convention and the accustomed ways of doing things – the sediment of habit – and which is continuously insisting that we must try now this, now that, in a creatively restless search for better means. It is a search that yields, as a by-product, better ends as well. One might take up ballet to improve one's posture and discover that one loves the ballet for its aesthetic qualities; a means would have become an end. Through such examples the charge that pragmatism is philistine is rebutted.

Dewey's approach is "democratic" in the sense of emphasizing the community over the exceptional individual. Knowledge is not produced mechanically by the repeated application of algorithmic procedures by expert investigators all trained the same way, but by the tug of communal demands, the struggle between doubt and habit, the diverse strivings of individuals of diverse background, aptitude, training, and experience, and the application of methods of inquiry, such as imagination and intuition, that owe little to expert training. No one, no elite even, has a pipeline to truth – truth is always just out of reach, like the grapes of Tantalus, at most a regulatory, an orienting, ideal – and if this is the case with scientific truth, it is all the more likely to be the case with moral and political truths as well. The project of Plato's Republic, the rule of experts, of the people who by virtue of aptitude, training, and experience have privileged access to scientific, moral, and political truth, is quixotic.

Conceiving of science as a branch of practical reason, that is, as oriented toward helping us cope rather than toward revealing the external world as it really is, Dewey was led to argue that scientific reasoning is not fundamentally different from the reasoning used to solve such "practical" problems as how to govern a society or organize its economy. Science is just better than our more common modes of inquiry because it has a more fruitful attitude toward inquiry, an attitude emphasizing openmindedness, intellectual flexibility, a practical orientation, and a readiness to be disproved, that is more likely to achieve useful solutions than the slapdash approximations to scientific inquiry that politicians and other "men of affairs" tend to use.

Dewey thought that because the scientific approach is not fundamentally different from the epistemic procedures used by the ordinary person, maybe the population as a whole could someday learn to use that approach in the moral and political domain (MacGilvray 1999: 551, 562). If so, political democracy would become unproblematic. But even short of that day, the theory of epistemic democracy has implications for political governance. If rule by experts is out, with it goes any theocratic or otherwise authoritarian conception of right political rule, any basis for the censorship of ideas and opinions, any legitimacy to having a fixed and durable political hierarchy. The idea that there are experts who have reliable techniques for getting in touch with the antecedently real in morality and science is inconsistent with democracy, which is rule by people who have no claim to have such a pipeline. So Dewey's philosophical project of overturning Platonic epistemology, to the extent it succeeds, makes the case by default for democratic political rule, the system in which the community as a whole rather than selected experts makes political decisions,[12] in just the way that Platonic epistemology leads to the authoritarian political system described in the Republic. Harvey Mansfield and Delba Winthrop, quoting Tocqueville, contrast "democratic eagerness to get practical applications of science to the 'ardent, haughty, and disinterested love of the true' characteristic of a few" (Mansfield and Winthrop 2000: xvii, xxxii).[13] Dewey turned Plato on his head.

A name for the bridge that connects epistemic or cognitive democracy to political democracy is "deliberative" democracy – not Dewey's term but a good description of how he related the two conceptions.[14] Deliberative democracy is political democracy conceived of as not merely a clash of wills and interests, or as an aggregating of preferences (the Benthamite conception of democracy), or as merely a check on the officials, elected and otherwise, who are the real rulers (Schumpeter's conception of democracy)[15] – none of these would be epistemically robust – but rather as the pooling of different ideas and approaches and the selection of the best through debate and discussion. The problem with the suggested linkage, the problem that gave rise to Dewey's pessimism about our actual existing democracy, is that deliberative democracy is almost as purely aspirational and hopelessly unrealistic as rule by Platonic guardians. With half the population having an IQ of less than 100 (not a point that Dewey himself would have been comfortable making, however), with the issues confronting modern government highly complex, and with ordinary people having as little interest in as they have aptitude for complex policy issues, it would be unrealistic to expect good ideas and sensible policies to well out of the intellectual disorder that is the political process. Part of what lay behind Dewey's interest in the reform of education was his belief that political democracy would not work well unless people learned to think about political questions the way scientists think about scientific ones – disinterestedly, intelligently, empirically. He seemed to think they could learn to think this way but he was not optimistic that they would, and this made him pessimistic about American democracy.

The history of the United States in the half century since Dewey's death suggests that his pessimism was misplaced, that he had succumbed to the intellectual's typical mistake of exaggerating the importance of intellect. He thought that until the American population as a whole had acquired the ethics of scientific inquiry, democracy would remain unsatisfactory, perhaps even vulnerable.[16] So far as we can judge today, he was wrong. It is probably the case (though India, with its 50 per cent illiteracy rate, seems to be a counterexample) that some minimum of education is required for a democratic political system to work in a large, complex, modern society; the system does require that the citizenry make occasional political decisions, and those decisions involve persons and issues that the average citizen cannot assess at first hand. But if we may judge from the US experience, the minimum required for viable (indeed vibrant) political democracy is low, perhaps low enough to be supplied by television rather than formal education, which seems increasingly less inclined to provide it. Political democracy has, as Dewey believed, decisive advantages, at least for wealthy, secure societies having relatively well informed populations, over alternative forms of government. But they are not advantages that depend on deliberation, on analogies to scientific inquiry, or on a lively and informed public interest in public issues. Democracy's only real epistemic advantage is one that Dewey did not emphasize: democracy enables public opinion to be reliably determined, thus providing vital feedback for the policy initiatives of political leaders and other officials. Nondemocratic regimes find it difficult to gauge public opinion, and as a result sometimes adopt, as it were inadvertently, policies so radically unpopular as to kill the regime. It is easy for nondemocratic rulers to get out of touch with the citizens.

But this epistemic advantage of democracy is not democracy's greatest advantage. Indeed, the epistemic disadvantage of the purest forms of democracy, such as Athenian direct democracy, a disadvantage resulting in part from the intellectual limitations of the citizenry, is decisive in the shape that modern democracy has assumed – that of representative democracy. The classical tradition regarded representative democracy as "aristocratic" in the Aristotelian sense (Manin 1997), rule by "the best" (hoi aristoi).[17] The characterization grates, but is apt. In representative democracy the people do not rule, though they decide who shall rule. The rulers are the officials, selected in an electoral competition among contestants who are by no means ordinary men and women but instead belong to an elite of intelligence, cunning, connections, or other attributes that enable them to present themselves to the public plausibly as "the best." The resulting division of labor in political governance, with the people only intermittently and remotely engaged and actual governance delegated to specialists in politics and government, is a sensible bow to the claims of expertise. But at least in the circumstances of modern government it is not democratic in a Deweyan sense, when one considers the role of parties and interest groups, the vastness and complexity of the issues that confront modern government, the political apathy and ignorance of the great mass of the people most of the time, and how much of the real power of government resides in unelected officials, many of them judges and civil servants with lifetime tenure. People's preferences and interests influence government, certainly, through the electoral process and otherwise, but not in the way that views expressed in a faculty meeting influence faculty decisions, through debate and pooling of ideas. The role of the people at large in the governance of a large democratic nation is altogether more passive than its role in the concept of deliberative democracy. People know when things are going well or going badly and will vote accordingly, but that is about it. And the relevant "well" or "badly" is well or badly for them. They vote their interests. Voting is rarely disinterested. The political parties know this, and so their campaigns appeal to interests, rather than to the Good.

It is even arguable that despite the expansion of the suffrage, there is less political democracy in the United States today than there was in the early nineteenth century, at least outside the slaveholding region. Much more of the business of government was done then by the states, and states are more democratic than the federal government; terms of office are shorter, judges' tenures are less secure, more officials (including judges) are elected rather than appointed; the issues with which state government deals are more comprehensible to the electorate; and there is less delegation to administrative agencies. Yet from a pragmatic standpoint, it is hard to argue that the shift in power from the states to the federal government has been on balance a bad thing; pragmatism and political democracy are not synonyms.

The real political spillover from a pragmatic theory of knowledge is, as John Stuart Mill recognized, not a boost for democracy but a boost for liberty. The first chapter of *On Liberty* explains the dependence of sound government on freedom of inquiry and expression. Liberty is at once a precondition of and a limitation on democracy – a precondition because without liberty the people lack the independence and competence to perform their role in democratic governance, that of controlling the officials. But liberty is not democracy. The right of just compensation for taking private property for public use, the right of association, the right of expression, the right of religious freedom – all these are rights primarily against popular majorities. They are legally protected rights because of fear that the people would sometimes want to infringe them. Granted, there is also the fear that democracy without rights against the democratic majority is unstable; that a temporary majority will entrench itself by intimidating the temporary minority that opposes it. But this is to say that the people cannot be fully trusted in the bestowal of authority, and must be protected by the curtailment of their power.

Dewey on law

If I am right, Dewey's democratic epistemology, this idea of "distributed intelligence" that is at the core of his political philosophy as well as his theory of knowledge, is unlikely to have much of a payoff with regard to the resolution of issues of political governance, which include issues about the role (and rule) of law. The bridge he tried to build between epistemic and political democracy is not strong enough to carry heavy traffic across the divide. But this is merely a hypothesis, which I shall try to test by examining Dewey's most extended foray into law, the essay "Logical Method and Law" (Dewey 1924), from the standpoint of his political philosophy. He wrote another major essay on law, "The Historic Background of Corporate Legal Personality" (Dewey 1926), in which he took on the theory (primarily Germanic) that corporations have "real personality," that they are not merely legal constructs, which was, when he wrote, as it is now for that matter, the prevailing view of Anglo-American lawyers.

Dewey made a nice pragmatic point in that essay – that the entire meaning of corporate "personality" resides in the legal consequences annexed to the corporate form. Thus, instead of asking whether a corporation has enough "personality" to be a "person" within the meaning of the Fourteenth Amendment, or to be exclusively liable for "its" debts rather than merely a conduit to the shareholders as under partnership law, we should ask whether the courts have given corporations the status of persons for Fourteenth Amendment purposes and whether they have limited the liability of the corporation's shareholders to their investment in the corporation, so that the corporation's creditors cannot sue the shareholders personally for the corporation's debts. All we care about is the answers to these practical legal questions, and not the metaphysical question of whether or not a corporation has a "personality."

This is fine as far as it goes but leaves unexplained what the courts should draw on to answer the practical legal questions concerning the corporation (Luban 1998: 275, 298). Dewey is characteristically of no help with that question. But he is correct that whatever the right source of wisdom for corporate law, it is not the metaphysics of personality. And that was a fresh and useful point when he made it. The article owes nothing to Dewey's concept of democracy, however, and neither does an interesting short piece on law that he wrote some years later. It repeats and generalizes the pragmatic point in his corporate law piece – "the standard [for evaluating law] is found in consequences, in the function of what goes on socially" – but with the further and arresting thought that:

from any practical standpoint, recognition of the relatively slow rate of change on the part of certain constituents of social action is capable of accomplishing every useful, every practically needed, office that has led in the past and in other cultural climes to setting up external sources such as the Will or Reason of God, the Law of Nature ..., and the Practical Reason of Kant.

(Dewey 1941: 81, 84, emphasis in original)

Apparently he meant by this that habit and custom, which shape law, change so slowly as to create the illusion of permanence, which we then reify as natural law, elevating our time-bound, quotidian concerns to eternal principles. We shall discover a closely related idea in "Logical Method and Law," to which I now turn.

The article begins by distinguishing between two types of human action: the instinctive or intuitive, which is swift and inarticulate yet not necessarily unreliable; and the deliberative. Actions of the first type are often reasonable; actions of the second type are reasoned (and may or may not be reasonable). "Logical theory" is Dewey's term not for logic in the orthodox sense best illustrated by the syllogism, but for "the procedures followed in reaching decisions of the second type." These procedures are similar to those followed by engineers, doctors, and businessmen and approximate the procedures employed by scientists (Dewey 1941: 17–18), for remember that Dewey believed science to be the model for all sound reasoning. Logic thus conceived "is ultimately an empirical and concrete discipline" (Dewey 1941: 19). When lawyers such as Justice Holmes describe law as existing in the tension between "logic and good sense," Dewey explains, they have in mind "formal consistency, consistency of concepts with one another irrespective of the consequences of their application to concrete matters-of-fact" (Dewey 1941: 20), or, in short, the syllogism. The problem for law is that "concepts once developed have a kind of intrinsic inertia on their own account; once developed the law of habit applies to them." This makes it difficult to adapt legal doctrines in a timely fashion to changing circumstances (Dewey 1941). To do that requires "another kind of logic[,] which shall reduce the influence of habit, and shall facilitate the use of good sense regarding matters of social consequence" (Dewey 1941: 21). Recall that Dewey had in his short essay "My Philosophy of Law" pointed out that the inertial force of habit is augmented by reifying the familiar, the customary or habitual, as a permanent, unchangeable Truth.

The problem with applying syllogistic reasoning to law, Dewey continues, is that such reasoning requires "that for every possible case which may arise, there is a fixed antecedent rule already at hand," whereas sound "general principles emerge as statements of generic ways in which it has been found helpful to treat concrete cases" (Dewey 1941: 22); in short, they are generalizations from experience. For "we generally begin with some vague anticipation of a conclusion (or at least of alternative conclusions), and then we look around for principles and data which will substantiate it or which will enable us to choose intelligently between rival conclusions" (Dewey 1941: 23). The distinction is thus between a logic ("method" would be a better term) of inquiry and a logic of exposition. Law needs the former as well as the latter: the former to reach the legal conclusion, the latter to set it forth in an articulate, coherent ("logical") form that will provide both a public justification and a guide for the future.

Regarding the justificatory role of the characteristic "logical" (syllogistic) style of judicial opinions, Dewey makes the interesting suggestion that "it is highly probable that the need of justifying to others conclusions reached and decisions made has been the chief cause of the origin and development of logical operations in the precise sense; of abstraction, generalization, regard for consistency of implications" (Dewey 1941: 24). Regarding the importance of making law predictable for the guidance of the community, Dewey insists on the difference between "theoretical certainty and practical certainty," the former based on "the absurd because impossible proposition that every decision should flow with formal logical necessity from antecedently known premises" (Dewey 1941: 25, emphasis in original). Practical certainty is highly desirable, but can be achieved to only a limited degree (that is the "practical" aspect) when social and economic conditions are rapidly changing, requiring law to change also if its rules are not to become obsolete. There is, as we might put it, a tradeoff between the social interest in the law's continuity or constancy, which is important to enable people to plan their affairs, and the social interest in the law's adaptability to change, which is important to the creation of sound legal rules.

Insistence on the former interest to the exclusion of the latter can actually undermine the law's predictability: "because circumstances are really novel and not covered by old rules, it is a gamble which old rule will be declared regulative of a particular case" (Dewey 1941: 26). The old rules breed a "virtual alliance between the judiciary and entrenched interests that correspond most closely to the conditions under which the rules of law were previously laid down," and so "the slogans of liberalism of one period often become the bulwarks of reaction in a subsequent era" (Dewey 1941: 26). Those slogans include "liberty in use of property, and freedom of contract" (Dewey 1941: 27), slogans that when Dewey wrote were being used to invalidate progressive (in the social-welfare sense) state legislation and that later would be used to invalidate New Deal legislation. He hoped the old slogans would give way to newer rules based on "social justice." But he warned against the hardening of such rules in their turn "into absolute and fixed antecedent premises" (Dewey 1941: 27), which would just be a modern version of Platonic absolutes or natural law. In fact, just such hardening has occurred in those precincts of legal thought in which the decisions of the Warren Court are regarded as sacred writ.

What is needed, Dewey's article advises, is "a logic relative to consequences rather than to antecedents," a logic that is forward looking rather than, as is the natural bent of lawyers and judges, backward looking; a logic that treats general rules and principles as "working hypotheses, needing to be constantly tested by the way in which they work out in application to concrete situations" (Dewey 1941: 26, emphasis in original). He concludes that "infiltration into law of a more experimental and flexible logic is a social as well as an intellectual need" (Dewey 1941: 27).

Dewey's essay is a clear statement of the pragmatic theory of adjudication,[18] and one of the founding documents of legal realism. His essential point, which as far as I know had not been made previously though it is implicit in much of what Holmes (heavily quoted in Dewey's essay) wrote, was that legal reasoning is *au fond* just like other practical reasoning. This is because all practical reasoning is alike, all a closer or more distant approximation to scientific reasoning. Since the law's concerns are practical, law cannot be "logical" in the strict sense; nothing practical can be. This point is the essential creed of pragmatic adjudication.

The shortcoming of the essay, as of so much of Dewey's policy-oriented writing, is its (paradoxical) lack of engagement with concrete problems and real institutions. It is top-down reasoning, rather than the bottom-up reasoning that he recommended. The same is true of his thinking about democracy and explains his pessimism. Instead of looking closely at our actual democratic system in comparison to the political systems of other countries, he compares our system with a democratic ideal of his concoction and so naturally is disappointed. "Logical Method and Law" is about practical reasoning, rather than being an example of practical reasoning. (Its brevity – the essay is only ten pages long – is suggestive.) Dewey was very good at reasoning about practical reasoning, but not very good at doing practical reasoning. Similarly, while he commended scientific reasoning as the model of reasoned inquiry, the scientific spirit is not conspicuous in his own writings.

Law and Deweyan democracy

One of the peculiarities of "Logical Method and Law," as of the other two essays of Dewey's on law that I've discussed, is that it owes relatively little to any of the concepts of democracy that engaged his attention. Democracy, as I said, is the bridge between his philosophy and his engagement with public issues; yet his most successful forays into those issues, his essays on law, make little use of the bridge. The notion of a logic of consequences is *echt* pragmatic; but it is not distinctively Deweyan. The emphasis on habit as reifying merely expedient legal notions, and the notion of legal reasoning as adaptive to changing circumstances, which is to say to a changing environment, are distinctively Deweyan; but they are not central to the essays.

I go further. The essays on law owe less to philosophical pragmatism than to what might be called "everyday pragmatism," which is to say the untheorized cultural outlook of Americans, an outlook rooted in the usages and attitudes of a commercial, materialistic society, with its emphasis on working hard and getting ahead.[19] Well described by Tocqueville more than 150 years ago, this is an outlook that predisposes Americans, not excluding philosophers, to judge proposals by the criterion of what works, to demand, in William James's memorable phrase, the "cash value" of particular beliefs, to judge issues on the basis of their concrete consequences for one's happiness and prosperity. It is this everyday pragmatism that seems to underlie, and that provides a sufficient explanation and justification for, the view of law that Dewey sketches in his legal essays. The concept of epistemic democracy adds little.

And yet that concept has two important implications for law, implications Dewey might have drawn had he engaged more closely with law. First, he might have pointed to the desirability of having a diverse judiciary (Posner 1990: 447–448). When lawyers, judges, and law professors talk about the qualities of a good judge, implicitly they assume that there is some optimum recipe of qualities; and since it is the optimum, the best, it is what every judge should have. So in an ideal world all judges would be alike. But Dewey's theory of "distributed intelligence," and its Darwinian underpinnings or analogy, imply, once the idea of a Platonic-logical conception of legal reasoning is rejected, the desirability of having judges of diverse origins, experience, attitudes, values, and cast of mind. This is especially true at the appellate level. The deliberations of a panel of appellate judges will be improved, Dewey's entire philosophy implies, if the judges have (within limits) diverse qualities. There is thus no single "ideal" judge. We want judges who are intelligent and learned, judges who are practical and down to earth, judges of austere intellectual independence and judges skilled at compromise, judges who have led worldly and those who have led sheltered lives, judges who are realistic and judges who are idealistic, judges who are passionate about liberty and judges who appreciate order and civility.

We can sense in Ronald Dworkin's heuristic of Judge "Hercules," the judge who combines all the moral and intellectual qualities requisite in a judge and in the optimum combination, and therefore deliberates alone, the remoteness of Dworkin's legal philosophy from Dewey's; and we are helped to understand Dworkin's disdain for pragmatism (Dworkin 1991: 359, 360). The disdain is unmerited. Hercules is a chimera. As Professor (now Judge) Noonan once cruelly but aptly observed, "It is strange to talk of Hercules when your starting point is Harry Blackmun" (Noonan 1976: 174). No sensible person would want a court of Harry Blackmuns, yet one might think (though I happen not to) that a Harry Blackmun would bring something to the judicial table that was worth having.

Second, and as it turns out related, Dewey's essay implies (or might seem to imply – a vital qualification, as we shall see) that courts either should not have the power to invalidate legislation, or should exercise the power only in the most extreme circumstances, when faced by a law patently unconstitutional or utterly revolting. For by invalidating legislation, courts kill diversity and frustrate experimentation. Holmes had already described the states as "laboratories" in which social experiments can be carried out without endangering the nation as a whole,[20] and he had done this in the context of protesting against his fellow Justices' willingness to forbid such experimentation in the name of the

Constitution. This was a Deweyan point, and one might have expected Dewey to make it in his essay on law. Constitutional invalidation of legislation, in the Deweyan intellectual universe, is more than just checking a political preference. It is profoundly rather than merely superficially undemocratic (superficially because the Constitution itself was a product of democracy, or at least what passed for democracy in the eighteenth century). It places expert opinion over the distributed intelligence of the mass of the people and prevents the emergence of the best policies through intellectual natural selection, which requires experimentation.

This point is missed by many of Dewey's current avatars in the legal academy. They not only applaud the snuffing out of democratic experimentation by the Supreme Court in areas such as abortion, school prayer, and criminal rights; many of them would like to see the Court do much more to override democratic sentiment – they would like to see it for example abolish capital punishment (which the vast majority of the population supports), institute rigid racial quotas, eliminate disparities among school districts in per-pupil funding, require interdistrict busing to eradicate traces of school segregation, require that states guarantee a minimum income for their citizens, and recognize homosexual marriage (invalidating the Defense of Marriage Act, passed by Congress with near unanimity and signed into law by President Clinton). Such judicial measures cannot plausibly be considered democracy-promoting, as might, in contrast, decisions invalidating unreasonable impediments to voting in political elections or limitations on freedom of political speech. The contemporary Deweyans who advocate judicial adoption of the current left-liberal political agenda, bypassing legislatures, can have little respect for distributed intelligence, democratic diversity, or social experimentation. At some level they must believe that Supreme Court Justices guided by the best thinkers in the legal academy can build a pipeline to moral, political, and juristic truth. They fail to recognize, as Dworkin, at least, recognizes, the incompatibility of so Platonic a conception of the judicial role in constitutional adjudication with Deweyan pragmatism.

Consider *Roe* v. *Wade*. Whatever its merits as a constitutional decision, they are not democratic merits. To suppose that the Supreme Court was merely applying a democratic decision made when the original Constitution was ratified, or the Fourteenth Amendment in 1868, would be ludicrous. The Court simply set a lower value on fetal life than on women's interest in the control of their reproductive activity. This was a legislative judgment, owing nothing to democratic theory or preference. The democracy-reinforcing argument that women burdened with unwanted children would be in effect expelled from the public sphere and prevented from participating effectively, whether as voters or candidates, in political activity, is unconvincing. Had the Court decided *Roe* v. *Wade* the other way, upholding the constitutionality of the Texas abortion statute despite its very limited exceptions, some states would have retained their prohibitions against abortion – but these are the states in which abortions are still very difficult to get because of hostility to and intimidation of abortion doctors and clinics and hospitals that perform abortions. In such states, probably the primary effect of a legal prohibition of abortions would be to induce greater caution in girls and women in engaging in sexual activity than if they had access to abortion on demand as a back up to contraception.

We might think of *Roe* v. *Wade* as a pragmatic decision, since it seems to have been based on a weighing of the consequences of the alternative outcomes, there being nothing in the text of the Constitution or in the case law to compel the Court's decision. But an important consequence was left out of consideration and that was the stifling effect on experimentation of establishing a constitutional right to abortion. The Court's pragmatism was truncated.

There is a complementary right-wing agenda which involves constitutionalizing laissez-faire economics and, in some versions, deeming the fetus a "person" whose life the due process clause of the Fourteenth Amendment requires the states to protect against abortionists. The right-wing school of judicial activism is profoundly (but unapologetically) anti-Deweyan.

If the agenda of the constitutional maximalists, whether of the Left or the Right, were adopted, the federal judiciary, advised by academic lawyers and by advocacy groups, would become the national legislature. Electoral politics would be reduced to choosing the officials to implement the judiciary's policies and to fill judicial vacancies. The President and the Senate would become, in effect, the electors of the national legislature through their exercise of the powers respectively to nominate and to confirm federal judges and Justices. I am exaggerating; nevertheless the domain of democracy would shrink dramatically if either school of judicial activism triumphed.

Yet Dewey might have been persuaded that given our actual existing political democracy that he thought so defective, even popular laws could not be considered fully authentic and therefore legitimate democratic products; and in that event there might be some scope for rule by judicial experts after all. Dewey could not easily see this, because at the time he wrote "Logical Method and Law" the Supreme Court was using its power of judicial review to invalidate legislation that he thoroughly approved of – such as legislation forbidding child labor, or fixing minimum wages, or fixing maximum hours of work – and that he may even have thought products of epistemic democracy. Skeptical about political democracy in what he conceived to be an era of propaganda and of a debased and ignorant political culture, Dewey could not consistently have denied the possibility that public policy might be improved by intermittent substitution of the rule of judicial experts for popular rule. I am not aware that he ever advocated it. Still, though he was not an elitist, he was not a populist either. He hoped that education would give the average person something approaching the intelligence of the elite – eventually; but in the meantime there was a nation to govern.

I don't think, however, that the following effort at a Deweyan justification of judicial review works: democracy is deliberation; judges deliberate; therefore judicial review is democratic (Peters 1997: 312). The Soviet Politburo, at least after Stalin's death, deliberated too; but this did not make it a democratic organ. A Supreme Court of nine judges is not a large enough slice of the electorate to be a statistically significant sample of, and hence an adequate stand-in for, the electorate; and it is not a representative sample of the electorate, either. We are not governing ourselves when we are governed by nine Supreme Court Justices, no matter how conscientiously they deliberate.

Dewey's theory of democracy evaluated

We must consider whether Dewey was right about democracy. I think his concept of epistemic democracy, what I am calling "distributed intelligence," has great merit, though maybe less than he thought. I am less persuaded by his belief that successful political democracy requires (or, I would add, at the risk of appearing paradoxical, is even consistent with) the adoption by the public at large of the ethics of scientific inquiry. Writing in the 1930s, the decade of many of his most emphatic warnings about the limitations of American democracy, Dewey had plenty of company in sensing a crisis of democracy. But from the perspective of the present day, his concerns seem excessive. I am not a pollyanna. But have we not muddled through quite well in the last six decades despite being a people increasingly disengaged from a serious and well informed interest in the political process? Election turnout, for example, is substantially lower than when Dewey was writing; education in civics and political history has dwindled; the funding of political campaigns has become a process of quasi-bribery. We may, I suggested earlier, be experiencing a long-term decline in the strength of the democratic principle in American politics, a decline connected with the growth of federal relative to state government. And yet the sky has not fallen. This may be in part because the (recent) growth in political apathy has paralleled and may indeed be the result of the recession of our most serious political problems, both foreign and domestic. But it may also reflect the fact that like most intellectuals, Dewey exaggerated the importance of knowledge and intelligence in public matters. Remember what I said about Franklin Roosevelt, a man far less learned, intelligent, or disinterested than Dewey, a man, indeed, who was intellectually lazy, manipulative, and not a little cynical – yet he was far more correct about the great issues of the day than Dewey. Which is what Dewey himself should have expected: as a consummate politician, Roosevelt was far better plugged into the distributed intelligence of American society than Professor Dewey.

Of course it is possible to imagine things having gone even better for us than they have. Utopian thinking is easy, especially for intellectuals, whose minds move easily from the actual to the imaginable. There is an "if only" quality about Dewey. If only hoi polloi were like us, and if only the educational system realized that and educated kids accordingly. But besides practical constraints on educational reform, and the persisting lack of a good educational theory 2,500 years after Plato first wrote about it, there is the unwarranted Socratic assumption that people are selfish and mean because they are ignorant. Education is a fine thing but above a threshold soon reached it doesn't seem to improve democracy. So if we are realistic about human nature (and hence about the edifying as distinct from the vocational effects of education), and consider realistically how the other nations of the world have done in the period since Dewey wrote, we shall be left with little reason for supposing we might have done even better if only we had been better Deweyans and conducted politics on the model of a faculty seminar.

Schumpeter's dyspeptic conception of democracy that so distressed Dewey[21] seems, in short, not only descriptively accurate but normatively adequate. I would go further and call it normatively superior to Dewey's hopes for democracy. One reason is that a strong interest in politics foments political discord, exacerbates conflict, and distracts people from private pursuits, including business, science, art, and the professions, that contribute substantially to social welfare, and in particular that build prosperity, a great emollient of political and social tensions. It is rather a strength than a weakness of representative democracy that, in contrast to direct democracy (especially in its town-meeting form, better described as participatory democracy and demanding a substantial investment in time) or plebiscitary democracy, it allows most of the people to tune out of politics most of the time. We don't have to spend all our time fending off crazy political initiatives. I shudder at Bonnie Honig's desire, superficially Deweyan, to restore "politics as a disruptive practice that resists the consolidations and closures of administrative and juridical settlement for the sake of the perpetuity of political contest" (Honig 1993: 4, 124).

Another reason not to want to raise the political consciousness of the US population is that even well educated and well informed people find it difficult to reason accurately about matters remote from their immediate concerns. People who vote on the basis of their self-interest are at least voting about something they know at first hand, their own needs and preferences. I am suspicious of the high-minded voter.

If my concerns are well founded, our society might be worse off rather than better off if people were to become as well informed about, attuned to, and engaged in politics as Dewey dreamed. But by the same token, because they are not very well informed or politically engaged, the political process cannot be expected to approximate the scientific, its products are not always entitled to the same respect as the products of scientific inquiry, and so the Supreme Court's interference in the name of the Constitution with political experimentation is not as untoward as it would be if the United States and its states were Deweyan polities. Yet he surely would have been cautious about judicial review – he who said that:

> In the absence of an articulate voice on the part of the masses, the best do not and cannot remain the best, the wise cease to be wise. It is impossible for high brows to secure a monopoly of such knowledge as must be used

for the regulation of common affairs. In the degree in which they become a specialized class, they are shut off from knowledge of the needs which they are supposed to serve.

(Dewey 1927: 206)

In the end, the implications of Dewey's legal philosophy for constitutional adjudication may be somewhat obscure. But his articulation of a pragmatic jurisprudence remains a permanent contribution to legal thought.

Notes

1 Judge, US Court of Appeals for the Seventh Circuit; Senior Lecturer, University of Chicago Law School. This is the text of a talk given at the First Annual Symposium on the Foundation of the Behavioral Sciences: "John Dewey: Modernism, Postmodernism and Beyond" held at Simon's Rock College of Bard under the auspices of the Behavioral Research Council of the American Institute for Economic Research, on 21 July 2001. I thank Eric Posner and Cass Sunstein for their helpful comments on a previous draft, the participants in the symposium for their helpful comments, and Bryan Dayton for his research assistance. A version of this chapter appears as chapter 3 ("John Dewey on Democracy and Law") in Posner 2003.

2 He has been cited in 582 articles published in law reviews in the Lexis database in the last decade.

3 On which see the excellent anthology *The Philosophy of John Dewey* (McDermott 1981).

4 For a notable example, see Sunstein 1993, described as "remarkably Deweyite" in Balkin 1995. Articles in recent years devoted to Dewey's legal thought have been rare. For an example of one, see Kendall 1995.

5 Dewey strongly opposed the election of Roosevelt in 1932. See Dewey 1984c: 246; 1984a: 252. He stated during the campaign, "Governor Roosevelt holds the same position as predatory wealth. ... Governor Roosevelt is speaking for the class he trains with" (1984d: 395). Dewey supported the socialist candidate for President, Norman Thomas.

6 Well illustrated by the New Republic essays collected in John Dewey, *Individualism Old and New* (1930). But those essays are merely illustrative; the thirty-seven volumes of Dewey's complete works, edited by Boydston, contain literally hundreds of usually very brief essays on current events and controversies.

7 See Posner 2001b: chs 8, 9.

8 See, for example, his essay on agricultural policy during the Depression, "What Keeps Funds away from Purchasers" (Dewey 1986).

9 This is not philosophical skepticism, for example skepticism about whether the external world is real or a dream. Pragmatism is resolutely opposed to philosophical skepticism because of its utter lack of practical significance.

10 A notion quite similar to Dewey's concept of distributed intelligence is Friedrich Hayek's concept of knowledge distributed throughout the community rather than concentrated in a handful of experts. See Posner 2003: ch. 7. From this Hayek drew policy implications antithetical to Dewey – that markets were the most efficient method of aggregating this knowledge. Dewey, in contrast, believed in central planning.

11 "True distributed processing has separate computers perform different tasks in such a way that their combined work can contribute to a larger goal" (Microsoft Press 1997: 154).

12 See, for example, Dewey 1993a.
13 Cf. Zaret 2000: 272–273, arguing that the successes of experimental science promoted faith in the power of reason to resolve public issues.
14 See Westbrook 1998: 128, 138, and references to essays by Hilary Putnam and Joshua Cohen at 139–140. Cf. Sunstein 2001: 37–39; 1985: 81–86.
15 Derided, unjustly as I shall argue, as "narrow[ing] democracy to little more than an *ex post facto* check on the power of elites, an act of occasional political consumption affording a choice among a limited range of well-packaged aspirants to office" Westbrook 1991: xv.
16 See, for example, Dewey 1927: ch. 4 and pp. 166–167; 1993b: 48, 56–57; Radin 1994–1995: 539, 543–544.
17 This sense of aristocracy is to be distinguished from hereditary aristocracy, which is rule by a privileged class determined by genealogy and (usually) ownership of land, as distinguished from rule by elected representatives of the people at large.
18 One that I have argued for on a number of occasions. See in particular Posner 1990; 1995; 1999; 2001a: ch. 4.
19 See Posner 2002, where this concept is elaborated.
20 See, for example, *Truax v. Corrigan*, 257 US 312, 344 (1921) (dissenting opinion). Cf. his defense, in his dissenting opinion in *Abrams v. United States*, 250 US 616, 630 (1919), of the First Amendment as an "experiment." Experimentalism, like judicial diversity, is another concept that is alien to Ronald Dworkin's jurisprudence, which is one of high rationalism.
21 And dyspeptic is the word. See Scheuerman 1999.

Bibliography

Balkin, J.M. (1995) "Book Review: Populism and Progressivism as Constitutional Categories," *Yale Law Journal*, 104: 1935.

Dewey, J. (1924) "Logical Method and Law," *Cornell Law Quarterly* 10: 17.

—— (1926) "The Historic Background of Corporate Legal Personality," *Yale Law Journal* 35: 655.

—— (1927) *The Public and Its Problems*, New York: H. Holt and Company.

—— (1930) *Individualism Old and New*, New York: Minton, Balch & Company.

—— (1941) "My Philosophy of Law," in *My Philosophy of Law: Credos of Sixteen American Scholars*, Boston, MA: Boston Law Book Company.

—— (1984a) "After the Election – What?," in A. Boydston (ed.), *John Dewey: The Later Works, 1925–1953*, vol. 6: 1931–1932, Carbondale: Southern Illinois University Press.

—— (1984b) "Apostles of World Unity: XVII – Salmon O. Levinson," in A. Boydston (ed.), *John Dewey: The Later Works, 1925–1953*, vol. 5: 1929–1930, Carbondale: Southern Illinois University Press.

—— (1984c) "Prospects for a Third Party," in A. Boydston (ed.), *John Dewey: The Later Works, 1925–1953*, vol. 6: 1931–1932, Carbondale: Southern Illinois University Press.

—— (1984d) "Roosevelt Scored on Relief Policy," in A. Boydston (ed.), *John Dewey: The Later Works, 1925–1953*, vol. 6: 1931–1932, Carbondale: Southern Illinois University Press.

—— (1986) "What Keeps Funds Away from Purchasers," in A. Boydston (ed.), *John Dewey: The Later Works, 1925–1953*, vol. 9: 1929–1930, Carbondale: Southern Illinois University Press.

—— (1993a) "Philosophy and Democracy," in D. Morris and I. Shapiro (eds), *The Political Writings*, Indianapolis, IN: Hackett Publishing Company.

—— (1993b) "Science and Free Culture," in D. Morris and I. Shapiro (eds), *The Political Writings*, Indianapolis, IN: Hackett Publishing Company.

Dworkin, R. (1991) "Pragmatism, Right Answers, and True Banality," in M. Brint and W. Weavers (eds), *Pragmatism in Law and Society*, Boulder, CO: Westview Press.

Grey, T.C. (1996) "Freestanding Legal Pragmatism," *Cardozo Law Review*, 18: 21; reprinted in M. Dickstein (ed.), *The Revival of Pragmatism: New Essays on Social Thought, Law, and Culture*, Durham, NC: Duke University Press.

Honig, B. (1993) *Political Theory and the Displacement of Politics*, Ithaca, NY: Cornell University Press.

Kendall, W.J. III (1995) "Law, China, and John Dewey," *Syracuse Law Review*, 46: 103.

Luban, D. (1998) "What's Pragmatic about Legal Pragmatism?" in M. Dickstein (ed.), *The Revival of Pragmatism: New Essays on Social Thought, Law, and Culture*, Durham, NC: Duke Universiy Press.

McDermott, J.J. (ed.) (1981) *The Philosophy of John Dewey*, Chicago: University of Chicago Press.

MacGilvray, E.A. (1999) "Experience as Experiment: Some Consequences of Pragmatism for Democratic Theory," *American Journal of Political Science*, 43: 542.

Manin, B. (1997) *The Principles of Representative Government*, Cambridge and New York: Cambridge University Press.

Mansfield, H.C. and Winthrop, D. (eds) (2000) "Editors' Introduction," in Alexis de Tocqueville, *Democracy in America*, Chicago: University of Chicago Press.

Microsoft Press (1997) *Computer Dictionary: The Comprehensive Standard for Business, School, Library, and Home*, 3rd edn, Redmond, WA: Microsoft Press.

Morris, D. and Shapiro, I. (eds) (1993) "Editors' Introduction," in J. Dewey, *The Political Writings*, Indianapolis, IN: Hackett Publishing Company.

Noonan, J.T. Jr (1976) *Persons and Masks of the Law: Cardozo, Holmes, Jefferson, and Wythe as Makers of the Masks*, New York: Farrar, Straus and Giroux.

Peters, C.J. (1997) "Adjudication as Representation," *Columbia Law Review*, 97: 312.

Posner, R.A. (1990) *The Problems of Jurisprudence*, Cambridge, MA: Harvard University Press.

—— (1995) *Overcoming Law*, Cambridge, MA: Harvard University Press.

—— (1999) *The Problematics of Moral and Legal Theory*, Cambridge MA: Belknap Press of Harvard University Press.

—— (2001a) *Breaking the Deadlock: The 2000 Election, the Constitution, and the Courts*, Princeton, NJ: Princeton University Press.

—— (2001b) *Public Intellectuals: A Study of Decline*, Cambridge, MA: Harvard University Press.

—— (2002) "Bush v. Gore as Pragmatic Adjudication," in R. Dworkin (ed.), *A Badly Flawed Election: Debating Bush v. Gore, the Supreme Court, and American Democracy*, New York: New Press.

—— (2003) *Law, Pragmatism, and Democracy*, Cambridge, MA: Harvard University Press.

Radin, M.J. (1994–1995) "A Deweyan Perspective on the Economic Theory of Democracy," *Constitutional Commentary*, 11: 539.

Scheuerman, W. (1999) *Carl Schmitt: The End of Law*, Lanham, MD: Rowman & Littlefield.

Sunstein, C.R. (1985) "Interest Groups in American Public Law," *Stanford Law Review*, 38: 29.
—— (1993) *Democracy and the Problem of Free Speech*, New York: Free Press.
—— (2001) *Republic.com*, Princeton, NJ: Princeton University Press.
Westbrook, R.B. (1991) *John Dewey and American Democracy*, Ithaca, NY: Cornell University Press.
—— (1998) "Pragmatism and Democracy: Reconstructing the Logic of John Dewey's Faith," in M. Dickstein (ed.), *The Revival of Pragmatism: New Essays on Social Thought, Law and Culture*, Durham, NC: Duke University Press.
Zaret, D. (2000) *Origins of Democratic Culture: Printing, Petitions, and the Public Sphere in Early-Modern England*, Princeton, NJ: Princeton University Press.

12 Truth but no consequences

Why philosophy doesn't matter

Stanley Fish

Introduction

When in the wake of 11 September a number of commentators began to draw lines of cause and effect between what had happened and the "rise" of postmodernism, a new chapter was opened in a very old story. It is the story of the supposed relationship between philosophy at its highest reaches and the events of history. The governing thesis that makes the story go is that philosophy matters and matters both at the societal level – the actions of a society will in some sense follow from the philosophical views encoded in its institutions – and at the level of the individual who will think or do something as a consequence of the philosophical views to which he or she is committed. My counterthesis is that philosophy doesn't matter and that when faced with a crisis or choice or decision you and I will typically have recourse to many things – archives, consultations with experts, consultations with friends, consultations with psychiatrists, consultations with horoscopes – but one of the things we will not typically consult (and if we did it wouldn't do us any good) is some philosophical position we happen to espouse.

Let me make clear what I do and do not mean by philosophical position. I don't mean a substantive idea, like the idea that gender differences justify discriminatory practices or the (opposing) idea that they don't. Ideas like those most certainly matter and have real world consequences as the history of the twentieth century amply shows. Moreover if you are committed to one of those ideas, you will be inclined to act in certain ways in certain situations. You say to yourself (for example), "since I believe that gender differences do not justify differences in compensation, I will take care that men and women receive equal pay for equal work." But if you say to yourself, "I believe that what is true is what corresponds to the independently specified facts," or, alternatively, "I believe that truths are internal to historically emergent and revisable frames of reference or interpretive communities," nothing follows with respect to any issue except the issue of which theory of truth is the correct one. That is to say, whatever theory of truth you might espouse will be irrelevant to your position on the truth of a particular matter because your position on the truth of a particular matter will flow from your sense of where the evidence lies, which will in turn flow from the authorities you respect, the archives you trust, and so on. It is theories of truth on that general level to which I refer when I say that philosophy doesn't matter.

An example of the opposing view is a statement by Professor Larry Hickman (2001) in a draft of an essay presented at the conference for which the present paper was written: "As long as it is accepted that the mind and the body are distinct ... insurance companies will appear to have rational grounds for insuring the health of the body while ignoring the health of the organism as a whole." The suggestion is that were the mind/body distinction to become discredited in philosophy, insurance companies would change their ways. But the rational grounds insurance companies have for their practices are derived from actuarial tables and other relevant statistics, not from any philosophical doctrine, whether self-consciously or unself-consciously held. In the unlikely event that insurance company executives believed anything about the mind/body distinction, that belief would be irrelevant to their decisions about what and what not to insure. In this chapter I will raise that irrelevance to the status of a general proposition and argue, first, that nothing of any consequence follows from one's philosophical positions of the abstract kind I have instanced,[1] and, second, that the philosophical position someone is known to hold tells us nothing about his or her views on anything not directly philosophical and tells us nothing about his or her character or moral status.

I propose to begin somewhat obliquely by introducing two arguments made by Matthew Kramer. The first argument is about truth, and the second is about the relationship between one's philosophical position on truth (or any other metaphysical concept) and one's performance in particular (or as Kramer puts it, "mundane") situations. Kramer's argument about truth is that the valuing of one's particular assertions because they are true does not commit one to valuing truth in general; conversely, he argues that one's general account of truth or of any other abstract, overarching notion (foundationalism, antifoundationalism, neopragmatism, social constructedness) does not direct one to act in any particular way when the issue is not general, but local, empirical, and mundane. These two interrelated theses, which neatly summarize arguments I have been making for some time now, at once clarify the claims and scope of a strong pragmatism and show why normative schemes for organizing political and social life – Habermas's communicative reason or discourse ethics will be my example – are incoherent and unworkable.

Kramer's argument about truth unfolds in the context of a critique of a chain of reasoning offered by John Finnis. Finnis begins with the unexceptionable proposition that if I assert "that P," I am implicitly committed to anything entailed by that assertion. He then argues that two of the things I commit myself to by asserting "that P" are, first, that I believe P to be true and that, second, I believe P to be worth asserting. Moreover, he adds, one of the reasons I believe P to be worth asserting is that I believe it to be true. That is to say (and here I quote Kramer's gloss), "one's ascriptions of desirability to one's statements will have flowed at least partly from one's sense that one is stating the truth" (Kramer 1999: 16).

Kramer has some problems (as do I) with the sequence so far, but his main difficulty is with Finnis's next step, which he sees as an unwarranted leap. Finnis concludes from the propositions I have already rehearsed that one of the things entailed by my asserting "that P" is that I believe truth to be a good worth pursuing or knowing. That is, the combination of my asserting "that P," believing that "that P" is true, and valuing my assertion "that P," adds up to my having committed myself to the value of truth in general, that is, as a meta-physical good to which I pledge allegiance independently of either my substantive convictions or my political/social situation. It is here that Kramer gets off the train (and I with him) because, as he puts it, "the fact that a person X must commend the knowledge of the truth of her own assertions does not per se justify our holding that X must commend the value of truth ... in general" (Kramer 1999: 16). Kramer's point is that X might well regard the truthfulness of her assertions as a bonus property added to their substantive goodness; she thinks, for example (the example is mine), that asserting "that P" at this moment is good because it furthers the objective of moving her target audience to act in a way she finds desirable – to cease quarreling, or to adjourn a meeting, or to come to a dinner party – and she is happy to assert the truth of P (in which she does believe) because she knows or suspects that her target audience will find in P's truth status an additional reasoning for acting in the way she desires. Asserting "that P" in this spirit will "involve no commitment to the belief that truth-in-general is good – in much the same way that one's ascription of goodness to rhetorical vigor for the crafting of one's own assertions will involve no commitment to the presumption that rhetorical verve is always estimable" (Kramer 1999: 17).

Indeed, there are plenty of occasions on which someone who commends the truth of her own assertions might find the truthfulness of an assertion made by someone else objectionable and morally flawed. Kramer's example is the hard-core truth teller who "truthfully tells a murderer about the hiding place of a victim." Surely, "one's commending of the truth of one's own asser-tions will decidedly not entail one's commending of the truth of the informant's disclosures" (Kramer 1999: 17). The example need not be so extreme and can even be commonplace. "It is good always to tell the truth" is a disastrous prescription for the health of any marriage. Doctors routinely withhold the truth from their patients because they deem it good to do so, even though in other contexts they will regard the truthfulness of their state-ments as a chief recommendation of them. And one can advise others to tell the truth without thereby having committed oneself to the goodness of truth in general or to any general view of truth whatsoever. I would advise politi-cians always to tell the truth because efforts to mislead or stonewall the public usually backfire and produce more harm than would have been produced by letting it all hang out. (Richard Posner remarked to me in conversation, however, that this conclusion rests on a skewed sample because it is reached in ignorance of all the cover-ups that have succeeded.) Politicians, addicted as they are to cover-ups, never seem to learn this lesson, but the lesson they don't learn is not a philosophical lesson about the general goodness of truth or the value of truth telling; it is a practical lesson about the likely empirical consequences of engaging in one form of behavior rather than another. Let us assume (against all the available evidence) that a politician actually learns that lesson and acts accordingly. Would he now have or be implicitly committed to a general account of truth and its value? Obviously not. Such an account is a very special achievement available only to those who have undergone a long and arduous training in those traditions of inquiry in the course of which large abstract questions about truth (and other metaphysical matters) have been posed and (variously) answered. It is not an achievement that comes to one simply because, in the course of everyday thought and action, he has asserted the truth of something and meant it.

That's the first half of Kramer's argument (and mine). The second half is simply, or not so simply, the flip side. If metaphysical theses and positions do not flow from mundane utterances and actions, the formulation by an actor of a metaphysical thesis commits him to no particular form of mundane utterance or action, nor does it rule out any form of mundane utterance or action. It has more than occasionally been said that the way one will behave in particular local contexts will be at least in part a function of one's metaphysical commitments or anticommitments. Thus we are told on one side that those who make antifoundationalist arguments – arguments asserting the unavailability of independent grounds for the settling of factual or moral disputes – cannot without contradiction assert their views strongly or be trusted to mean what they say (on the model of the old saw "if there is no God, then everything is permitted"); and we are told on the other side that those who make foundational arguments – arguments identifying general and universal standards of judgment and measurement – are inflexible, incapable of responding to or even registering the nuances of particular contexts, and committed to the maintenance of the status quo. Kramer responds (and again I am with him) by warning against the confusion of two levels of consideration and against the mistake (resulting from the confusion) of drawing a direct line from one to the other. It is a mistake because on one level – the level of metaphysical or general propositions such as "all things are socially constructed" or "all things are presided over by a just and benevolent God" – the point is to describe the underlying bases of reality, those first principles that rather than arising from particulars confer on particulars their shape and meaning. Such principles or basic theses or all-embracing doctrines are, Kramer (1992: 51) says, "ultimate in their reach and are thus fully detached from any specific circumstances and contexts." It is because they are fully detached from specific circumstances – that is how they are derived, by abstracting away from specifics – that metaphysical doctrines like the social constructedness of everything or the God-dependent status of everything can be neither confirmed nor disconfirmed by specifics:

> A metaphysical view can hardly undergo either confirmation or refutation through empirical methods. Precisely because a metaphysical doctrine must abstract itself from specifics … in an effort to probe what undergirds all specifics of any sort, it retains its lesser or greater cogency regardless of the ways any specific facts … have turned out.
>
> (Kramer 1992: 7)

The cogency it does have for those persuaded of it is a philosophical or theoretical cogency, a cogency fashioned in the course of philosophical argument where the typical questions are, "What is the nature of reality?" or, "Where do facts come from?" – questions the answers to which will not be found in the observable facts; when the answers are found (to the satisfaction of one or more of the participants) the observable facts will have been explained (at least within the framework of particular general theses), but they will not have generated or confirmed or falsified the perspective that explains them. For example, the doctrine that a benevolent God presides over all things will not be disconfirmed by the existence of poverty, war, oppression, injustice, genocide, and so on, for it is precisely the claim of the doctrine to account for these and other facts in its own terms (which typically will include attendant doctrines such as the doctrine of original sin and the doctrine of the mysteriousness of God's ways), and that claim will be made good (if it is) by abstract theoretical arguments and not by empirical investigation. Someone defending the benevolence of God in the face of the Nazi Holocaust will be trafficking in theological concepts like sin, redemption, retribution, suffering, patience, the last days, and so on. He will not be considering whether its perpetrators were the unique products of a virulent German anti-semitism or exemplars of a bureaucratic mentality found everywhere in the modern world; he will not be poring over diagrams of gas chambers or assessing the effects either of resistance movements or of the failure to resist. His is a thesis not about how a particular thing has happened but about how anything – of which this particular is an instantiation and an example – happens, and happens necessarily. His job is not to precipitate an explanation of the event out of the examination of documents and other sources but to bring the fact of the event into line with an explanation already assumed and firmly in place. (The master teacher of this skill is Augustine who, in his On Christian Doctrine, advises those who find biblical passages that seem subversive of the faith to subject those passages to "diligent scrutiny until an interpretation contributing to the reign of charity is produced" (Augustine 1958: 93).) He is, in short, a theologian, maintaining and elaborating an ultimate perspective, and not a historian who has set himself the disciplinary task of relating a historical, mundane occurrence to its contingent and multiple causes. (I know that there are those who argue that the Holocaust is not an appropriate object of ordinary historical analysis; but this merely means that they have switched jobs and become philosopher/theologians rather than historians.)

This independence of metaphysical doctrine from empirical or mundane matters (in the sense that empirical mundane matters have nothing to say about the cogency of metaphysical doctrine, although they provide the materials on which metaphysical doctrine works itself out) goes in both directions: those who are immersed in mundane and empirical problems will get no help from metaphysical doctrine. Historians concerned to trace out the historical causes of the Holocaust will not be able to do anything with the declaration that everything happens under the dispensation of a benevolent God. They may even believe it on the metaphysical level, but this belief will not aid them with the questions historians ask by virtue of their membership in the discipline and answer with the tools – archives, testimonies, dated events, and so on – that same discipline authorizes. Neither will the belief they may have in an all powerful and benevolent deity rule out any answers or discredit the search for answers altogether. This latter is another instance of confusing the two realms of consideration and thinking that there must be a connection between them, thinking that if you really believe in a benevolent all-powerful deity, you couldn't possibly engage seriously in ordinary historical investigation. But a God who is ultimately benevolent (whether we can see the springs of his benevolence or not) can in his unsearchable benevolence allow or direct all kinds of mundane things to happen, and those mundane things, when they happen, will have mundane (in addition to ultimate) causes of which one might want to give an account independently of what one believed on the level of eschatology. The questions, "How is the universe ultimately disposed?" and, "How, in the context of the cause-and-effect patterns within which our mundane lives are lived, did this happen?" are entirely different questions, and the answers we might give to the one have no necessary relevance to our attempts to answer the other. (This is a truth known and lived out by those many scientists who are at once good, dedicated researchers and deeply religious bearers of a faith, even of a fundamentalist faith.)

Perhaps an example where the stakes are not cosmic might help. Currently in the small world of Milton studies, there is a controversy about the authorship of a large theological treatise, *De Doctrina Christiana* first discovered in an archive in 1823. The person who found it and almost all of those who were made aware of it (including the King of England) believed it to be the work of John Milton. There was at least one early dissenter from this view, but Milton's authorship was long assumed as a matter of undoubted fact by everyone in the field, and it is only in the last ten years that a challenge to that attribution has been mounted, a challenge that has sparked considerable debate. One of those who has been persuaded to become at least an agnostic on the subject has recently written a lengthy essay tracing in detail the history and provenance of the manuscript (which he is one of the few to have examined) and flagging the many points at which the line of transmission is blurred or broken. He is, in short, doing the usual work one does when arguing a case for or against attribution, and he comes to the conclusion that on the evidence now available the question cannot be settled and must remain open.

Twice, however, he thinks to support this conclusion by invoking arguments made by Roland Barthes and Michel Foucault, arguments that call into radical question the very notion of an author or of a singular voice that owns its utterances. But these arguments (as I told him) are too general to suit his purpose. Not only do they not support his conclusion; they take away its interest because they dictate it in advance and dictate also the reaching of the same conclusion in all cases, including those in which there is no controversy about authorship at all. That is, entering into a debate about authorship only makes sense if you believe that there are in principle facts the discovery of which could settle the matter one way or the other; but if what you believe is that attribution of a work to a single author will always be a mistake – not an empirical mistake but a metaphysical mistake – because the idea of an individual voice is myth and an artifact of bourgeois culture or because authorship is always and necessarily multiple, that belief can have no significance or weight in relation to empirical questions (did Milton write it or did someone else write it?) it renders meaningless. The general account of authorship put forward by Barthes and Foucault is of no use to someone trying to figure out who wrote something (or who didn't) because it tells you that figuring out who wrote something is a task both impossible to perform and evidence of a large philosophical error. I accordingly urged my friend the Miltonist (who does believe that there is a fact of the matter but that we are not now in a position to determine what it is) to drop the references to Barthes and Foucault if he wanted to be taken seriously by parties to the dispute, and I am pleased to report that he has done so.

To summarize the argument thus far: considerations on the metaphysical level and considerations on the quotidian, mundane level are independent of one another; you can't get from one to the other; the conclusions you come to when doing metaphysical, normative work (if you are one of the very few people in the world who perform it) do not influence or constrain you when you are concluding something about a mundane matter; and the fact that you have concluded something about a mundane matter and said so in a form like "that P" commits you to no normative/theoretical presuppositions. The two levels of consideration are different practices or, if you prefer, different games; and your ability or inability to play the one says nothing about your ability or inability to play the other.

So what? What follows? Well, one thing that follows is that the normative project of the Enlightenment – the project, generally, of abstracting away from practical contexts to a context or noncontext from the vantage point of which you might bring back to practical contexts normative help – is a non starter because if Kramer and I are right there is no commerce between the two contexts and therefore no way to get from what Jürgen Habermas calls pragmatic discourses – discourses formed by the intersection of already in-place interests, goals, and value systems – to the realm of normative discourse where present interests are suspect and under scrutiny and the only interest in place is the interest in searching for interests that would be acceptable to everyone, interests that would be universal. And if you can't get from the pragmatic to the normative, you can't make a return journey and bring back to local mundane practices the universal perspective that would constrain and guide them, and the entire normative project is dead in the water.

Habermas is quite aware of what is required, and in these two passages from Between Facts and Norms he stipulates the conditions that are necessary for the advance of his project:

> In moral [that is, normative] discourse, the ethnocentric perspective of a particular collectivity expands into the comprehensive perspective of an unlimited communication community, all of whose members put themselves in each individual's situation, world view, and self-understanding, and together practice an ideal role-taking.
>
> (Habermas 1998: 162)

> Entrance into moral discourse demands that one step back from all contingently existing normative contexts. Such discourse takes place under communicative presuppositions that require a break with everyday taken-for-granted assumptions; in particular it requires a hypothetical attitude toward the relevant norms of action and their validity claims.
>
> (Habermas 1998: 163–164)

The reasoning here is familiar to anyone schooled in the tradition of political theory that includes Hobbes, Locke, Kant, Mill, and continues in our time in the writings of Berlin, Rawls, Ackerman, Guttman, Nagel, Dworkin, Kymlicka, Korsgaard, and others. It goes like this: contingently existing normative contexts equip those who live within them with values that are themselves contingent, in that they flow from the historical accident of having been born into a certain culture and geographical location, or from the rhetorical authority of a charismatic leader, or from the entrenched power of a religious orthodoxy, or from the apparently pressing priority of a political goal (to defeat an enemy, to stabilize the economy, to maintain the purity of the collectivity, and so on). How, then, do you get to a place where the partisan and parochial visions that have so immediate an appeal for embedded subjects can be countered and corrected by a vision that belongs to no one but includes everyone? The general answer to this question is also Habermas's: you have to break with the existing normative contexts with their "taken-for-granted assumptions." But the recommendation begs the real question: how exactly do you do that? One strategy often urged is implicit in Habermas's mention of a "hypothetical attitude toward the relevant norms of action and their validity claims," that is, an attitude toward the norms and claims now yours by virtue of your historical situation that renders them hypotheses – things to be entertained and probed – rather than accepted truths. In the words of Thomas Nagel:

> from the perspective of political argument we may have to regard certain of our beliefs, whether moral or religious or even historical or scientific, simply as someone's beliefs, rather than as truths – unless they can be given the kind of impersonal justification appropriate to that perspective, in which case they may be appealed to as truths without qualification.
>
> (Nagel 1987: 230)

But again the question is how do we do that? (There is also the question of why should we, why should anyone, do that, but for the moment I will lay it aside.) You can't simply strike the Nike stance and say, just do it, because the ability to do it – to "break" with the norms and assumptions that currently fill your consciousness and move to a level more universal – is what the project of discourse ethics is supposed to produce; and if you assume that the ability is one we already have, you render the entire project unnecessary and superfluous. There has to be some bite to the problem – there has to be somewhere to go, some place you're not yet at – and there has to be some route by which you can get there.

Habermas claims to provide both when he asserts (and this is an argument he has been making for some time now) that the universal perspective we must rise to if the ideal speech situation of the public forum is to be realized is already implicit in the speech activities we perform in the very contexts that are to be transcended. An early strong statement of this thesis is found in the essay "What Is Universal Pragmatics?": "I shall develop the thesis that anyone acting communicatively must, in performing any speech action, raise universal validity claims and suppose they can be vindicated [or redeemed: einlösen]" (Habermas 1979: 2).

The key word here is "must," and it is a must independent of any speaker's conscious intention. The intention belongs to the communicative context in general. Merely by stepping into that context, the argument goes, a speaker commits himself or herself to everything that communication as an action implies, which includes, according to Habermas, the goal of bringing about "an agreement [Einverständnis] that terminates in the intersubjective mutuality of reciprocal understanding, shared knowledge, mutual trust, and accord with one another" (Habermas 1979: 3). "Our first sentence," Habermas declares in another place, "expresses unequivocally the intention of universal and unconstrained consensus" (Habermas 1971: 314). We may think that we are merely making a point or asserting a truth, but if we are serious and not insincere or basely instrumental we are doing much more:

> Whoever makes natural use of a language in order to come to an understanding with an addressee about something in the world is required to

take a performative attitude and commit herself to certain presuppositions; … natural language users must assume, among other things, that the participants pursue their illocutionary goals without reservations, that they tie [the possibility of] their agreement to the intersubjective recognition of criticizable validity claims, and that they are ready to take on the obligations resulting from consensus and relevant for further interaction. … That is, they must undertake certain idealizations – for example ascribe identical meanings to expressions, connect utterances with context-transcending validity, and claims, and assume that addressees are accountable, that is, autonomous and sincere with both themselves and others.

(Habermas 1998: 4)

So, for example, if I say to some discourse partner, assisted suicide is immoral or inflation is an unreliable index of the health of an economy, I commit myself not only to the truth of what I've said but to the giving of reasons should it be challenged and to the desirability and possibility of reaching an agreement rooted for both of us (and for all other potential discourse partners) in the recognition and acceptance of universal norms of validation. In short, and to return to Kramer's vocabulary, by asserting "that P" I have committed myself to future discourse actions, to a belief that such future actions will participate in and help bring about an intersubjective mutuality of reciprocal understanding, and to a normative theory of how autonomous agents can achieve a transparent consensus in a communicative context that is free and undistorted. In the words of William Rehg, the translator of *Between Facts and Norms*, by making the simplest of statements, I have bought into "the strongly idealizing, context transcending claims of reason" (Rehg, introduction in Habermas 1998: xii).

I believe this to be at once false and mildly insane, an exemplary instance of the mistake of thinking that mundane, pragmatically situated utterances contain and (implicitly) declare theoretical presuppositions. I will agree that (except in specifiable strategic contexts such as parenting, marriage, faculty meetings, job interviews, automobile purchases, classroom teaching, talk shows, labor disputes, legal proceedings, party politics, psychoanalysis, real estate transactions, medical procedures, and international negotiations) when I assert something I commit myself to its truth. But that's about it. Other commitments might follow if I am a certain kind of person or have a certain job (philosopher, facilitator, experimental scientist) or a certain local goal, but those commitments would be contingent, not necessary. Among the commitments I would not have bought into simply by asserting "that P" is the commitment to give reasons and the commitment to bring about an agreement. I could very well assert "that P" just because I was pleased to have worked it out or because I knew it would irritate my enemies, and I might not care a whit if anyone agreed with me, and I would therefore feel no obligation at all to give reasons to those I had no interest in persuading in the first place. And even if I were to care about persuading someone or persuading everybody, I would not simply by making the effort to persuade commit myself to any likelihood that my effort will succeed (it might or it might not, but that's the chance you always take); nor would I be committed to the reasonableness of my target audience or to its possession of communicative norms just like mine; and, in the event that my persuasive effort should fail, I will not have committed myself to a reconsideration of my assertion in the name of "mutual and reciprocal intersubjective agreement" or any other fancy concept that never entered my head and was no part of either my hope or my aspiration. I could simply attribute my failure to the blindness of those who will not see and go on to other more rewarding pursuits. So when Habermas declares that the motivation toward reciprocity – to mutual agreement rooted in universal norms – "belongs *eo ipso* to the interactive knowledge of speaking and acting subjects" (Habermas 1979: 88), or that, in the gloss of a commentator "the motivation toward (cognitive) consensus" is "always embedded in the very possibility of speech" (Warren 1995: 180–181), he is flat wrong and philosophically inflationary. The only things that belong to the interactive knowledge of speaking and acting subjects – to competent speakers in the world – is the knowledge first of what they mean to say and second of what is locally at stake in saying it; and the only motivations built into speech are the motivations that come along with the pragmatic contexts in which speech is uttered.

Another way to put this is to say that there is no such thing as an orientation toward understanding as such, as a general rather than a local and particular goal. A general orientation toward understanding is not (as Habermas sometimes asserts) the basic or original communicative impulse of which all other impulses – strategic, instrumental, persuasive – are derivative fallings-off; it is rather a very special impulse, indeed so special as to be impossible. The oddness of the notion of an orientation to understanding as such is apparent as soon as we ask the question, "Orientation to the understanding of what?" From Habermas's perspective this is exactly the wrong question because it is freedom from substantive, local, context-bound concerns and issues that distinguishes this orientation from the orientation – more or less the content of practical conscious activity – to understand what your wife is saying or what the Republicans are proposing or the benefits and dangers of genetically altered foods, or the benefits and dangers of allowing prayer in the public schools, or any of the other questions raised in the course of ordinary domestic and civic life. When you are oriented just to understanding in general (if that were a possible attitude of mind, and I am saying that it is not), no specific matter occupies your attention; rather, your attention is focused solely on the normative conditions within which the experience of ordinary understanding and concluding and justifying occurs or should occur. The elucidation of those conditions is your goal, and when that goal has been achieved (or at least furthered), you can then return to the precincts of context-bound, discourse specific understanding, at once better equipped and more confident in the rightness of your assertions. "The firmly retained orientation to truth [to understanding as such] permit[s] the translation back of discursively justified assertions into reestablished behavioral [mundane] assertions" (Habermas 2000: 48–49).

The distinction between the two orientations – one to understanding within the values and norms given to you (without your self-conscious and deliberative assent) by the discursive context in which you happen to live, and the other to understanding within the values and norms so general as to be pertinent, applicable, and probative no matter what local, historical context you inhabit – is for Habermas also a moral distinction that affords reflective actors a choice:

> For self-interested actors, all situational features are transformed into facts they evaluate in the light of their own preferences, whereas actors oriented toward understanding rely on a jointly negotiated understanding of the situation and interpret the relevant facts in the light of intersubjectively recognized validity claims.
>
> The binding energies of language can be mobilized to coordinate action plans only if the participants suspend ... the immediate orientation to personal success [i.e. to having your views prevail and be accepted] in favor of the performative attitude of a speaker who wants to reach an understanding [and not to prevail] with a second person [and if a second, why not a third and a fourth, and so on] about something in the world.
>
> (Habermas 1998: 27, 18)

Obviously, this is a ramping up of the argument about single assertions into an argument about contexts of discussion and inquiry. Just as every assertion (according to Habermas) raises universal validity claims and commits the speaker to acts of investigation and justification implied by those claims, so does everyone who enters a discussion or debate commit himself or herself to seeking out in the company of others those general, intersubjectively recognized norms of understanding that will then constrain all interlocutors – that is, check any orientation to "personal success" – and guide the subsequent (and now radically cooperative) process of coming to agreement.

My critique of this picture is implied in what I have already said: (1) speakers in ordinary contexts commit themselves only to the interests thought to be at stake in those contexts and not to a more general interest; and (2) there is no more general interest. There is no more general interest because all orientations toward understanding, including those that advertise themselves as context-transcending, are context-bound. This does not mean that there are no moments like those Habermas describes in which participants in discussion or debate step back and consider the premises within which they have been operating. Such moments when, as Habermas puts it, actors temporarily adopt "a reflexive attitude in order to restore a partially disturbed background understanding" occur all the time (Habermas 2000: 47). What they mark, however, is not a movement away from mundane pragmatic contexts to a normative, transcending context, but another stage in the unfolding of a pragmatic context that has not been (even temporarily) transcended at all. You can label that stage the "orientation to understanding stage," but only in the sense that you (and/or your partners) are trying to get agreement on some basic definitions and presuppositions before returning to the specific matter at issue.

In short, the "orientation to understanding" move is strategic, not normative. I might be oriented to understanding – that is, to foregrounding the assumptions implicit in our discussions to date – because I want to keep the conversation about our marital problems alive. Or, I might be oriented to understanding – to stepping back and surveying the forensic field – so that I might better gauge what arguments are likely to persuade you to vote a certain way in a committee meeting. Or, I might be oriented to understanding – to uncovering the deep anxieties producing your surface behavior – so that I would have a better chance of bringing you into a healthy relationship with your neuroses. But in all of these instances, and any others that might be imagined, I would be moved (as would you if you joined me) to seek mutual understanding because of, and within the purview of, some mundane purpose that gripped me and rendered what I was doing intelligible. This holds too even for those contexts in which the realm of the normative is the primary focus – philosophy seminars where the community effort is precisely to discover and formulate intersubjectively recognized and mutually shared norms of agreement and validity. For that too is a mundane, pragmatic space, the space of philosophy, not as a natural kind, but as an academic/institutional discipline with its own special history, traditions, exemplary achievements, canonical problems, honored and scorned solutions, holy grails, saints and sinners. Those who work (usually professionally but not exclusively so) within that history and tradition join in the search for context-transcending norms because that is what the local, professional, pragmatic context they belong to directs them to do, in the hope (never to be realized) that if they do it, they will, in an act of noblesse oblige, provide normative help to all of us who are not philosophers.

The mistake – made by Habermas in spades but made by many others, too – is to think that normative philosophy is not a local, pragmatic practice like any other, but a special practice in which the local and pragmatic have been left behind. From this mistake follows the mistake of thinking that the conclusions arrived at in the course of doing normative philosophy can be imported back into the local and pragmatic where they will function as guides and constraints; and this is part and parcel of the self-inflating mistake of thinking of philosophy as a master discipline whose definitions, formulations, and criteria are pertinent to all disciplines, even though practitioners of these other disciplines don't seem to realize it; this is just an indication of how much they need philosophical help.

It is in the context of philosophy's self-embraced mission to bring us normative help that Habermas comes up with the idea of the orientation to a general understanding or understanding as such. The idea is his response to the usual objections lodged against the program of reasoning downward from normative insights, objections that show, as he says, "that an idealization of justificatory conditions cannot achieve its goal because it either distances truth too far from justified assertibility or not far enough" (Habermas 2000: 45). That is, the ideal formulation is either so high above ordinary contexts of practice that you can't get from here to there (and vice versa), or traces of the ordinary already reside in the idealization, which is thus contaminated by what it claims to transcend.

> Either [the idealizations] satisfy the unconditional character of truth claims by means of requirements that cut off all connection with the practices of justification familiar to us, or else they retain the connection to practices familiar to us by paying the price that rational acceptability does not exclude the possibility of error even under these ideal conditions.
>
> (Habermas 2000: 45)

If you take this objection seriously (as Habermas does) and yet wish to continue the normative project, you must come up with a notion of the universal that neither scorns particulars and therefore has nothing to say about them nor is so responsive to particulars that its status as a universal is called into question. Habermas's solution, as we have seen, is to locate the universal in the particular, to assert that a claim to universal validity is presupposed by every mundane act of communication. The imperative of making good on that claim produces the program of discourse ethics that, if followed, will generate the ideal speech situation participated in by discourse partners wholly committed to the universal norms now filling their consciousnesses. Habermas's claim is that this claim to universal validity is unavoidable, but in fact it is avoidable by everyone except those philosophers for whom presupposing it is necessary if the project of discourse ethics is ever to get started. The directions that accompany that project – directions like "start with concrete speech action embedded in specific contexts and then disregard all aspects that these utterances owe to their pragmatic functions" – are impossible to follow and themselves presuppose the ability (to transcend the local and mundane) the project is supposed to generate (Habermas 1979: 31). If you disregard all aspects that utterances owe to their pragmatic functions, what remains will not be the kernel of the universal, but nothing.

Habermas would no doubt respond by saying that the universal must reside implicitly in the particular, else it would be difficult to understand why anyone ever says anything or enters into debate; speakers must assume (at least as a hope and a general outline) a normative communicative structure into which their utterances step. But, as I have already argued, speakers need assume no such thing and can enter into conversations for all kinds of reasons and in the absence of universal hopes. Habermas's "must" belongs entirely to his theory of discourse ethics; he and his fellow rationalists must presuppose a normative structure of understanding; it is an artifact of their scheme and not a necessary component of every particular act of assertion or debate. Particular acts of assertion or debate never mention or refer to it; those who engage in particular acts of assertion and debate feel themselves under no obligation to comport themselves according to its requirements (by giving reasons, by regarding their interlocutors as free and equal, by self-consciously seeking a shared intersubjective form of understanding), and if you were to insist that they fulfill those requirements, they would look at you as if you were crazy.[2]

In short, the entire program is both unnecessary and unworkable; an orientation to general understanding moves no one (except as an artifact of a professional desire); claims of universal validity are no part of any ordinary assertions; the only presuppositions built into discourse are those on the surface, and they are the only presuppositions utterers need; the first step in the supposedly unavoidable agenda – the step of abstracting away from specifics and toward the universal – cannot be taken because there is nothing that would give it traction. If an orientation to understanding as such is not built into every communicative act and thus cannot function as a bridge to itself, if intersubjective norms name a desire but not a possible human achievement, then there is no Habermasian project, nowhere to start, nowhere to go, and no possible payoff except the employment of a few rationalist philosophers.

But, say those who cling to normative hopes, if what you say is so, the basis for our decisions and the confidence we might have in their rightness is entirely eroded, and we are left to stand on the shifting sands of custom, opinion, accidental and contingent configurations of power and authority, with no defense against the suspect persuasiveness of arguments that just happen to mesh with the temper of the times. This is Habermas's point against Richard Rorty when he complains, first, that "in losing the regulative idea of truth, the practice of justification loses that point of orientation by means of which standards of justification are distinguished from 'customary' norms," and, second, that "without a reference to truth or reason ... the standards themselves would no longer have any possibility of self-correction and thus would ... forfeit the status of norms capable of being justified" (Habermas 2000: 51). These comments owe their apparent force to an assumption that Habermas apparently thinks self-evident, the assumption that the norms and standards built into everyday practices are deficient and in need of support from transcontextual norms and standards. This, however, is the very assumption contested so vigorously by the pragmatist/postmodernist thinkers against whom he writes. Their thesis is that the norms and standards to which we have an unreflective recourse most of the time are by and large up to their job, which is not the job of being transcontextual and universal, but the job of helping us in our efforts to cope with and make sense of the exigencies of mortal life and to shape and alter those exigencies in accordance with our human needs. For these thinkers the fact that a norm or a standard or an evidentiary procedure cannot be justified down to the ground (whatever that would mean) is less significant than the fact of whether or not it is useful to us in finding a cure for the common cold, or in fashioning a tort reform that would protect consumers without bankrupting industry, or in coming up with a policy that would enhance minority opportunities without flying in the face of ordinary notions of fairness and equality, or in devising a method of literary evaluation that would not force us to choose between canonical works and works that are innovative and even occasionally indecorous. And should it happen that a norm or standard we have been deploying no longer helps us to do these things, we respond, say pragmatists, by trying to come up with another one (perhaps by borrowing the vocabulary of a neighboring discipline or by seizing on a generative metaphor) and not by trying to come up with a norm or standard detached from any and all possible situations of use. In this picture "self-correction" is not forfeited but located in the very goal-driven context within which the norm or standard is expected to do its work; the fact that something is not working – not helping us to get on with the job – is the self-triggering corrective mechanism, and no other more general or abstract mechanism is necessary.

Now whatever one might think of this argument (which has its modern roots in the writings of Dewey and James), it gives an account of everyday norms that shows them emerging from the crucible of mundane situations of practical problem solving, and it also shows them maturing, and failing and becoming tired, and being replaced in that same crucible. In Habermas's account this thickness is lost and everyday norms and standards are reduced to the status, as he says, of the "customary" – in place only because they have been there for a long time or because they serve the interests of entrenched authorities. In effect he turns the pragmatist's detailed and historicist account of how things work and don't work into an assertion of the will to power, and with this diminished target in place he aims and fires his normative guns, and – surprise, surprise – scores a hit.

The diminished target is useful not only because it affords an easy victory but also because it is crucial to the raising of the fears in the context of which victory seems necessary in the first place; it is only if a world without transcendent norms and intersubjectively agreed upon standards of validity is a world without constraints, without warranted direction, without any operative sense of right and wrong, legitimate and illegitimate, better or worse that you will be moved to take philosophical arms against it and believe yourself to be carrying out a high moral purpose. But if a world without transcendent norms and intersubjectively agreed upon standards of validity leaves us in possession of all of these things (albeit in quotidian, not eternal forms) and provides us with all the equipment we shall ever need (or be able to recognize) for the solving of problems and the making of judgments, then there is nothing to be bothered about and no reason to search for what we shall never find, and every reason to continue with our projects, dedicate ourselves to their success, and make do (as we always did before the normative project was ever invented) with the resources our traditions and histories afford us.

Not only does nothing dire follow from the fact (if it is a fact) of a world – the world of human discourse – bereft of transcendent norms, nothing follows of either a psychological or epistemological kind for the thinker who believes in a human world bereft of transcendent norms and says so. This is the other fear and accusation hurled at the strong pragmatist by his or her rationalist opponents: if you proclaim the unavailability of regulative ideals and independent grounds, you lose the right and ability to be confident in your own assertions; and what's more, by strongly asserting the unavailability of the independent grounds that would underwrite that very assertion, you fall into the dreaded performative contradiction, declaring certainly that certainty is not to be had. It is in this spirit that Habermas declares, "we would step on no bridge, use no car, undergo no operation … if we did not hold the assumptions employed in the production and execution of our actions to be true" (Habermas 2000: 44). In the same spirit, historian James Kloppenberg declares that historians face a choice between the older pragmatic traditions of Dewey and James, and "newer varieties of … pragmatism that see all truth claims as contingent," and declares too that the choice is crucial for historians because the newer pragmatists (Rorty, Fish, and company) would undermine "the legitimacy of our practice in studying the past" and saying true things about it (Kloppenberg 1998: 116, 84). Thomas Haskell, another historian, counsels that people who disbelieve in an independent reality that underwrites our assertions are not to be trusted, for "if nothing at all constrains inquiry, apart from the will of the inquirers, … if there is nothing real for one's convictions to represent, then they … may as well be asserted with all the force one can muster" (Haskell 1996: 69–70).[3] Susan Haack sharpens Haskell's point:

> if one really believed that criteria of justification are purely conventional, wholly without objective grounding, then, though one might conform to the justificatory practices of one's own epistemic community, one would be obliged to adopt an attitude of cynicism towards them, to think of justification always in covert scare quotes.
>
> (Haack 1995: 136)

And Alan Sokal takes this line of reasoning to its inevitable conclusion when he crows, in his infamous exposé of his infamous hoax, that new pragmatists, postmodernists, and social constructionists of any stripe would, presumably, feel no hesitation at stepping out of a window in his twenty-first-floor apartment.

Linking all these (and similar) statements is the assumption that the theory you have about fact, truth, evidence, justification, and so on, is part, and a crucial part, of the equipment you bring with you when you enter the world (and leave off theorizing); and were that assumption true, it really would matter which of the range of theories – realist, foundationalist, antifoundationalist, conventionalist, pragmatist, relativist, nihilist – you held to. But the assumption is false because of what it itself assumes: that ordinary mundane actions are performed within, or in the company of, beliefs about their underpinnings or lack thereof. But ordinary mundane actions are not underwritten or accompanied by any metaphysical beliefs and receive both their shape and warrant from the pragmatic contexts that call them into being. You don't step on a bridge because you could produce some theoretical account of the relationship between its construction and the weight it can bear, but because you know that a bridge isn't opened until some state agency has certified it as safe, and the faith you have (which can certainly be shaken in the event of a disaster) is in that agency, and not in some realist notion of truth. Your confidence in the methods of historical research does not flow from your assent to a foundational argument about the bottom-line reality of facts, but from the training you received in graduate school, training that taught you how to find archives, how to read them, and what to do with the data you derive from them. You don't inhabit the routines, including the routines of justi- fication, of your practice loosely and with metaphysical reservations or cynicism because you are unable to ground them in some independent calculus; the grounding of their own soil – the soil of their histories, hierarchies, received authorities, standards of achievement, and so on – is more than sufficient to sustain them and you, and the search for some further abstract grounding is undertaken only when philosophers ask impertinent questions. And you don't refrain from jumping out of a window in Sokal's twenty-first-floor apartment because you are a foundationalist, but because you don't believe you can fly and because you've seen what happens when flowerpots or air conditioners fall from twenty-first-floor windows and are smashed to bits.

Consider, as an example, the ordinary mundane action of writing an histor- ical account of an event, say the execution of Charles I of England in 1649. What will determine the statements you might make about that event will be the archives you consult, the predecessors you respect, the conversations and disputes you have engaged in, the weight you give, respectively, to religious factors, to economic factors, to geopolitical factors, to the personality and char- acter of various key figures, and a host of other disciplinary considerations the knowledge of which has been internalized by every historian. What will not determine the statements you might make is your theory of fact, truth, and evidence, should you happen to have one, or your self-identification as a new or old pragmatist, should you have ever hazarded one. You might for example hold to the general belief that facts only emerge and are perspicuous within partic- ular, contingent and revisable frames of reference and that therefore, as some have said, history is through and through textual; but when you are asked or ask yourself "What exactly happened in 1649?" your belief in the textuality of history will not be a component of your answer because it is a component of another game, the game of theorizing history as opposed to doing history.

Similarly, I might have a radically textual view of literary interpretation and believe that the establishment of literary meaning is at bottom a matter of rhetoric, but when I open my copy of *Paradise Lost* and begin to read it, meanings – definite, clear, perspicuous, undoubted meanings – just leap out of the page at me; and if someone who saw other meanings thought to argue against me by reminding me of my general belief about the bottom-line rhetoricity of literary readings, I would dismiss his argument as being beside the point because the meanings I saw would have been the product not of my general belief but of the disciplinary and institutional investments that are the literary equivalent of the disciplinary and institutional investments internalized by historians. To be sure, someone could ask me to defend my specification of the meanings in Milton's text, and I might well respond, and I might even respond by rehearsing some general assumptions; but they would be assumptions about what kind of poet Milton thought himself to be, or assumptions about the relationship between a poet's art and his strong religious convictions, or assumptions about poetic conventions in the Renaissance, or assumptions about the degree to which poets in the mid-seventeenth century were drawn into the political maelstrom, even if politics was not the specific subject of their work. They would not be assumptions about whether or not interpretation is grounded because at that moment I would not be theorizing about interpretation, but doing it; and were I to have a theory about whether or not interpretation is grounded, there would be no way to get from it to the particulars of any interpretive act; or, rather (and it amounts to the same thing), my theory of interpretation at that level would accommodate any and all interpretive acts, neither approving some nor rejecting others. I might believe that interpretation is grounded in, say, the author's intentions, but I still have to argue for the meanings I see as intended by the author, and it will not be an argument if I just keep saying that interpretation is grounded in the author's intention. And, conversely, I might believe that interpretation rests on nothing firmer than the historically emergent and always challengeable conventions in place in the discipline at any moment, but, again, I still have to argue both for the precise shape of those conventions and for the meanings they render perspicuous, and it will not be an argument – that is, it will not help make my case for a specific meaning – if I just keep saying that literary interpretation is not grounded in an extra-conventional reality.

The point is the one we began with: there is no relationship between general metaphysical accounts of human practices and the performance of human practices. There is no relationship in any direction. If I am a foundationalist, my foundationalism directs me or inclines me to no particular acts, nor does it forbid any. If I am an antifoundationalist (in the sense that when asked certain philosophical questions I give antifoundationalist answers), my antifoundationalism neither tells me what to do in particular situations nor tells me what I cannot or should not do. (It certainly doesn't tell me to jump out of Sokal's twenty-first-floor window.) Moreover my declaration that I am a foundationalist does not mean that it would be inconsistent for me to say that I am radically uncertain about something; nor would my declaration that I am an antifoundationalist mean that it would be inconsistent for me to say that I am absolutely certain about something, for my certainty or uncertainty would have emerged from whatever mundane context had given rise to the question at hand and not from the context of metaphysical talk. (That is why general accounts of interpretation – say the strict constructionist or originalist theories of interpretation in the law – often migrate from one side of the political divide to the other, as partisans find them more or less useful to the substantive interests they wish to further.) And in the other direction, you cannot tell from my particular performance whether I hold to foundationalist or antifoundationalist views. You cannot say that since Fish believes that the last line of many of Milton's sonnets is indeterminate in meaning, he must be an antifoundationalist, and you cannot say that since Fish believes that the overriding message of *Paradise Lost* is clear and absolutely unambiguous, he must be a foundationalist and a believer in the capacity of texts to constrain their own interpretations. (I might have to explain why I thought that Milton was ambiguous in one place and unambiguous in another, but the explanation would take the perfectly mundane form of specifying different intentions for Milton or of elaborating a generic distinction between epic and lyric conventions, or of declaring that Milton's poetic practice changed from one period of his career to another.) There just is no commerce between the mundane and metaphysical levels, no bridge except the contingent and strategic bridges constructed by those who wish to make rhetorical use of general theories for either psychological reasons (they wish there to be a homology between their most abstract commitments and the commitments they enact in everyday life) or political reasons (they know that a certain theoretical vocabulary will have resonance with those they wish to influence).

Now, if there is no commerce between the mundane and theoretical levels (which is where we began with the arguments of Kramer), then there is no performative contradiction. A performative contradiction occurs (we are told) when someone asserts that there are no shared intersubjective norms of communication (either already available or waiting to be realized), yet implicitly relies on or presupposes just such norms in making that very assertion. You are doing what you are saying cannot be done. But it depends on what you are in fact doing when you say something like "there is no independent, metaphysical backup for assertions of fact; there are only the backups available and in place in our various contexts of practice." What you are doing is making (or performing) a claim and initiating a discussion the shape of which follows from the claim. The claim is that there are no independent backups; the discussion, if there is one, will begin when someone puts forward a candidate for the status of independent backup, giving you the assignment (in some sense you have given it to yourself) of showing that it is not independent or freestanding, but local and tied to some historical, contingent, and mundane discursive structure.

Note that the antifoundationalist does open himself up to challenges by saying what he says; if he cannot contextualize his opponent's candidate for independent ground, his assertion that there is no independent ground is compromised, perhaps fatally. But the assertion is compromised because he has failed to make good on the claim implicit in it, not because it has the internal flaw of a performative contradiction. It would have that flaw if it were made in a foundationalist spirit, if the claim were that there are no foundations or backups at all. That is how a foundationalist understands (or, rather, misunderstands) the antifoundationalist's assertion (a foundationalist is an all-or-nothing creature: give me independent ground or give me relativist death); but the antifoundationalist understands himself to be saying that there are plenty of grounds or backups – in the elaborated structures of disciplines and practices – just no independent ones and no need for independent ones.

That is how the notion of a performative contradiction gets its apparent force: the foundationalist rewrites the antifoundationalist's assertion so it has the form it would have if he (the foundationalist) made it and then declares it (a transubstantiated it) to be a contradiction of itself. The foundationalist thinker is simply unable to imagine serious discourse absent the independent grounds that in his view must underwrite it. He can only think of discourse as serious if it links up with or desires to link up with intersubjectively established communicative norms that have the character or aspiration of being universal. If assertions are untethered to such norms or do not aspire to be so tethered, what is the point of making them? Well, in making an assertion I might just want to get it off my chest or make someone mad or put it on the record, so that when someone looks at the record later on I will be seen to have stood up for what I believe to be true. And I might perform that act of testimony even though I thought there to be almost no chance it would persuade anyone, and even if it were not clear at all that anyone in the future would note and approve what I had done.

It is in this spirit, and in the conviction that his cause is lost, that John Milton writes a pamphlet in 1660 against the imminent restoration of the monarchy and declares at its end, "Thus much I should perhaps have said though I were sure I should have spoken only to trees and stones; and had none to cry to, but with the Prophet, O earth, earth, earth!" (Milton 1974: 7/462). That is, I am saying this and I am saying this seriously even though I don't think that anyone will hearken to me, even though I have no faith in a community of speech partners who will join with me in a search for truth undistorted by instrumental motives (everyone in England, he says, is busily choosing for themselves a "captain back to Egypt")(Milton 1974: 7/463) and even though, as far as I can tell, the light of universal reason has been extinguished. Nor is this necessarily a (self) counsel of despair. The fact that Milton disbelieves in the existence of any universal communicative norms and assumes that the lines of communication are massively distorted does not mean that he (or someone like him) proceeds without any hope and therefore without a reason for speaking. There is always the possibility, although not the certainty or even the likelihood, that something said will touch a nerve in a listener, even a listener who is for all intents and purposes on the other side, but who hears something (what that something might be is not predictable) and pauses to rethink. In a world where persuasion is always a contingent matter because there is no rational procedure for achieving it, speakers necessarily take their chances, hazarding speech even in the absence of intersubjectively shared norms in the hope that something shared with some members of a potential audience (it's not all or nothing) will advance the conversation in a productive way. It's not perfect, and it doesn't hold out the possibility of becoming perfect in some future state of communicative grace, but it does sometimes succeed – people do get persuaded and come to agree – and that is enough to motivate those who lack the presuppositions Habermas thinks unavoidable and who yet utter and debate and do so without falling into any performative contradiction.

In fact, as I have been arguing throughout, there are no consequences whatsoever to lacking the presuppositions Habermas thinks unavoidable. Of course a foundationalist is committed to believing that there are consequences (that's what it means to be a foundationalist) and to believing that they are disastrous. Hence another version of the performative contradiction argument in which the antifoundationalist, by declaring independent grounds to be unavailable, deprives himself of the right to do or say anything sincerely and with vigor, on the reasoning that a metaphysical shadow – the shadow of his unfortunate antifoundationalist convictions – hangs over everything he utters or does. If you say the antifoundationalist thing about truth or fact or evidence in our theoretical debates, then you will be unable to say that something is true or stipulate something as a fact or invoke a piece of evidence when you turn to doing history, or anthropology, or law, or literary criticism, or the living of everyday life. But it has been my thesis all along that no metaphysical shadow – foundationalist or antifoundationalist – hangs over our every day lives and that the commitments we profess in metaphysical discussions (such as there are or are not normative backups for our assertions) do not follow us when we leave those discussions, but remain where they are, waiting for us should we leave the context of some mundane practice and return to the practice of debating metaphysical points. In short, and to repeat a point made many times, your general metaphysical position commits you to nothing outside of the limited sphere in which such matters are debated (so that it would be a contradiction to say simultaneously or serially that you think facts can be grounded in independent normative structures and that you think that they cannot be), and therefore there cannot be a contradiction (or for that matter a relation of homology) between your general metaphysical position and anything you say or do when your are not discussing and debating general metaphysical positions. Different games are different games, and your performance in one is independent of your performance in another.

Ty Cobb had a theory of how to hit a baseball that was anatomically impossible, but hit the baseball nevertheless and hit it better than anyone in the history of the game, the game not of theorizing baseball but of playing it. A theorist may be right or wrong about his foundationalism or antifoundationalism, but his assertion of one or the other will neither enable him nor disable him when he sets himself the task of doing something other than theory.

It should be obvious that pulling the sting from the charge of performative contradiction is part of my effort to explain why antifoundationalism – the thesis that independent grounds are unavailable (which doesn't mean that there are none in some suprahuman realm, only that they are unavailable to us as limited creatures) – has none of the bad consequences often attributed to it by Habermas, Haskell, Haack, Kloppenberg, and many others. Antifoundationalism does not leave its proponents unable to assert anything strongly. It does not amount to relativism because the flip side of the unavailability of extracontextual/universal norms is the firmness of our attachment (too weak a word) to the norms of everyday practices and the impossibility of our having a distance from those norms that would allow us to relativize them (relativism is the name of a position in philosophy, not a possible program for living). Antifoundationalism does not lose hold of objectivity, for, as Rorty once said, objectivity is the kind of thing we do around here, by which he meant that within the pragmatic worlds in which we live and move and have our being, the distinction between what is objective and what is not is always alive and fairly perspicuous (what is not alive, at least not for us, is a standard of objectivity entirely removed from any of our pragmatic worlds; what would it be like and how would we recognize it?). Antifoundationalism does not deprive us of the hardness of facts, for facts are all around us at every moment, and we are always and already registering them. We are not, however always and already believing in them; that is, it is not a requirement of our encounter with facts that we believe in them in the sense of having a theory of them first; that requirement is just one more version of the mistake of thinking that you get your theory in place and then everything follows (you do or do not jump out of Sokal's window). The truth (a word I do not shrink from) is that everything – facts, decisions, judgments, justifications, evaluations, and so on – is already in place and configuring the landscape, and theory is sometimes brought in to provide a high abstract gloss to what was going on and getting along quite nicely without it. No one gets up in the morning and has to decide whether or not to believe in facts; you just open your eyes and there they are.

But if antifoundationalism leads to none of the bad consequences often attributed to it, neither does it lead to any of the good consequences sometimes claimed for it. Holding antifoundationalist views does not make you more generous and less absolutist (generosity and absolutism are possible modes of engagement within local contexts, and whether you are one or the other in no way depends on what account you would give, if you were asked to give one, of general contexts). Holding antifoundationalist views will not make you less judgmental (you will be judgmental, if you are, in relation to the local norms and standards to which you are attached). Holding antifoundationalist views will not make you more open; you will be more or less open to the extent that your opinions on some specific matter of concern or debate are or are not settled; there is no general stance of openness, and therefore the resolution to be open in a general way is empty (for the same reason that being oriented to understanding as such is empty). The only advantage you will have as an antifoundationalist is the advantage of believing that you have the better argument, but your foundationalist opponent will have the same advantage, and there will be no further cash value for either of you.

This is, I think, the only point, or half a point, Habermas scores against Rorty in their exchange. Rorty, says Habermas, can provide no normative reason for anyone to move in the directions he thinks good – a more and more inclusive sense of us, breaking out of parochial contexts, reaching beyond our peer groups, becoming less dogmatic, leaving behind more and more forms of cruelty and discrimination. "As soon as the concept of truth is eliminated in favor of a context-dependent epistemic validity-for-us, the normative reference necessary to explain why a proponent should endeavor to seek agreement for 'p' beyond the boundaries of her own group is missing" (Habermas 2000: 51). My criticism of Rorty, however, is not that his desire for a more inclusive sense of us lacks a normative backup but that he sometimes thinks it has one in the antinormativism he preaches. He thinks that if you give up on context-transcending norms, stop worrying about them, and learn to do without them – that is, if you become a Rortian – you will thereby become a better, less dogmatic, more open-minded person. This is more than implied when he says, "I see pragmatism, and the neo-Darwinian redescription of inquiry it offers, as part of a ... general anti-authoritarian movement" and opposes it to the project of "universal rationality" which he derides as a "relic of patriarchal authoritarianism" (Rorty 2000: 62).

This is just wrong and wrong in ways Rorty of all people should recognize. Someone who holds pragmatist views (as opposed to just acting pragmatically in real-world situations) can be as authoritarian as anyone else (I am living proof), if, in the mundane context he presently occupies, he is absolutely sure of the rightness of his position (not the normative rightness, but the context-bound rightness). In another mood, a philosophical mood, when the pragmatist was asked if anything could ever be absolutely certain, he would, as a pragmatist, answer no; but in mundane contexts he's not being asked or asking himself questions like that; he's being asked to come down on one side or the other of a particular dispute, and if he is strongly convinced of his position and of the danger of the opposite position (a strong conviction in no way unavailable to him because of his general pragmatist views), he might well stick to his guns fiercely and give no quarter at all to the opponent. And, on the other side, nothing bars someone who holds to the existence and necessity of a universal rationality from arguing against parochialism and in favor of openness if he sees that the consideration of his ideas is being blocked by the powers that be or by entrenched custom.

Rorty concludes his response to Habermas by declaring that persons brought up to accept pragmatist, quasi-Humean beliefs would "end up being just as decent people" as "the ones who were brought up to understand the term 'universal rationality'" (Rorty 2000: 63); but as the sentence itself indicates, this goes both ways. Decency, like all the other virtues invoked in discussions like these – tolerance, straightforwardness, sincerity, accuracy, reliability, honesty, generosity, objectivity, truth telling – is a quality independent of the metaphysical views you happen to hold, if you hold any. Indeed, everything, except for your profile in the narrow world of high theory, is independent of the metaphysical views you happen to hold. As Keats said of something else, that's all there is to know on earth and all you need to know; but I know that very few on either side of this philosophical divide will be satisfied with an argument so parsimonious and minimalist.

Notes

1 I should add that nothing follows from the general proposition that nothing follows from general propositions in general. That is to say, if you are persuaded by my argument, you will not be directed either to do something or to refrain from doing something. On this point, see Fish 2000.

2 Habermas might reply – on the model of Chomsky's deep and surface structure distinction – that the fact that normative presuppositions aren't mentioned and that speakers do not ordinarily live up to the normative implications of their speech acts only marks the degree to which they are insufficiently aware of what they are doing and remain trapped in distorted forms of communication; but that would be a moral judgment made against those who are quite happily getting along without all the normative machinery he wants to saddle them with.

3 In order to reach this conclusion, Haskell must assume, falsely, that inquiry is a willful activity in need of an external constraint. In fact, inquiry is only possible if constraints – the constraints of some particular discipline or interpretive community – are already in place and have been internalized by the inquirer who proceeds within them. Constraints, in short, are constitutive of inquiry – were there none in place, inquiry would be directionless – and need not be sought in some external authority.

Bibliography

Augustine (1958) *On Christian Doctrine*, trans. D.W. Robertson, Indianapolis: Indiana University Press.

Fish, S. (2000) "Theory minimalism," *San Diego Law Review*, 37: 761–777.

Haack, S. (1995) "Vulgar pragmatism: an unedifying prospect," in H.J. Saatkamp Jr (ed.), *Rorty and Pragmatism: The Philosopher Responds to His Critics*, Nashville: Vanderbilt University Press.

Habermas, J. (1971) *Knowledge and Human Interests*, trans. Jeremy J. Shapiro, Boston: Beacon Press.

—— (1979) *Communication and the Evolution of Society*, trans. Thomas McCarthy, Boston: Beacon Press.

—— (1998) *Between Facts and Norms: Contributions to a Discourse Theory of Law and Democracy*, trans. William Rehg, Boston: MIT Press.

—— (2000) "Richard Rorty's pragmatic turn," in Robert B. Brandom (ed.), *Rorty and His Critics*, Oxford: Blackwell.

Haskell, T. (1996) "Justifying the rights of academic freedom in the era of 'power/knowledge'," in Louis Menand (ed.), *The Future of Academic Freedom*, Chicago: University of Chicago Press.

Hickman, L. (2001) "Dewey: modernism, postmodernism, and beyond," paper presented at the symposium sponsored by the Behavioral Research Council, a division of the American Institute for Economic Research, Great Barrington, MA, July 2001.

Kloppenberg, J. (1998) "Pragmatism: an old name for some new ways of thinking?" in Morris Dickstein (ed.), *The Revival of Pragmatism: New Essays on Social Thought, Law, and Culture*, Durham, NC: Duke University Press.

Kramer, M.H. (1992) "God, greed and flesh: Saint Paul, Thomas Hobbes, and the nature/nurture debate," *Southern Journal of Philosophy*, 30: 51–66.

—— (1999) *In the Realm of Legal and Moral Philosophy: Critical Encounters*, New York: St Martin's Press.

Milton, J. (1974) "The readie and easie way," in Robert W. Ayers (ed.), *Complete Prose Works of John Milton*, 8 vols, New Haven, CT: Yale University Press.

Nagel, T. (1987) "Moral conflict and political legitimacy," *Philosophy and Public Affairs*, 16: 215–240.

Rorty, R. (2000) "Response to Habermas," in Robert B. Brandom (ed.), *Rorty and His Critics*, Oxford: Blackwell.

Warren, M.E. (1995) "The self in discursive democracy," in Stephen K. White (ed.), *The Cambridge Companion to Habermas*, Cambridge: Cambridge University Press, 167–195.

13 The logical necessity of ideologies

Tom Burke

In this chapter I want to define formally what an ideology is, assuming we understand that term in a non-pejorative way – that we do not view the term as an invective or accusation. My primary aim is to show how a properly conceived notion of ideology can be profitably incorporated into John Dewey's theory of inquiry.

The word "ideology" can have at least three distinct uses or senses. In its original sense, as introduced around the time of the French Revolution, it meant simply an objective "science of ideas," or a "science of the origin of ideas." The aim of such a science was the objective analysis of the origins and development of ideas, to clarify whatever can be clarified free of metaphysical and religious prejudices. In this sense, we might say that an ideologue is (or would have been) to ideology what a biologist is to biology, or what a mathematician is to mathematics.

Due primarily to Marx, drawing on Hegel's reflections on Napoleon's political displeasure with certain intellectual challenges to his monarchy, the term has now come to denote particular "isms," especially with regard to social, cultural, political, and economic practices. An ideology is an ism – Fascism, Nazism, Capitalism, Communism, Liberalism, Conservatism, Radicalism, Theism, Atheism, Pragmatism, Positivism, Absolutism, Relativism, and so on – and an ideologue is a dyed-in-the-wool, true-believing, prejudiced proponent of any such ism. As a result of the battles of ideas that have characterized recent global political and economic developments, it is easy to see how the term would take on pejorative connotations, coming to denote a pernicious system of false or otherwise dubious concepts or ideas – usually someone else's. To escape or avoid the clutches of ideology would be to embrace a fair and even-handed perspective on the world, avoiding conceptual perversions and mere pseudo-science, attaining instead some measure of fair and equitable objectivity. The drumbeat here is for "the end of ideology."

It may be convincingly argued that any such pejorative reading of the term "ideology" is inherently inconsistent. A non-pejorative reading of the term need not suffer this inconsistency. This speaks in favor of maintaining a non-pejorative reading of the term. To see how this is the case, first assume that under either kind of reading, pejorative or non-pejorative, one endorses an ideology concerning (among other things) ideologies. This is the case regardless of one's claims to "non-ideological" objectivity. We cannot establish that we are free of ideology simply by insinuating that we are neutrally objective. The status of such claims is the very thing at issue here. It is safe to say that in endorsing a pejorative reading of the term "ideology," one endorses an ideological preference against ideologies. It follows that this ideological preference against ideologies (as an ideology about ideologies) should itself be avoided. The proponent of this view unavoidably is doing what one allegedly must not do – namely, advancing an ideology. This is a performative inconsistency.

On the other hand, in endorsing a non-pejorative reading of the term, one must admit simply that one has an ideology about ideologies. This indicates that one has a conceptual perspective on conceptual perspectives, one that of course may be erroneous or may otherwise fall short in its applicability or workability. This is typical of any conceptual perspective, in the sciences or otherwise. It is better that we be aware of this limited and potentially error-laden perspectivity and adopt a suitably fallibilistic attitude toward any given ideology. This suggests that ideologies must remain open to criticism if they are to remain viable. This fallibilism may be distasteful to anyone who craves unwavering certainty, but it is not inherently inconsistent. Indeed one may legitimately claim objectivity, but one should be wary of claims to ideology-free objectivity. Any such claim is suspect insofar as it is subject to the inconsistency outlined earlier. This is particularly true of any claim that would pit objectivity against ideology and thereby cast ideology in a negative light. Pitting objectivity against ideology simply presents a false dichotomy.

A third sense of the term "ideology" is the one I want to work with here. It is similar to the first sense in being non-pejorative, but it is like the second in denoting a system rather than a science of ideas. It is unlike the second insofar as it regards ideologies not just as unavoidable and even ubiquitous but also as indispensable. Ideologies are not illegitimate simply because they are ideologies. Rather, the legitimacy or illegitimacy of specific ideologies depends as much on the attitudes one takes towards them as on the details of their actual use in one's experience. The drumbeat in this case is for the intelligent functioning of ideologies in human affairs, particularly in regard to their role in critiques of just about anything we say or do (as economists or otherwise). As a corollary, this calls for the end of ideology alone, i.e., the end of holding to given ideologies without sufficient attention to the sources of one's ideas or to practical consequences of implementing those ideas. Ideology in this view is not a threat to science. The main threat to science lies rather in ignoring ideology and thus being insufficiently cognizant of the manner and consequences of its function in scientific inquiry.

Nor does this view pit principle against practicality (viewing ideologies as background sources of principles that we live by). "Being pragmatic" versus "resting on principle" is another false dichotomy. In many cases it may be quite legitimate on practical grounds to rest on principle. But in such cases this should be done in light of and as a result of rationally and diligently surveying potential long-term consequences of such an option. What is not legitimate is always holding fast to certain principles come what may, ignoring considerations of the relevance, propriety, and circumstantial efficacy of those principles. This of course should be read as a cautious admission of fallibility, not an endorsement of unfettered relativism. It is hard to tell which is worse: the unconstrained relativism stemming from abuses of the admission of fallibility that goes with "being pragmatic" or the unwavering fundamentalism stemming from abuses of the desired sense of certainty that goes with "resting on principle." We should avoid these extremes. We do not have to choose exclusively between principle and practicality. We should wield ideologies as reliable but improvable tools whose proper use requires skill, vigilance, and finesse, regarding them neither as throwaway conveniences nor as sacrosanct gifts from on high.

In this third sense, an ideology is just a particular type of system or scheme of ideas relevant to some subject matter (not limited to social, cultural, political, or economic affairs). Specifically, the definition I want to present here is based on a notion similar in many respects to the notion of a semantic model for a modal logic. But in place of related possible worlds, we should think of an ideology in terms of classes of related world-views. What is distinctive about world-views, as opposed to possible worlds, is that each world-view is associated with a class of abstract theories consisting entirely of universal propositions (in Dewey's sense of "universal proposition," not in the common extensional quantificational sense of propositions sporting appropriate quantifiers; more will be said about this later).

Our task, then, will be to see how such a definition might capture an acceptable notion of ideology, and to show specifically how this characterization of ideologies comports with Dewey's overall theory of inquiry. Admittedly this project will be more useful to readers who have an interest in understanding Dewey's philosophy of logic, with few if any commitments one way or another concerning how the term "ideology" is currently used elsewhere. Our primary goal is to elucidate Dewey's conception of logic and only secondarily to clear up the current muddle of views about ideology. It should also be stated up front that while ideas from economics will be used to illustrate various features of inquiry in general, the true relevance of this chapter to economics is less direct than that. Its relevance to economics lies rather in its concise characterization of a particular methodological notion (the notion of ideology) that is germane especially (though not exclusively) to the social sciences. This chapter is thus addressed to the economist qua scientist, not just to the economist qua economist.

Before going on, I should say something about the title of this chapter. The word "necessity" in the title has two possible meanings, and I mean both of them. On one hand it refers to the essential (unavoidable and indispensable) function of ideologies in all types of inquiry – being thus a necessary component of inquiry, competent or otherwise. It follows that logical theory must in a substantial way accommodate ideologies (in an appropriate sense of the term "ideology").

On the other hand, the word "necessity" refers to the abstract character of implication, consequence, and proof typical of the ideas, hypotheses, definitions, and theories that constitute world-views and thus ideologies – in contrast with existential entailments characteristic of matters of fact. That is to say, as a complex association of universal propositions, an ideology consists in part of systems of relations of ideas that are characterized by a type of abstract "logical" necessity. Just what this amounts to should become clear as we proceed.

The following discussion falls into two parts. First, we need to review Dewey's conception of experience, his conception of inquiry in particular (as a kind of experience), and at least a rudimentary outline of his theory of propositions, as a prelude to explaining the essential function of ideologies in inquiry. The second part looks at how certain methods and concepts from mathematical logic fit within Dewey's theory of inquiry, employing those techniques to characterize ideologies in a wholesale fashion while at the same time preserving their non-analytical aspects.

Experience and inquiry

Dewey casts logic broadly as a theory of inquiry. It is not just a study of formal languages, though that is an integral part of its subject matter. Dewey's notion that inquiry is a clarification and transformation of some concrete problematic situation (Dewey 1938: ch. 6) is well known. This pattern of inquiry is essentially the basic pattern of experience – a redirection of life activities against disturbances or imbalances (Dewey 1916: ch. 11; 1925: ch. 1; 1930; 1934: ch. 3). But inquiry also involves deliberate observation and experimentation guided by theoretical reflection. In short, competent inquiry is a type of concrete experience that involves experimentally applied thinking. Of special interest here is the notion that inquiry involves the correlative development and manipulation of both existential and ideational contents:

> Inquiry is progressive and cumulative. Propositions are the instruments by which provisional conclusions of preparatory inquiries are summed up, recorded and retained for subsequent uses. In this way they function as effective means, material and procedural, in the conduct of inquiry, till the latter institutes subject-matter so unified in significance as to be warrantably assertible. It follows (1) that there is no such thing as an isolated proposition; or, positively stated, that propositions stand in ordered relations to one another; and (2) that there are two main types of such order, one referring to the factual or existential material which determines the final subject of judgment, the other referring to the ideational material, the conceptual meanings, which determine the predicate of final judgment. In the words of ordinary use, there are the propositions having the relation which constitutes *inference*, and the propositions having the serial relation which constitutes reasoning or *discourse*.
>
> (Dewey 1938: 310; also see 1942: 37–38)

This passage ranges widely over matters we need not delve into here. Of special importance though is the identification of two types of ordered relations among propositions, namely, existential and ideational. In his 1938 *Logic* (and in several articles written at roughly the same time: 1935; 1936a; 1936b; 1936c) this distinction serves as the basis for a rather elaborate scheme for classifying different sorts of propositions and their constituent terms. In particular this distinction supports acknowledgment of three distinct sorts of relational terms corresponding, respectively, to qualities, universals, and kinds.

In the first place, we use predicates like green, sweet, or soft to denote sensory qualities of things. There are other types of qualities besides sensory qualities. We also value various goods in an immediate qualitative way. We have qualitative preferences for certain goods over others. We have a qualitative sense of ownership of property. In light of such examples, it should be emphasized that, for Dewey, qualities, while not limited to simple or atomic sense data, are the most immediate results of exploiting various operational capabilities and empirical sensitivities. A so-called "particular proposition" is one in which a quality is attributed to some discernible this or that: *this is mine, that is preferable to these.* We should also allow that qualities may be binary, tertiary, etc.---that is, qualities may be relational, not just attributive. Hence, *that this is more valuable than that* may be as much a qualitative proposition as any simple value attribution. Things like voter preferences or salary levels as recorded by means of some properly administered survey instrument may also be regarded as qualities of individuals in a given population. Or the mean income of a given sample of households may be regarded as a quality of that sample. Generally speaking, observational results – data – are expressed by particular propositions in this sense.

Second, some predicates function in inquiry to denote abstract ideas, or what Dewey sometimes prefers to call universals. By themselves, universals and the abstract propositions they constitute (so-called "universal propositions") are not directly answerable to experimental or observational methods. They are subject rather to standards of comprehensive systematic coherence. It must be emphasized though that Dewey's conception of universals is markedly non-traditional. He identifies ideas as plans of action and thus espouses a kind of operationalism in which ideas designate possible practices, possible ways of acting, possible modes of being, abilities to act or be in specific ways, etc. (1936c: 107–112; 1938: 263, 269, 289, 350–351, 516): "Ideas are operational in that they instigate and direct further operations of observation; they are proposals and plans for acting upon existing conditions to bring new facts to light and to organize all the selected facts into a coherent whole" (1938: 116). It is of course this operational, practicable content of universals that ultimately renders them applicable to existential affairs even if such implementation need not be a factor in abstract discourse. "The 'universal' is not something metaphysically anterior to all experience but is a *way in which things function* in experience as a bond of union among particular events and scenes" (Dewey 1934: 291).

It is not by accident that Dewey often refers to ways of acting and modes of being in one breath. They are in one sense the same thing. You can act or you can be, but in either case, you are engaged in a certain manner of practice. You can drive, or you can be driven, but either way, you are on the road to some destination. The notion of "universal" by itself need not distinguish these two manners of being on the road, though of course we will want to make this active/passive, agent/patient distinction in specific cases on various independent grounds. Dewey sometimes draws this distinction in terms of our capacities to do and to undergo various activities. In either case we have various abilities to engage in certain activities or processes. Insofar as such abilities are engrained and ready-to-hand, they are subject to serving as the contents of ideas formulated in universal terms.

Ideas, denoting possible ways of acting or modes of being, are termed universals by Dewey in virtue of their abstract function in inquiry, not so much because of any specific grammatical features of language. In particular, universal propositions are not well represented once and for all by strings of predicate symbols and individual variables with upside-down-A quantifiers ranging over some given domain of individuals. Indeed it is not useful to think of them as first- or second- or third-order propositions in any familiar extensional sense insofar as their "ontological commitments" are not based on domains of individuals but rather on repertoires of possible ways or modes of acting or being. A universal proposition is universal insofar as it expresses relations among ideas that allegedly obtain in any inquiry in which those ideas are at all relevant. Perhaps we could regard universal propositions as "quantifying" over some domain of possible situations. But it is somewhat questionable whether one can legitimately pre-specify a domain of possible situations or inquiries in an interesting and substantial way (Dewey 1938: 66–69). The universality of universal propositions hinges more on intrinsic structural and functional relations among the possible activities to which they refer, not just with respect to any particular situation but with respect to the general standing of such relationships as warrantably reliable invariants in our ongoing experience. As such, the functional role of universal propositions is to formulate such operational invariants as guiding principles in the unfolding course of inquiry. Clearly this characterization of universals and universal propositions is not anything like what one finds in a standard object-based extensional semantics.

Dewey's characterization of universals in terms of possible modes of action is rooted in a natural history of human biological and socio-cultural developments. He discusses such genetic matters in the opening chapters of his 1938 *Logic* (and elsewhere) as essential background for his logical theory. Human beings are typically capable of various distinguishing ways of acting or modes of being. Different human groups or individuals also have various relatively unique capabilities shaped and refined by evolutionary and developmental processes. On the whole, these capabilities are rooted in basic animal abilities tempered by distinctively human cultural forces. In saying that they are functionally universal, we allow: (1) that such abilities are malleable; (2) that their relevance and availability for use depends on contingencies of ongoing experience and of our growth as organic social creatures; but (3) that taken together they constitute a hopefully stable operational perspective that should serve us well from situation to situation. To whatever extent these abilities serve as the contents of ideas, they function as if they were fixed (as "pillars of thought") – that is their role in our experience. But because of their contingent and evolving character it behooves us to be able to continually critique and refine these abilities and their relations as we encounter new and unusual situations. Failure to appreciate this fallible, functional role of universals in inquiry and the consequent neglect of the need to continually attend to their existential adequacy has no doubt all too often led to misconceptions about their nature and to such perversions as recalcitrance, dogmatism, and tenacious intolerance in "battles of ideas" devoid of honest and intelligent (self-)criticism.

While genetic considerations are crucial to understanding the functional nature of universals in inquiry, our primary focus here will be on certain structural features that facilitate their function in inquiry. Engrained abilities may function as universals insofar as they are possibly relevant and thus available for use in virtually any situation that comes about. Such abilities embody ideational aspects of inquiry insofar as a specimen inquirer has the capacity to consider different options regarding how to act or to be in given circumstances, rather than simply being driven mechanically by established habits. Existential conditions will support certain suggestions as to feasible options, and these suggestions take on the status of "ideas" when developed symbolically in relation with other ideas (Dewey 1938: 58, 113, 275, 300, 350). Reflection upon ideational aspects of a problem constitutes a significant portion of our abstract discourse in a given inquiry, including (but not limited to) mathematical modeling and mathematical discourse (1938: 20).

Third, we use predicates in inquiry to denote what Dewey refers to as kinds. Classifying a particular job skill as being of the kind *capital asset* (a "singular proposition") or subsuming a kind *job skill* under a kind *capital asset* (a "generic proposition") differ in important ways both from subsuming a universal *job skill* under a universal *capital asset* and from attributing a quality *capital asset* to some particular job skill. A kind is neither a quality nor a universal, but it is a systematic synthesis of various qualitative and universal contents, that is, an integration of existential and ideational contents (1938: 274–275). If anything is basic in Dewey's philosophy of logic, it is the claim that we cannot rectify an agent's grasp of things in the world except in terms of that agent's operational abilities and possible qualitative results of exercising such abilities. Quality predicates and universal predicates serve to denote each of these aspects of human experience, respectively. Attunements to kinds, as well-behaved systematic associations of such abilities and the possible qualitative events to which these abilities provide access, are the primary means by which an inquirer finds structure and meaning in the world. Actual objects or populations of objects (or substances or fields of substances) serve as actual or potential instantiations of kinds insofar as they are capable of evidencing an array of characteristic qualitative traits resulting from prescribed systematic activities. Clearly the classification of an object or substance as one of a kind is subject to direct experimental and observational methods, as are claims about general relationships among kinds themselves. Qualitative propositions express supporting (confirming or disconfirming) data for such claims, while universal propositions should convey whatever systematicity there is in the activities that might yield those data. Kinds thus incorporate a significant integration of operational and empirical factors into the basic fabric of inquiry, where the operational contents of kinds may be directly related to ideational matters while the empirical contents of kinds are directly existential in nature.

To further illustrate these three distinct sorts of predicates, consider again a notion such as *capital*. This one word, as a predicate symbol, may be used in three fundamentally different ways.

1   At least part of our qualitative sense of scarcity and need is an immediate sense of capital-differentials. We also try to determine quantities of at least some types of capital using certain accounting instruments and methods. Respective economic and financial data in certain contexts can be taken to indicate qualities attributable to activities to which such accounting methods are applied. You fill out your tax forms after the end of the year; and when you finally get that last calculation that is the "amount you owe" or the "amount you overpaid," you have an immediate sense not just of a number but of a certain impact on your cash reserves.

2   The abstract idea of capital (or capital as a universal), on the other hand, may be grounded in various econometric methods, but these methods remain mere possibilities when the idea of capital is employed abstractly in relation to other ideas, for instance, in theories of markets, money, property, or production. The idea of capital is meaningful because it is rooted in operational measurement activities, though its full meaning is expanded greatly by explicating its relations to other universals. Thus, on one hand, ideas which are perhaps not so simply grounded – e.g., ideas of wealth or prosperity, – are rendered (more) meaningful through their abstract linkage with ideas such as that of capital. On the other hand, by virtue of such linkages, types and quantities of capital may be determined indirectly by measuring related variables (e.g., productivity levels, market share, employment rates, and so forth) – all by virtue of abstract relations among universals that one has chosen to work with.

3   Capital as a kind may be specified with respect to certain econometric methods and would thus be articulated in terms of specifications for the proper use of particular survey and accounting instruments and techniques and the range of possible results of their employment. Capital as a kind term is inherently a general term applicable in certain existential circumstances – integrating numerous abstract ideas and their relations to

one other with a respective range of registrable qualities (namely, survey and accounting data). Another kind that we might call *profitable enterprise*, for instance, would incorporate, among many things, specifications referring to the kind *capital* with allowable economic data falling within certain ranges, disallowing data outside of these ranges (in a simplest characterization anyway, applicable under normal economic conditions). This type of general term would be wielded frequently by CEOs and CFOs intent on actually running their respective businesses – as opposed to engaging merely in abstract discourse typical of economic theory.

The point of these illustrations is that we need to distinguish (a) the abstract universals embodied in possible econometric methods; (b) the potential qualitative data we get from exploiting such methods; and (c) systematic pairings of these methods and their possible results in the constitution of kinds. This identifies three sorts of predicates associated with the one word "capital" – one or more universals, respective qualities, and one or more kinds – all of which function rather differently, though in an understandably coordinated way, in the language of economics. Failing to distinguish these predicates can easily lead to nonsense insofar as different uses of one and the same word can fail to be intersubstitutable as we move between ideational and existential (pure and applied) considerations in economic inquiries (Burke 2002b).

Ideologies and models of ideologies

We may turn now to the notion of ideology, focusing specifically on possible structural relationships among universals as they might arise in inquiry. The first point to make is that ideas do not arise in isolation but rather in systematic "constellations of related meanings" (Dewey 1938: 55–59, 82, 116, 312). Contemporary mathematical logic can help to articulate details of this possible systematicity of ideas. To make this work, we need to introduce two technical notions that help to explain how frameworks of ideas are brought to bear in specific inquiries. These are the notion of an ideology and the notion of a world-view (where I am basically imposing these notions on Dewey's logical theory, since he does not often use these terms himself).

Recall that inquiry, for Dewey, is an existential process of transforming a situation, seeking a satisfactory resolution of a given problem – from making a purchase or sale, renewing a contract, or keeping a company solvent, to revitalizing a depressed economy, securing the political and economic reconstruction of some post-war country, or stabilizing and strengthening prospects for peace and prosperity in a chronically conflict-ridden region of the world. The issue to consider here is how possible systems of ideas may play a role in guiding and constraining such transformations. An inquiry may involve competing systems of ideas. In particular, these systems may fail to be satisfactorily systematic, or they may fail singularly or together to address the problem at hand, or they may tend to conflict with one another in determining what is most appropriate for the given existential situation. The primary question here concerns what it means to say that a system of ideas is indeed systematic.

Traditional conceptions of scientific inquiry acknowledge experimental versus theoretical aspects of science. With regard to inquiry more generally, scientific or otherwise, the notion of a theory is not rich enough by itself to characterize the ideational aspects of inquiry. To provide anything approaching an adequate account of the systematicity of ideas, we need to introduce a notion of ideology.

To do that, we first need to take care to distinguish systems of universals from our models or representations of systems of universals. This is important given that we are now trying to formulate conceptions of conceptions, ideas about ideas. We should not confuse specific features of our ideas about ideas with general features of the object ideas themselves, blithely drawing conclusions about one based on assumptions about the other. The transformation of a situation in and through inquiry is guided largely by the development and application of one or more systems of ideas that are functionally universal in character. We want to refer to actual systems of universals in the broadest sense as ideologies. A logician's task would be (in part) to formally "model" ideologies, where a formal description of the use and development of ideologies in a given inquiry will often involve changes in how those ideologies are modeled.

Also, it should be emphasized again that the term "ideology" will be taken in neither a laudatory nor a pejorative manner. We might say that an ideologue is a person who makes decisions and otherwise acts uncritically if not blindly on the basis of some tenaciously favored ideology. But that is not our main concern here. Ideologies for better or worse are just ideational contexts characterized by systems of universals, where universals are understood to be not just representational or explanatory but potentially instrumental in laying out programs of action in or with respect to some situation at hand. That universals are social and cultural in their origins and constitution – that certain ways of acting or modes of being are not just reinforced by social relations but are irreducibly shared (and thus socially distributed) – speaks in favor of employing the term "ideology" here in the sense intended. But this term should not carry only the limited meaning given to it in social and political discourse where it most often arises. In the present view any inquiry, political or otherwise, is ideological insofar as ideas are employed (well or badly) in that inquiry. The notion of an ideology is needed only to allow reference to abstract contexts in which systems of universals are couched.

To accommodate the pluralistic nature of ideational aspects of inquiry, we cannot assume that an ideology can always be represented by a single theory. If we think of theories as systems of definitions and hypotheses and everything that follows from them by certain consequence relations or by given proof rules, then many of our ideas arise in "constellations" that could not properly be called theories at all. To better understand what a theory is, we need a more general construct, formally analogous to a possible world in the semantics for modal logics. This analogue of a possible world will be termed a world-view. A world-view will accommodate possibly many theories; and an ideology will consist of a class of systematically related world-views. We want to acknowledge that in any inquiry we bring to bear different families of world-views (in varying degrees of salience or relevance). These families will be distinguished by various systematic relations among their constituent world-views, and by what systems of abstract hypotheses obtain in each world-view.

Recall from the passage quoted earlier (Dewey 1938: 310) that the eventual outcome of a successful inquiry will be a judgment with a subject–predicate structure. Obviously this (seemingly) simple structure is not typical of assertions in general; but the "final judgment" issuing from a given inquiry, broadly speaking, will state facts of the matter (the subject of final judgment) plus options and choices regarding what is to be done about them (the predicate of final judgment). More precisely, we want to think of a "predicate of final judgment" not just as a single idea, nor as a single theory, nor as a single world-view, nor even as a single ideology, but as a possibly fuzzy class or family of ideologies. A single ideology can be modeled by a triple (V,R,T), where V is a (possibly fuzzy) set of world-views. If Λ is a grammar for a language of abstract hypotheses, the (possibly fuzzy) function $T: \Lambda \rightarrow 2^V$ will associate basic abstract hypotheses and their constituent terms (universals, modes of being) with various world-views. In this sense T may be regarded as a specification of a set of ontologies, one for each world-view.

If we acknowledge various ways of operating with universals (e.g., introducing or removing terms, definitions, or axioms; redefining old terms or constructing new ones; specifying or changing principles of argumentation or rules of proof; performing calculations and derivations; proving theorems or producing arguments (analogous to existential test-programs), etc.), then these operations may be composed or combined in simple or complex, standard or innovative ways to yield a repertoire Γ of possible forms of reasoning or discourse. In a given ideology-model (V,R,T), the (possibly fuzzy) function $R:\Gamma \rightarrow 2^{V \times V}$ will specify ways in which world-views are mutually accessible through transitions in discourse, e.g., by these methods of reasoning.

An abstract theory, then, will be a coherent set of definitions, axioms or basic hypotheses, and implications thereof, holding within a given world-view, possibly shared across many world-views. A given world-view may countenance several competing theories, not all mutually consistent. Moreover, there need be no assurance or requirement that theories in this abstract sense will be existentially applicable insofar as they are systems of strictly universal propositions – as in mathematics, for instance, but also in sciences where existential applicability often both motivates and constrains their development. For this reason, Galilean kinematics, Bohr's model of the hydrogen atom, Keynes's theory of the business cycle, or even Marx's theory of capital will not (or should not) be disposed of because of their lack of empirical adequacy. Much of their value and legitimacy rests elsewhere, namely, in how they serve to systematize certain ideas clearly and simply.

Note how this view of ideologies supports several different notions of "necessity." We might say that a given universal proposition P is necessarily true in a given world-view v just in case P is true in every world-view accessible from v (by means of appropriate methods of reasoning). This sense of necessity is formally tractable along the lines of a Kripkean modal semantics. But there are other feasible notions of necessity – such as an abstract principle being true (and thus necessarily true) in every world-view in a given ideology. Or an abstract principle may be said to be necessarily true in a given ideology (not just in a world-view) if it is true in every world-view in every ideology which is in some sense "accessible" from the given ideology, that is, if we could speak in some systematic way about wholesale accessibility relations among ideologies (in a prescribed class of ideologies, as in a "final predicate of judgment"). Or, addressing the functional nature of ideologies as instruments of existential inquiry, we can think of abstract principles as "universal" (and in a way, "necessary") insofar as they are presumed to hold good in every situation to which or in which they might be employed as guides to action. In this case the relevant contexts with respect to which necessity is determined are possible concrete situations rather than abstract world-views and/or ideologies.

Notice too how this scheme accommodates various non-analytical, non-structural aspects of ideologies. To assert a predicate of final judgment (with respect to the subject of final judgment), so the claim goes here, is to adopt and apply a class of ideologies – possibly a singleton class, but a class nonetheless. Why a class of ideologies? Often in making concrete judgments we cannot or will not be so precise as to narrow the predicate of final judgment to a single ideology but will instead make do with a rough characterization sufficient for specifying only a class of ideologies. Such a class will not necessarily be systematic in its constitution. We should expect that there will not always be (if ever) a formula or construction or calculus or decision procedure that can tell us once and for all what should go into these classes. Too often this is just not a formal exercise, though in some cases these classes may be formally specifiable. Of course, even without the aid of formal procedures, such classes might still be products of diligent inquiry propelled by innovative insight. But more often, for better or worse, it will be forces of habit, tradition, and convention that constitute these classes. It may be just a matter of "constant conjunctions" or "family resemblances" among ideological factors in our ongoing experience that form these classes – forces that simply are not amenable to analytical determination.

This point runs deeper. Even within a single ideology, we have a class of world-views. Again, what determines such classes? Constant conjunctions? Family resemblances? Happenstance? Whatever holds these classes together, it may not be analytically determinable. This of course highlights the lack of fit between many of our models of ideologies and actual ideologies themselves, insofar as modeling, for better or worse, is essentially an analytical enterprise.

The point runs deeper still! Any given world-view will be characterized by some class of theories (the latter consisting of systems of universal propositions). Different theories in a given world-view may be mutually compatible takes on a certain subject matter, or they may be competing alternatives that are singularly plausible on various grounds but mutually incompatible. In this sense a world-view taken as a whole may be "inconsistent." In any case the question again arises: why this class of theories and not that one? This need not be analytically determinable, but we have such classes nonetheless.

We get to where formal consistency and the possibility of analytical determination is the norm only at the level of single theories – at which point, of course, the full arsenal of formal logical techniques is at our disposal and can have free play. By building non-analytical elements into the constitution of ideologies, we have not sacrificed precise logical analysis. We have only identified where it is possible and where it is not – we have only located its proper place in inquiry.

These remarks indicate one place, by the way, where logic, at least in Dewey's sense, is or can be decidedly empirical in nature. Namely, if we look at ideologies not as social or political commentators regard them but as logicians should regard them, intent on understanding the general pattern of inquiry in both its better and worse aspects, then ideologies may become in themselves a type of existential subject matter. It becomes an empirical question, quite pertinent to logical theory, of what sorts of ideologies are actually out there in the world affecting people's thoughts and actions. Where and, perhaps, why do we find these as opposed to those sorts of classes of classes of classes of systems of universal propositions at work, and how do they actually function in our experience? Those are empirical questions.

To go on then, if we adopt this way of modeling predicates of final judgment (in Dewey's sense) as classes of ideologies, we could afford to say still more about what we mean by a universal proposition. We will want to say that universal propositions (that is, propositions whose terms are universals) will have both unarticulated and articulated features (Burke 2002a). If an utterance of "Income equals consumption plus accumulation" functions as the utterance of a universal proposition relative to some given inquiry, then it would occur in some stage of that inquiry relative to some class of ideologies, as a constituent of one or more theories that characterize one or more world-views in those ideologies. The articulated features of a universal proposition will be what is actually expressed when the proposition is stated in some natural language, whereas unarticulated features will include (at least) ideological contextual factors which must be shared or otherwise grasped in order to understand the import of what is articulated.

We would expect the articulated features of such a proposition to respect compositional rules for the given natural language in which it is couched, along with certain other constraints. Namely, the basic lexical terms for its expression-types will designate universals or compositions of universals. The main "verb" (like *is*) in an atomic universal statement will designate an abstract identity relation (not that there is just one such identity relation) or perhaps some reduction relation. Complex universal propositions will trace implications and equivalences entailed by the postulation or stipulation of such relations. It is in this stipulative or postulational sense that universal propositions will be definitional in character, and most likely contrary to fact, as opposed to existentially descriptive (Dewey 1938: 259–260, 270–271, 300–303, 404–405; see also 1936c: 107).

A universal term, as part of a symbol system, is an abstraction denoting an ability (a possible practice or way of acting or mode of being). Various existing mathematical formalisms can be used to model ways in which such abilities may be systematically composed or otherwise related. For instance, a lambda calculus (Barendregt 1984; Hindley and Seldin 1986; Stansifer 1995) could describe how complex abilities may be composed systematically out of simpler abilities. A lambda calculus is of course just one sort of Cartesian closed category. The type of systematization of universals that Dewey discusses in the 1938 *Logic* (chapters 16–20) thus could be cast more broadly in category-theoretic terms (Arbib and Manes 1975; Barr and Wells 1990; Pierce 1991; Rydeheard and Burstall 1988). Of course pure category theory as a going concern in mathematics is not beholding to Dewey's logical theory. But category theory can play a role in clarifying what Dewey had to say about ideational aspects of inquiry, specifically by describing possible structural properties of systems of universal terms and universal propositions.

Such formalisms as the lambda calculus or category theory more generally thus make possible a rigorous treatment of Dewey's conception of "abstract hypotheses," as sketched in chapters 16–20 of the 1938 *Logic*, particularly when it comes to dealing with "formal relations of completely abstract subject matters, in which transformation as abstract possibility takes the form of trans-form*ability* in the abstract" (1938: 394). A theory in this kind of framework will be a consistent extension of such a formalism, closed under respective modes of transformability. Such a theory is obtained from a set of abstract hypotheses by adding the latter as axioms to the axioms and rules of the given formalism (e.g., Barendregt 1984: ch. 4). A given world-view in a given ideology will then correspond to a class of (possibly incompatible) alternative theories each of which is based on its own system of universals. Overall, then, a world-view will correspond to some space of categories, each constituting a system of universals in Dewey's sense, and each supporting the systematic formulation of abstract hypotheses.

We might emphasize the relevance here of fuzzy set theory and fuzzy logic. The present account should accommodate fuzzy ideology-models (V,R,T), world-views v, accessibility relations R, ontologies T, etc. But also the basic systems of universals that populate these various structures may themselves be formulated in terms of fuzzy categories (Dubois and Prade 1980: 120–122). An account of the possible systematicity of ideas need not be so crisp and rigid as words such as "systematicity" or "formalism" may suggest. The increased determinacy that should characterize acceptable conclusions of inquiry would not be a matter of eradicating fuzziness but rather of finding suitable levels and forms of fuzziness that best accommodate the problem at hand in a world that inevitably evades constraints imposed by rigid ideologies. Crisp ideologies may well be typical only of early stages of inquiry where issues are established in a merely preliminary fashion. Hence we should expect a positive correlation between increased determinacy and more explicit and more precisely specified fuzziness. Fuzziness thus would represent a high-point of formal analysis and consistency, rather than a lack thereof. If this is the case, then fuzzy set theory would have a key role to play in explicating the analytical aspects of ideologies and the ideational aspects of inquiry.

The sort of systematicity of ideas outlined above (fuzzy or not) suggests a rather abstract manner of discourse – one that is characteristic of mathematics, mathematically sophisticated sciences, and other types of inquiry in which abstract discourse plays a key role. One measure of the coherence of a system of ideas would be the degree to which those ideas lend themselves to systematic composition and transformation – describable, for example, by means outlined above. Systematic coherence in this sense and to this degree is not always to be expected, as is the case apparently with many social and political problems we face on a regular basis. This is not a normative admonition but merely a descriptive observation. If and when systematic coherence of ideas is expedient or advantageous, the techniques outlined here simply provide ideal standards. We will have achieved some useful results simply by describing some standards in this regard.

Conclusion

Taking stock of where we are, hopefully it is clear that what has been presented here captures various crucial aspects of the notion of ideology or is otherwise commendable on its own terms. Namely, (1) this account accommodates non-analytical (even irrational) as well as analytical aspects of human experience, being fully open to any and all logical methods to whatever extent various components of ideologies can be subject to logical methods at all. (2) The present account indicates how a common failure to appreciate the functional and fallible nature of ideas and universal propositions may have understandably though unjustifiably engendered abuses of the notion of ideology. (3) This account explains how ideologies function not just in economic or political spheres but in all types of inquiry and all arenas of human endeavor, including any and all sciences. (4) This account fully allows that ideologies are characteristically social in nature insofar as universals may be constituted by irreducibly shared ways of acting or modes of being. (5) It casts ideologies in a succinct and precise way that provides at least a strong hint of the possibility of practical applications in the analysis and critique of human affairs. And not least of all, (6) the present account of ideologies is by no means the whole story, but it helps to elucidate Dewey's theory of inquiry in a way that illustrates the value of that theory as a positive contribution to logic and epistemology – so long as we regard ideologies as indispensable and call not for their eradication but for a better understanding of their intelligent use in inquiry.

Bibliography

Page and chapter numbers in citations of Dewey's works refer to versions of those works in Dewey 1976–1980 (*MW*); and 1981–1990 (*LW*). Some general studies of the notion of ideology are also included in the following list of references. Treatments that at least in part are compatible with the third (non-pejorative) sense of ideology developed here include Boudon 1989, Brown 1973, Cormack 1992, Eagleton 1991, Freeden 1996, Geuss 1981, McLellan 1995, Plamenatz 1970, Samuels 1977, and van Dijk 1998. Treatments more in line with the second (pejorative) sense of the term include Barth 1976, Drucker 1974, Halle 1972, Larrain 1979, and Thompson 1984.

Arbib, M.A. and Manes, E.G. (1975) *Arrows, Structures, and Functors: The Categorical Imperative*, New York: Academic Press.

Barendregt, H.P. (1984) *The Lambda Calculus: Its Syntax and Semantics*, revised edn, Amsterdam: Elsevier.

Barr, M. and Wells, C. (1990) *Category Theory for Computing Science*, Prentice Hall International Series in Computer Science, New York: Prentice Hall.

Barth, H. (1976) *Truth and Ideology*, trans. Frederic Lilge, Berkeley: University of California Press; originally published as Wahrheit und Ideologie (Stuttgart: Eugen Rentsch Verlag, 1945, enlarged 2nd edition 1961).

Bernstein, R.J. (ed.) (1960) *On Experience, Nature, and Freedom: Representative Selections by John Dewey*, New York: Bobbs Merrill Company.

Boudon, R. (1989) *The Analysis of Ideology*, trans. Malcolm Slater, Chicago: University of Chicago Press; originally published as *L'idéologie: ou l'origine des idées reçues* (Paris: Librairie Artheme Fayard, 1986).

Brown, L.B. (1973) *Ideology*, London: Penguin Books.

Burke, T. (2002a) "Prospects for Mathematizing Dewey's Logical Theory," in F. Thomas Burke, D. Micah Hester and Robert Talisse (eds), *Dewey's Logical Theory: New Studies and Interpretations*, Nashville: Vanderbilt University Press.

—— (2002b) 'Qualities, Universals, Kinds, and the New Riddle of Induction," in F. Thomas Burke, D. Micah Hester and Robert Talisse (eds), *Dewey's Logical Theory: New Studies and Interpretations*, Nashville: Vanderbilt University Press.

Cormack, M.J. (1992) *Ideology*, Ann Arbor: University of Michigan Press.

Dewey, J. (1903) "Logical Conditions of a Scientific Treatment of Morality," in *Investigations Representing the Departments*, Part II: Philosophy, Education, University of Chicago decennial publications, first series, 3: 115–139, Chicago: University of Chicago Press; reprinted in Dewey 1946: 211–249; and in *MW* 3: 3–39.

—— (1916) *Democracy and Education*, New York: Macmillan Company; reprinted in *MW* 9.

—— (1925) *Experience and Nature*, Chicago: Open Court; reprinted in *LW* 1.

—— (1930) "Qualitative Thought," *The Symposium*, 1: 5–32; reprinted in Dewey 1931: 93–116; and in *LW* 5: 243–262.

—— (1931) *Philosophy and Civilization*, New York: Minton, Balch and Company.

—— (1934) *Art as Experience*, New York: Henry Holt and Company; reprinted in LW 10.

—— (1935) "Peirce's Theory of Quality," *Journal of Philosophy*, 32: 701–708. Reprinted in Bernstein 1960: 199–210; and in *LW* 11: 86–94.

—— (1936a) "Characteristics and Characters: Kinds and Classes," *Journal of Philosophy*, 33: 253–261. Reprinted in LW 11: 95–104.

—— (1936b) "General Propositions, Kinds, and Classes," *Journal of Philosophy*, 33: 673–680. Reprinted in LW 11: 118–126.

—— (1936c) "What Are Universals?" *Journal of Philosophy*, 33: 281–288. Reprinted in LW 11: 105–114.

—— (1938) *Logic: The Theory of Inquiry*, New York: Henry Holt and Company. Reprinted in LW 12.

—— (1942) "Inquiry and the Indeterminateness of Situations," *Journal of Philosophy*, 39(11): 290–296. Reprinted in Dewey 1946: 322–330; and in LW 15: 34–41.

—— (1946) *Problems of Men*, New York: Philosophical Library. Essays reprinted separately in The Later Works (LW), except for Dewey 1903, MW 3: 3–39.

—— (1976–1980) *The Middle Works* (MW), vols 1–15 (1899–1924), ed. Jo Ann Boydston, Carbondale: Southern Illinois University Press. Citations of items in this edition are indicated by MW followed by volume and page numbers.

—— (1981–1990) *The Later Works* (LW), vols 1–17 (1925–1953), ed. Jo Ann Boydston, Carbondale: Southern Illinois University Press. Citations of items in this edition are indicated by LW followed by volume and page numbers.

Drucker, H.M. (1974) *The Political Uses of Ideology*, London: Macmillan Press.

Dubois, D. and Prade, H. (1980) *Fuzzy Sets and Systems: Theory and Applications, Mathematics in Science and Engineering*, No. 144, New York: Academic Press.

Eagleton, T. (1991) *Ideology: An Introduction*, New York: Verso Books.

Freeden, M. (1996) *Ideologies and Political Theory: A Conceptual Approach*, Oxford: Oxford University Press.

Geuss, R. (1981) *The Idea of a Critical Theory: Habermas and the Frankfurt School*, Cambridge: Cambridge University Press.

Halle, L.J. (1972) *The Ideological Imagination: Ideological Conflict in Our Time and Its Roots in Hobbes, Rousseau, and Marx*, London: Chatto and Windus.

Hindley, J.R. and Seldin, J.P. (1986) *Introduction to Combinators and Lambda-Calculus*, London Mathematical Society Student Texts, vol. 1, Cambridge: Cambridge University Press.

Larrain, J. (1979) *The Concept of Ideology*, London: Hutchinson and Company.

McLellan, D. (1995) *Ideology*, 2nd edn, Minneapolis: University of Minnesota Press.

Pierce, B.C. (1991) *Basic Category Theory for Computer Scientists*, Foundations of Computing Series, Cambridge, MA: MIT Press.

Plamenatz, J. (1970) *Ideology*, New York: Praeger.

Rydeheard, D.E. and Burstall, R.M. (1988) *Computational Category Theory*, Prentice Hall International Series in Computer Science, New York: Prentice Hall.

Samuels, W.J. (1977) "Ideology in Economics," in Sidney Weintraub (ed.), *Modern Economic Thought*, Philadelphia: University of Pennsylvania Press, pp. 467–484.

Stansifer, R. (1995) *The Study of Programming Languages*, Englewood Cliffs: Prentice Hall.

Thompson, J.B. (1984) *Studies in the Theory of Ideology*, Berkeley: University of California Press.
van Dijk, T.A. (1998) *Ideology: A Multidisciplinary Approach*, London: Sage.

14 Pragmatism as criticism

John J. Stuhr

From abstraction to expedience

Claiming that "theories thus become instruments, not answers to enigmas, in which we can rest" (1979 [1907]: 32), William James wrote in his *Pragmatism* that the true is only the expedient in thought, just as the right is only the expedient in action:

> Expedient in almost any fashion; and expedient in the long run and on the whole of course; for what meets expediently all the experience in sight won't necessarily meet all farther experiences equally satisfactorily. Experience, as we know, has ways of boiling over, and making us correct our present formulas.
>
> (James 1979 [1907]: 106)

Truth, James summarized, is a "class-name for all sorts of definite working-values in experience" (1979 [1907]: 38). As a "working-value," it thus is "one species of good"; it is "good in the way of belief, and good, too, for definite, assignable reasons (1979 [1907]: 42)."

Contemporary pragmatist philosophers are familiar with this sentiment or attitude, and they are fond of repeating this claim and ones like it in the writings of Peirce, James, Dewey, and Mead that link truth to action, intellect to will, theory to practice, and belief to experience.

This familiarity and fondness of philosophers aside, this pragmatic point is often forgotten or ignored. It is nowhere to be found, for example, when philosophers treat pragmatism itself not as an instrument but as an answer to abstract, intellectual enigmas about the nature of reality or the nature of method and intelligence or the nature of values. For example, consider this enigma: What is the nature of truth? Now sit back, put your feet up, and take a rest with this answer: Truth is pragmatic.

There is, of course, nothing useful about saying this sort of thing. Accordingly, a more genuinely expedient pragmatism thus is absent when philosophers write and read papers that pretend to establish by themselves and independent of purpose, action, practice, experience and what Dewey called their particular selective emphases, the truth of pragmatism, or the truth of whatever other views they profess. Similarly, this genuinely pragmatic attitude is overlooked by academics who write tedious papers that propose to establish conclusively and solely by the argument in their papers the truth or falsity of the views of writers such as Peirce, James, Dewey, Mead, Lewis, Smith, Bernstein, McDermott, or Lachs, or the resources or limitations of movements such as modernism, postmodernism, or pragmatism. These academics too frequently fail to demonstrate, or even address, whether their arguments have any definite, concrete, assignable expedience in experience – beyond, perhaps, bringing their authors institutional and professional status and some opportunities to speak to one another at conferences or publish together in scholarly tomes. When this happens, pragmatism in name has little to do with pragmatism in life.

Accordingly, here are some abstract questions that pragmatists and everyone else should not ask: Is pragmatism like or unlike modernism? Is it like or unlike postmodernism? Is pragmatism like both, or is it an alternative to both modernism and postmodernism? Is Dewey's pragmatism in, say, *Experience and Nature* and *Logic: The Theory of Inquiry* continuous or discontinuous with his views in, say, *Knowing and the Known*? Are these two former books filled with more insights than this latter one? Is Dewey's pragmatism like or unlike the work of particular more recent pragmatists? Is it more correct for pragmatists to talk in terms of experience and transactions or in terms of language and vocabularies? Which pragmatist is best? Which one says the most true things? Would it be a good thing for philosophers to talk more frequently with economists? When these and similar questions are posed like this – in the abstract and unconnected to use – their responses, whatever the responses, have no expediency at all. When this happens, pragmatism fails to be pragmatic.

To acquire expediency, these questions must be linked to:

1   matters of use – in relation to what ends is a particular answer to a particular question better?
2   matters of purpose – in relation to what selves and whose selective interests is a proposed answer better than alternatives? and
3   matters of power – from the perspective of whose judgments, what standards and practices, and whose abilities to act, institutionalize, and authorize those judgments is a given belief warranted?

When these links are made explicitly, pragmatism becomes genealogical.

From the valued to the valuable

James's stress on truth as a value is paralleled by Dewey's account of philosophy as criticism concerning values. Philosophy, Dewey wrote in the final chapter of *Experience and Nature*, "is inherently criticism":

Criticism is discriminating judgment, careful appraisal, and judgment is appropriately termed criticism wherever the subject-matter of discrimination concerns goods or values. ... Primitive innocence does not last. Enjoyment ceases to be a datum and becomes a problem. As a problem, it implies intelligent inquiry into the conditions and consequences of a value-object; that is, criticism.

(Dewey 1985 [1925]: 298)

Upon what conditions do specific values, enjoyments and sufferings, depend? How can those conditions be secured and extended? How can specific values be deepened and intensified? To what further enjoyments and frustrations do these enjoyments lead, and how are they, in turn, valued? What alternatives can be imagined, invented, and pursued? In this light, what values become in specific contexts valuable? These questions go to the heart of Dewey's conception of philosophy: "We are criticizing, not for its own sake, but for the sake of instituting and perpetuating more enduring and extensive values" (Dewey 1985 [1925]: 302).

It is important to be clear about what exactly is being criticized when one philosophizes pragmatically. Criticism, Dewey wrote, is discrimination, judgment, appraisal about subject matters that concern values – not about values themselves, but about subject matters that concern values. Values themselves, values as occurrences, values as they are had and undergone, values as existences, are simply qualitatively immediate. They are experienced rather than known.

As such, Dewey repeatedly pointed out, they cannot be reflected on or theorized about. Does this mean criticism is impossible? No, as Dewey explained in a crucial passage:

After the first dumb, formless experience of a thing as a good, subsequent perception of the good contains at least a germ of critical reflection. For this reason, and only for this reason, elaborate and formulated criticism is subsequently possible. The latter, if just and pertinent, can but develop the reflective implications found within appreciation itself. ... Criticism is reasonable and to the point, in the degree in which it extends and deepens these factors of intelligence found in immediate taste and enjoyment.

(Dewey 1985 [1925]: 300)[1]

Beginning with experiences of values, criticism is inquiry into the relations that give rise to, and issue from, this experience. This inquiry is not a method for finding values in experience, because, as might be thought, values antedate and are presupposed by critical inquiry. Instead, this inquiry is a method for making values in belief, making the valuable. Critical inquiry thus is transformative: it turns the valued into the valuable. The valuable is a consequence produced by, not an antecedent revealed by, critical inquiry.

Now, just as both James and Dewey repeatedly say that truth, for pragmatists, is an affair of truths, plural truths, multiple truths, a collection of truths, so too critical inquiry is an affair of plural, multiple, collected inquiries, appraisals, discriminations. Landscapers, medical doctors, economists and financial planners, to pick a few examples from a nearly endless list, all deal with the antecedent and eventual causal relations of immediate values of particular experiences.

To say that all these inquirers employ a common, shared "method of intelligence" is just to say that they all proceed as best they can according to the practices that so far have been found to be most effective in solving the many different problems they face. For careful pragmatists, intelligence and science are just "class-names" for all sorts of definite, fallible, best available, never final inquiries that relatively significantly secure "working-values in experience." The method of intelligence is a method only in the abstract – and in the rather rarely expedient abstract at that.

From criticism to multiple criticisms

How is inquiry into the conditions and consequences of immediate value distinctively critical? Is criticism anything different from, or more than, employing an understanding of the causal relations of immediate values – and thus funding the subsequent appreciations of these values?

And, how is philosophy, among all these many inquiries, any sort of criticism at all? Like most literature and unlike most science, it seems to investigate very little, if at all, causal relations "found only by search into the antecedent and the eventual." Is there anything expedient or pragmatic or true about philosophy?

If criticism really is something more than determination of causal relations, and if philosophy really undertakes this something more, it won't be found in the pure, clear, noble abstractions and "skinny outlines" of the thinkers James called rationalists, monists, absolutists, and ultra-abstractionists. Look instead, James said, in "the rich thicket of reality."

OK. In my three-acre backyard in Pennsylvania that rich thicket is a dense strip of trees on either side of a small stream. My family and I, from the moment we arrived after many years living in the Northwest, have walked through these deciduous woods under the high canopy of branches and leaves, listening to birds breaking the silence, stepping over the undergrowth sheltering wildflowers, sometimes spotting as many as fifty deer and sometimes following their tracks in the snow. These are experiences of appreciation and enjoyment, aesthetic experiences, consummations.

However, just as Dewey wrote, a brief course in experience enforced reflection; enjoyment became a problem. Subsequent perception of the good contained a germ of critical reflection: the walks seemed to be followed by terrible rashes and blisters and allergic reactions. One of our neighbors, Divya, is a medical doctor, and she diagnosed the cause as substantial contact with poison oak or poison ivy or poison sumac, and she prescribed various ointments, tablets, and shots with long needles. This criticism – an inquiry into causes – extended and deepened our experience of these rashes and blisters, and we became very good at differentiating the first signs of poison oak, ivy, and sumac, from heat rash, hives, insect bites, and minor abrasions and irritations.

Of course, this inquiry also transformed our experience in walking through the woods. We came to view the walks as games of chance. My son, who likes to fish, began to call it "trolling for poison oak." We asked Eric who mows our yard and does landscaping work for several people in the neighborhood to see what could be done. He identified thickets of poison sumac and dozens of huge poison oak vines along the ground and climbing high into trees they were beginning to choke. He said he thought he could eliminate the poison sumac and poison oak in two years by cutting and uprooting them in the late winters, applying organic pesticides in the springs and early summers, using some tarps to smother new growth, and planting in autumns some native willow bushes and mountain laurel that would crowd out the poison sumac and oak. He cautioned that this would not be inexpensive and that some of the trees choked by poison oak vines might die anyway. And, he insisted that it most likely would not work unless he also did this work on the neighboring woods to the north.

My neighbors on the north, Nigel and Kata, are economists. They don't have any interest in walking in the woods, but they thought it would help their property value to eradicate the poison sumac and oak, and so we all agreed to hire Eric. It took him three seasons instead of two to succeed totally, but the poison sumac and oak are now gone. Unlike Nigel and Kata, I carefully watched Eric's work as much as I could, and sometimes worked with him. I understand why and where he chopped, uprooted, sprayed, or covered with a tarp – though I do not understand just how the organic pesticide worked. I understand why and where he planted competitor shrubs, and how he sought to alter the limestone soil and sunlight conditions to discourage any return of these poison plants. I can see the markings on the bark of maples where the poison oak vines twisted, deformed, and choked. And when my family walks at dusk, we now often see wild turkeys on the ground and in low branches, and understand that they had avoided the area because the poison oak vines provided too little space for their wide wingspan.

Eric's inquiry into causes and consequences is criticism because it takes immediate possession of values not as an occurrence but as a problem, because it develops the reflective implications found within possession and appreciation, and because it extends and deepens these factors of intelligence in later experience. In order to extend and deepen factors of intelligence in experience, the results of criticism have to fund subsequent experience. This does not mean that results of inquiry are applied externally to experience, but rather that they enter into experience in its new immediacies. To pay someone to eradicate poison plants that you have never encountered in woods that you have never entered may be to better secure your property's value, but it is barely to extend and deepen experience and barely to engage in criticism. Inquiry that does not fund experience is not criticism.

Of course, not all criticism is philosophy. In fact, very little criticism is philosophy. Landscaping, for example, is not philosophy – fortunately for landscapers and their clients. Eric gave me an estimate for the cost of his work, but of course he could not tell me if I could afford to pay for it. It may be tempting to say that his landscaper inquiries produced only instrumental knowledge, only knowledge about means rather than ends. Pragmatism, via its insistence on means–ends continuums and fierce opposition to value dualisms, resists and rejects this temptation. Eric's inquiries did not merely make use of new instrumentalities. Rather, they effected new consummations. We now walk differently the different woods.

Nigel and Kata, my neighbor economists, probably could have counseled me about whether I could afford to hire Eric for this purpose. They teach principles of economics and personal finance and financial planning. No doubt they could have helped me budget well this expense and understand more fully not just the price but also any lost investment income, opportunity costs, tax implications should I sell my home, and so on. This is the kind of inquiry characteristic of their specialization in their profession. But even Nigel and Kata could not tell me, assuming I could hire Eric, whether or not I should hire him. If it is tempting here again to say that an economist's inquiries produce only instrumental knowledge – that economists know the price of everything and the value of nothing – then here too this temptation must be rejected. To understand that paying a landscaper is not just paying to eradicate poison sumac and poison oak but, for example, holding on to a ten-year-old car for another three years is to undergo – immediately have – different experience.

But, should I have hired Eric to make my woods safe for human walking? Or would it have been better to use the money to buy new books on philosophy and economics at philosophy meetings. Or should I have made a donation to a local charity that provides housing for battered women and children? Or should I have provided financial support to advance the agendas of Aryan Nation and Neo-Nazi groups? If I had decided to do any of these things, there are expert inquirers, such as landscapers and economists, with their expert methods of intelligence ready to tell me how best to do them, what is necessary for the highest chance of success, and what longer range consequences most reasonably would follow.

But if landscapers and medical doctors and economists and others do not engage in the kind of criticism that determines which of these, or other, options I should pursue, then is there some other kind of criticism that does address this sort of issue?

From hierarchy to difference

Expert in special pleading, philosophers frequently have viewed philosophy as some other kind of criticism, some other kind of intelligence, some wisdom other than knowledge, something higher and more useful in its uselessness than the concerns of landscapers and doctors and economists. By contrast, James and Dewey viewed philosophy as criticism that is not different in kind or higher in principle than other critical inquiries. I would like to push pragmatism further in this direction.[2]

In this context, Dewey made three important points about philosophy as criticism. First, he wrote that philosophy is "criticism of criticism," distinctive among other modes of criticism not in principle but only in its generality (Dewey 1985 [1925]: 298). This is frequently quoted but rarely explicated or assessed. What does it mean? As criticism, by Dewey's own definition, this would mean that philosophy seeks to determine antecedents and eventualities, causal relations. But, the causal relations of what? Well, the causal relations of other kinds of inquiry. What conditions brought about the development of particular critical inquiries in landscaping – or medicine, or economics, or liberalism or sexuality? What subjects, interests, practices, institutions, in turn, do these critical inquiries produce?

This view usefully renders philosophical criticism simultaneously genealogical and instrumental in its orientation. But does it render philosophical criticism more general than other forms of criticism? Is a critical study of other modes of criticism more general than a critical study of soils, viral infections, or markets? It would be more accurate, I think, to say simply that this kind of criticism is different from other modes of criticism, just as they are different from it; they all have different subject matters. To say that philosophy is the most general mode of criticism is to give in to fading nostalgia for the view of philosophy as Queen of the Sciences. I think pragmatism now can be more modest, more democratic, and more embracing of difference.

Second, Dewey wrote that philosophical criticism is not different in principle from science and literature. At the same time, philosophy is not science, as some modernists would have it, or literature, as some postmodernists would like it to be. Rather, its "discourse partakes both of scientific and literary discourse" (Dewey 1985 [1925]: 304ff). It is like literature, Dewey explained, in its aim and in its lack. Its primary aim is clarification, liberation, and extension of the values already in "the naturally generated functions of experience." Its primary lack is any "stock of information or body of knowledge peculiarly its own" and, thus, "no private access to good" except "the good diffused in human experience." But here, Dewey continued, philosophy parts with literature. It does not seek to "vivify in imagination" experienced goods. It is not fiction, and its focus is not language or vocabularies. It does not take a "linguistic turn." Instead, it has what Dewey called a "stricter task." It is criticism, appraisal of relations, and its focus is experience. Dewey wrote: philosophy "has to appraise values by taking cognizance of their causes and consequences. ... If its eventual concern is to render goods more coherent, more secure and more significant in appreciation, its road is the subject matter of natural existence as science discovers and depicts it" (Dewey 1985 [1925]: 305).

This sharp separation between literature and science is far, far too sharp, and it underplays the role of imagination in philosophy. Still this connection of philosophy to literature in aim, and connection of philosophy to science in critical method is a largely promising if incomplete (and not side-effect free) antidote to post-Deweyan versions of pragmatism that reduce philosophy to conversation, academic quibbles, and professional chest puffings and poundings cut off from inquiry. These impractical pragmatisms leave us with appeals to experienced values separated from the cultural resources for reconstructing them.

Third, Dewey characterized philosophy as criticism of criticism as a counter-force to professional and institutional forces that isolate and petrify goods. Philosophy, he contended, must become "a generalized medium of intercommunication," "an all around translation from one separated region of experience into another": "Thus philosophy as a critical organ becomes in effect a messenger, a liaison officer, making reciprocally intelligible voices speaking provincial tongues, and thereby enlarging as well as rectifying the meanings with which they are charged" (Dewey 1985 [1925]: 306). Dewey was right to worry about the effects of institutionalized professionalism and specialization, though I think their production of specific new values is more problematic than their compartmentalization of existing ones.[3]

Nonetheless, his remedy is also worrisome for three reasons. First, there is no reason to think that different regions of experience always or generally can be translated from one into another. Indeed, because different regions of experience – say, landscaping, medicine, and economics – have their own distinctive qualitative immediacies, there is reason to think that, to the extent they are different, they cannot be wholly translated to other regions. Moreover, even if they somehow always could be translated into one another, why would it be good always to strive to do this? In concrete cases – say Eric, Divya, and Nigel and Kata – this might have no expedience and no point. Consider this notion of omni-translatable experience. Surely here is a value sorely in need of criticism. What are its historical sources, how is it used, and what are its political effects?

Second, no criticism – not even pragmatic criticism – can be merely a medium of communication, and no philosophy can be merely a method. There simply is no value-free medium or content-free method. Translation is always in part selective transformation, reconstruction, revaluation, emphasis, and violence. As Dewey stressed elsewhere, a critical philosophy must acknowledge, not deny, this selective emphasis.

Third, when philosophers or any other critics do this, they must realize that any effort to make provincial tongues mutually intelligible is itself the work and hope of a provincial tongue – their own tongue, a different tongue, perhaps, but one no less provincial and no less bound up with specific uses, purposes, and powers. Experience, as James recognized, has a way of "boiling over" any philosophy, even a pragmatism, that proclaims otherwise. But a pragmatism, as Dewey (without Bentley) observed, that extends and deepens factors of intelligence identified in experience – identified in our always provincial, always local thickets of experiences – such a pragmatism can be reasonable and to the point. It can even be good for definite, assignable reasons.

Notes

1   Criticism is possible, on Dewey's view, because criticism draws on, and is based in, experience. Criticism thus has a historical basis, but no logical foundation. This means that we may be able to transform through intelligence the experiences and values of those with whom we initially disagree. It also means that there is no guarantee that we can do this, and also that those who hold views other than our own – even radically other views – are not necessarily illogical in maintaining their views. Finally, it means that whether intelligence is valued and what counts as intelligence is a function of matters of use and purpose and power.
2   See Stuhr 2003: 167–205.
3   See Stuhr 1997: ch. 1.

Bibliography

James, William (1979 [1907]) *Pragmatism, The Works of William James*, Cambridge, MA: Harvard University Press, p. 32.

Dewey, John (1985 [1925]) *Experience and Nature, John Dewey: The Later Works, 1925–1953*, vol. 1, ed. Jo Ann Boydston, Carbondale, IL: Southern Illinois University Press, p. 298.

Stuhr, John J. (1997) *Genealogical Pragmatism: Philosophy, Experience, and Community*, Albany: State University of New York Press, chapter 1.

——— (2003) *Pragmatism, Postmodernism, and the Future of Philosophy*, New York and London: Routledge, pp. 167–205.

15 Corrigibilism without solidarity

Isaac Levi

Charles Peirce declared himself a fallibilist. John Dewey elaborated on the hope-lessness of the quest for certainty. And although William James acknowledged that we can have knowledge we can never know for certain when we have it.

Contemporary commentators (e.g. Menand 2001) have taken such remarks as expressions of an attitude towards uncertainty that, in my opinion, conflicts with one of the distinctive insights that all three classical pragmatists endorsed.

When Peirce came out for fallibilism, he did not mean that his current beliefs might be false but rather that he might change his current beliefs for good reason. The two claims are quite different.

I am absolutely certain there is an Indian reservation near to Brantford, Ontario. I rule out the logical possibility that the reservation at Brantford is nonexistent. In James's terminology, that logical possibility is not alive. It is dead. I have no living doubt that it is true.

At the same time, I do not rule out the logical possibility that new consid-erations will surface in the future that will warrant me changing my mind. Of course, I now am convinced that if this should happen, I will make a mistake. Yet, if I should change my mind and come to believe that there is no reserva-tion near Brantford, I will then become certain of the truth of my new conviction.

I prefer to call what Peirce termed "fallibilism" corrigibilism. A fallibilist denies that inquirers should be absolutely certain of current extralogical beliefs. All propositions are conjectures that are more or less probable. According to my terminology, Peirce was an epistemological infallilibilist and a corrigibilist.[1]

I understand James to be emphasizing the revisability of our doctrines when he claims that we can never be certain when we have knowledge. The quest for certainty that Dewey took to be a will of the wisp is a quest for beliefs immune from future criticism. Dewey insisted that points of view may be so settled that they can serve as resources for subsequent inquiry. They are not so settled that they are immune to emendation in future inquiry (Dewey 1938).

That the classical pragmatists were committed to a distinction between fallibilism and corrigibilism is evidenced by the most original component of the views that they shared in common.

Peirce insisted that efforts to justify or explain current beliefs that characterize epistemology since Descartes ought to be abandoned. Insofar as we should be concerned with justifying belief, the concern ought to be focused on justifying changes in belief. Inquirers ought to be concerned with justifying replacing doubt by full belief and presumably with replacing full belief with doubt. Moreover, justification for changes in belief ought to be grounded in the methods and information currently free of living doubt. Both James and Dewey shared this interest in redirecting the focus of epistemology.

According to this view, the current point of view relative to which changes in point of view are to be assessed is judged true with as much certainty as is needed to qualify as an evidential basis for inquiry currently undertaken. Epistemological infallibilism is presupposed by the belief–doubt model just as is corrigibilism.

Dewey sought to extend this preoccupation with justifying changes in belief to justifying changes in points of view in ethics, politics, in approaching the creation and critical evaluation of works of art.

Dewey, for example, insisted that moral struggle to acquire the resolve needed to fulfil what are antecedently recognized to be one's moral obligations receives an undeservedly lion's share of attention from moralists, politicians, therapists and philosophers. The attention is excessive not because of the absence of questions that in a given context are more or less non-controversially answered. Too often, however, the answers are prepackaged according to allegedly secure incorrigible moral principles backed by reason or the solutions are derived from moral intuitions that to the skeptic seem (rightly in my view) to express uncritically accepted prejudice. Neither moral intuition nor pure practical reason secures the settlement of moral judgment concerning much more than moral truisms.

The neglected issue concerns how to engage in inquiry to remove doubts as to what one's moral obligations are. Like Berlin and Williams, Dewey was a value pluralist who insisted on the multidimensional aspect of the value commitments of individual agents. Such value commitments, however, are liable to come into conflict just as Berlin and Williams later acknowledged. But unlike Berlin and Williams, Dewey thought that the conflicts that arise are the occasions of moral inquiries quite unlike the efforts to overcome original sin that confronts us, for example, when we seek to conform to the diet we know we ought to follow. In such cases, therapy aimed at getting us to do what we know we ought to do and not inquiry seeking to determine what we ought to do is the order of the day. Occasions of moral conflict are occasions of "real and living doubt" and call for removal of doubt through inquiry just as surely as do doubts about the chemical composition of the Sun. The structure of the inquiry and the character of the doubt may differ from the scientific case in some respects; but in broad outline there should be important similarities.

Similar observations apply mutatis mutandis to Dewey's view of politics. He wrote: "If we look in the wrong place for the public we shall never locate the state" (Dewey 1954: 37). According to Dewey, the problem of "discovering the state" is a "practical problem." It concerns assessing "the degree of organization of the public which is attained" and "the degree in which its officers are so constituted as to perform their function of caring for the public interests."

> But there is no a priori rule which can be laid down and by which when it is followed a good state will be brought into existence. ... The formation of states must be an experimental process. The trial process may go on with diverse degrees of blindness and accident, and at the cost of unregulated procedures of cut and try, of fumbling and groping, without insight into what men are after or clear knowledge of a good state even when it is achieved. Or it may proceed more intelligently, because guided by knowledge of the conditions which must be fulfilled. But it is still experimental. And since conditions of action and of inquiry and knowledge are always changing, the experiment must always be retried. The state must always be rediscovered. ... The belief in political fixity, of the sanctity of some form of state consecrated by the efforts of our fathers and hallowed by tradition, is one of the stumbling-blocks in the way of orderly and directed change; it is an invitation to revolt and revolution.
>
> (Dewey 1954: 33–34)

One should change one's view in order to address some difficulty, doubt or problem. The change in point of view may concern one's judgments concerning what is true, one's goals, one's judgments of value including what is better than what, and what, all things considered, ought to be done in a given context of deliberation. More generally, any change in attitude that may come up for critical reflection could be grist for problem solving inquiry.

Jeffords inadvertently stumbled into moral inconsistency because initially he was convinced that the obligation to be a loyal member of the Republican Senatorial Party and the further obligation to keep the faith with his commitment to education, medical care issues, etc. could both be satisfied. In the past, he may have been convinced that the options he faced in political decisions could be evaluated in a manner consonant with both his commitment to the Republican party and to his political projects. Contrary to his initial expectations, the facts as he came to see them did not support the joint implementability of his several value commitments.[2]

Jeffords needed to change his beliefs about the facts just as Michelson did when he obtained a null result in his initial experiments with the interferometer. Both Jeffords and Michelson needed to adjust in order to save consistency. But Jeffords also needed to alter his value commitments. He could no longer require that the evaluation of the options he faced satisfy the demands of the Republicans and his political projects. He could suspend judgment in the sense that he could recognize the demands of the Republicans as a permissible way of evaluating his options and recognize the demands of his projects in education, on the environment and medical care as a permissible standard for evaluating his options. From that perspective, he was in a position to inquire as to whether he should rule out one of these permissible standards or the other or pursue some other standard that somehow qualifies as a potential resolution between the two. He could do this without begging any questions.

Dewey's brand of value pluralism thus integrates well with the belief–doubt model of inquiry extended to questions of value and with an insistence on separating infallibilism from incorrigibilism. A value pluralist of Dewey's persuasion can endorse value commitments with full and sincere conviction and no shred of doubt. Nonetheless, the value pluralist can inadvertently confront a situation that clashes with these convictions and find him- or herself with good reason to call into doubt several elements of such commitments. And Dewey claimed that through inquiry, one might hope to remove the doubt subsequently and, in that sense, to resolve the conflict.

There is, to be sure, one respect in which moral inquiry so conceived seems to differ from inquiry where the output is a change in doxastic commitments. In practical deliberation, choice is often peremptory. Yet properly conducted inquiry takes time. No preestablished harmony can guarantee that deliberating agents will have the opportunity to resolve conflicts before the moment of choice.

Existentialists, behaviorists and subjectivist Bayesians all agree that the peremptoriness of choice requires that the agent create his or her preference by his or her choice whether or not the agent has had the opportunity to obtain and sift through all the considerations relevant to his or her deliberation. This view supports the idea that inquiry aimed at resolving conflict can be replaced by existential choice.

Pragmatists should resist this idea. Choice theoretic machismo is a poor substitute for inquiry. If we cannot identify options as being for the best all things considered, we may have to make a decision. But we don't have to pretend that what we have chosen is for the best when we have no basis for doing so.

If Jeffords had to reach a decision without having abandoned his loyalty to the Republican Party or to his legislative agenda, he should have had to declare that his choice was not for the best because there is no best. To have to make a choice without having removed all doubts is tantamount to making a choice without having eliminated all conflict. And that is equivalent to making a decision without choosing for the best all things considered.

Dewey is indeed a value pluralist. There is no single standard of value as utilitarians or cognate theorists insist that reduces all ignorance concerning what ought to be done to ignorance of non-evaluative facts. Nor is there a system of moral principles hierarchically organized so that, in case two or more of them conflict in their recommendations, instructions are already prepackaged as to what overrides what. It is this value pluralism that provides much of the motivation for Dewey's view of moral inquiry as moral problem solving and sharply differentiates it from the pluralism of Berlin and Williams.

What would an implementation of the extension of Dewey's belief–doubt model to changes in values look like? In the scientific context, pragmatists claim that we seek to fix belief and thereby to remove doubt. The beliefs currently held are judged true and, indeed, certainly true. There is no serious possibility that they are false. There are potential beliefs, however, that are conjectures – candidate potential answers to questions inquirers take seriously. Analytic philosophers ask whether such "propositions" carry truth-values according to the pragmatist view. Peirce and James explicitly answered in the affirmative. They acknowledged that such propositions might be true and might be false and could not be anything else. And I think that Dewey would have endorsed a similar position had he deigned to answer it.

Unfortunately in the current climate, the issue is not so trivial. For a potential belief (a proposition) to carry a truth-value, it must be coherent for an inquirer to suspend judgment as to its truth, to judge it possible or impossible, to impute a probability to it (whether numerically determinate or not), to attribute a value to its being true. The nontriviality of this point emerges when we consider propositional attitudes other than truth. Frank Ramsey (1990) famously and correctly noted that judgments of probabilistic degrees of belief lack truth-values. L.J. Savage (1954) showed that one cannot coherently assign "higher order" probabilities to judgments of subjective probability. Similar qualitative arguments may be advanced for showing that one cannot assign probabilities to judgments of serious possibility, or to judgments of utility.

I cannot enter into the details of these arguments here. It is important to emphasize that the difficulty in suspending judgment with respect to the truth of value judgments and assigning subjective probabilities to them sustains the view embraced by a variety of expressivists and emotivists in ethics, that judgments of value lack truth-values. In this respect, desires and values are no different than doxastic attitudes like degrees of belief or judgments of serious possibility.

On the other hand, the outlook that emerges undermines the widely held view (endorsed by Williams and by emotivists and expressivists) that there is a fundamental difference between theoretical rationality (associated with belief) that is related to objective truth, and practical rationality that is not. Doxastic attitudes, like probability judgments, and conative and evaluative attitudes, like preferences, for the most part, lack truth-values. Degree of belief and desire are in the same boat.

The main exception is full belief. I do not claim that the classical pragmatists recognized this fact. But they certainly were in favor of an integrated understanding of practical and theoretical rationality. Science differs from what Dewey called "common sense" in its goals. As a consequence, it also differs in its methods. But insofar as rationality plays a role, it is means–ends rationality in both cases. That is to say, it is practical rationality.

Now the significance of the exceptional status of full belief is this. Inquirers can, in changing full beliefs, seek to avoid error. As James correctly pointed out, it is not a good idea to avoid error to the exclusion of all other considerations; for then one should never remove doubt. One needs some incentive to risk error. In some contexts, it is seeking explanations. In others, it is making predictions. In others it is seeking cures for diseases, etc. Information that in the context of the particular problematic is judged relevant and important provides the incentive. So the common feature of the proximate goals of particular efforts to change belief is to seek new error-free information.

Peirce placed great emphasis on seeking the true, complete story of the world at the End of Days as the ultimate aim of inquiry. I have argued elsewhere that this view is disastrous for Peirce's own pragmatism and should be abandoned, as it was I believe by Dewey.

But Dewey seems to have thrown out the baby with the bathwater. Avoiding error still matters! It remains possible for pragmatists to respect the concern to avoid the importation of false belief into the evolving doctrine as part of a proximate aim of inquiry. Both Peirce and James either did endorse such respect or could have done so consonant with what they wrote. Dewey is a more vexing case.

Dewey was concerned to extend the belief–doubt model of inquiry to issues of ethics, politics, art and culture. His concern was neither "to raise the rest of culture to the epistemological level of the natural sciences" nor "to level down the natural sciences to an epistemological par with art, religion and politics" (Rorty 1991: 36.) This vision of raising or lowering epistemological levels is one that Richard Rorty has sought to impose on the pragmatists and most notably on Dewey. Rorty used to speak of the leveling down of the natural sciences and attributed such a view to Dewey. Now he somewhat grudgingly admits that this might not be historically accurate. What he does not admit, however, is that, for Dewey, the question was not the jejeune issue of raising or lowering levels at all. It is not a question of academic pecking order.

What is true is that the pragmatists thought that both scientific inquiry and other forms of intellectual deliberation are, when well conducted, efforts to find optimal solutions for the problems under investigation. What Dewey saw is that value commitments may become legitimate targets for inquiry aimed at removing doubts. This does not mean that the goals of science, morality, art, politics, etc. are all the same. A fortiori the methods cannot be the same. But the kind of intelligence or rationality that ought to govern one kind of activity or another exhibits a similar structure that it is important to emphasize.

The apparent obstacle to this vision is that value commitments and the value judgments that express them do not seem to carry truth-values. Dewey in point of fact sometimes denied this and Rorty has insisted that one can allow attributions of truth-values to value judgments satisfying Tarski-like requirements.

But can one suspend judgment concerning the truth or falsity of value judgments? Can one judge them probable in varying degrees in a coherent manner? I have offered an account of how an agent might suspend judgment between rival ways of evaluating options. But this suspense is not suspense with respect to truth-value. And the rival ways of evaluation cannot be judged to be more or less probable.

Seeking to avoid error requires taking risk or probability of error seriously. Inquirers do not risk error in changing their probability judgments on the information available. They do not risk error in changing their values either. But, by their own lights, they risk error in adding new beliefs to their evolving doctrines.

To give an account of how changes in value commitments and probability judgments can be justified that identifies avoidance of error as a goal of efforts to make such changes thus becomes incoherent.

Now Dewey was justly famous for urging that "the fundamental unity of the structure of inquiry in common sense and in science be recognized, their difference being one in the problems with which they are directly concerned, not their logics" (1938: 79). The "fundamental unity" Dewey is urging here is not that of a standardized program for problem solving. The methods that will work well in solving certain kinds of problems may work poorly in solving others. There is no "scientific method" for Dewey any more than there was for Peirce that was common to all of the sciences and to the activities of use and enjoyment that Dewey called common sense. The scientific method that Dewey was constantly touting was what he called the logic shared by the structure of all well conducted inquiries.

All problem-solving inquiry concerns the adaptation of means to ends. The common logic or method, if one likes, concerns the minimal requirements for practical rationality in such goal directed activity. Thus, all problem solving activity involves clarifying the goals to be satisfied in solving a problem, identifying potential solutions to a problem, exploring ways to assess the relative merits of potential solutions and coming to a judgment as to which solution to adopt. These are among the common features shared by scientific inquiry, the creation of works of art and moral struggle. But Dewey never denied that there are differences in these activities as well as similarities. Intellectual anarchists like Feyerabend and pseudo-pragmatists like Rorty profess to be against method. Rorty chastises Dewey and Sidney Hook for a certain "scientism" that heaps encomia on the scientific method. But, of course, Dewey and Hook alike understood well that addressing different types of problems calls for adopting different methods and procedures. The methods of physics and biology clearly differ. The methods of both differ from the techniques employed in economics, sociology, history and literature, painting, politics, and entrepeneurial activities. Dewey thought it urgent to emphasize, however, the commonalities in the structures of such deliberations and inquiries.

To maintain that a common feature of the goals of inquiries aimed at modifying full beliefs – i.e., judgments of truth – is a concern to avoid error is quite compatible with denying that avoidance of error is a feature of other types of problem solving activity. Dewey, the value pluralist, could have readily acknowledged avoidance of error as a cognitive value ingredient in certain kinds of activities that is not reducible to economic, political, moral, aesthetic or other values. He could have done so without compromising the anti-reductionist and pluralistic attitude he so famously espoused.

But unlike both Peirce and James he did not do so. Scientific inquiry for Dewey was instrumental to the concerns of use and enjoyment. But scientific inquiry had no autonomous aims independent of the aims of common sense. Dewey failed to take seriously the concern to avoid the importation of false belief into one's evolving doctrine as a desideratum of inquiry. Rorty admires this aspect of Dewey. But this attitude is a reductionist and anti-pluralistic one hostile to attitudes that both Dewey and Rorty seek to inculcate. Why not concede that in some important problem solving activity avoidance of error is a desideratum irreducible to the other concerns of use and enjoyment?

However, if some changes in values do not involve importing new beliefs, in such changes there can be no issue of risk of error. If avoidance of error is not a concern in changing judgments of value that do not entail changes in judgments of full belief, a certain problem arises. Inquiry aimed at removing doubts about values involves removing ways of evaluating options as permissible for use in decision making. The more we remove, the more doubt is eliminated. What will deter us from going all the way and removing all ways of evaluating options as better or worse?

We may point out that one desideratum we may have in such inquiries is to avoid incoherence. This suggests that we should rule out as an option removing all ways of evaluation as permissible. But this desideratum leaves us with the recommendation that we remove all but one way of evaluating options as permissible. This is better than encouraging incoherence; but not by much. It encourages opinionation even in situations when there is no basis for ruling out one way of ruling out all but one option over another.

Responding that we should privilege a ranking that is settled or that is relatively so will not do. Such an alternative is not open to us here because we are in a setting where the agent or community is in doubt as to which of many rankings to privilege.

Nor can we take into account risk of error, for, as just pointed out, the ways of evaluation are neither true nor false. There is no good sense to the notion of risk of error.

By leaving the Republican Party, Jeffords abandoned a lifelong network of personal associations he held dear. But by betraying his environmental causes, he will forfeit the trust of his constituents. Perhaps the resolution of his conflict should be based on a decision to embrace "solidarity" with the point of view of one community rather than another. According to Rorty, pragmatists ground the "objectivity" of their views in solidarity with a community. "For pragmatists, the desire for objectivity is not the desire to escape the limitations of one's community, but simply the desire for as much intersubjective agreement as possible, the desire to extend the reference of 'us' as far as we can" (Rorty 1991: 23).

This is the view that Rorty himself sometimes calls "postmodernist" (1991: 198–199). He seems to think of Dewey as being a postmodernist ahead of his time. But this is surely a mistake. Whether in scientific inquiry, moral deliberation, the creation of works of art or anywhere where there is genuine doubt as to what to believe or do, the decision facing the inquirer does not, in general, concern with which of several communities to form solidarity. Nor is the pragmatic inquirer seeking in such inquiries to extend consensus as far as possible.

What is true is that if X is concerned not only to fix X's belief but to justify X's conclusions to members of community Y, the initial body of settled beliefs will be constituted by relevant shared agreements between community Y and X. That is to say, X will have to pretend not to believe many things X takes for granted. But then the effort to remove doubt should be undertaken with the aim to obtaining information generally recognized as valuable while minimizing risk of error as evaluated from the shared initial viewpoint. X hopes that by pretending to have an open mind in this fashion, Y and X can come around to the conclusion X already endorses. It does not mean that should the joint inquiry come to a conclusion other than the one that X hopes will eventuate, X will or should genuinely convert from X's initial view for the sake of solidarity with the community.

When it comes to resolving conflicts in value, as in Jeffords' predicament, to suggest that it is merely a question of the community with which one identifies in the hope of maximizing agreement trivializes the issue. Leaving the Republican Party may, indeed, have been a genuine loss for Jeffords not to be dismissed. But surely that loss would be cheapened if it were incurred merely to join forces with another community. Jeffords had to somehow come to the conclusion that the values promoted by the conservationists override loyalty to the Republican Party. I say "conclusion" because in order to justify either to himself or to others that he should leave the party, the assumptions from which he began ought not to take for granted one of the issues under dispute. That is to say, even if we utilize Rorty's misleading way of speaking and identify Jeffords's decision as a choice between solidarity with one of two communities, neither of these communities is the community with which the inquirer has solidarity when reaching the decision. And neither of these communities is the community whose point of view yields a warrant for the decision Jeffords made. Once we see this, the issue of solidarity with a community drops out of the picture as a consideration to invoke in resolving doubts about values.

Is there any way to reason to a resolution of value conflict that avoids question begging? Dewey surely thought there was. Otherwise there would have been little point in moral inquiry. How should such reasoning be described? I wish I had a crisp answer. But I do not. And I am not sure I understand Dewey's answers well enough to explain them accurately.

We might rely on the distinction between those beliefs and value judgments the inquirer takes for granted and the values held in suspense to render a verdict. Jeffords had lived a long time as a loyal member of the Republican Party even though the prevailing tenor of the party was out of step with his own thinking. But, perhaps, he was prepared to stay as long as he entertained hope that he could ameliorate the policies to which he was opposed. When he lost that hope, he could still have concluded that loyalty to the party overrode his commitment to the environment, healthcare and education. But membership in the kind of party in which he could have no effective voice might have fit poorly with ideals of public service that he continued to take for granted. Becoming an Independent cohered better with these ideals. Perhaps the settled background provided in this way a warrant for bolting the party. As my colleague, Akeel Bilgrami has suggested, some value commitments held in doubt cohere better with the value commitments already taken for granted than others in some sense of "coherence" that can somehow be rendered intelligible.

Alternatively, engaging in the kind of moral *Gedankenexperimenten* with potential resolutions of value conflicts that Dewey sometimes contemplated might warrant a resolution of conflict.

I am not sure how to develop either of these lines of thinking in a well-structured way. What I do think, however, is that pursuing questions like this, giving them form and proposing tentative answers is a line of inquiry that is well worth pursuing.

Perhaps I have been too uncharitable to Rorty's notion of solidarity with a community. Both John Dewey and Charles Peirce could endorse as an ideal solidarity with a community of inquirers engaged in intelligently conducted problem solving inquiry. And Rorty appears to do the same.

But appearances are deceiving. For Dewey and Peirce, such solidarity amounts to a shared commitment to respond to difficulties with intelligently conducted inquiry. According to Rorty, such intelligently conducted problem solving inquiry attains "an appropriate mixture of unforced agreement with tolerant disagreement" (Rorty 1991: 41.) For a pragmatist, by way of contrast, intelligently conducted problem solving or adaptation of means to ends is not to be characterized in terms of the extent and quality of agreement and disagreement achieved.

Continued squandering of our energy resources might be an expression of an uncoerced consensus accompanied by tolerance of those who dissent. But the dissenters from this consensus may be convinced that this is not an intelligent adaptation of means to ends. Have they removed themselves thereby from the community of intelligent inquirers? In general, the intelligence with which problem solving inquiry is undertaken is only imperfectly correlated with the way agreement is reached and disagreement tolerated.

Rorty seems to think that toleration of dissent should be promoted because of our recognition of the fallibility of our views and our sense of solidarity with and, to that extent, respect for the dissenter. Such a view reflects the all too familiar tendency to conflate fallibility with corrigibility.

If each of us recognizes a difference between what is certainly true and settled and what is doubtful and possibly false while acknowledging that each of us draws the distinction differently, we should distinguish between two kinds of dissent. In the one case, we are certain that the dissenter is in error and recognize no reason good enough to change our minds. In the other case, the character of the views advanced or some merit in the dissenter may afford a justification for changing from firm refusal to take the dissenting view seriously to a position of suspense.

In the first case, the attitude taken to the dissenter's view is one of contempt. We put up with the dissenter's expression of his or her views out of politeness, friendship or refusal to engage in cruel repression. But we rule the dissenting views out as live alternatives. They receive no serious hearing. In the second case, sufficient respect for the dissenting views is achieved to warrant our opening up our minds.

Rorty's ideas about agreement and disagreement register no sensitivity to the difference between contemptuous toleration and respect. This insensitivity is an expression on the level of social interaction of an insensitivity to the distinction between fallibilism and corrigibilism.[3]

Pragmatists who insist on rejecting fallibilism while maintaining corrigibilism maintain that we may have contempt for the views of a dissenter because we have no doubt that his or her beliefs are false and values deplorable. But when the views of the dissenter somehow offer us a good reason to change our minds, they merit our respect.

Intelligently conducted inquiry such as the pragmatism of Peirce and Dewey understands it is a serious business. It is not always obvious when one should open up one's mind any more than it is when one should close it. The pragmatists saw that both kinds of change call for justification through intelligently conducted inquiry. Rorty's postmodernism, by way of contrast, eviscerates the most valuable insights of Peirce, James and Dewey in a manner that deprives us of the possibility of taking agreement, disagreement and inquiry very seriously at all.

Notes

1   In "What Pragmatism Is," *The Monist*, 15 (1905): 161–181 (reprinted in Peirce 1998: ch. 24), Peirce writes: "Now that which you do not at all doubt, you must regard as infallible, absolute truth" (1998: 336.) In spite of his official declaration of his view to be fallibilistic, Peirce explicitly endorsed infallibilism as I intend it here. First person commitment to the infallible truth of his or her views is not to be confused with the claim that he or she is an infallible oracle as the doctrine of the infallibility of the Pope claimed for the Pope speaking *ex cathedra*.

2   The motives I am attributing to Jeffords are speculation on my part. There are those who think that the sole issue of concern to him was a committee chairmanship. I have no way of knowing what went on in his mind. Even if it is true, however, that interest in a chairmanship played a role in his deliberations, it seems

unlikely to me that it was the sole value or interest involved. It is enough for the purpose of this illustration to suppose that he faced a conflict between several strands in his value commitments.

3   For more on this topic, see Levi 1997: ch. 12.

Bibliography

Dewey, John (1938) *Logic*, New York: Holt.

—— (1954) *The Public and Its Problems*, Chicago: Swallow Press.

Levi, I. (1986) *Hard Choices*, Cambridge: Cambridge University Press.

—— (1991) *The Fixation of Belief and Its Undoing*, Cambridge: Cambridge University Press.

—— (1997) *The Covenant of Reason*, Cambridge: Cambridge University Press.

Menand, L. (2001) *The Metaphysical Club*, New York: Farrar, Straus and Giroux.

Peirce, C.S. (1998) *The Essential Peirce*, vol. 2, ed. Houser *et al.*, Bloomington: Indiana University Press.

Ramsey, F.P. (1990) *Philosophical Papers*, ed. D.H. Mellor, Cambridge: Cambridge University Press.

Rorty, R. (1991) *Objectivity, Relativism and Truth*, Cambridge: Cambridge University Press.

Savage, L.J. (1954) *The Foundations of Statistics*, New York: Wiley.

Williams, B. (1973) *Problems of the Self*, Cambridge: Cambridge University Press.

—— (1981) *Moral Luck*, Cambridge: Cambridge University Press.

Part IV

Economic methodology

16 Pragmatism, knowledge, and economic science

Deweyan pragmatic philosophy and contemporary economic methodology[1]

D. Wade Hands

Introduction

This paper will examine the relationship between pragmatism – specifically the classical pragmatism of John Dewey – and economic methodology. I will argue that while pragmatism was relatively ill-suited for the self-defined tasks of mid-twentieth century economic methodology, those tasks have substantially broadened during the last few decades, and the changes that have taken place allow for pragmatic ideas to play a more important role in contemporary methodological debates than in the debates of a previous generation. In a sense the changes that have taken place within the field of economic methodology simply mirror substantive changes that have taken place within science theory more generally, and in order to understand the opportunity that currently exists for a pragmatic approach to economic methodology, it is necessary to understand the corresponding changes within contemporary science theory.

The chapter is divided into three parts. The first section discusses the changes that have taken place within science theory during the closing decades of the twentieth century and how these changes accommodate, and have increasingly allowed for the re-emergence of, pragmatic philosophical ideas. While it is important to understand these general developments, the discussion in this section will be relatively brief, in part because a thorough examination of such a wide-ranging subject would carry us far beyond the scope of the current chapter, but also because I have previously examined these issues in more detail (Hands 2001a). The second section turns from science theory in general to economics and economic methodology in particular. While recent developments within general science theory have reopened the door to pragmatic philosophical ideas, there are also a number of features specific to economic science that make its methodology particularly accommodating to the pragmatic turn. A few of these discipline-specific features will be the focus of the second section. The third section considers Dewey's political economy, focusing particularly on the fact that Deweyan ideas within economic methodology (the subject of the second section) can be separated from Dewey's particular ideas about the economy. While this topic certainly deserves a more careful examination, the purpose of the third section is simply to emphasize that it is possible to separate these two different sets of arguments and concerns. The final concluding section briefly summarizes the argument and reflects more generally on the subject of economics and pragmatic philosophy.

The pragmatic turn in contemporary science theory

The so-called Received View of scientific knowledge – or what Philip Kitcher (1993) aptly termed "Legend" – is of course far behind us. Not only does it no longer have the status of a "received" view, the empiricist-foundationalist version of the Legend that once dominated Anglo-American philosophy of natural science is increasingly being written out of the disciplinary history of modern philosophy. According to Nancy Cartwright, Thomas Uebel, and others (Cartwright *et al.* 1996; Uebel 1992) Otto Neurath never endorsed such a view; Michael Friedman (1999) adds another big-name positivist, Rudolf Carnap (and to a lesser extent Moritz Schlick), to the list of dissenters; and Malachi Hacohen (2000) joins other Popperians who deny that Karl Popper ever advocated anything like the Legend view of scientific knowledge. To add to the confusion, not only are most of the names being scratched off the membership roll of the Received View, the individual that had previously been given most of the credit for overthrowing the Legend – Thomas Kuhn – is now being described as much less revolutionary than previously believed (Fuller 2000). Despite these recent changes in the genealogy of the Received View, it remains the case that there was a fairly strong consensus within mid-twentieth century Anglo-American philosophy of natural science; it was positivist-inspired and broadly empiricist-foundationalist in epistemological focus; and it is now gone.

Of course there is more to science theory than the philosophy of natural science, and it is clear that alternative approaches to the subject of scientific knowledge have experienced an exponential growth during the years since the fall of the Legend. The sociology of scientific knowledge (including, but not restricted to, the Strong Program and Social Constructivism), Actor Network Theory, Reflexive Science and Technology Studies, Feminist Epistemology, various naturalistic approaches (including, but not restricted to, those drawing on evolutionary biology and cognitive science), the Rhetoric of Science, and even a few attempts to analyze the activities of natural scientists in terms of economic theory (what I have previously termed the Economics of Scientific Knowledge (Hands 1994a)), are but a few of the many post-positivist, but not philosophy of science-based, approaches to scientific knowledge that have emerged within the contemporary literature. While a small number of these views emphasize the radical debunking of the epistemic standing of science, most are not intent on undermining the cognitive position of scientific knowledge or the social position of the scientific community. For most contributors to the vast literature on contemporary science theory, the goal is still to understand the unique cognitive virtues of science; it is just that the Legend's demise has significantly transformed the framework, or intellectual terms of engagement, for arriving at such understanding. In general, most investigators are seeking some form of middle ground between the Received View and relativism; science is cognitively special, but it is not special because it can be justified on the basis of some (or any) version of empiricist-foundationalist philosophy of science.

Given the wide array of different approaches, interests, and concerns that are currently at work within science theory, it is very difficult to identify a small set of key features that adequately summarize this post-Legend literature. Nevertheless, despite these vast differences, if one paints with a relatively wide brush, it is possible to identify a few, very general, family resemblances that can be discerned among the wide variety of competing perspectives (at least among those that are actively seeking some kind of middle ground). I will mention four such family resemblances.

Perhaps the most important is that science is fundamentally social and must be understood in social terms. There are many different competing views about what it means to say that science is social – what "social" means, what sociality implies about scientific knowledge, scientific behavior, or scientific culture, as well as how it affects the proper approach to investigating science – but there is a general consensus that the social character of the scientific enterprise is fundamental to scientific knowledge and that any adequate view of scientific knowledge will need to recognize this sociality in a substantive way.

A second point of relative consensus concerns the way that one should approach the subject of scientific knowledge; again there is a vast array of specific approaches, but they all consider the actual practice of science to be essential to understanding scientific knowledge. For some this means studying the history of great science, for others conducting anthropological investigations of contemporary site-specific scientific practices, for still others examining the general characteristics of scientific culture, but in any case armchair a priori philosophizing about the essential character of scientific knowledge is no longer sufficient for the job of doing science theory (even among philosophers of natural science).

The third feature, and one that is clearly related to the previous two, is an inclination towards pluralism. This pluralism can also take a variety of different forms depending on the author's particular philosophical focus; but in almost every case, despite the wide variation in detail, there seems to be the agreement that science is not a single homogeneous thing, but a heterogeneous cluster of things (and for many authors an unstable and shape-shifting cluster of things). There may be broadly identifiable features of the behavior of scientists – or of the culture of science, or of the institutional structure of scientific communities – that differentiate scientific activities from other aspects of human culture, but they are generally recognized as much broader, more permeable, and more flexible, than the "demarcation criteria" traditionally provided by the philosophy of science. Science is many things, not one thing.

The fourth characteristic of science, and one that seems to be more controversial, is the emphasis on naturalism. There are a variety of ways that naturalism is interpreted within the contemporary literature, but in general it is the idea that science, or the scientific approach, should be employed in the investigation of scientific knowledge; that epistemological questions should be approached in some sense, like scientific questions. This might mean that insights from cognitive science regarding human belief acquisition, or biological models of evolutionary change, are employed in the investigation of how scientific beliefs are acquired or stabilized within the scientific community; it might be simply the idea that scientific knowledge is a phenomenon to be studied scientifically like any other natural phenomenon; or it might be the argument that since contemporary science seems to be so much more stable and reliable than contemporary philosophy, it is the latter that should be judged by the standards of the former (rather than vice versa) – but in any case science will be employed in the investigation of scientific knowledge.

Given these general features of, or family resemblances within, contemporary science theory, the revival of pragmatism is no surprise; these characteristics represent fertile ground for the germination of pragmatic ideas. Consider first the very idea that scientific knowledge is special and yet not justified on the basis of some version of foundationalism. This is exactly the characterization of scientific inquiry within classical pragmatism. Despite their differences on many subjects, Peirce, James, and Dewey all agreed that beliefs fixed by intelligent scientific means possessed value that was not possessed by beliefs fixed by other means (tradition-authority, tenacity, etc.) and that the world would be a better place if more beliefs were formed intelligently; and yet all three would also agree that philosophical positions that sought to "ground" knowledge on the basis of some set of absolutely certain, incorrigible, epistemological "foundations" (sensory, rational, or other) were an absolute dead end – not only a failure, but socially pernicious. Pragmatists not only believed that the scientific form of life was virtuous and sought to extend it into other areas of human culture, they also agreed that one of the main barriers to that extension was the foundationalist epistemic vision (or short-sightedness) that had dominated Western philosophy since the Greeks. For Dewey in particular, the origin of the idea that the fundamental philosophical problem was the question of mental "representation" – the mirror metaphor that asks how our thoughts and beliefs can accurately reflect an independent, objective, nature "out there" – was to be found in Greek slave society where the purified, true, and universal objects of knowing (by the elite) were radically separated from the earthly, instrumental, and practical objects/activities of doing (by slaves). The result was a spectator theory of knowledge: "the model of a spectator viewing a finished picture rather than after that of the artist producing a painting" (Dewey 1948 [1920]: 122–123). Western philosophy amounts to little more than one very long and unproductive excursus on this essentially representational characterization of the fundamental philosophical question. So for classical pragmatism, science was something special to be encouraged, but the spectator theory of knowledge (and thus the philosophy of science contingent upon it) needed to be overthrown; this view is shared by most contributors to contemporary science theory.

Not only does pragmatism sit comfortably with the general tenor of the current problem situation within the various fields that study scientific knowledge, it also shares the four more specific features listed above. The classical pragmatists all held that scientific knowledge (intelligence) was fundamentally social. While there were differences in detail – with Peirce perhaps going the farthest in extending sociality to a metaphysical vision – they all viewed the particular features that allowed for the development and extension of scientific intelligence (or instrumental reason, or cause-and-effect thinking, or experimental inquiry) to originate in, and be affected by, the inexorably social nature of human society and human existence. In Dewey's own words:

> philosophy held that ideas and knowledge were functions of a mind or consciousness which originated in individuals by means of isolated contact with objects. But in fact, knowledge is a function of association and communication; it depends upon tradition, upon tools and method socially transmitted, developed and sanctioned. Faculties of effectual observation, reflection and desire are habits acquired under the influence of the culture and institutions of society, not ready-made inherent powers.
>
> (Dewey 1991 [1927]: 158)

There is also convergence with respect to the second and third features, attention to the actual practice of science and pluralism. Of the three – Peirce, James, and Dewey – only Dewey lacked training as a scientist, and all three viewed their philosophical endeavors as an application of experimental reasoning gleaned from the actual practice of successful science: believing that their philosophical conclusions depended "upon an analysis of what takes place in the experimental inquiry of natural science" (Dewey 1929: 168). Obviously James and Dewey were committed pluralists (Peirce is more controversial); James is even credited with introducing the term "pluralism" into English-language philosophy (Menand 2001: 143). Not only were they some kind of pluralists, Dewey in particular, was a pluralist in essentially the way that pluralism has emerged within post-Legendary science theory. He separated the scientific attitude from the subject matters of the various sciences, and insisted that the scientific method did not imply there was but one science: "In the house which science might build there are many mansions" (Dewey 1970: 34).

Finally, there is the issue of naturalism, and here too the perspective of classical pragmatism corresponds nicely with contemporary developments. Although not every classical pragmatist endorsed "naturalized epistemology" in the narrow contemporary sense, they were all certainly naturalists in the broader sense of regarding human knowledge and intelligence as something to be explained as one would explain any other object of interest (i.e., scientifically). It is also clear that certain pragmatists (Dewey in particular) often did employ evolutionary biology in a more narrow sense – like contemporary "evolutionary epistemologists" (see Bradie 1986 for a survey) – as a naturalizing "base" for the characterization of human knowledge in general. Intelligence in the human mind has evolved, like any other feature of the human anatomy, to help us cope with our environment. Knowledge – like fins, horns, or an opposable thumb – is not about accurate mental representations; it is about helping us get on in the world. As Louis Menand summarizes Dewey's position:

> Philosophers, Dewey argued, had mistakenly insisted on making the problem of the relation between the mind and the world, an obsession that had given rise to what he called "the alleged discipline of epistemology" – the attempt to answer the question, How do we know? The pragmatist response to this question is to point out that nobody has ever made a problem about the relation between, for example, the *hand* and the world. The function of the hand is to help the organism cope with the environment; in situations in which a hand doesn't work, we try something else, such as a foot, or a fishhook, or an editorial. ... Dewey thought that ideas and beliefs are the same as hands: instruments for coping.
>
> (Menand 2001: 360–361, emphasis in original)

Pragmatism and economic methodology

Even if much of classical pragmatism is consistent with many of the recent developments within general science theory – or perhaps a different way of characterizing the situation is to say that science theory is now in a position to accept many of the pragmatic ideas from the late nineteenth and early twentieth centuries – this still leaves open the specific question of the relationship between pragmatic ideas and economic methodology. Are there specific ways that pragmatism is relevant to the field of economic methodology that go above and beyond the simple fact that pragmatism connects up with recent debates within science theory and that economics is a social science?

In a sense, the most immediate answer to the above question is "No." Economic methodology, at least as it has traditionally been defined, does not emphasize sociality, plurality, naturalism, or any of the above features that linked pragmatism to the recent developments within the general theory of scientific knowledge. At least during the latter half of the twentieth century, economic methodology focused primarily on finding a small set of relatively simple rules for the proper conduct of economic science – 3'×5' card philosophy of science (McCloskey 1998) – and the philosophical resources involved in the search for these simple rules generally came from the Received View, or a Popperian falsificationism not easily distinguished from it (see Blaug 1992 for instance). This traditional view of economic methodology – what I have called the "shelf-of-scientific-philosophy" view of economic methodology (Hands 1994b) – is basically an exercise in taking various ideas off the philosophy of natural science "shelf" and then applying them to the science of economics; during the course of such exercises it was generally assumed that the items on the shelf were: small ($3' \times 5'$ card), relatively easy to apply (simple rules of demarcation), effectively ready to use (no assembly required), applicable to the behavior of individual economists (individual, not social, in character), and that they provided a suitable philosophical justification for the epistemic quality of the resulting scientific product (provided solid epistemological foundations).

Pragmatism does not really help if one is searching for such simple, universal, rules for the proper conduct of economic (or any other) science. Dewey was perhaps the classical pragmatist who came closest to such concerns, but even his view of experimental inquiry most certainly did not focus on the identification of a few simple rules for the proper behavior of individual scientists. While Dewey did exclude certain ways of thinking/acting from the realm of scientific intelligence, his characterization of the scientific "method" was extremely latitudinarian (Westbrook 1991: 142) – simply the method "of analytic, experimental observation, mathematical formulation and deduction, constant and elaborate check and test" (Dewey 1991 [1927]: 164) – and he clearly (and self-consciously) did not provide anything that would fit on a $3' \times 5'$ card, offer any strict rules, or guarantee that the resulting knowledge was grounded in epistemically incorrigible foundations.

Fortunately for this discussion, recent economic methodology has started to broaden its focus and it now looks more like contemporary science theory than the $3' \times 5'$ card methodology of a few years ago. Without rehashing the entire story (it is discussed in detail in Hands 2001a and 2001b), the bottom line is that the same issues and concerns that have affected science theory in general have also affected methodological inquiry about economics. But while they are certainly important, these changes are not the whole story about the relationship between pragmatic philosophy and economic methodology. Economic methodology has substantially broadened its focus; it is now concerned with the social character of the discipline, the actual practice of the economics, various pluralist issues, and is (more) naturalistic; but pragmatism and economics connect up in a number of different ways that go beyond, and actually existed prior to, the recent convergence of economic methodology, general science theory, and pragmatic philosophy. Let me just briefly discuss three of these specific features.

First, pragmatism fundamentally connects scientific rationality and economic rationality; for pragmatism economic interests are not one thing and epistemic interests something else. The view of knowledge that pragmatism sought to replace characterized knowledge as a particular kind of individual mental representation – a perfect/privileged representation – of objects independent of human interests and concerns. For pragmatists of course, knowledge is inexorably intertwined with those human interests and concerns; "knowing about" and "doing with" are two sides of the same coin. Such a view moves human interests, including economic and industrial interests, immediately onto the epistemic center stage. Knowledge in industry is not fundamentally different from knowledge in science.

> In principle, the history of the construction of suitable operations in the scientific field is no different from that of their evolution in industry. Something needed to be done to accomplish an end; various devices and methods of operation were tried. Experiences of success and failure gradually improved the means used.
>
> (Dewey 1929: 124)

I would note that one particular example of the pragmatic convergence of scientific and economic rationality is provided by Peirce's explicitly microeconomic cost–benefit analysis of the process of scientific decision making (Peirce 1879), but Peirce's work on the economics of science is just one, perhaps a rather extreme, example of this connection. The linkage between scientific knowledge and economic interests is not something that just emerges in the work of a single author or in a few papers, it is a general characteristic of all pragmatic philosophy.

The second deep and long-standing connection between economic methodology and pragmatic philosophy involves the fact that for pragmatists the scientific way of thinking applies to the social and moral sciences, not just natural science. Focusing specifically on Dewey, one might respond that the potential inclusion of social sciences like economics into the domain of scientific intelligence is simply an implication of the pluralist or latitudinarian nature of Dewey's position: "there is no kind of inquiry which has a monopoly of the honorable title of knowledge" (Dewey 1929: 220). While Dewey's pluralism certainly does prevent him from defining scientific knowledge solely in terms of natural science, the desire to subsume social and economic analysis under the rubric of science runs much deeper than the mere fact that experimental reasoning is not restricted to the natural sciences. The goal of applying the experimental reasoning characteristic of natural science to other aspects of human social life is the driving force behind Dewey's (and most pragmatists') philosophizing. For Dewey many aspects of modern life are governed by instrumental scientific rationality, but many others – our values – are viewed as originating elsewhere: in God, in nature, in sprit/soul, in rite and cult (Dewey 1929: 223). The result is a crisis of culture that defines the philosophical problem.

> Man has beliefs which scientific inquiry vouchsafes, beliefs about the actual structure and processes of things; and he also has beliefs about the

values which should regulate his conduct. The question of how these two ways of believing may most effectively and fruitfully interact with one another is the most general and significant of all the problems which life presents to us.

(Dewey 1929: 18–19)

If scientific inquiry is not relevant to questions of social life and social values, the separation of these two aspects of culture – and the associated crisis – will remain with us. Pragmatic philosophy can, and for Dewey should, serve an emancipatory role within the process of social reconstruction, but in order to do so it must affect the values that individuals hold. But these values are products of the social environment, and thus in order to succeed pragmatic philosophy must hook-up effectively with social life; the most significant hooks for pragmatic philosophy and social life are the social and moral sciences. Philosophy that says nothing about social life leaves our practical (instrumental, experimental, scientific) life separated from, and in tension with, our most cherished values. Such a philosophy is part of the problem; pragmatism intends to be part of the solution.

The third connection is that for Dewey in particular, the experimental form of life has grown up and begun to assert itself, along with economic development and industrial progress. As mentioned above, Dewey attributed the representationalism characteristic of Western philosophy to the economic conditions of Greek society (slavery), but the relationship between economic institutions and scientific reasoning did not end with the Greeks. The slow but systematic inroads that experimental reasoning made into Western life were accelerated by the industrial revolution and economic progress; industrial rationality and scientific rationality grew up together. As Dewey explained the process:

> New-found wealth … tended to wean men from preoccupation with the metaphysical and theological, and to turn their minds with newly awakened interest to the joys of nature and its life. … The demands of progressive production and transportation have set new problems to inquiry; the processes used in industry have suggested new experimental appliances and operations in science; the wealth rolled up in business has to some extent been diverted to endowment of research. The uninterrupted and pervasive interaction of scientific discovery and industrial application has fructified both science and industry, and has brought home to the contemporary mind the fact that the gist of scientific knowledge is control of natural energies.

(Dewey 1948 [1920]: 40–42)

While it is clear that Dewey thought of experimental rationality – not the economic, particularly market, institutions – as the prime mover, it is also quite clear that he believed the two developments were substantively related.

The growth of science facilitated the industrial revolution, which in turn precipitated changes in economic (and other social) institutions, which in turn can (though for Dewey, need not always) further accelerate the growth of experimental rationality. This is not (as we will see in the next section) an argument for linking the spread of scientific rationality to the spread of capitalist-market institutions, but it certainly is yet another example of how deeply intertwined experimental reasoning and economic relations were for Dewey (and to a lesser extent other pragmatists). Compare this to the Received View and the shelf-of-scientific philosophy characterization of economic methodology, where scientific knowledge is something that is produced when individual scientists follow the foundationalist-inspired rules laid down by philosophers of science, and then economics enters at the very end, with the only question being whether it is, or is not, capable of living up to the philosopher-decreed scientific standards. With pragmatism there is no such caricature; knowledge evolves through its associated doing, and doing is what economic life is all about.

Deweyan economic methodology and Dewey's economics

Today when economists, and for that matter most others, refer to the economy and economics, they are normally referring to the market: market prices, market institutions, and production for profit by business firms. Economists of course discuss a variety of other topics, but there certainly is the general presumption that what gets produced in the modern economy is produced for sale in markets by profit maximizing business firms. This presumption rests in part on the belief that market-oriented relations of production and distribution in fact (now) prevail in most of the world, but also, and perhaps more importantly, on the belief that such relations constitute a rational, and for some, even a natural way of organizing economic activity. While Dewey would have agreed with the first part (the fact of market institutions), he would not have agreed with the argument that such arrangements are either rational, or natural. For Dewey, production for profit and the associated institutions of industrial capitalism were neither rationally/scientifically designed, nor "natural" in Adam Smith's sense. For Dewey, the ownership rights and institutional arrangements of capitalism are simply hold-overs from feudal social conditions: "chargeable to the unchanged persistence of a legal institution inherited from the pre-industrial age" (Dewey 1991 [1927]: 109). Industrial arrangements could be determined by the (democratic) application of scientific intelligence – the extension of experimental reasoning to social and economic life – but were not in his day (and Dewey would say, still are not today); rather than being socially applied, the technical applications of science "are utilized by those in positions of privileged advantage to serve their own private or class ends" (Dewey 1929: 252). While never sympathetic to Marxism, Dewey clearly supported a version of democratic socialism and economic planning; he endorsed the application of science and technology to industrial production, but not the private control of that technology in the hands of business owners who used it to produce goods for sale at a profit. Dewey's political economy was, as is generally recognized, very close to the American Institutionalism of Thorstein Veblen and later Veblenians such as Clarence Ayres.

Dewey's political economy raises an obvious question. Since the first two sections of this chapter argued that Dewey's pragmatic ideas had much in common with the major themes of contemporary science theory, and that there are independent reasons to connect pragmatism and economic methodology, the question is: Does endorsing an economic methodology informed by Deweyan pragmatic ideas necessarily commit one to endorsing Dewey's particular political economy?

This is a very complex question that frankly deserves a lot more attention than I can give it here, but I want to suggest a few reasons why the answer might be "no." There are tensions between Dewey's philosophical position and his political economy, and when these tensions are viewed from the perspective of contemporary debates within philosophy, science theory, political economy, and our general intellectual culture, there seems to be much more reason to support Dewey on the philosophy side of the tension than on the economic side. This said, it is important to emphasize two points. First, I am not suggesting that the tension between Dewey's pragmatism and his economics is any more, or any worse, than the tensions exhibited in the work of any other wide-ranging intellectual with substantive philosophical and social/economic ideas; and second, consistent with a general commitment to pragmatism, leaning in the direction of one side of the tension at this particular time, in this specific social context, and in this cultural environment, says absolutely nothing about what the better pragmatic choice might be at a different time, in another context, or an alternative environment. I will briefly consider three such tensions – they are closely related, but clearly separable.

First, there seems to be a tension between Dewey's pragmatic instrumentalism – with its fallibilism, context-sensitivity, and anti-teleology – and his acceptance of the idea that it is possible to engage in wide-scale social engineering and economic planning. The amount of information one would need for such planning seems to be precisely the type of universal and certain knowledge that Dewey denies intelligence provides (and the suggestion that it exists he finds pernicious). It seems problematic to be against the quest for certainty, and yet to be for a type of economic planning that requires it. As John Patrick Diggins explains the tension:

> During the depression Dewey criticized the New Deal for lacking purpose, direction, and systematic social control. The public philosophy and the good society could only be, he was convinced, a society of applied intelligence, a "great community" scientifically planned, designed, organized, and managed along with citizen participation. The irony here

> is that Dewey's epistemology could give little support to his politics. ...
> Dewey's idea of rational social control could scarcely take account of the
> uncertainty, obscurity, and paradoxes inherent in reality itself. Convinced
> that a planned society was within human conception and design, he
> claimed cognitive abilities in politics that his epistemology denied in
> philosophy.
>
> (Diggins 1994: 304–305)

The second tension begins with the previous point about the pragmatic
view of natural science and Dewey's view of social science, but puts a slightly
different spin on it. The spin involves criticizing not Dewey's social science,
but rather his general methodological view of social science. Dewey (consistent with contemporary science theory) clearly sees science as social, but he
seems to draw from this fact the additional (invalid) inference that whatever
the general experimental approach says about the method of natural science
applies equally well to social and economic phenomena. He seems to deduce
"social problems can be solved by the (natural) scientific method" from
"science is social," when in fact these two things are entirely separate. This
criticism was raised by Frank Knight (1936) and is certainly consistent with
the ideas of the Austrian tradition in economics (among others); in a sense it
is the criticism that Dewey was not sufficiently pluralist. Dewey's desire to
think of the scientific-experimental method in ways that would allow it to be
applied to social, economic, and cultural life, seemed to block him from seeing
any possibility of there being aspects of human and social life that are not
amenable to the experimental method. It is possible to agree entirely with
Dewey's general view of science – particularly the social character of science
– and yet not agree that all social and economic problems can be solved, or
even approached, by the application of the method of intelligence derived
from the natural sciences. As Knight characterized the problem:

> Professor Dewey's theories of liberalism and his program for its salvation
> go definitely and catastrophically wrong. He seems to confuse the
> unquestionable fact that scientific and technological knowledge is in a
> fundamental sense social in genesis and transmission with the view that
> this style of intelligence is applicable to social problems, which is the
> antithesis of the truth.
>
> (Knight 1936: 231)

Even if one disagrees with Knight's claim that such applications are "the
antithesis of the truth," there does seem to be a problem with Dewey's jump
from the sociality of scientific knowledge to his belief in the general applicability of instrumental rationality to social and economic problems.

The third tension I would like to discuss concerns Dewey's treatment of
"natural laws" in physical science versus his treatment of such laws in social
and economic science. Dewey argues that a pragmatic conception of knowl-

edge not only undermines the notion that physical laws are absolute, universal, and representationally true, it also undermines the notion that social and economic laws are "natural laws" with these same features. For Dewey what happens in society is a result of human will, intention, agency, and values; neither physical nor social laws are "out there," universal, and independent of human purposes. The quite reasonable conclusion that he draws from this is that undermining the purported natural basis of such economic laws undercuts the intellectual grounds for laissez-faire inherited from eighteenth-century political economy. As he explains:

> Its paralyzing effect on human action is seen in the part it played in the eighteenth and nineteenth century in the theory of "natural laws" in human affairs, in social matters. These natural laws were supposed to be inherently fixed; a science of social phenomena and relations was equivalent to discovery of them. Once discovered, nothing remained for man but to conform to them; they were to rule the conduct as physical laws govern physical phenomena. They were the sole standard of conduct in economic affairs; the laws of economics are the "natural" laws of all political action; other so-called laws are artificial, man-made contrivances in contrast with the normative regulations of nature itself.
>
> Laissez-faire was the logical conclusion. For organized society to attempt to regulate the course of economic affairs, to bring them into service of humanly conceived ends, was a harmful interference. … But if man in knowing is a participator in the natural scene, a factor in generating the things known, the fact that man participates as a factor in social affairs is no barrier to knowledge of them. On the contrary, a certain method of directed participation is a precondition of his having any genuine understanding. Human intervention for the sake of effecting ends is no interference, and it is a means of knowledge.
>
> (Dewey 1929: 211–212)

So Dewey's pragmatism replaced the Newtonian conception of "natural" physical laws and therefore undercut the justification for laissez-faire based on such a Newtonian-based conception as "natural" economic laws. So what is the tension? The tension surfaces in the way that Dewey applies these discredited laws; what we are supposed to do, or not do, with these laws once their philosophical foundations have been successfully devitalized. When it comes to Newtonian physics, or any other theory within the natural sciences, the fact that we reject the traditional philosophical justification for, and explanation of, these laws and replace it with a pragmatic characterization, does not mean that we quit using these laws in practical life. Accepting the pragmatic critique of the standard philosophical characterization of Newtonian mechanics does not mean that we should quit using such physics in engineering applications such as bridge building. Yet, when it comes to economics, this seems to be precisely what Dewey is arguing; since the characterization of economic laws in Adam

Smith and others should be rejected, the competitive market must necessarily be rejected as an instrumentally efficient means for dealing with practical problems such as coordinating economic activity and allocating resources. In the case of natural science, Dewey's rejection of the philosophical characterization of natural laws never led him to reject those laws as pragmatically useful – the problem lies with philosophy, not with natural science – and yet, when it came to economic laws, rejecting the philosophical defense of competitive markets led automatically to the position that competitive markets cannot be pragmatically useful instruments for solving practical economic problems. Why? A more pragmatic response appears to be: "Yea, there is no natural tendency to truck, barter, and exchange – competitive markets are as Karl Polanyi (1957 [1944]) and others have argued, entirely human constructs – but as pragmatists we do not much care what philosophers say about 'foundations' or 'natural laws'; perhaps competitive markets can be instrumentally useful for solving various problems in the allocation of economic resources; let's try them out and see how they work." That might be a reasonable pragmatic response, but it is not Dewey's response. For Dewey markets are not instruments for efficient resource allocation, they are (backward looking) reflections of dominant property rights; a pragmatism that undermines the foundations of those rights necessarily undermines the reason for markets. Of course one can understand Dewey's position on this matter and yet reject his particular (rather backward looking) characterization of competitive markets.

These three tensions are only the tip of the iceberg regarding the complex relationship between Dewey's pragmatic philosophy and his economics. I realize that none of the three criticisms provides anything like a knock-down argument; they are merely suggestions for why it is not necessarily the case that one would need to accept Dewey's attitude about markets just because they find his pragmatism to be a useful framework for helping tread their way through the labyrinth of contemporary science theory and economic methodology. The issue of the relationship between Dewey's philosophy and Dewey's economics clearly remains an open question; the purpose of this section was merely to point out a few issues that might lead one to question whether a tight (or perhaps any) connection exists between the two.

Conclusion

I have tried to make the case that pragmatism is consistent with many of the recent developments within the general theory of scientific knowledge; that pragmatism connects up nicely with economic methodology for a number of reasons that go above and beyond the (important) fact that it is consistent with contemporary science theory; and finally that (at the very least) it is an open question whether approaching economic methodology from a pragmatic perspective necessarily means endorsing Dewey's view of the economy.

It is important to remember that in such discussions, pragmatism (like any other very general philosophical program) is not a view that can be "applied" to questions about economic methodology in the way that positivist or Popperian falsificationist ideas were previously "applied." The changes that have taken place in the general way that questions about scientific knowledge are approached – particularly the emphasis on the social character of such knowledge – has fundamentally changed how both disciplinary philosophy and social science "work" in theorizing about scientific knowledge. It is an environment that is much more conducive to the (re)emergence, survival, and reproduction of pragmatic ideas than the environment where armchair philosophizing was king and the social sciences were (at best) second class epistemic citizens. This is not to say that pragmatism, Dewey's or any other, is going to provide some nice neat (certain, absolute, universal, etc.) answer to all of the questions in general science theory or in economic methodology. Philosophical positions, after all, are ultimately just tools for coping with the vicissitudes of an uncertain environment; our current intellectual environment just seems to be one that is particularly well-suited for the application of pragmatic tools.

Notes

1   Earlier versions of this chapter were presented at the AIER Conference "John Dewey: Modernism, Postmodernism, and Beyond" at Simon's Rock College of Bard, Great Barrington, MA, 20–22 July 2001, and at the Amsterdam Research Group in History and Methodology of Economics, University of Amsterdam, Amsterdam, The Netherlands, 2 November 2001. I would like to thank John Davis, Ross Emmett, Frank Ryan and various members of the two audiences for helpful comments on earlier drafts. Errors and omissions are of course solely my responsibility.

Bibliography

Blaug, M. (1992) *The Methodology of Economics: Or How Economists Explain*, 2nd edn, Cambridge: Cambridge University Press.

Bradie, M. (1986) "Assessing Evolutionary Epistemology," *Biology and Philosophy*, 1: 401–459.

Cartwright, N., Cat, J., Fleck, L. and Uebel, T. (1996) *Between Science and Politics: The Philosophy of Otto Neurath*, Cambridge: Cambridge University Press.

Dewey, J. (1948 [1920]) *Reconstruction in Philosophy*, enlarged edn, Boston: Beacon Press.

—— (1991 [1927]) *The Public and Its Problems*, Athens, OH: Swallow Press Reprint.

—— (1960 [1929]) *The Quest for Certainty: A Study of the Relation of Knowledge and Action*, New York: Capricorn Books.

—— (1970) "Unity of Science as a Social Problem," in O. Neurath, R. Carnap and C. Morris (eds), *Foundations of the Unity of Science: Toward an International Encyclopedia of Unified Science*, vol. 1, Chicago: University of Chicago Press, pp. 29–38.

Diggins, J.P. (1994) *The Promise of Pragmatism: Modernism and the Crisis of Knowledge and Authority*, Chicago: University of Chicago Press.

Friedman, M. (1999) *Reconsidering Logical Positivism*, Cambridge: Cambridge University Press.

Fuller, S. (2000) *Thomas Kuhn: A Philosophical History for Our Times*, Chicago: University of Chicago Press.

Hacohen, M.H. (2000) *Karl Popper – The Formative Years, 1902–1945*, Cambridge: Cambridge University Press.

Hands, D.W. (1994a) "The Sociology of Scientific Knowledge," in R. Backhouse (ed.), *New Directions in Economic Methodology*, London: Routledge, pp. 75–106.

—— (1994b) "Blurred Boundaries: Recent Changes in the Relationship Between Economics and the Philosophy of Natural Science," *Studies in History and Philosophy of Science*, 25: 751–772.

—— (2001a) *Reflection without Rules: Economic Methodology and Contemporary Science Theory*, Cambridge: Cambridge University Press.

—— (2001b) "Economic Methodology is Dead – Long Live Economic Methodology: Thirteen Theses on the New Economic Methodology," *Journal of Economic Methodology*, 8: 49–63.

Kitcher, P. (1993) *The Advancement of Science: Science without Legend, Objectivity without Illusions*, Oxford: Oxford University Press.

Knight, F.H. (1936) "Pragmatism and Social Action," *International Journal of Ethics*, 48: 229–235.

McCloskey, D. (1998) *The Rhetoric of Economics*, 2nd edn, Madison, WI: University of Wisconsin Press.

Menand, L. (2001) *The Metaphysical Club: A Study of Ideas in America*, New York: Farrar, Straus and Giroux.

Peirce, C.S. (1879) "A Note on the Theory of the Economy of Research," in *United States Coast Survey* for the fiscal year ending June 1876, US Government Printing Office. Reprinted in Operations Research, 15 (1967): 642–648; and as an appendix to Wible 1994.

Polanyi, K. (1957 [1944]) *The Great Transformation*, Boston: Beacon Press [1957].

Uebel, T.E. (1992) *Overcoming Logical Positivism from Within: The Emergence of Neurath's Naturalism in the Vienna Circle's Protocol Sentence Debate*, Amsterdam: Editions Rodopi.

Westbrook, R. (1991) *John Dewey and American Democracy*, Ithaca, NY: Cornell University Press.

Wible, J.R. (1994) "Rescher's Economic Philosophy of Science," *Journal of Economic Methodology*, 1: 314–329.

17 A Deweyan economic methodology

Alex Viskovatoff

Introduction

Philosophy – the philosophy of science in particular – has played varying roles at different stages in the development of economics. As political economy developed and refined a well-defined paradigm, philosophy played a guiding role. Thus, it is rather likely that Adam Smith's philosophical reception of the Newtonian revolution in science, as articulated in his essay, "The History of Astronomy" inspired him to develop the comprehensive vision of the economy as a system he presented in his *Wealth of Nations*; similarly, John Stuart Mill wrote his *Principles of Political Economy* only after he had already written his *System of Logic*, which dealt at length with the social sciences.[1] Mainstream economics essentially adopted the methodology articulated by Mill. In the twentieth century, as the failure of Mill's attempt to graft inductive procedures onto Ricardo's "geometric" economic method became increasingly apparent, methodological writings centered around the question of whether economics had become too deductive and not sufficiently inductive, with Hutchison (1938) arguing in the affirmative and Friedman (1953), influentially, in the negative.

In that debate, methodologists were able to argue about whether or not economics possessed a sufficient empirical component, and hence in effect whether it was a proper science, because there existed a shared background philosophy of science which allowed them to do so – logical empiricism.[2] With the demise of logical empiricism however, and with the increasing marginalization of non-mainstream approaches to the study of economic phenomena, economic methodology seems to have lost its inclination to consider "big questions" like what the scientific status of economics is. In 1983, Alexander Rosenberg posed the question "If economics isn't science, what is it?" The question was never answered, but today it is seldom even posed. What Hands (2001) proposed we call "the new economic methodology" pursues "local" methodology, either describing what economists do in practice by looking at specific case studies, or interpreting the practice of economists in terms of a novel philosophical model. Neither approach takes a stand on the scientific status of economics, or attempts to *guide* economics with regard to how it should go about constructing its theory and conducting its empirical investigation, in the way that philosophy previously guided economics.[3]

John Dewey would not have been happy with this situation. To him philosophy, like all inquiry, must be *practically engaged*; what distinguishes philosophy from other forms of inquiry is its generality:

> [p]hilosophy is inherently criticism, having its distinctive position among various modes of criticism in its generality; a criticism of criticisms, as it were. Criticism is discriminating judgment, careful appraisal, and judgment is appropriately termed criticism whenever the subject-matter of discrimination concerns goods or values.
>
> (Dewey 1981 [1925]: 298)

One way to define philosophy is thus to say that it is the study of how well values are grounded or justified. And values, for Dewey, lie at the bottom of any conscious human activity, including science:

> If the use made of scientific resources, of techniques of observation and experiment, of systems of classification, etc., in directing the act of judging (and thereby fixing the content of the judgment) depends upon the interest and disposition of the judger, we have only to make such dependence explicit, and the so-called scientific judgment appears definitely as a moral judgment.
>
> (Dewey 1977 [1903]: 19)

The implications of this for economics are that economics, like any science or aspiring science, is guided by values, and that the task for philosophy, in relation to economics, is to determine whether or not those values are sound, offering more appropriate values if they are not.

Contemporary economic methodology

Most contemporary economic methodology falls under one of three traditions: Millian, Popperian, or realist (Hands 2001).[4] Since mainstream economics essentially follows Mill's economic methodology, we shall only consider his methodology here.[5]

Mill (1965 [1843]) divided sciences into experimental and deductive sciences. In general, sciences start out as experimental, but as a science accumulates empirical knowledge, gradually one comes to learn about the laws that obtain in its domain of interest, at which point the science becomes deductive. Physics is the principal example here; chemistry (at least in Mill's time) has yet to make the transition to being a deductive science. Economics is exceptional in that it *starts off* by being a deductive science. The reason for this is that experiments are very difficult in economics: in the social domain it is difficult to disentangle a multitude of causes which gives rise to a multitude of effects, as can in general be done in the physical domain.

The fact that from its origins economics has avoided the experimental method does not compromise it empirically, for two main reasons. First, in the economic domain, it is not difficult, simply by means of "casual empiricism," to determine what the important cause that should be looked at is: it is people's desire to increase their wealth. Thus, one's inability to perform experiments does not compromise one's ability to know the appropriate causal factor: one knows it from the start. Second, even though one develops the theory deductively, this does not mean that the science as a whole does not maintain an empirical contact. This is because when the theory is *applied*, one does aim to verify its conclusions. (Certainly, when one applies the theory, one tends to add causal factors other than the one considered by the theory, namely, wealth-maximization.)

Mill's "isolation" of the cause "driving" economic processes was very influential on the further development of economics: it in effect led to the conflation of two senses of rationality – acting appropriately, given the circumstances, and acting so as to gain one's own advantage – which has largely been constitutive of the development of mainstream economics. Mill's legitimation of the deductive method for economics was of course also highly influential. When the mathematics of constrained optimization was introduced into economics, that, together with the deductive method, amounted to a directive to do precisely what theoretical economists actually do: take any social phenomenon, and see how it can be modeled as the result of the interaction of utility-maximizing agents. On one level, the methodology does not suffer from the "conventionalism" or "relativism" that follow from logical empiricism: the methodology says that using the constrained optimization approach is precisely the way to proceed. On another level of course, the conventionalism is still there, since no attempt is made to empirically justify the theoretical framework.

The difficulties of Mill's economic methodology can be seen by reflecting upon the title of a book by the main current "disciple" of Mill in the field: *The Inexact and Separate Science of Economics* (Hausman 1992). The Millian claim is that economics is a science: it is just an inexact and separate one. Let us consider each of these aspects in turn. First, a main misgiving of Hausman about mainstream economics is the degree to which it tries to maintain its "separate" status by ignoring empirical psychological evidence that people do not behave as is postulated by rational choice (i.e., utility maximization) theory. But such behavior of ignoring the empirical evidence is precisely what is required by Mill's methodology: one confronts theory with observation when one *applies* it for practical purposes, not when one is "developing" it. Second, the Millian supposition is that while there are no "exact" economic laws, there are "inexact" ones. Carrying over a particular methodology from a domain in which there are exact laws to one in which there are only "inexact" ones however is a risky undertaking: how does one know if there are indeed laws in the second domain, if only "inexact" ones, or if there are no laws at all in the sense relevant to that methodology?[6] In the latter case, there is nothing for the theory to be a theory of. The theory then turns out to be a pure formalism, not about anything that actually exists (or could exist). This would take it outside the realm of science.

Before closing this section, we should consider one "methodological" idea that is seldom stated openly, but one which is widely shared among mainstream economists, and is in fact the only thing that can explain the high prestige that mainstream economics enjoys relative to the other social sciences, both among economists, and among policy makers and "opinion makers." This is that mainstream economics is unique among the social sciences in being a "genuine" science, because it follows the same method as do the natural sciences: "Like the physical sciences, economics uses a methodology that produces refutable implications and tests these implications using solid statistical techniques" (Lazear 2000: 99). The basic argument is the following:

1   (Physical) science proceeds by using mathematics and confronting its models and theories with empirically obtained data in some way.
2   Economics does both of these things, i.e., it follows the method of the natural sciences.
3   Therefore, economics is a science.[7]

This is a methodological idea that we can latch on to, and one to which Dewey provides us with a response.

Dewey's philosophy of natural and social science

As we have seen, economists to this day tend to follow the methodology prescribed by J.S. Mill. Since the notion of laws, as that which links causes with effects in a regular way, is central to that methodology, and since Dewey had much to say about the Millian understanding of laws, a good place to start our consideration of Dewey's philosophy of science is with his account of natural laws, in chapter 22 of *Logic: The Theory of Inquiry* (1986 [1938]).

Dewey's account of lawfulness and causality is somewhat obscure, but we must get to grips with it, since it is the point at which his thought relates most directly to economic method. The overall train of his argument is as follows. Since Mill, the generally accepted understanding of causality has involved the combination of the common sense notion that effects are temporally preceded by their causes and the scientific notion that the relation between causes and events is necessary. A scientific law is thus discovered when one determines that there is a constant conjunction of a certain kind of cause with a certain effect, where both cause and effect are taken as events. Upon a correct analysis of what is involved however, one finds that this account of causality and of scientific laws is untenable. This is because the combination of the common sense and the scientific notions of cause and effect is unworkable: no event is necessarily followed by any other event, since when there is an observed succession of events, this succession occurred only because other events occurred, a state of affairs which is contingent; and at a sufficiently fine level of analysis, "causes" and "effects" will be seen to occur not at discrete points of time, but simultaneously. The response must be to replace the prevalent ontological understanding of laws, as dealing with ordered sequences of events, with a *logical* understanding of laws, as expressing if–then relations which are of use in the practical process of intervening in nature.

When philosophical analysis of natural phenomena begins, and it is noticed that the objects we encounter seem to be "separated from one another by their singular qualitative natures," it is felt that something is required to bridge the gap between them. Thus, when it is observed that a burning match lights a piece of paper, "[t]he burning match and the burning paper are two distinct qualitative objects. The conception of a *force* was introduced to get over the difficulty constituted by this qualitative gap." Gradually, the notion of force was generalized, to gravitational force, electrical force, the vital force possessed by living creatures, and so on. Eventually however, Hume recognized that there is no empirical basis for believing that such forces exist, and they "were then ruled out of science along with other 'occult' qualities and forms – of which they were perhaps the most conspicuous example" (Dewey 1986 [1938]: 445). Unfortunately, the solution which Hume presented (and which Mill took over from Hume) of treating laws as constant conjunctions of events – without saying anything about what "underlies" this constant conjunction if nothing observable can be found – was unsatisfactory. Dewey shows this by means of an example. Consider a man found dead under suspicious circumstances. How does one determine if a murder was committed? Say it is known that a shot was fired. This would mean that there is a tentative cause-and-effect sequence of events – the shot followed by the death. To determine whether this amounts to a murder, the consideration of many facts other than just those two events is required. It is necessary to "look" outward, to investigate the whereabouts of different suspects at the time of the shooting, their possible motives, the move-ments of the victim up to the time of his death, and so on. Also, it is necessary to look "inward," to consider the "event" of death at a finer level than that of a single event: one needs to consider the physiological sequence of events that lead to the cessation of normal metabolic processes in the body. From all this, two points follow. First, to determine what *kind* of event occurred (i.e., a murder as opposed to a suicide or an accident), it is necessary to consider information in addition to that provided by the two events in question. And second, one finds that the two events in question do not actually form a sequence, as it had at first appeared:

> A common conception, derived from loose common sense beliefs, is that an event can be picked out as *the* event in question, and that this antecedent is its cause. For example, it would be said that *the* antecedent of the death of the murdered person is a shot fired from a revolver by another person. But examination shows that this event is not temporally

antecedent, leaving out the matter of its being the antecedent. For the mere firing of the shot is not sufficiently close in temporal sequence to be a "cause" of death. A shot may have missed the man entirely. Only a bullet which actually enters some vital part of the organism in such a way that the organic processes cease to function is "causally" connected with the occurrence of death. Such an event is not an antecedent of the event of dying, because it is an integral *constituent* of that event.

(Dewey 1986 [1938]: 443, emphasis in original)

The proper response to these reflections is to recognize that the correct characterization of lawfulness is not an ontological but a logical one. Say it is noted that certain kinds of infection and poisonings are followed by death. These regularities can be expressed in the form of "physiological laws." Such laws will not express constant conjunctions of events. This is because an instance cited as verifying one of the laws in question "concerns a *singular* event, and the *event* is unique in its singularity, occurring at one and only one time and place, so that, at any rate, there is no recurrence in the event in its singularity" (Dewey 1986 [1938]: 448). What recur are the kinds of events or, to put it differently, one finds that certain *traits* of various events are found to be associated with each other:

But the more the soundness of this affirmation of constancy is admitted (or insisted upon) the clearer it becomes that the uniform or constant relation in question is not a temporal and sequential one. For the traits are *logically*, not temporally, conjoined. They are selected and ordered (related to one another) by means of the operations that resolve a gross qualitative occurrence into a definite set of interactions. The law or generalizations that expresses the conjunction of traits determined by these interactions contains no temporal and *a fortiori* no sequential relations.

(Dewey 1986 [1938]: 449)

Dewey concludes his chapter on scientific laws with the observation that his "view that the category of causation is logical, that it is a functional means of regulating existential inquiry, not ontological, and that all existential cases that can be termed causal are 'practical,' is not a view that will receive ready acceptance" (1986 [1938]: 456).[8]

And indeed, it has not. One reason for this may be the type of the examples Dewey uses: the fact that Dewey uses as his main example demonstrating the non-ontological nature of *natural* laws an instance of *intentional* action (murder) is disconcerting. But that need not trouble us here. Whether Dewey's point about the logical nature of laws holds for natural laws is of no direct interest to us, since we are interested in social science.[9] We can take Dewey's point as holding for social phenomena. That has profound implications for economics, since as we have noted, economics follows Mill's methodology, and that methodology calls for looking for laws which express the constant conjunction of events. Thus a different methodology is required for economics.[10] What can we find in Dewey's writings that would help us to formulate such a methodology?

Before we answer that question, we should first confirm that the views that Dewey holds on social science are consistent with his general philosophy of science which we have just presented. The following passage demonstrates that they are:

> The exposed myth is that the existing social order is a product of natural laws which are expounded in a rational, a scientific, way in the traditional sciences of society. ... Economic science regards the dynamic order of society as the result of the cumulative intelligence of an indefinitely large number of beings, each devoting his own intelligence to the things to which it is peculiarly adapted, namely, the pursuit of interests which lie within personal control. The net result in the existent social order is supposed to be resolvable into an immense assemblage of minute and wonderfully interwoven acts of intelligent adaptation.
>
> (Dewey 1982 [1918]: 89)

Not only does this passage demonstrate that Dewey believed that economics was in error when it held that it had isolated economic "laws": the passage also shows that the type of economics Dewey had in mind was Anglo-American, free-market economics and so, by extension, the mainstream economics of today. Dewey goes on to describe his alternative vision of what constitutes economic phenomena:

> If the war has revealed that our existing social situation is in effect the *result of the convergence of a large number of independently generated historic incidents*, it has shown that our *ordinary rationalizing and justifying ideas constitute an essential mythology* in their attributions of phenomena to basic principles and intelligently directed forces. ... [I]t appears that any science which pretends to be more than a description of the particular forces which are at work and a descriptive tracing of the particular consequences which they produce, which pretends to discover basic principles to which social things conform, and inherent laws which "explain" them, is, I repeat, sheer mythology.
>
> (1982 [1918]: 90, emphasis added)

As we have seen, mainstream economists believe that their discipline is justified because it follows the method of the natural sciences. Dewey used the same premise to explain why the general conclusions of the discipline are, as he put it, "sheer mythology": "the existing limitations of 'social science' are due mainly to unreasoning devotion to physical science as a model, and to a misconception of physical science at that" (1985 [1931]: 64). One reason the social sciences are not genuine sciences is that they look for laws which do not exist. Another is that their empirical research is not useful, since the data they collect have little or no connection with human needs and conditions:

> I may illustrate the present practice of slavishly following the technique of physical science and the uselessness of its results by the present zeal for "fact finding." Of course, one cannot think, understand and plan without a basis of fact, and since facts do not lie around in plain view, they have to be discovered. But for the most part, the data which now are so carefully sought and so elaborately scheduled are not social facts at all. For their connection with any system of human purposes and consequences, their bearing as means and as results upon human action, are left out of the picture.
>
> (1985 [1931]: 64–65)

It is in chapter 24 of his *Logic*, entitled "Social Inquiry," that Dewey gives his most complete account of what a proper social science methodology would be like. The general structure of the argument, as in Mill, is to see what conclusions from the example of the natural sciences can be drawn for the social sciences, but of course Dewey draws conclusions quite different from Mill's. Dewey begins by making some general points about natural science by way of review. First, he observes that all sciences are socially determined, so that in its early stages, a science will be influenced by values external to itself. Thus today, "to many persons the 'physical' seems not only relatively independent of social issues (which it is) but inherently set apart from all social context" (1986 [1938]: 482). (This was of course not the case in Galileo's time.) Next, Dewey makes the pragmatic point that theoretical science cannot be separated from its practical application. He also notes that scientific inquiry, once it has properly "taken off," becomes "self-correcting" in that one scientist's conclusion will be treated as merely a hypothesis by the scientific community until his fellow workers accept it. Dewey further observes that "the ultimate end and test of all inquiry is the transformation of a problematic situation (which involves confusion and conflict) into a unified one" (1986 [1938]: 484). That is, one can tell that one is dealing with a genuine science to the extent that instances of conflict and confusion eventually become resolved.[11] Dewey finally notes that social inquiry must satisfy the joint conditions that factual determinations are made empirically and that "operational conceptions" allow that to be done. He observes that the social sciences markedly do not satisfy this requirement:

> [T]he necessity of this conjugate relation indicates the most important way in which physical science serves as a model for social inquiry. For if there is one lesson more than any other taught by the methods of the physical sciences, it is the strict correlativity of facts and ideas. Until social inquiry succeeds in establishing methods of observing, discriminating and

arranging data that evoke and test correlated ideas, and until, on the other side, ideas formed and used are (1) employed as *hypotheses*, and are (2) of a form to direct and prescribe operations of analytic-synthetic determination of facts, social inquiry has no chance of satisfying the logical condition for attainment of scientific status.

(1986 [1938]: 485)

According to Dewey, the way that the natural sciences have been able to achieve the conjugate relation between factual and conceptual subject matter is by following what he calls the "experimental method." What Dewey evidently means by this is what we usually mean by doing experiments – that is, setting up controlled conditions in order to test a particular theory – but understood more broadly, so that under this notion it is understood that we creatively and energetically try various combinations of experimental setups to see what will happen, and inventively use our present knowledge to create instruments that will allow new kinds of phenomena to be observed in the laboratory or elsewhere. Dewey is quite clear that, to become genuine sciences, the social sciences must also follow the experimental method:

The special lesson which the logic of the methods of physical inquiry has to teach to social inquiry is … that social inquiry, as *inquiry*, involves the necessity of operations which existentially modify actual conditions that, as they exist, are the occasions of genuine inquiry and that provide its subject-matter.

(1986 [1938]: 486)

The practical difficulties in the way of experimental method in the case of social phenomena as compared with physical investigations do not need elaborate exposition. Nevertheless, every measure of policy put into operation is, *logically*, and *should* be actually, of the nature of an experiment. For (1) it represents the adoption of one out of a number of alternative conceptions as possible plans of action, and (2) its execution is followed by consequences which, while not as capable of definite or exclusive differentiation as in the case of physical experimentation, are none the less observable within limits, so they may serve as tests of the validity of the conception acted upon. The idea that because social phenomena do not permit the controlled variation of sets of conditions in one-by-one series of operations, therefore the experimental method has no application at all, stands in the way of taking advantage of the experimental method to the extent that is practicable.

(1986 [1938]: 502, emphasis in original)

I turn later to the problem of how the experimental method can be implemented in economics. To conclude the present section, I will briefly consider the remarks that Dewey makes about Millian economic method, since they can be taken as directed also at current mainstream economics. Dewey writes that the classical political economists, from Adam Smith to J. S. Mill, held that

> first principles were ... derived inductively, instead of being established by *a priori* intuition. But once arrived at, they were regarded as unquestionable truths, or as axioms with respect to any further truths, since the latter should be deductively arrived from them. The actual content of the fixed premises was taken to be certain truths regarding human nature, such as the universal desire of each individual to better his condition. ... The net consequence of the procedure of classical economics was reinstatement of the older conception of "natural laws" by means of a reinterpretation of their content. For it was concluded that the "laws" of human activity in the economic field, which were theoretically deducible, were the *norms* of proper or right human activity in that field. The laws were supposed to "govern" the phenomena in the sense that all phenomena which failed to conform to them were abnormal or "unnatural."
>
> (Dewey 1986 [1938]: 498)[12]

The situation has not changed significantly to the present day, as one sees from the often-made observation that the subjects that tend to "defect" in prisoners' dilemma-type experiments are those that have taken economics courses, and from the degree to which free market solutions to social problems are currently favored in English-speaking countries.

Dewey's views on science reconsidered

In the previous section, we ran into two potential problems. These were: (1) that Dewey may be too anti-realist in his claim that natural laws do not have an ontological basis; and (2) that it may be difficult to follow the experimental method in economics, in which case Dewey's methodology would have little to offer us. In this section, we shall use Kantian ideas to try to resolve both these problems. We will start with the second problem, since it directly concerns economic methodology, and since the solution proposed to it will lead to a solution to the first problem.

A major theme of Dewey's philosophy of science is that science does not passively accept "information" that is provided to it by nature, but instead learns about nature by actively examining and interacting with it. Thus, Dewey concludes that "the special lesson" which the natural sciences have to offer the social sciences is that the latter must use the experimental method, if they are to progress. For Dewey, progress would involve an increase in the "correlativity" of what he calls "facts and ideas," which we can restate as an increase in the match between theoretical concepts and the structure of the physical world, which increase would lead in turn to an increase in the effectiveness with which that world can be studied. Now, the problem here, as already noted, is that it is not practical to perform experiments in economics.[13] It would thus be desirable to have an alternative, or at least additional, set of values with which to judge the acceptability of different approaches to studying the economy, and which one could employ in the pursuit of such inquiry, rather than simply the stipulation to "act experimentally."

A place to start is Dewey's remark that there should be a "correlativity" of "facts and ideas." Dewey tells us that experimentation is the way to reach this objective, and that we know we have reached it when we can manipulate the world successfully, but he tells us little about what the theories themselves are like in disciplines that have reached this objective. As I have argued (Viskovatoff, forthcoming), the philosopher who has had the most to say about this is Kant.[14] Kant shared Dewey's insight that science does not passively study nature: as he wrote, as scientists started employing the experimental method,

> [t]hey comprehended that reason has insight only into what it itself produces according to its own design; that it must take the lead with principles for its judgments according to constant laws and compel nature to answer its questions, rather than letting nature guide its movements by keeping reason, as it were, in leading strings; for otherwise accidental observations, made according to no previously designed plan, can never connect up into a necessary law, which is yet what reason seeks and requires.
>
> (Kant 1997 [1781]: B xiii)

This passage conveys two additional Kantian insights which we can use to lead us to and justify an economics that Dewey would find acceptable. Kant supplemented the standard empiricist account, according to which scientific knowledge is justified by empirical confirmation, by holding that it has two additional "components"; these relate to (1) the laws of nature being in some sense "necessary"; and (2) empirical observations being conducted by comparing them with what one would expect from a theory made according to a "previously designed plan."

From a Kantian point of view, scientific knowledge consists of three components: a probative, an explicative, and a systemic component.[15] The probative component involves the collection of experimental and observational data and using the data to confirm a given theory by induction. The explicative component consists of making the concepts of a given theory "comprehensible" by showing how they relate to other concepts that are more or less accepted and understood and providing a "metaphysical foundation" for those concepts, and thus showing how the entities or mechanisms they postulate are possible, given our other scientific knowledge.[16] Examples of the operation of the explicative component from the history of science are the redefinition of the concept of matter so that matter "inherently" exhibits gravitational attraction, thus making – contra Dewey – gravitational force no longer appear "occult," and the demonstration by Darwin that natural selection was *possible*, given that artificial selection was a well-known phenomenon.[17] The systemic component involves the construction of the whole body of theory within a given discipline in such a way that it is *system-atic*, so that the various theories are unified with each other, and the degree to which theory is unified and general – in the sense that Newton's theory of motion was more unified than Aristotle's, in that Newton could explain terrestrial and celestial motion with one theory, whereas Aristotle needed two.[18]

As I have argued (Viskovatoff, forthcoming), the systemic component can be used to direct the construction of a unified and general theory of society: as noted in the introduction, contemporary economic methodology does not provide social scientists with such a guide. For our present purposes however, the explicative component is of particular importance. By developing it for economics, we will be able to follow Dewey in holding that the task of philosophy is to be critical and that the task for economics is not to seek law-like uniformities in the economy. We will differ from Dewey on one point, however. Unfortunately, it appears that the case that Dewey makes that economics is misdirected when it looks for law-like regularities, and that it should instead look for the particular historical events that gave rise to a given institutional structure – which in turn produces a given pattern of behavior – is weak. This is because in those articles, such as "A new social science," in which he makes the point that the economy is not governed by laws analo-gous to physical laws, he is only able to provide arguments such as "the war has revealed to us that our existing social situation is in effect the result of the convergence of a large number of independently generated historic incidents" (Dewey 1982 [1918]: 90). This point gets its "force" from the shared collective shock and horror of having lived through the First World War; it is not a philosophical argument. When Dewey does make a philosophical argument that society and the economy are not governed by laws (in the sense of phys-ical, not legal, law), his argument is quite general, and applies to physical, as well as social, science. This is a drawback, since it must be admitted that his non-ontological interpretation of laws *in general* is not very convincing: if one observes what they teach in college courses and also what they say among themselves, one finds that physicists very much believe that physical laws are an actual feature of the way nature really works, as opposed to mere calcu-lating devices that are of practical value to humans. Thus, it is possible for economists to respond to Dewey: "You say that there are no economic laws, but you say that there are no physical laws either; it may well be that we have not found any economic laws, but there certainly are physical laws; so how can we exclude the possibility that there are economic laws too, but we have simply not yet found them?"

To deal with such a response, we can pursue the following Kantian strategy: we will make conceivable why there are physical laws, by offering a transcendental argument; when we examine that argument, we will find that it does not go through for the social domain; and finally, when we make an analogous argument for the social domain, we will find that it leads to the conclusion that there are no social laws.[19] As is often the case in such discussions, it is useful to go back to Hume. Intuitively, we understand causation to exhibit *necessity*: if I hold a ball above the ground and then release it, my releasing the ball will *necessarily* make the ball fall to the ground. It will not be the case for instance that most of the time, the ball falls to the ground, but that very rarely, for no discernible reason, this does not happen; if things suddenly started behaving that way, we would be very puzzled indeed. Its necessary aspect is what makes a causal regularity a law; we call such a regularity a law because things *must* behave as specified by the law. Hume argued that nothing in the world deserves the name of causal necessity. Causes do not exhibit necessity, according to Hume, because no matter how many times we observe a given cause to be followed by a given effect, there is no way of demonstrating with absolute, logical certainty, that the cause will be followed by the same effect in the future; at most there are what Hume called "constant conjunctions" of events, and the feeling of certainty we have that a ball will fall when we release it comes merely from the force of habit, and has no rational basis.

Kant argued that this argument of Hume's is self-refuting. For us to be able to make the argument, we must live in a world with persistent objects which behave according to stable laws. If we did not live in such a world, we would not be able to identify objects in it in the first place, since if the world did not exhibit regularity, we could not come to associate perceptions of a certain kind with physical objects of a certain kind. In other words, if causation did not exhibit necessity, experience would not be possible. This grounding of the concept of causation, Dewey's misgivings notwithstanding, legitimates the notion of physical laws as actually governing the objects of our experience, as opposed to being merely devices that we use to control the world, without giving an objective description of that world.

Can we make a similar argument work for the social domain? Consider an example of such causation: when I present a book at the library circulation desk together with my library card, the person working there checks the book out to me. Does my action necessarily cause the attendant to check the book out? Yes, in a sense: if the book is classified as circulating, and my library card is valid, the attendant is *obligated*, by the rules of his or her job description, to check the book out. But this necessity is not the necessity of physical law: if the attendant doesn't check the book out, but instead walks away from the circulation desk in disgust, I would wonder what had brought on this bizarre behavior, but not stop dead in my tracks, as I would if a heavy object started to float in the middle of the room. The necessity is that of obligation, as in our society obliging us not to break the law against theft; it is not the machine-like necessity of physical law. Because the necessity is that of obligation and obligations are not always followed, there are no social laws, in the strict sense of the term.

With this different notion of necessity in place, let us see what the corresponding transcendental argument for the social domain would be. As we have seen, social causation involves people following rules, as when the library worker follows the rules of the circulation desk. Now, we can make the argument that people *must* be following rules, successfully most of the time. (We must leave open the possibility that people could make a mistake in following a rule. If they could not, the causation involved would be of the machine-like kind exhibited by the physical world, not the normative kind exhibited by the mind.) Say I see a cat on a mat, and think to myself, "The cat is on the mat again." To do so, I would need to apply rules such as "Cats are furry four-legged creatures with pointy ears," "Mats are flat rectangular objects that tend to collect dirt," and "One object is on top of another when they are contiguous and the image of the former is higher than the image of the latter in my visual field." If I could not regularly follow rules such as these, I would not be able to think. If sometimes when I saw a furry four-legged creature with pointy ears I would think it is a cat, but at other times I would think it is a brick, my "inner experience" would be such that I couldn't accumulate knowledge about my world, so that in a sense, my inner experience would be empty or non-existent.

We are now in the position to reach an important conclusion. The way in which the social and the physical domains exhibit persistence is different: the physical domain exhibits persistence through its laws, which do not change; the social domain exhibits persistence through its rules, which are fairly stable, although they do change over time.[20] (If they were not somewhat stable, meaningful social interaction would not be possible.) Since the goal of science is to identify the structures determining the behavior of the phenomena in a given domain, the goal of the natural sciences must be to discover physical laws, while the goal of the social sciences must be to study the rules of a given society. Because we cannot "read off" physical laws simply from observing physical phenomena, while physical phenomena have "machine-like" regularity and are quantifiable, the way to discover physical laws is to measure physical parameters. Because there are no social laws, that is, because rules do not determine behavior with machine-like regularity, there are no laws to discover by collecting quantitative data. (Engaging in that kind of behavior has as much scientific legitimacy as does technical analysis ("charting") as an investment "style." That is not to say that collecting data cannot be useful, to learn for instance how well people in one part of the world live compared to those in another.) The rules themselves can be discovered however through a means for which no equivalent exists in the natural domain – interpretation. By means of interpretation, we can put forward accounts of the rules that were in play in a given time and place. To understand how those rules gave way to another set, we can again use the process of interpretation. But this amounts to using a historical method of analysis.

We have thus arrived at conclusions about what one should look at in studying society similar to those that Dewey reached: it is the combined effect of a series of "independently generated historic incidents," like those that led to the First World War, that constitutes a social order. But we have done so without having to make implausible claims, namely, that nature does not obey objective physical laws.

The experimental method for economics

As we have seen, according to Dewey, mainstream economics – by holding that it has found "laws" analogous to physical laws and by taking empirical inquiry to involve the collection of statistical data which have little relation to actual human concerns – is seriously flawed. To be a genuine science, economics must abandon the position it effectively holds that there is a natural order in the economy that should not be tampered with, countenance intervention in the economy, and learn about the economy in the only way that a science really can learn about the world – by acting in the world and seeing what the outcome is. As we have noted however, the pursuit of such an "experimental" method in the social sciences is rarely possible; this is especially the case in countries such as the United States where – largely as a result of the influence of the very economics of which Dewey was critical – "free market solutions" to social and economic problems tend to be preferred. But here, we can make use of another example from the physical sciences. Physics, clearly, is an experimental science.[21] Nevertheless, even in physics, experiments are not always possible: in astronomy, one cannot move planets around at one's will, but must be satisfied with observing the motions that the planets themselves exhibit. One can proceed similarly in social science. Each society is different in some way from all other societies, so each society itself actually constitutes a kind of experiment. One can thus compare different societies, and see what kinds of institutional arrangements lead to what results. To be sure, because in society many causal factors are active simultaneously – one does not run across cases in which a given system-state is affected by only one force, as the inertial motion of the planets is disturbed only by gravity – and for the reasons we have seen in the previous, we will not discover any social or economic "laws." But if we ask good questions and consider a sufficiently wide range of societies, we should be able to find that certain kinds of institutional arrangements benefit people more often than other kinds.

As examples, we can briefly consider two issues: what form of economic organization leads to the highest level of technological innovation, and what form of the welfare state is most effective at reducing poverty. If there is one thing on which mainstream economists are virtually unanimously agreed, it is on the principle of free trade (Samuels 1989). Their reason for believing in this principle is the persuasiveness of Hume's argument of comparative advantage, which is still included in elementary economics textbooks. That argument is of course wholly deductive, but this has not stopped economists from accepting the validity of the principle. Another principle that is only slightly less widely believed is that free markets lead to the optimal allocation of resources. This idea goes back to Adam Smith's invisible hand argument: capital will be guided to its best uses by investors seeking the highest rate of return. This is also a deductive argument. What is common to both arguments is that they take the production technologies that are employed as given – this despite the fact that the factor that at bottom determines living standards in the long run is precisely technology, since that is a main determinant of productivity. Thus these arguments, while being correct as chains of deductions, do not really get at what we should be most interested in as economists: for them to go through, we must take technology as given, whereas really, we should be asking ourselves how society should be "configured" so that technology can be improved at the greatest rate possible. The arguments are thus subject to the following Deweyan admonition:

> The syllogism "All satellites are made of green cheese; the moon is a satellite; therefore it is made of green cheese" is formally correct. The propositions involved are, however, *invalid*, not just because they are "materially false," but because instead of promoting inquiry they would, if taken and used, retard and mislead it.
>
> (Dewey 1986 [1938]: 287–288, emphasis in original)

So how can we promote inquiry into our first question: what kind of institutional arrangements best promote technological progress? Following what we have said above, the obvious answer is to see what "experiments" history has performed for us, in the form of obvious instances of periods in which one country or a small group of countries has excelled at technological innovation. Several instances come to mind: Britain at the time of the first industrial revolution, the United States roughly from the start of the twentieth century to sometime in the 1960s, and Japan after the Second World War. For a time, each of these countries was the world leader in manufacturing. If one could explain how each of these countries came to have manufacturing pre-eminence and then lost it, one would have an understanding of what would be needed to increase a given country's productivity and ability to innovate.

Explaining productivity growth

That task has been undertaken by the economic historian William Lazonick. Lazonick (1991) argues that these three countries exhibited three different patterns of organization of their productive enterprises, which he calls proprietary capitalism, managerial capitalism, and collective capitalism, respectively. In proprietary capitalism, firms were managed by their owners. This limited the size to which firms could grow, and led to their specializing in particular kinds of products. This specialization was not a problem, since a firm would tend to be located in areas in which many other firms with which it needed to trade were located. When an industry grew, new firms entered the industry, instead of old firms growing larger. Firms did not train workers: workers were trained by other workers. Workers were skilled, so that management did not need to take a detailed interest in the manufacturing process. Firms thus relied upon the market for many functions, such as the provision of trained workers, providing British firms a competitive advantage at the time.

In managerial capitalism, through managerial coordination, firms developed the combined productive capabilities of human and physical resources in ways that market coordination, with its unplanned interaction of specialized producers, could not. The innovative modern American corporation was able to plan and coordinate production, research and development, and marketing activities to generate the types of products that buyers wanted at prices they could afford.[22] As opposed to English firms, American firms were run by managers who did not own the firms, but were employees. This allowed firms to expand dramatically, their size limited in principle only by the size of their market. In order to produce as much output as possible to service a large market, mass production techniques were introduced. The employment of assembly lines required that managers take control of production from workers. This entailed the de-skilling of workers. Workers went along with this, even though it meant their jobs became tedious and boring, because unions were able to get the workers higher wages and guarantees of promotion in exchange. As opposed to workers, managers and engineers needed to be specially trained. The expanding public system of colleges and universities provided for this.

In collective capitalism, the maintenance of long-term relations between firms allows for planned coordination by groups of firms, not just within firms. A hierarchy between firms is set up, with prominent, well-known firms buying parts from less prominent firms, with which they have a long-term relationship. This allows the high-status firms to give guarantees of life-long employment to their employees – workers as well as managers and engineers. These firms can afford to do so, because in a downturn, they can simply order less from their less prestigious suppliers, and the latter will lay off or fire workers to adjust to the new market conditions without the high-status firms needing to do so. The latter firms cut costs in a downturn not by laying off workers, but by reducing their orders from other firms. Because they follow a policy of lifetime employment, they can entrust workers with greater responsibilities. Therefore, in contrast to what is the case in the American system, workers are considered to be essential partners in the production process, so that they are skilled and well-trained, and participate in the planning of production with managers and engineers. Lifetime employment also makes managers and engineers see their destinies as being closely tied to the destiny of the company they work for, so that they are more likely to make an effort to try to save it when it runs into trouble, as opposed to simply trying to find employment elsewhere. Finally, in the Japanese system, firms that are in the same group tend to own each other, as opposed to being owned by shareholders who have no interest in the long-term prospects of a firm they happen to own. This means that Japanese firms do not have to worry as much about paying their shareholders dividends as American firms do, so that they have more funds left over for investment, and hence innovation.

The implications of this analysis for the United States are the following. Since the 1970s, American firms have responded to new competition in manufacturing industries by, as Lazonick puts it, adapting rather than innovating. What this means is that rather than trying to maintain market share by innovation, US firms try to live off past accomplishments, by, for example, making use of their distribution channels and brand names to sell products which they no longer manufacture themselves, but obtain from foreign suppliers who are their former competitors. While this allows US firms to maintain profits at levels that are acceptable to their shareholders, it has the effect of reducing workers' wages, since on the national level this process leads to a net loss of manufacturing jobs, which pay more than jobs in the service sector requiring comparable levels of education. Such a historical analysis leads to policy implications which are different from what one gets from the perspective of mainstream economics which, as Dewey observed, deductively obtains its views on policy from first principles. A major policy implication is that a way must be found to reduce pressure on US firms to maintain high short-term profitability at the expense of investment in innovation, which leads to long-term growth. Thus, from the standpoint of a historical approach, the pressures that financial markets exert upon firms are, in the current environment at least, a bad thing, rather than the good thing that they are supposed to be according to mainstream economics. This is consistent with the fact, noted by Lazonick, that firms have financed innovation and expansion by means of retained earnings, not through the stock market: historically, the function of stock markets has been to allow entrepreneurs to capitalize the wealth contained in the firms they created.[23]

Varieties of welfare capitalism

In their recent book *The Real Worlds of Welfare Capitalism*, Goodin *et al.* pose the question: "What are the best institutional arrangements for promoting each of a variety of social, political, and moral values which the welfare state has historically been supposed to serve?" (1999: vii). Following a widely recognized typology, the authors distinguish between three kinds of institutional approaches to reducing poverty: the liberal welfare regime, the social democratic welfare regime, and the corporatist welfare regime. The authors evaluate the effectiveness of these regimes by using panel data.[24] The countries chosen to represent the three different types of regime were the United States, the Netherlands, and Germany, respectively.[25]

All three types of regimes aim to reduce poverty, but they aim to do so in different ways, and each regime has different additional objectives. The authors resolve the problem of how to compare the effectiveness of regimes that are intended to accomplish differing objectives by evaluating each on its own terms, by seeing how well each accomplishes the objectives it is intended for. According to the liberal approach, the point of welfare programs is to reduce the suffering that is caused by poverty. Only the *deserving* poor, that is, the poor that are poor through no fault of their own, are to be helped, however: to help those who could work but choose not to would be to create harmful disincentives to work. Also, since the aim is simply to reduce suffering, the benefits are kept small compared to the average income of people who work: income redistribution on grounds of equity is not pursued.[26] On the contrary, keeping in mind the equity/efficiency tradeoff emphasized by liberal theorists (Okun 1975), by keeping welfare payments to a minimum and precisely targeting benefits to only the "truly" needy, the distortions produced by state interference into the economy are also kept to a minimum, leading to higher efficiency than is possible under more generous welfare regimes, and thus to higher incomes for all. Finally, it is hoped that private donations will be effective in reducing poverty and will avoid the bureaucratic overheads involved when the state serves this function, which it does as a last resort.

The objective of the social democratic regime is not only to reduce poverty, but also to make the distribution of income more fair. It is hoped that doing the latter will also help foster other objectives, such as enhancing societal stability and increasing personal autonomy: a person who is not able to provide for his needs, for whatever reason, becomes more autonomous and "free" when satisfaction of these needs is treated as a basic human right, so that the state ensures that they are satisfied, as opposed to the individual needing to depend upon the discretionary charity of others. (The liberal theory of course views welfare programs as leading to the opposite result – "dependency.")

The corporatist regime lies in many ways between the other two. Promoting equality is not a major concern. It is accepted that some will have significantly higher incomes than others; the objective is to make society more stable by strengthening the connections of individuals to the groups to which they belong, and to protect individuals from circumstances beyond their control, by giving for example workers who lose their jobs benefits which closely match the wages they received. Thus benefits paid to different individuals will vary considerably, depending on the "social rank" a given individual falls under. Like the liberal regime, the corporatist approach hopes that much financial support to individuals and families will be supplied by institutions of civil society.

The authors' basic finding is that any success of the liberal and corporatist regimes was not the result of the reasons posited in their theories. From the perspective of liberal theory, the market should have accomplished much more than it actually did, and according to corporatist theory, organizations in civil society should have accomplished much more. However in both cases, to the extent that goals other than economic growth were met, this was the result of government action. In social democratic theory, in contrast, government action is central, so that there the goals are achieved through the prescribed mechanism. The authors conclude:

> [I]t turns out that the social democratic welfare regime is "the best of all possible worlds." … [N]o matter which … goals you set for your welfare

regime [whether they be its own goals, or those of the other two regimes], the social democratic model is at least as good as (and typically better than) any other for attaining it.

(Goodin *et al.* 1999: 260)

What is surprising is that this holds for the goal of increasing average income. In the period under study (1983–1992 for the USA and 1985–1994 for Germany and the Netherlands), per capita income increased more in the Netherlands than in the USA. Furthermore, the authors argue that real equivalent household income (i.e., income adjusted for household size) is a better measure of economic well-being than per capita income, and on this measure, expressed as the change in the median or in the proportion of households showing improvement, the Netherlands (as well as Germany) performed much better than the United States. It is of course possible that generous welfare programs did have the negative impact upon economic growth postulated by liberal theory, and that the Dutch economy would have grown even faster if they did not exist.[27] But as the authors note:

> An equally plausible interpretation of our general pattern of findings, however, is to say that they simply call into question the "necessary truths" of neoclassical economics. There seem to be several different paths to economic productivity. It seems possible, in certain circumstances, to sustain generous welfare benefits without greatly increasing the numbers of people relying upon them. And it also seems possible, in certain circumstances, to sustain high rates of welfare dependency while at the same time achieving relatively high rates of economic growth. Thus one upshot of our study is to cast doubt upon the necessity of Okun's ... "big trade-off" between equity and efficiency, between social and economic objectives.
>
> (Goodin et al. 1999: 261)

To see whether the existence of this trade-off can be definitively rejected, further studies of this type are of course needed. These are precisely the types of studies – the use of "experiments" to inquire into issues that are of direct importance to human beings – that a Deweyan economic methodology calls for.[28]

Conclusion: realizing the practical implications of an empirical economics

In this chapter, we have considered the implications of Dewey's philosophy for economic methodology. Economic methodology as currently practiced tends to be descriptive rather than normative. This would have disappointed Dewey: economic methodology is essentially philosophy applied to economics; and for Dewey, philosophy is essentially *criticism*. Therefore, a proper economic methodology is inherently normative; it must either justify economists' practice or, if that cannot be done, it must criticize that practice, and show how that practice must be changed.

The practice of (mainstream) economics has not changed fundamentally since it was first codified by J.S. Mill, who argued that economics must explain phenomena by deducing them from certain "laws" of human behavior. We discover these laws not from systematic empirical inquiry, but already know them from common sense "experience" before we initiate any inquiry, in the way that we "know" the "law" that people act so as to maximize their wealth. According to Dewey, this Millian methodology is wrong, because there are no general laws of human behavior – the regularities exhibited by different societies are the consequences of particular properties of those societies, not of some universal "human nature" – and because, more fundamentally, the very notion of a scientific law as commonly understood is incoherent. On this last point, we have disagreed with Dewey: it is hard not to read the history of physics and physics as currently practiced as indicating that there are *physical* laws. Therefore, to obtain Dewey's result that there are no social laws, we have taken the very non-Deweyan route of arguing that while there is a transcendental argument for the existence of physical laws, the parallel argument for the social domain leads to the result that there are no social laws: regularity in the social domain is not the machine-like regularity of physical law, but the comprehensibility that results from the fact that humans are rule-following creatures.

Dewey holds that what distinguishes genuine scientific inquiry is that it is *experimental*, and we have supported Dewey's point that economics can be experimental in Dewey's sense by means of two examples, a historical study comparing different ways of organizing innovation in manufacturing, and a study comparing the effectiveness of three different regimes for providing social welfare services. Surprisingly, the social democratic regime, represented by the Netherlands, performs better than the liberal regime, represented by the USA, in terms of economic growth, not just in terms of reduction of poverty. This falsifies the "law," derived from a priori considerations, that there is a trade-off between equity and efficiency.

Dewey would have been pleased with the finding that greater equity need not imply lesser efficiency, and that in some cases at least, economies of social democratic societies exhibit higher growth rates than economies with much less generous social welfare policies, because he was a firm believer in social democracy. In fact, Dewey was a significant figure in the process of expanding the requirement of liberalism that individuals be as free as possible from interference from the church and state to the requirement that individuals be guaranteed a certain level of income necessary for "human flourishing" to be possible. To conclude, and to complete our review of what we as economists can learn from Dewey, it is useful to consider in a little detail Dewey's views on liberalism, to which mainstream economics is so intimately related.

In his *Liberalism and Social Action* (1935), Dewey argues that liberals often make the mistake of seeing their political philosophy in "absolutist" terms, as holding for all times and social conditions, instead of understanding it historically. Liberalism is usually seen as having originated with the political philosophy of John Locke. As Dewey argues:

> The outstanding points of Locke's version of liberalism are that governments are instituted to protect the rights that belong to individuals prior to political organization of social relations. These rights are those summed up a century later in the American Declaration of Independence: the rights of life, liberty and the pursuit of happiness. ...
>
> The whole temper of this philosophy is individualistic in the sense in which individualism is opposed to organized social action. ... It defined the individual in terms of liberties of thought and action already possessed by him in some mysterious ready-made fashion, and which it was the sole business of the state to safeguard. Reason was also made an inherent endowment of the individual, expressed in men's moral relations to one another, but not sustained and developed because of these relations. It followed that the great enemy of individual liberty was thought to be government because of its tendency to encroach upon the innate liberties of individuals.
>
> (1987 [1935]: 6–8)

An important right for Locke was the right to property. But as Dewey points out, "Locke was interested in property already possessed." A century later, interest shifted to "*production* of wealth, rather than its possession" (1987 [1935]: 8, emphasis in original), giving rise to a new, *laissez-faire* version of liberalism. The canonical argument for why individuals should be protected not merely from interference with the possession of their wealth but also from interference with the production of it was of course provided by Adam Smith, who transferred the physiocrats' doctrine of economic natural law from an agrarian to an industrial context.

Its claims to being a "positive science" notwithstanding, mainstream economics still operates with this normative political theory in the background. But as Dewey argues, the individualistic liberal theory of Locke and Smith is not appropriate under contemporary conditions. Under the influence of Coleridge and others influenced by German romanticism, for J.S. Mill,

> [t]he problem of achieving freedom was immeasurably widened and deepened. It did not now present itself as a conflict between government and the liberty of individuals in matters of conscience and economic action, but as a problem of establishing an entire social order, possessed of a spiritual authority that would direct the inner as well as the outer life of individuals. The problem of science was no longer merely technological applications for increase of material productivity, but imbuing the minds

of individuals with the spirit of reasonableness, fostered by social organization and contributing to its development.

(1987 [1935]: 24–5).

It was realized that contrary to what was supposed by Locke's liberalism, individuals are not taken up pre-formed into society, but are produced by the society to which they belong; therefore, that society has an obligation to see to it that those individuals are placed under conditions that allow them to form properly.[29] Because of the learning process of people such as Mill,

> [g]radually a change came over the spirit and meaning of liberalism. It came surely, if gradually, to be disassociated from the *laissez-faire* creed and to be associated with the use of governmental action for aid to those at economic disadvantage and for alleviation of their conditions. In this country, save for a small band of adherents to earlier liberalism, ideas and policies of this general type have virtually come to define the meaning of liberal faith.
>
> (1987 [1935]: 18)

Dewey wrote "Liberalism and Social Action" just before the New Deal. Today the "small band of adherents" has swollen to virtually all of the Democratic Party, and Dewey's "earlier liberalism" now has a name, "neo-liberalism," and is indeed held to represent the very quintessence of modernity, as opposed to the half-way stage on the way to modernity's full development which the earlier liberalism really represents. The USA never established a social democratic welfare regime in the way that the northern European democracies did, merely a "safety net," but today even that is under attack. It is hard to deny that such neo-liberal measures, and neo-liberalism in general, get their intellectual support and "scientific" credibility largely from mainstream economics, with its *laissez-faire* implications.

Dewey argued that mainstream economics gets its substantive implications not from empirical evidence, but from a priori deductions. Those indicate that a society can provide in a thoroughgoing way for the welfare of all its citizens only by sacrificing the overall level of that society's income. The most thorough empirical study done to date indicates that that is not the case, and the simple idea of "human capital" suggests we have no reason to believe that further studies would not yield the same conclusions. Therefore, a good way to start creating a public call for a more rational and just economic policy would be to induce economics to follow what Dewey called an "experimental," rather than its current a priori, method. This is a worthy task for economic methodology.

What are the chances of a Deweyan economic methodology replacing the current one? A sense of this can be obtained by considering when the last time was that the USA embraced ideas in keeping with Dewey's philosophy –

the New Deal.[30] The latter was preceded by a period similar to the present one, with the prevalent social and political climate being a free-market boosterism, the presence of a financial bubble, and so on. What made reform acceptable then was the economic collapse, and there is no reason to think that things would be any different now. How likely is a collapse of comparable severity to occur today?

To answer this question, it is necessary to pick up the story of the US economy's position in the world from where we left it earlier, in the 1980s. Initially, US policy makers shared the widespread concern in the USA with relative decline in manufacturing, which was reflected in the countless books that were published in that decade about the Japanese economy. A concerted effort to arrest, and indeed reverse, this decline was undertaken with the Plaza Accord of 1985, which reversed the strong dollar policy which had been in place since the Reagan–Thatcher monetarist "revolution" of 1979–1980. It was hoped that the lower dollar would increase US exports by making them cheaper; simultaneously, complaints about "unfair trade practices" of other countries, particularly Japan, were stepped up, and legislation to close off the US market to leading (mostly East Asian) foreign competitors was passed in 1989. Although these steps did usher in a revival of US manufacturing, the increase in US competitiveness was almost wholly the result of differences in wage growth and the exchange rate, as opposed to any speed-up in US manufacturing productivity growth (Brenner 2002: 61). Thus, the revival did not indicate that the problems that Lazonick had delineated had been resolved, but merely that foreigners were now more willing to buy US goods, since they had become cheaper for foreigners.

Unfortunately, the weak dollar was taking its toll on the Japanese economy, highly dependent on the US market for exports. After Washington rescued the Mexican peso in response to the peso crisis of 1994–1995, there was a further run on the dollar, bringing the yen to its highest levels ever. "Japanese producers could not even cover their variable costs, and ... the Japanese growth machine appeared to be grinding to a halt" (Brenner 2002: 130–131). The world economy could not afford a Japanese crisis of similar proportions to the Mexican one, so the USA entered into an arrangement with Germany and Japan, later called the "reverse Plaza accord," to reverse the upward trend of the yen and the downward trend of the dollar. At the same time, during spring and summer 1995, the USA "summarily dropped its campaign to force open the Japanese auto parts market," thus making clear that support of US manufacturing was no longer a major US policy goal. This entirely unexpected change in policy of both the USA and its trading partners set the stage for the boom of the late 1990s. The strong dollar policy was implemented by lowering Japanese interest rates with respect to those of the USA, and also by substantially enlarging Japanese purchases of US Treasury bills, as well as purchases of dollars by Germany and the US government. The USA-bound foreign capital largely found its way into the US stock market, thus leading to the continual increase in US equity prices during this period. This effect was magnified by the Federal Reserve's easy money policy; American firms used the abundant liquidity to buy back their own shares in order to get the high growth rates in their stock prices expected during the period, thus increasing the size of the bubble (Brenner 2002: 146–152). One can expect that the severity and duration of the period of low growth brought on by the collapse of the bubble will be augmented by the overabundance of physical capital resulting from the high levels of investment stimulated by the bubble.

At the same time that the shift from a policy supporting US manufacturing to one supporting a strong dollar occurred, one can also detect a shift in US geostrategic policy which has been pointed out by the demographer/political scientist Emmanuel Todd (2002). As late as 1993, books with titles such as *The Competitive Advantage of Nations* (Porter 1990) (which dealt with various types of capitalism, such as Japanese, German, or Korean, held to be superior to the Anglo-Saxon variety) or *Head to Head: Coming Economic Battles among Japan, Europe, and America* (Thurow 1992) were being published. It was still expected that the USA would exist in a bi- or at least multi-polar world, since Russia was still a formidable power, despite the dissolution of the Soviet Union. The USA would thus be one liberal market society among others, and thus formulate its economic policy accordingly – that is, it would have to be concerned with the problem of its decreasing economic competitiveness. However, as the collapse of the Russian economy progressed, the idea of the USA being the world's sole superpower, and accordingly acting in its own interests alone, became increasingly seductive. Thus, in 1997, Brzezinski (1997) advocated the domination of the Eurasian continent through the encirclement of Russia with US military bases. Perhaps decreasing economic competitiveness was not such a problem after all, since it could be compensated for by leveraging US military power and the disproportionately high (relative to its present share of world GNP) influence of the USA over international organizations such as the United Nations, the World Bank, and the International Monetary Fund, a legacy of the immediate post-Second World War situation. To make such a posture more palatable both to US citizens, who tend to view their country as a republic or indeed a democracy, and to other governments, this policy could be called imperial, rather than imperialist: creating the world order that would best serve US interests would "require that Americans re-conceive their role from one of a traditional nation-state to an imperial power. An imperial foreign policy is not to be confused with imperialism. The latter is a concept that connotes exploitation, normally for commercial ends, often requiring territorial control" (Haass 2000).[31]

As Lazonick has pointed out, US manufacturers responded to the new competition they faced from East Asia by adapting, rather than innovating. Therefore, their ability to innovate is now as low as it has ever been. Consequently, the USA imports more (relatively higher-quality/cheaper) goods than it exports (relatively lower-quality/more expensive) goods, at the current exchange rate. To be sure, demands for many types of foreign goods are relatively insensitive to the exchange rate, since many types of goods (particularly electronic ones such as flat-panel computer displays or the laser engines used in laser printers) simply are not produced in the USA. Nevertheless, when a country persistently exhibits a large trade deficit as the USA has done since the early 1980s, normally a self-corrective mechanism comes into play: in order to attract the foreign capital to counterbalance the trade deficit, the country must raise interest rates; this lowers its aggregate demand, and hence its imports, up until the point that the trade deficit disappears. As Michael Hudson (2002) has shown, US policy makers came upon, more or less by accident, a means to evade this classical balance-of-payments adjustment mechanism. It is this that allows the USA to finance its persistent balance-of-payments deficit.

As is often the case when a country wages a war, the US government was not willing to pay for the Vietnam War by raising taxes. Instead, it ran a budget deficit; the military spending that was financed by this deficit created a balance-of-payments deficit. Since the Bretton Woods system that was set up after the Second World War operated under a gold standard, because the USA could not sell enough goods and services or financial assets to pay for the goods and services it was consuming to run the war, it needed to make up for this shortfall by allowing foreigners to obtain gold in exchange for the excess dollars that they were receiving. However, by 1971 it became clear that the USA did not have sufficient gold reserves to continue honoring foreign central banks' requests for gold, and the USA got off the gold standard. From now on, the USA would no longer release gold that it held in its reserves for dollars. As an economist working for the Chase Manhattan Bank gloatingly pointed out as this process was beginning, this would leave the central banks of other countries in an unfortunate predicament:

> With their dollars no longer freely convertible into gold, they would have to decide what to do with the dollars they own, and how to deal with the dollars that would be presented to them by their own commercial banks for conversion into local currencies.
>
> But this would be a most disagreeable choice. On the one hand, if they permitted the dollar to depreciate, prices of U.S. goods would drop relative to domestically produced goods. Furthermore, it would make U.S. exports more competitive in third markets. This solution would be vigorously opposed by most exporters and businessmen abroad.
>
> On the other hand, if foreign central banks continued to support the dollar at its present [foreign exchange] rate, this would place them more unequivocally than ever on a dollar standard. ... If it is made unmistakably clear that in the event of a crisis the U.S. would simply terminate the privilege now given to foreign central banks of buying [U.S.] gold freely, then the burden of decision regarding the defense of the dollar would be shifted even more than now from the U.S. to the shoulders of European and other central banks.
>
> (Deaver 1967, cited by Hudson 1977: 24)

We are back in the same situation today, with the difference being that instead of the balance of payments deficit being caused by a war, it is the product of the inability of US industry to meet the requirements of US consumers and businesses.

The USA has created a world financial system in which it can amass arbitrarily large trade deficits indefinitely, and these will be financed by foreign central banks accumulating more and more dollar reserves. Hudson calls this system the "Treasury-bill standard," because when a foreign commercial bank turns in dollars to its central bank to receive its local currency, the central bank can do nothing with those dollars but recycle them back into the US economy, financing the US federal government deficit by buying US Treasury bills. If foreign central banks exchanged their dollars for other currencies instead, eventually the dollar would plummet, destabilizing the world financial system. (The central banks are not able to buy more "tangible" assets such as US corporate stocks or real estate because their holdings are reserves, which must be liquid.) As Hudson has noted, under this system, the US balance of payments deficit amounts to a kind of tribute, since the US indebtedness (mostly in the form of its Treasury bill liabilities) is already so large that it can never be repaid (in any case, the USA has made clear that it will never repay it), and it is growing ever larger. Foreigners provide the USA with real goods and services, and receive in return only US Treasury bills, which will never be redeemed, but only rolled over into further debt. By buying these bonds, they also do the USA the favor of financing its budget deficit. By not taking any measures to curb its balance of payments deficit, the USA is daring the creditor central banks to provoke a world economic crisis, which is what would occur if they refused to continue to be subject to this exploitation by declining to accept any more dollars. The situation continues because creditor countries believe they would be more vulnerable if a break occurred than would the world's main debtor, the USA, which has a continental economy and has traditionally been economically self-reliant, with its international accounts being relatively small in proportion to its GDP.

But does the world need the USA more than the USA needs the world? Todd (2002) has made the case that it does not. The USA is dependent on the world for many goods that it cannot produce itself, and it is only able to pay for all the goods and services it consumes by running a persistent balance of payments deficit, accumulating debt in the form of US Treasury bills which will never be repaid.[32] What the world receives from the USA in turn is merely effective demand, which the USA cannot even fully finance itself. Japan and other East Asian countries continue to amass holdings of dollar reserves, in order that their companies can keep on selling products to American consumers. It is clear that such a situation cannot last forever. Eventually foreigners, and then their governments, will begin to resent this exploitative policy to such an extent that they will not allow it to go on any further, even if the dislocations to the world economy that would result would cause them short-term costs.[33] The USA could not credibly make the threat to use its nuclear arsenal to preclude this: Mutually Assured Destruction (MAD) still works, since Russia is still a *nuclear* superpower (Todd 2002). A replacement could be found for the effective demand that the USA provides for the world economy by writing off Third World debt.

It is also possible that the dollar will collapse, due to foreign central banks no longer being able to support it, before that point is reached. Under either scenario, the USA would lose its present ability to finance both its balance of payments and its government budget deficits, something which would have disastrous consequences for the US economy, as would the supply shock resulting from the many high-tech components – going into consumer and other products – which the USA is unable to produce itself, becoming suddenly much more expensive in US dollars. When that time comes, there will be a new openness to Deweyan economic methodology, since it will have become difficult not to recognize the degree to which mainstream economic methodology serves to obscure and mystify, not describe and explain, the true nature of the economy.

Notes

1 Indeed, as Dewey notes, "it was interest in social inquiry and discussion that underlay the work of John Stuart Mill in composing his classic treatise on Logic" (1984 [1929]: 168).
2 For essentially historical reasons, this philosophical influence manifested itself in economic methodological debate mostly as the pronouncements of Karl Popper.
3 An exception is Lawson (1997), the most prominent proponent of critical realism in economics. Lawson is uncompromising in his rejection of mainstream theory, and is explicit in wishing his methodology to serve as a "handmaiden" for a more empirically adequate economics.
4 All three of these approaches are empiricist, in that they hold that the sole grounds for judging the truth of a theory is empirical evidence. As I have argued elsewhere (Viskovatoff, forthcoming), there is another tradition in the philosophy of science according to which other factors, such as unifying power of theory and comprehensibility of theoretical concepts, enter into such judgments: Kantian philosophy of science. That this tradition is essentially ignored by mainstream economic methodology indicates how philosophically narrow this field's perspective actually is.
5 Readers wishing to get a broader sense of contemporary economic methodology can turn to Hands (2004, 2001) and Dow (1997).
6 We shall encounter this possibility later in the chapter.
7 Of course, this is not a valid argument – the structure of the argument is (1) p → q; (2) q; (3) ∴ p – but this would not be the first time that rhetoric employs faulty logic. I argue that this is the principal actual justification of mainstream economics in Viskovatoff, forthcoming.
8 As Manicas (1998: 52) notes, in other works Dewey was more of a realist on physical causes.
9 As we shall see in the next section however, we shall need to return to this matter after all.
10 This is essentially Lawson's (1997) critique of mainstream economics.
11 To put this in Kuhnian terms, the point is that if, in cases when an anomaly appears, a new paradigm emerges which eventually becomes generally accepted,

and for which the former anomaly is no longer problematic, one would have reason to think that one is dealing with a genuine science. In economics, conflicts that existed between the so-called Mercantilists and Adam Smith exist to the present day, not fitting this picture at all. Avoiding the obvious conclusion that would follow from this according to Dewey's philosophy of science may be one reason why mainstream economists tend not to favor methodological pluralism.

12 Rüstow (1942, 2001 [1945]) argues that this attitude is of a religious, mystical nature, ultimately deriving from Stoicism, of which Adam Smith was a strong admirer.

13 When mainstream economists make the claim that economics follows the method of the natural sciences and hence is itself a genuine science, they almost invariably note as the one difference the difficulty of performing experiments in economics. One economic experiment was performed in the USA however – a study of how workers' labor participation rate is affected by a negative income tax, carried out in New Jersey in the 1970s – but this is the only example that ever gets mentioned. There has recently appeared in mainstream economics a field called "experimental economics." This involves investigating in the laboratory, by having undergraduates sit in front of computers simulating a theoretical economic model, the degree to which the predictions of highly idealized economic models can be "confirmed" – hardly what Dewey had in mind.

14 It should not be surprising that Kant was able to explicate this aspect of science more extensively than Dewey: Kant actively engaged in physics, the theoretical science *par excellence*, whereas the science to which Dewey made contributions was psychology, which even today is primarily an experimental science, with no widely accepted general theory.

15 I am here presenting the description of science of Gerd Buchdahl (1992), who places Kantian ideas within the context of recent philosophy of science.

16 The result of conceptual explication of a given theory will be, to put it in Lakatosian terms, the theory's "hardcore" (Lakatos 1970). Thus, according to the Kantian account, the "hardcore" elements of a given discipline are rationally justified by showing how they "make sense," whereas for Lakatos, as for Kuhn, they are essentially held by the adherents of a given paradigm because of "conversion experiences" they have had.

17 The main place where the explicative component comes up in the economic methodology literature is with Friedman (1953) in effect advocating its suppression, by arguing that the more "unrealistic" assumptions are, the better.

18 Mainstream economists often claim that their theory is superior to other approaches because there is no other theory of comparable generality: mainstream economics can "explain" everything with one theory – that people maximize their utility. Thus mainstream economics does give the systemic component its due, instead of ignoring it as it does the explicative component.

19 As Pihlström (1998) and Westphal (2001) have argued, pragmatists can make good use of transcendental arguments. As I argue in Viskovatoff (2002), so can critical realists (see footnote 3).

20 An economic example illustrating this is provided by Lawlor's chapter in this volume. In the 1990s, economists discovered that a "law-like" relationship between money supply M2 and gross domestic product ceased to hold; as Lawlor observes, a similar relationship between M1 and GDP accepted earlier by economists ceased to hold in the 1970s. Evidently, the amount of money in circulation is determined partly by the demand for money, and, as Keynes argued, the amount of money that economic actors will require will be influenced by the amount of interest they forgo by holding their wealth as money as opposed to in the form of less liquid, interest-bearing assets. Since people hold money to make purchases, there will be a relationship between the amount of money in the

economy and total purchases, which is the statistical relationship that economists observed. However, when new kinds of assets are introduced which provide liquidity while still earning interest, economic agents' behavior will change, as happened in the 1970s and 1990s. Note that the observed "law-like regularities" disappeared, while the rule followed by agents – hold only as much liquid assets as you need, keeping in mind the opportunity cost of doing so – remained the same.

21 Mill's claim that mature sciences like physics increasingly become deductive as opposed to experimental sciences notwithstanding.

22 In keeping with his view of scientific rationality as paradigmatic, Dewey tended to advocate planning by the state as superior to reliance upon the free market. (See, e.g., Dewey 1985 [1931].) We see here that he was half-right: planning does allow the economy to deal with more complexity than does the market. Where Dewey was wrong was in not realizing that this planning is often done by corporations.

23 Another discrepancy between mainstream economics and the historical record is the fact that all three countries pursued protectionist policies during their periods of industrialization.

24 As they argue, the more usual approach of using time series of various indicators of economic well-being does not tell us enough, since that approach merely takes periodic snapshots of groups, without being able to say how individuals got into one group or another, or what happens to particular individuals at different points in time.

25 Holland rather than one of the Scandinavian countries was chosen as the social welfare state to examine because no panel data for any Scandinavian country exists.

26 This is Friedrich Hayek's position, which suggests that it might be more appropriate to call this regime *neoliberal*: after all, Dewey was a liberal, and he certainly believed in income redistribution!

27 It is also possible that the US economy would have grown faster in the period under study if the negative impact of the financial system upon manufacturing industry, noted elsewhere in this chapter, had not been present, or if the huge drain on the US economy produced by military spending, which the 2001 terrorist attacks on New York and Washington, DC have shown has little or no discernible benefit, had been avoided.

28 Interestingly, although this book has received favorable reviews in the *American Political Science Review*, the *Journal of Sociology*, and the *American Journal of Sociology*, it has not received reviews of any kind in any economics journal to my knowledge. Evidently, when a central tenet of mainstream economics is empirically refuted, the response is not to try to refute the refutation, but simply to ignore it.

29 This was also the position of Hegel, who was a major influence on Dewey:

> [C]ontingent physical factors and circumstances based on external conditions ... may reduce individuals to *poverty*. In this condition, they are left with the needs of civil society and yet – since society has at the same time taken from them the natural means of acquisition ... [since individuals can no longer provide for themselves autarchically, as Locke assumed, but depend on the market for their existence], and also dissolves the bond of the family in its wider sense as a kinship group – they are more or less deprived of all the advantages of society, such as the ability to acquire skills and education in general, as well as of the administration of justice, health care, and often even of the consolation of religion. For the *poor*, the universal authority [i.e., the state] takes over the role of the family.
>
> (Hegel 1991 [1821]: 241, emphasis in original)

30 Dewey himself of course did not think the New Deal went far enough, and as Goodin *et al.* (1999) suggest, he was correct.

31 At the time of writing, Haass was Director of Policy Planning for the State Department.

32 The standard textbook story is that if there is a deficit in trade in goods and services – the current account – this must be compensated for by a surplus in the capital account. The fact that if the capital account surplus is insufficient to make up for the current account deficit, the shortfall must be covered by the reserves account is treated as an afterthought. It is never mentioned that if one currency functions as the international reserve currency, no mechanism exists to limit the balance of trade deficit that the country "owning" the currency can run. If the dollar were not the world's reserve currency, the US would have had to sell off assets, such as real estate and corporate equity, to finance its current account deficit.

33 The decision for when to make the break would thus be primarily political, not economic. It would doubtless be influenced by the apparent increasing divergence between European and American values, with Europeans still adhering to modernity – requiring real, not just simulated, democracy and that international disputes be resolved through international law, not violence. Why should one expect Europeans and East Asians to go on financing wars they themselves do not want? Currently, the US current account deficit is nearly 50 per cent bigger than its military expenditures.

Bibliography

Brenner, R. (2002) *The Boom and the Bubble: The US in the World Economy*, London and New York: Verso.

Brzezinski, Z. (1997) *The Grand Chessboard: American Primacy and Its Geostrategic Imperatives*, New York: Basic Books.

Buchdahl, G. (1992) *Kant and the Dynamics of Reason*, Oxford: Blackwell.

Deaver, J.V. (1967) "Deficits, dollars and gold," *Business in Brief*, 73.

Dewey, J. (1977 [1903]) "Logical conditions of a scientific morality," in *The Middle Works*, vol. 3, Carbondale: Southern Illinois University Press, pp. 3–39.

—— (1981 [1925]) *Experience and Nature, The Later Works*, vol. 1, Carbondale: Southern Illinois University Press.

—— (1982 [1918]) "A new social science," in *The Middle Works*, vol. 11, Carbondale: Southern Illinois University Press, pp. 87–92.

—— (1984 [1929]) "Philosophy," in *The Later Works*, vol. 5, Carbondale: Southern Illinois University Press, pp. 161–177.

—— (1985 [1931]) "Social science and social control," in *The Later Works*, vol. 6, Carbondale: Southern Illinois University Press, pp. 64–68.

—— (1986 [1938]) *Logic: The Theory of Inquiry, The Later Works*, vol. 12, Carbondale: Southern Illinois University Press.

—— (1987 [1935]) "Liberalism and Social Action," in *The Later Works*, vol. 11, Carbondale: Southern Illinois University Press, pp. 1–68.

Dow, S. (1997) "Critical survey: Mainstream economic methodology," *Cambridge Journal of Economics*, 21(1): 73–94.

Friedman, M. (1953) "The methodology of positive economics," in *Essays in Positive Economics*, Chicago: University of Chicago Press, pp. 3–43.

Goodin, R.E., Headey, B., Muffels, R. and Dirven, H.-J. (1999) *The Real Worlds of Welfare Capitalism*, Cambridge: Cambridge University Press.

Haass, R.N. (2000) "Imperial America," paper presented at the Atlanta Conference, November 11. Online at: http://www.brook.edu/dybdocroot/views/articles/haass /2000imperial.htm (accessed 1 June 2003).

Hands, D.W. (2001) *Reflection without Rules: Economic Methodology and Contemporary Science Theory*, Cambridge: Cambridge University Press.

—— (2004) "Pragmatism, knowledge, and economic science: Deweyan pragmatic philosophy and contemporary economic methodology," in E. Khalil (ed.), *John Dewey: Modernism, Postmodernism and Beyond*, London: Routledge.

Hausman, D.M. (1992) *The Inexact and Separate Science of Economics*, Cambridge: Cambridge University Press.

Hegel, G.W.F. (1991 [1821]) *Elements of the Philosophy of Right*, ed. A.W. Wood, trans. H.B. Nisbet, Cambridge: Cambridge University Press.

Hudson, M. (1977) *Global Fracture: The New International Economic Order*, New York: Harper & Row.

—— (2002) *Super Imperialism: The Origin and Fundamentals of U.S. World Dominance*, 2nd edn, London and Sterling, VA: Pluto Press.

Hutchison, T.W. (1938) *The Significance and Basic Postulates of Economic Theory*, London: Macmillan.

Kant, I. (1997 [1781]) *Critique of Pure Reason*, trans. and ed. P. Guyer and A.W. Wood, *Cambridge Edition of the Works of Immanuel Kant*, Cambridge: Cambridge University Press.

Lakatos, I. (1970) "Falsification and the methodology of scientific research programs," in *Criticism and the Growth of Knowledge*, Cambridge: Cambridge University Press, pp. 91–196.

Lawson, T. (1997) *Economics and Reality*, London: Routledge.

Lazear, E. P. (2000) "Economic imperialism," *Quarterly Journal of Economics*, 115(1): 99–146.

Lazonick, W. (1991) *Business Organization and the Myth of the Market Economy*, Cambridge: Cambridge University Press.

Manicas, P.T. (1998) "John Dewey and American social science," in L.A. Hickman (ed.), *Reading Dewey: Interpretations for a Postmodern Generation*, Bloomington: Indiana University Press, pp. 43–62.

Mill, J.S. (1965 [1843]) *A System of Logic Ratiocinative and Inductive Being a Connected View of the Principles of Evidence and the Methods of Scientific Investigation*, in Collected Works of John Stuart Mill, vol. 7–8, Toronto: University of Toronto Press; London: Routledge and Kegan Paul.

Okun, A.M. (1975) *Equality and Efficiency: The Big Tradeoff*, Washington, DC: The Brookings Institution.

Pihlström, S. (1998) "Peircean scholastic realism and transcendental arguments," *Transactions of the Charles S. Peirce Society*, 34 (2): 382–413.

Porter, M. E. (1990) *The Competitive Advantage of Nations*, New York: Free Press.

Rosenberg, A. (1983) "If economics isn't science, what is it?" *Philosophical Forum*, 14: 296–314.

Rüstow, A. (1942) "Appendix: general sociological causes of the economic disintegration and possibilities of reconstruction," in W. Röpke, *International Economic Disintegration*, London: William Hodge.

—— (2001 [1945]) "*Das Versagen des Wirtschaftsliberalismus*," in F.P. Maier-Rigaud and G.M. Rigaud (eds), *Das Versagen des Wirtschaftsliberalismus. Das neoliberale Projekt*, Marburg: Metropolis, pp. 19–200.

Samuels, W.J. (1989) "Economics as a science and its relation to policy: the example of free trade," in M.R. Tool and W.J. Samuels (eds), *The Methodology of Economic Thought*, 2nd revised edn, New Brunswick, NJ: Transaction Publishers, pp. 406–428.

Thurow, L.C. (1992) *Head to Head: Coming Economic Battles among Japan, Europe, and America*, New York: Morrow.

Todd, E. (2002) *Après l'empire: Essai sur la décomposition du système américain*, Paris: Gallimard.

Viskovatoff, A. (2002) "Critical realism and Kantian transcendental arguments," *Cambridge Journal of Economics*, 26(6): 697–708.

—— (forthcoming) *Critique of Economic Reason*, London: Routledge.

Westphal, K.R. (2001) "Can pragmatic realists argue transcendentally?" manuscript, University of East Anglia.

18 Dewey and economic reality

Michael S. Lawlor

Now reality is, I fear, more than a double-barreled word. Its ambiguity and slipperiness extend beyond the two significations which Hocking mentions in such a way as to affect the interpretation of "independence" and "dependence," in the view taken by him. For there is a definitely pragmatic meaning of "dependence" and "derivation," which affects the meaning of that most dangerous of all philosophical words, "reality." The objects of knowledge, when once attained exercise, as I have already said, the function of control over other materials. Hence the latter in so far depend for their status and value upon the object of knowledge. The idea of the ether was dropped when it ceased to exercise any office of control over investigations. The idea of quanta has increased its role because of its efficacy and fertility in control of inquiries. But this interpretation of dependence is strictly functional. Instead of first isolating the object of knowledge or judgment and then setting it up in its isolation as a measure of the "reality" of other things, it connects the scientific object, genetically and functionally, with other things without casting the invidious shadow of a lesser degree of reality on the latter.

(Dewey 1940: 160)

Real: Its use to be completely avoided when not as a recognized synonym for genuine as opposed to sham or counterfeit.

Reality: As commonly used, it may rank as the most metaphysical of all words in the most obnoxious sense of metaphysics, since it is supposed to name something which lies underneath and behind all knowing, and yet, as Reality, something incapable of being known in fact and as fact.

(Dewey and Bentley 1949: 300)

It depends on what you mean by reality

For an economist, even one sympathetic to the Pragmatism(s) of Peirce and James, the most jarring and difficult to comprehend aspects of Dewey's epistemology are his provocative statements on the open, unfinished and ultimately plastic character, not of knowledge, but of reality. Consider for instance the following statement from 1907, which is particularly pregnant with hints as to his complex ideas on this subject:

> If knowing be a change in a reality, then the more knowing reveals this change, the more transparent, the more adequate, it is. And if all existences are in transition, then the knowledge which treats them as if they were something of which knowledge is a kodak fixation is just the kind of knowledge which refracts and perverts them. And by the same token a knowing which actively participates in a change in the way to effect it in the needed fashion would be the type of knowing which is valid. If reality be itself in transition – and this doctrine originated not with the objectionable pragmatist but with the physicist and naturalist and moral historian – then the doctrine that knowledge is reality making a particular and specified sort of change in itself seems to have the best chance at maintaining a theory of knowing which itself is in wholesome touch with the genuine and the valid.
>
> (Dewey 1907: 126)

The exploration of what Dewey means by such statements as "knowledge is reality making a particular change … in itself" and its applicability to economic analysis is the subject of this chapter. To immediately state my premise, I believe that Dewey offers insightful, coherent views on the ultimately tentative and revisable character of the objects of real live inquiry. I also believe that these lessons, which can only be won by what Dewey would have called a thorough reconstruction of our philosophical outlook, are valuable and perhaps uncomfortable realizations for an economics profession that is accustomed to a self-conscious self-image of itself as positivistic science. But once this lesson has been learned, once one adopts Dewey's full conception of inquiry, including its unfamiliar and jarring language regarding "reals," I think the history and current practice of applied economic analysis – the only kind that Dewey would consider legitimate – offer many examples of the knowledge process as he saw it. I will briefly offer one such example at the end of the chapter. From the perspective of this chapter, what a Deweyan view on the evolution of economics adds is not so much a matter of substance or methodological prescription. Rather it offers a change in perception about how economists conduct inquiry in the social world

Before tackling those large topics, however, it will be useful to offer some preliminary arrangement of the props used in the argument to be staged. Properly this would require a starting point in Dewey's total philosophical outlook, its antecedents and context and its own development over time. Philosophers, in other chapters in this volume, treat this task. My goal is more narrow, as can be seen from the just-mentioned statement of purpose. It may be useful, however, to advertise up front some of the things I will and will not be doing. Most importantly I am using the Dewey oeuvre very purposefully and selectively. Thus I will admittedly avoid much of the intricacy of the voluminous primary and secondary literature on Dewey. In particular I will brush over the many subtleties of the precise theoretical form, and especially the long development of the language of Dewey's conception of truth, reality and the process of inquiry. More positively put, it is my reading that there is an underlying unity of outlook that, from his conversion to Pragmatism around the turn of the century onward, runs through all the zigs and zags of Dewey's massive output – from his earliest essays on pragmatism at the turn of the century, through his struggles with the theory of truth, underpinning his views on education,[1] to his mature statements of *The Quest for Certainty* and *Experience and Nature*, and even up to his last efforts to restate his case, such as the collaboration with Bentley on *Knowing and the Known*.

In the next section I will try to offer a statement of what I think this consistent message is. But as my final preliminary, I wish first to comment on the one aspect of this dynamic development in Dewey's writings (that I am otherwise suppressing) that must be addressed in the present discussion. It is a general aspect of his lifework that does strikes me as relevant to understanding his conception of the relationship between the process of inquiry and its object. That aspect is the continual frustration Dewey expressed about his ability to state his case in such a way that made his intended point and his consequent continual search for a "language" that would be appropriate to this task. This search saw him successively experiment over his career with various terms, such as truth, reality, importance, significance, meaning, and warranted assertion. It was responsible for his repeated and subtle recourse to the analysis of definitions. The dictionary makes numerous appearances in Dewey's writings. Significantly, these definitional excursions were used to show the ambiguity and double-barreled nature of words. Often Dewey's concern was to show that the multiple senses of a word revealed a common sense acknowledgment of the multiple perspectives in which a sign could be seen as signifying its object. More often than not, his complaint was that philosophy had idealized one meaning only, and so had lost touch with the more ambiguous, but meaningful, common usage. This linguistic aspect of Dewey's problem is nowhere as important as in his writings on "that most dangerous of all philosophical words, 'reality.' "

Reality was dangerous for Dewey because it embodied in one word the common conception of all idealist conceptions of knowledge. He labored throughout his career to counter this traditional use of the concept, and as with the term truth, finally felt forced to abandon it for what he called in his last formulations, summarized in *Knowing and the Known* (with A. Bentley, 1949), "the total transactional field." In fact it was in the presentation of the transactional analysis – where transaction was to stand for the model depiction of the continuously dynamic process by which inquiry is involved with the world – that Dewey also came finally to abandon the term "reality" altogether. His final posititon is indicated by definitions quoted at the top of this chapter. It was also in *Knowing and the Known* that Dewey's concern with definitions, a trait he shared with Peirce, reached its ultimate limit in his and Bentley's attempt to "name" the terms of a system that might consistently relate his conception of knowing.[2] I recognize the usefulness of the transactional description of knowing as a way to avoid unnecessary dualism between subject and object. I wish only to enter a simple, perhaps philosophically naïve, plea for what I see as the greater suitability for my purposes – those of a philosophical economist – of Dewey's previous attempts to cover the same ground with more common sense language.

From the perspective of an outsider to professional philosophy, but a sympathetic student of pragmatism and Dewey, the whole idea of a Deweyan system appears strangely antithetical to the spirit of his life work. Style is not all there is to the man, but in most of Dewey's writings it seems to fuse into a whole that is a natural complement to his message. Calm reasoned exploration of difficult topics is presented as a series of experimental forays. With homely language and examples, he slowly dismantles his absolutist opponents and tentatively builds an alternative conception. Thus he shows, as he is saying, that knowing occurs in the specific context of a live problem and that its terms must be adapted to the needs of that problem. In this context the notion of a system, at least stylistically, appears to contradict the specificity of knowing. Furthermore, the notion of a set of predetermined definitions postulated to code discussion of Dewey's ideas seems even more anathema to this spirit. This may be especially so in the present case. Isn't it possible that abandonment of the term "reality" would likely limit, not enlarge, chances for discussion with the vast majority of readers for whom reality, used in a very common sense manner, is so much seen as a "useful guide in enlarging the functioning of experience?" Also, doesn't such a list fail on Dewey's own previous grounds, as a frozen idealization of terminology, far removed from the actual life experiments of non-philosophical readers? Again I am reminded of Dewey's life-long commitment to dethroning eternals – what he calls "kodak fixations" – and his continual elevation of the flexible, adaptive knowings of real live actors as the key to understanding the epistemological problem. Isn't this one of the meanings of his championing the sense of common sense?

For my purposes this introduction should also serve as a notice that most of the material from Dewey that I will use comes from the period before he had rejected the term "reality." These works are written in the congenial style I have described earlier, and thus make a more vital connection to me than perhaps they would to one more enamored of the modern precision of philosophical debate. As is clear from Dewey's vast writings for more popular, non-philosophical readers, he obviously valued different horses for different courses. This is the horse I have chosen. Hopefully there will be some value in at least seeing how far we can take his argument with living, but ambiguous, common language. In any case, we cannot do away with the problem of the confusion of what reality signifies by new names, especially for an audience at the crossroads of social science and philosophy, for whom these names are not signs of a knowing. Thus for audiences like me, "slippery" and "more than double-barrelled" though it may be, perhaps we are stuck with "reality."

In the next sections I try to explain Dewey's views on the practical character of reality, and fit them into his general position on the "quest for certainty." In the process we will be forced to contend with the linguistic problem just raised. We will also be led to the consequent terminological tangle that Dewey came to lament concerning the topic of reality. I will end by suggesting an example from economics that I think suggests the validity of Dewey's pragmatism and the real intellectual vertigo it lands us in. I hope my brief comments will both exemplify in what sense it is possible to be a pragmatic realist and how difficult it is to use traditional terminology to present such a case.

The quest for certainty

The setting for our discussion of reality is what I see as the most difficult and vulnerable aspect of Pragmatism, its soft underbelly if you will. This is the problem of how do we judge the validity of beliefs if, along with Dewey and all the Pragmatists, we reject the classical view of "Reality" as an inaccessible and unchanging realm of pure certainty and truth, and center our attention on the pragmatic consequences of belief? In *The Quest for Certainty* Dewey shows that this idealistic view of truth and reality extends all the way back to the Ancients. It is also common to the otherwise incompatible British empiricist tradition (Locke, Hume) and the more rationalistic idealism of the continent (Kant and Hegel). This pairing is a dichotomy that crudely characterizes the world of epistemology that Dewey was challenging. In this tradition a further common outlook was the notion that human cognition was at best a mere glimpse, a dim and imperfect reflection, of the perfect forms of reality. Dewey also thought he saw in this tradition an intellectual source of the common social denigration of "practical" knowledge, just because practical knowledge, being uncertain and changeable, only imperfectly compared with ideal, immutable, certain "reals."

As a co-conspirator in Pragmatism with Peirce and James, this divorce of knowledge from experience, and knowing from practice, did not sit well with Dewey. Like them, he took aim at the very form in which the question was posed. Why must we analyze knowledge with reference to the abstract unknowable? In fact, looking at science as his model, it was clear to Dewey that the advances in knowing that we observe were made by a process much closer to that observed in the "profane" everyday professions than they are to the world of certainties of which previous philosophies had spoken. In experimental settings there is no certainty. This gives to ideas and theories a constitutionally mutable, revisable, character. Concepts evolve as the experience in using them to guide investigation evolves. Given the obvious success of science, might we do well to attend to this example for our model of knowing, says Dewey? In arguing his affirmative response, he also rejects the traditional ranking of ways of knowing – ideal versus practical. Instead, Dewey conflates the theoretical knowing of the sciences with the profane knowing of practice and common sense action. In the process he "evades" the traditional epistemological categories and explodes their questions.

On the uncertain reception of *The Quest for Certainty*

Such is the content of Dewey's mature project as expressed in *The Quest for Certainty*, *Experience and Nature* and elsewhere. Having taken my first philosophical milk from Peirce and having been raised as a Pragmatist, I have no trouble accepting Dewey's consequently radical "reconstruction of philosophy." Yet Dewey spent a lifetime trying to get this point across in a convincing manner. As Peirce and James had before him, he found the reception of this pragmatic epistemology a mare's-nest of mis-communication and controversy. The very fact of the current revival of Pragmatic philosophy, not to mention the controversy it has aroused, is evidence that the difficulty of his message persists. It behooves pragmatic thinkers to ask why, and to attempt to alter his formulation for our purposes, to make the points that still seem valuable.

I would say that one of the principle sources of this problem is that the very language of epistemology is drenched through with implications derived from this older classical "certainty" tradition. Combined with this is the difficulty, for communication, of too radically departing from ordinary usage in language. My reading of Dewey suggests that his early immersion in professional philosophical debate left him exhausted and dissatisfied with his attempts to use ordinary language to communicate his view of the knowledge process. His later abandonment of discussion of the "double-barreled" word reality, and his concentration on "experience" as the primary process to be focused on, was one move to reassert his ideas differently.

In particular, the problem can be stated as: How do you make Dewey's point about the ultimate revisability of knowledge, its essential lack of certitude, using the terminology of "truth" and eternal "reality," whose everyday meaning is colored by unstated preconceptions derived from the idealist tradition? Alternatively, we will see how difficult it can be to either try to use these terms in an entirely novel fashion, or, most difficult of all, not use them at all. As a partial exploration of this treacherous terrain, let's continue with our interpretation of Dewey's position on epistemology presented in *The Quest for Certainty* by examining some of his middle period writings where he was directly engaged in hand to hand combat with his philosophical critics over the very question of the character of reality. In the process I will try to pay particular attention to his struggle to convey his meaning with the language-cum-philosophical baggage, what Pierce called the signs, of the more traditional philosophical discussion.

"Does reality possess a practical character?"

A good starting point is an article by that title from 1908, in which Dewey tries to show how the pragmatic view of knowing relates to the traditional notions of reality as the realm of unchanging essences. To use Dewey's formulation, borne of a controversy over his denial of the traditional dichotomy of profane human knowledge and pure reality, the question is "why should the idea that knowledge makes a difference to and in things be antecedently objectionable?" His first pass at an answer already involves a contrast between his interpretation of reality and that of the classical epistemology:

> If one is already committed to a belief that Reality is neatly and finally tied up in a packet without loose ends, unfinished issues or new departures, one would object to knowledge making a difference just as one would object to any other impertinent obtruder. But if one believes that the world itself is in transformation, why should the notion that knowledge is the most important mode of its modification and the only organ of its guidance be a priori obnoxious?
>
> (Dewey 1908: 125)

Taking science as our model of knowing suggests that the epistemological question is not how do we ever know anything of the ideal world, but rather, what is the character of the knowledge that we use everyday? Dewey's solidly pragmatic answer is that the distinguishing feature of actual observed human knowing is that it serves our purposes. This means knowing will result in action that is adapted to reality – not the ideal reality of the philosophers but our own living reality to which we are intent on adapting. Such knowledge will be fallible and so open to revision, and thus will not result in absolute certainties like the Platonic forms. In fact it is "practical" that it be so flexible. Flexible knowing allows one to more easily adapt to the changing encounters of experience. As can be imagined, however, this process of accumulating a body of experimental knowledge will be one that is fraught with error. So arises a complement of questions that parallel those of the search for certainty and truth in the older view, now updated by Dewey's experimental outlook. What are the criteria of deciding the validity (usefulness, degree of instrumental power, etc.) of an idea? Is it possible to compare this evolving body of belief with traditional notions of confirmation and error? Put most crudely: How do we know if such useful beliefs are true?

> The realness of error, ambiguity, doubt and guess poses a problem. It is a problem which has perplexed philosophy so long and has led to so many speculative adventures, that it would seem worth while, were it only for the sake of variety, to listen to the pragmatic solution. It is the business of that organic adaptation involved in all knowing to make a certain difference in reality, but not to make any old difference, any casual difference.

The right, the true and good, difference is that which carries out satisfactorily the specific purpose for the sake of which knowing occurs. All manufactures are the product of an activity, but it does not follow that all manufactures are equally good. And so all "knowledges" are differences made in things by knowing, but some differences are not calculated or wanted in the knowing, and hence are disturbers and interlopers when they come – while others fulfill the intent of the knowing, being in such harmony with the consistent behavior of the organism as to reinforce and enlarge its functioning.

(Dewey 1908: 129)

Here we see Dewey grappling with the notion of truth as it is conceived in his pragmatic approach. Truth is not found by appeal to an ideal world of essences. Instead, true knowing "fulfill(s) the intent of the knowing." Alternatively, error (bad knowings) must be beliefs that frustrate the intent of the knowing. The fundamental nature of knowing is found in the ability of an idea or concept to further enlarge our functioning. Our inquiry will cease when this purpose is achieved, or replaced by a new intent. But is such knowledge true to reality?

For ordinary purposes, that is for practical purposes, the truth and realness of things are synonymous. We are all children who say "really and truly." A reality which is so taken in organic response as to lead to subsequent reactions that are off the track and aside from the mark, while it is existentially real, is not a good reality. It lacks the hallmark of value. Since it is a certain kind of object we want, that which will be as favorable as possible to a consistent and liberal or growing functioning, it is this kind, the true kind, which for us monopolizes the title of reality. Pragmatically, teleologically, this identification of truth and "reality" is sound and reasonable: rationalistically, it leads to the notion of the duplicate versions of reality, one absolute and static because exhausted; the other phenomenal and kept continually on the jump because otherwise its own inherent nothingness would lead to its total annihilation. Since it is only genuine or sincere things, things which are good for what they pretend to in the way of consequences, that we want or are after, morally they alone are real.

(Dewey 1908: 130)

This is quite a breathtaking statement. It shows Dewey probing his new conception of things with language forged in another realm. He is seemingly attempting to explain reality and truth by using the traditional words but self-consciously avoiding our traditional view of them. In the process he works down to the root of the problems of communication that his radical attempt to "reconstruct philosophy" leads. Perhaps an attempt at translation might be in order. For Dewey we shouldn't ask for the difference between a truth and an error. Instead "the right, the true and good, difference is that which carries out satisfactorily the specific purpose for the sake of which knowing occurs." Real error and doubt do exist. But they do not reflect a comparison between our meager belief and ideal reality. From a "practical" standpoint, there is no distinction between the truth and realness of things. But there are degrees of truth, and better and worse realities. The "good" reality is that which in knowing it leads to behavior that will be "as favorable as possible to a consistent and liberal or growing functioning." And so, finally, it is admitted, "it is this kind, the true kind [of belief], which for us monopolizes the title of reality."

So truth does not "approach" reality, but ideas of the class that are well adapted to our purposes are good and so "monopolize the title of reality." Is this mere word play? Dewey claims not, and his argument rests on his interpretation of science again. As he sees it, science (he mentions both Darwinian biology and physics) suggests a dynamic, evolving universe and not a static ideal one. Thus, if we are to "know" such a universe our concepts themselves will have to be as dynamic and open to change as the reality that we are trying to understand. For Dewey "reality" is a process in the making. Moreover, as befits the practical emphasis of a pragmatist, we need not stop to consider the ultimate and general reality of things except in so far as these bear upon the practice our knowing is engaged in.

> Hence the appropriate subject-matter of awareness is not reality at large, a metaphysical heaven to be mimeographed at many removes upon a badly constructed mental carbon paper which yields at best only fragmentary, blurred, and erroneous copies. Its proper and legitimate object is that relationship of organism and environment in which functioning is most amply and effectively attained; or by which, in case of obstruction and consequent needed experimentation, its later eventual free course is most facilitated. As for the other reality, metaphysical reality at large, it may, so far as awareness is concerned, go to its own place.
>
> (Dewey 1908:129)

Finally, lest we think of him as partaking in the supernatural, Dewey cautions, from "the teachings of sad experience" of being misunderstood, that this does not imply that we are free to construct our own individual fantasy realities:

> The change in environment made by knowing is not a total or miraculous change. Transformation, readjustment, reconstruction all imply prior existences: existences which have characters and behaviors of their own which must be accepted, consulted, humored, manipulated or made light of, in all kinds of differing ways in the different contexts of different problems. Making a difference in reality does not mean making any more difference than we find by experimentation can be made under the given

conditions. … Still less does it mean making a thing into an unreality, though the pragmatist is sometimes criticized as if any change in reality must be a change into non-reality.

(Dewey 1908: 132).

Viewed through the glasses of the cook-book positivism and text-book accounts of "scientific method" typical of a modern economist's training, Dewey's discussion can seem jarring and strange. What is a "change in reality?" What could it mean to say that "knowledge is reality making a particular and specified sort of change in itself?" What happened to falsification tests and the progressive nature of science revealing to us an unchanged essence of things as they really are?

One way of putting this "radical" departure from our preconceptions is that Dewey was taking seriously what formulaic treatises on scientific method merely ape. That is to say that the traditional view of science as a series of (seemingly random) hypotheses which are held up to a direct test of "Reality" and then either rejected or not, does not fully capture what Dewey is describing as the method of experimental rationality. For him scientific knowledge is at once more and less than this tradition has led us to believe. It is more in that it ends up radically challenging the traditional notions of an unchanging certain Reality. The formulaic notion of progressive science does not at root conflict with an idealist view of reality. In it each experiment is merely an instance of the classic view by which we refract and distort true reality by our imperfect thinking. It may be a more successful way (in an instrumental sense), but still it results in a knowledge that is imperfect by comparison with the world of certainties. Dewey's rejection of the certainty view says that we can never have any more "perfect" or "real" a reality than the set of circumstances we currently know. But we can have one that allows us to do more. As we can do more we transactionally change what we know of reality and cumulatively this alters reality for us. This doesn't mean we necessarily ignore or forget older elements of reality, so long as they continue to have an influence over our actions. But new actions which occur with new knowing will open up possibilities never before entertained. Thus, we don't just passively compare our ideas to ideal realities, as in the cook-book view. We interact with reality and our conception of it changes as our ideas do.

Second, Dewey's science is less exalted than the conventional picture because it does not constitute a fundamental departure from everyday ways of knowing. For Dewey, just like we do in our everyday activities, scientists are groping around in their environment, trying to alter the circumstances that they are faced with to a specific purpose. The inquiry they conduct results in new knowledge which itself becomes part of the world in which they are operating. If pragmatically the whole meaning of a concept is found in its practical consequences, then new concepts imply new practical consequences. Thus each successful experimental result, each successful habit in our personal and social lives will imply some alteration of those environments that have to be taken account of in subsequent investigations. Thus he claims that at bottom his view of reality coincides with common sense views of knowledge and judgment:

> Popularly, good judgment is judgment as to the relative values of things: good sense is horse sense, ability to take hold of things right end up, to fit an instrument to an obstacle, to select resources apt for a task. To be reasonable is to recognize things in their offices as obstacles and as resources. Intelligence, in its ordinary use, is a practical term; ability to size up matters with respect to the needs and possibilities of the various situations in which one is called to do something; capacity to envisage things in terms of the adjustments they make possible or hinder. Our objective test of the presence or absence of intelligence is influence upon behavior. No capacity to make adjustments means no intelligence; conduct evincing management of complex and novel conditions means a high degree of reason. Such conditions at least suggest that a reality-to-be-known, a reality which is the appropriate subject-matter of knowledge is reality-of-use-and-in-use, direct or indirect, and that a reality which is not in any sort of use, or bearing upon use, may go hang, so far as knowledge is concerned.
>
> (Dewey 1908: 126)

Science and the dangers of honorific knowing

Shifting focus for one last pass on this slippery argument, let us look briefly at some other comments of Dewey's concerning the role played by the concept of reality and knowledge in elaborately developed systems of science. In particular, I would like to explore the issue of how the sciences themselves, in their own self-image, often profess a view very much at odds with Dewey's. Understanding how and why this occurs will prove useful in our attempt to link up with economics.

In the process of his critique of Bradley, "The intellectualist criterion for truth," Dewey (1907) restates his pragmatic conception of inquiry, starting with something "out of joint between our desires and experience", and terminating when we "modify our conception of the situation so that our desires are fulfilled." The end result, again, is that "we make a new Truth – an adjustment of reality for us."[3] But here a possible difference between common knowing and scientific investigation is presented. In common everyday practice, says Dewey, most such adjustments to reality are left aside completely, they disappear as a problem with an answer and are thenceforward not thought about at all, treated as just another fact of existence. "Such however is conspicuously not the case with our scientific ideas."

For some of the products of science the process of making them true reveals so startlingly new an adjustment to reality that it becomes a basis for numerous rethinkings of other questions and activities, often widely separated from the original inquiry in which they were conceived:

The idea operates in many other inquiries, and operates no longer as mere idea, but as a proved idea. Such truths get "eternal" status – one irrespective of application just now and here, because there are so many nows and heres in which they are useful.

(Dewey 1907: 71)

Dewey here brings in a very interesting aspect of science, one often noted by philosophers and historians of science, which is the tendency of scientific knowledge to be clustered around breakthrough ideas. Today, after Kuhn and Lakatos, these clusters are most familiar as paradigms or research programs. What is intriguing about Dewey's pragmatic take on paradigms is that he calls our attention at the same time to both their practicality and the thoroughly human, natural origins – and dangers – of such honorific ideas.

First there is the pragmatic quality of such paradigmatic core concepts – also called by Dewey "truths in general," "truths in themselves," or "in the abstract," to which positive value is assigned on their own account. Dewey urges us to recognize that despite this status, these concepts are not the absolute copies of reality of Idealism. These concepts should instead be seen as valuable because they have derived, in a genuinely Deweyan dynamic formulation, a "generalized energy of position." This power is partly derived from repeated use, to be sure, but is also due to the wide potential future uses to which it is anticipated they may be put.[4] Thus they are not dead, static, eternals, in the sense of an ideal unchanging reality so much as they are highly likely to be useful in the foreseeable future (though conceivably they could ultimately be superseded):

so to say that an idea is "eternally true" is to indicate prospective modes of application which are indefinitely anticipated. Its meaning, therefore, is strictly pragmatic. It does not indicate a property inherent in the idea as intellectualized existence, but denotes a property of use and employment. Always at hand when needed is a good enough eternal for reasonably minded persons.

(Dewey 1907: 71)

Yet, as always, Dewey hastens to humanize the process of science as inquiry, to emphasize that its vast prestige should not blind us to the fact that it too is an ordinary human behavior, not completely different from more common-sensical activity. In this case he warns that the idea systems which have secured such a permanent status can become dangerously attractive in themselves, for more than pragmatic reasons alone:

They naturally and properly add to their intellectual and to their practical a certain aesthetic quality. They are interesting to contemplate, and their contemplation arouses emotions of admiration and reverence. To make these emotions the basis of assigning peculiar inherent sanctity to them, apart from warrant in use, is simply to give way to that mood which in primitive man is the cause of attributing magical efficacy to physical things. Aesthetically such truths are more than instrumentalities. But to ignore both the instrumental and the aesthetic aspect, and to ascribe values due to an instrumental and aesthetic character to some interior and a prior constitution of truth is to make fetishes of them.

(Dewey 1907: 74)

Through distance from the origin of such truths in an original practical problem, such honorific status often creates its own dogma. For Dewey, this is the cause of science itself often being seduced by the superiority of the results of its own knowing.[5] In enthroning epistemology in the experimental method of science, Dewey is also simultaneously dethroning science from this realm of unchanging and hence unknowable absolutes. Let us end with a warning he issues on this head, one that I hope to show in the next section is particularly applicable to the development of economics:

We may not exaggerate the permanence and stability of such truths with respect to their recurring and prospective use. It is only relatively that they are unchanging. When applied to new cases, used as resources for coping with new difficulties, the oldest truths are to some extent remade. Indeed it is only through such application and such remaking that truths retain their freshness and vitality. Otherwise they are relegated to faint reminiscences of an antique tradition.

(Dewey 1907: 74)

An economic example: the changing relationship between money and output

> Monetary theory is less abstract than most economic theory; it cannot avoid a relation to reality, which in other economic theory is sometimes missing.
>
> (Hicks 1967: 156).

All of this talk of practical consequence, common sense and the specific nature of knowledge-in-use, seems to beckon us to provide an example. What type of adjustment to reality can we practically say has resulted from the knowing experience of things, and in particular from the formal process of inquiry? I think there are many examples of such evolutions of knowledge in use from the economics field.[6] One currently very relevant topic is that of the changing meaning of money's relationship to aggregate economic activity in recent economic analysis.

The history and practice of monetary economics is a fantastic example of a complex system of inquiry, which has continually updated itself in pursuit of its subject. Of all aspects of the discipline of economics, the field of monetary economics is sometimes cited as the one least likely to fall into a tired scholasticism, what Dewey would have called a fetish above. The reason for its experimental character is at least two-dimensional. On the one hand its subject – roughly the manner in which financial institutions and markets provide the services of intermediation and media of exchange to the economy – is itself a vitally dynamic and changing phenomenon. Consideration of the evolution of forms of money and types of banking service and accounts over the last 300 years is one hint of this inherently dynamic character. The other is that for at least 200 years, the theory and practice of monetary economics has been tied up with – in a true organic Deweyan fashion – monetary policy, in all that term's multifarious meanings, depending on current social, legal and historical conditions (e.g. the Bank of England in the gold standard era versus the Federal Reserve in the era of fiat money). This is not to say that there have not been episodes of torpor and unchecked error by policy makers and economists, as well as examples in monetary economics of the "attribution of magical efficacy" to formulaic conceptions.

To try to quickly get to my example, it is perhaps useful to start with one such magical formula:

$$MV = PT$$

To economists, this familiar equation, where M represents the money stock, V the average turnover rate of that money in a given time period, P a suitably chosen average of prices, and T a suitably chosen aggregate of quantities of transactions in the same time period, is best thought of as an identity. It identifies the tautology that the sum value of all transfers of goods and services in a monetary economy in any time period (the right hand side) must equal the sum value of all monetary transfers that take place in the same period (the left hand side). I use it here to represent a view that started from this formula and, by a series of assumptions and deductions that are sufficiently familiar to economists but which don't really concern us here, came to be known as "Monetarism." The most basic and characteristic monetarist doctrine was the conception that all macroeconomic events and policy are intelligible via the postulation of a stable link between the money supply and the nominal value of total gross economic output, nominal Gross Domestic Product (GDP). As a prominent proponent of this view put it in a formal dictionary entry on the topic (Cagan 1987: 195): "Monetarism is the view that the quantity of money has a major influence on economic activity and the price level and that the objectives of monetary policy are best achieved by targeting the rate of growth of the money supply."

Without going into detail, this notion, which goes back at least to David Hume, was developed in the post-Second World War era into a theoretical paradigm, one of Dewey's "truths in themselves." Adding complexity, it was also proposed as a tool by which the "judgments" of central bank policy makers could predict the effects for inflation and economic growth of their attempts to exercise "control" over the money supply (control being a term commonly used by both Dewey and the Federal Reserve). It is not at all clear if the central bankers themselves ever took this very seriously, but the "quantity" of money and its empirical counterparts in Federal Reserve aggregates (M1, M2, etc.) clearly became more and more a part of the Fed's self-conscious presentation of its policy stance to the public. So by the 1980s for instance, when the Fed was called upon to semiannually justify its policies to Congress, there were regularly trotted out "target" growth rates for these monetary aggregates. Ignoring the question whether this was a serious constraint on their policy behavior (the evidence, say many monetary economists, indicates it was not), it was an addition to their rhetorical stance that depended on the same newly sanctified monetarist position. As a result, the public, particularly those whose job it is to forecast economic activity in the private sector (however inaccurately), were also thus implicated in this new state of things. An example of the reality of the latter is the Fed's quick retreat from weekly money supply announcements in the early 1980s when they found the markets reacting so strongly to their interpretations of them vis-à-vis the almost complete early missing of those "targets."

An extremely complex "transactional field" would have to be specified to do justice to the factors responsible for the rise to prominence, temporary widespread acceptance, and eventual demise of this "knowing." They would include (but are not limited to): concrete social factors such as the high inflation of the 1970s, the search for political cover amongst Federal Reserve officials hoping to bring this inflation under control, as well as intellectual factors, such as the fall from prominence of some "Keynesian" ideas about macroeconomic relationships, which itself can be traced to prior social and intellectual factors. It would also be grossly misleading to suggest that there were not throughout this episode constant internal professional and external empirical and policy "puzzles" associated with this approach that continually dogged it. In any case there was a time (echoes of Camelot!) when much of what passed for monetary economics was motivated – either negatively or positively – by the "generalized energy of position" associated with the core monetarist concept that changes in the money supply are tightly and causally linked (with a short lag of appropriate length) to changes in the level of nominal economic activity, and (with an even longer lag) to changes in the rate of inflation. I am stating this as broadly as possible to indicate the use of this framework in organizing scientific explorations and inquiries, its basis as a forecasting tool by real economic actors (however inaccurate) and possibly even as part of the inquiry behind some policy decisions

And then this "model," like so many presumed stable empirical economic relationships before it, fell apart. Starting in the early 1990s, using an operational measure of money that goes by the term M2 (essentially a collective count of existing cash, plus checking accounts plus certain savings deposits), the rate of growth of money began to lag behind the rate of growth of nominal GDP (see Duca 1992, 1995, for a non-technical account). It continued to do so in a progressive manner until the relationship stabilized again, around a completely different gearing ratio between the two series (for monetary economists, the "velocity of money") by the end of the decade. In the process, the total transactional field just described was altered. In economics proper there began an inquiry to "explain" the loss of predictive power of the former gearing ratio. Many explanations have been offered. One of the most persuasive, for instance, focuses on the simultaneous changes in costs and returns associated with holding wealth in the form of bond mutual funds as opposed to the bank assets being counted as M2 (Duca 2000). Meanwhile, both policy makers and financial market participants, who had been growing accustomed to using M2 data for making forecasts, were left scrambling for a new form of prognosis. Such is the most recent episode of missing money, sketched in its very barest bones only.[7] What of the Deweyan interpretation?

For a pragmatist, inquiry only starts from a real doubt, in a real live context. The breakdown of the traditional link between measures of the money supply and measures of aggregate economic growth offers many examples of such real live doubt in at least two contexts. First, monetary economists interested in ex-post explanations of economic behavior have been puzzled by the erratic performance of old, previously reliable, models. In Dewey's sense the traditional monetarist approach had ceased being adaptive to its environment and so needed to be revised. Thus for the "purpose" of understanding alone, this set the profession off on a real inquiry. In addition to the interest of professional knowers, this case also exhibits perhaps even more than the usual pragmatic urgency due to the doubt it created for the Federal Reserve itself. The Fed was not just "idly" interested as the academic economists were, it had come to depend on the instrumental use of these relationships for the very practical reason that they helped inform the Fed's ex-ante process of monetary "control."

Also interesting here is the issue of the pragmatic conflation of definition with practical consequences. What should the "real" definition of money be? That will depend on one's theoretical needs for the concept, what the pragmatists would call one's "purpose." If you want to define the ultimate media of settlement, the last stage in the cancellation of debits and credits in the economy by which accounts are finally settled, then a high-powered money definition (currency plus reserves of the Federal Reserve system) will do just fine. But it gets more slippery when as a monetarist theorist or as a Fed policy maker, you want to specify a transmission mechanism from changes in reserves to changes in the real economy. In succession, M1, M1A, M2, M2-MarkII, all ceased to perform the function of being an accurate predictor of GDP growth. As each was abandoned, the concept of aggregate money was redefined to one that, as Dewey would say, "was the difference which carries out satisfactorily the specific purpose for the sake of which knowing occurs." Note that this may be the point at which the Fed's interest and the more academic monetary specialist's interest might diverge. The Fed wants to know what works for its fuller functioning in its environment. If a definitional change in the list of accounts and instruments that perform a short-run forecasting function can help in this purpose, then all to the good for them. In this regard they may be the purest of instrumentalists in the sense of a lack of any inherent theoretical tastes or qualms other than pure predictive content. If the entrails of goats really were predictively useful, surely Mr Greenspan would have them in his bathtub each morning along with his other reams of "data." But the academic economist, free of the necessity of policy action and possessing allegiances instead to a scholarly community of his fellows, which imposes many implicit standards of "scientific" validity, may have further interests in terms of changing the conception of money. Here one can legitimately pose the less practical (in the sense of policy urgency) but no less pragmatic question of the criteria by which economists learn from the dialectic of theory, policy and evidence. We could take this a step further and ask what is it about the profession of economics that makes it intent on this search for statistically "stable" – and more elusively, "policy relevant" – relationships, all based on a seemingly inviolable theoretical paradigm, its standard way of knowing? After all, Monetarism is still with us professionally speaking. This raises the issue of what the purpose of professional economics is. It is not just prediction. Ex-post, by some standards of statistical validity,[8] the quantity theory can explain the long-run association of inflation and money growth, but often only by ex-post redefinitions of the empirical money supply. Yes, the purpose of theoretical allegiances is also manifestly not just description and explanation. In at least some fashion it has become the maintenance of a protective shield of theoretical propositions and mathematical methods that define its status, and demarcate its pronouncements, vis-à-vis non-professional economists. Also, in a very Dewey-like fashion, it is obvious that each knowing environment will have its own procedures of inquiry (naming, testing, communication, etc.), presumably adapted to its own needs. Consider for instance the very different ways in which such an episode is discussed by the economics profession internally, with formal modeling and statistical tests, and the more informal policy and financial market discussions in popular media.[9]

Conclusion: is Dewey's Pragmatism realistic, postmodern or both?

So we are brought back to our initial interest in this tricky business of reality – the concept that so troubled Dewey, as we have seen. I chose the parts of Dewey's *Middle Works* I used above to show his most extended grappling with the issue in a language that was congenial to crossing over into the discourse of economists. His position there is consistent with his mature work, if not as systematically philosophized. But if other evidence is needed we can find similar, later, statements in a 1931 essay (Dewey 1931: 209) where he complains of a common recourse by philosophers to a non-problem-centered, general view of reality as "without intellectual import." Also, in a reply to his critics in 1940, cited as our epigraph earlier (Dewey 1940: 160), he cautions against too loose a use of the word, because reality is a term which, in its "ambiguity and slipperiness," is, he fears, "more than a double-barreled word." We can see some aspects of this slipperiness in the case of the monetary problem just visited. Is the reality of money something different for the Fed, the monetary economists and the money-using public? Is there any genuine sense in which the reality of the monetary economy can be said to have changed along with our knowing of it over the last forty years? Let's explore this question from the standpoint of Dewey's characterization of epistemology, surveyed earlier in the chapter.

Dewey's universe is open and subject to change. Perhaps no other social spectacle than a capitalist economy offers as ready an example of such a dynamic, constantly self-transforming universe. Of all the sectors of the economy, no other has been so rapidly evolving itself as those associated with the handling and use of information. Information is the stuff in which financial markets trade. Thus when we look at the social reality behind the money demand equations and their recent breakdowns, we can quite clearly point to the transformation that has been wrought by information technology in the activities and services of the financial sector over the last two decades. As costs have come down for all types of transactions, whole new industries have arisen in mutual funds, new financial services have been created and financial institutions have experienced a surge in evolution. In the process we have witnessed a transformation in the way money is conceptualized. There are many levels on which to view this transformative change and they correspond to the various different purposes and ways of knowing of the public, the financial economist and the Fed. First note that these are not independent of each other. The institutional and consequent conceptual changes were the result of and part of the cause of – transactionally – the dramatic change in the behavior of the public in conducting its financial affairs. One of the professional economist's explanations cited earlier (Duca 2000) shows that the public holds many fewer M2 deposits because they now have the option of a myriad of diversified bond funds. Furthermore, changes in technology have absolutely decreased the need for monetary transactions due to better control of disbursements and receipts, clearinghouse transactions and the like. The question then is: Where does reality start and end in this social change?

Looked at from the standpoint of the public this change stands as a fact of "reality" to each of them individually. They personally adapt by altering their portfolios and financial routines. But from the standpoint of the bankers and the other suppliers, they are both anticipating what this public wants, as well as observing the successes and failures of their competition. These observed preferences of the faceless "public" (nothing is so anonymous as a mutual fund) and the trends of the market are the "reality" faced by each individual supplier. But the interaction of both of these is what the economist and the Fed observe. Further, the Fed must try to predict the outcome of the joint creation of "the markets" by the public and its suppliers of financial services, to react to them, and even, perhaps, to effect some "control" over them. The reality of the monetary economists meanwhile encompasses all of this, including the interaction of the Fed with the public and the markets – perhaps even trying to predict the predicting Fed – while now bearing the additional burden of estimating the possible (self-referential) impact of economics on this process. If this is not a process of transactionally constructing reality, a reality that thereby is changing as and because of our "knowing," nothing is.

But note that such an admission is not a license for either fantasy or theoretical nihilism. For one this reality is not recreated anew each day. Second, the construction of reality is a purposeful – not a senseless – process in which market participants reinterpret and recreate the world of finance. Dewey reminds us that the changes in "reality" he envisages are not radical miraculous ones. There are many antecedents to the recent monetary developments that, though partly changed, remain constituent of the same continuous reality. In some way, banking is still the business of processing information and providing services of intermediation and liquidity that it has been since the first Italian bankers opened shop in the fifteenth century. Moreover, we have a well-documented history of central banking that offers many insights and relevant parallels to current events. Also, monetary economics does have a useful theoretical and empirical experience to offer us. Money, in fact, defined by its most basic functions, its ability to make a complex trading society possible, has remained constant throughout. But these antecedents are constantly evolving, and thus the concepts of them have had to evolve as well. Dewey would say that this means the interactive process of inquiry, knowing and action has been updating "reality." It's hard to fault him in this particular case. Things do change, yet we are not thereby barred from understanding or without recourse to "testing" procedures. But we are thus forced to recognize that our knowledge is not certain. (One would hope this last point is finally now clear in the case of the demand for money.)

This is the place at which Dewey leaves us as scientists trying to be pragmatically rational. It is less than ideally satisfying if we still cling to the ideal of the quest for certainty. Perhaps that quest itself, given its persistence, is an adaptive behavior, a kind of beneficial myopia or optimism. Yet even if it were so adaptive for non-philosophical practitioners, Dewey would seem to imply that it is not useful for the purpose of understanding the process of knowing. His message may at least partially be captured as, "watch what they do, not what they say." And in watching science and all problem-centered human knowing, Dewey saw the operation of pragmatic thinking and the consequently revisable conception of reality. Somewhat surprisingly for us, but not for him due to his own brand of Darwinism, this changeable, growing universe was for him epitomized by the physical and biological sciences. I say surprisingly because it seems more natural to us to say that we can alter the social and intellectual world by our knowing than the physical (though, upon reflection, there is ample room for his view in the modern biological notions of changing ecological environments). This is surprising also because perhaps the most prominent modern day expression of Pragmatism is in its Postmodernist incarnation as a descriptive and prescriptive account of the evolution of ideas in history and interpretations in literature. Here we can see the sense in which Dewey's rejection of the quest for certainty, his abandonment of the simple view of reality, opens up inquiry to the possibility of multiple socially constructed realities.

In this recognition we can see a different aspect of the slipperiness of the term reality than that which Dewey speaks of. We can also more readily understand the philosophical source of the Postmodernist uses to which Dewey has more recently been put. It is but a small step from "appropriate realities for the legitimate objects of an organism in its environment," to a total shattering of reality into non-intersecting personal worlds. But how to navigate the middle ground between the nightmare of totally private realities and the modernist dream, now shattered and fallen, of an ultimate, unique, unchanging "real" world, is the live question for today. Dewey shows us – and this seems also to be one message of so called Postmodernist thought – that the only guides here are an attention to the suitability of our conceptions for the purposes of our inquiry. If they become dominated by standards of political preferences or so freed from common sense notions of intelligence that they reveal a lack of natural good judgment – "the ability to take hold of things right end up" – then they will presumably not be adapted to their environment. In this case we could say such maladapted knowings should fall away when they begin to frustrate the purposes of our inquiry.

Perhaps the fairly widespread incredulity about some extreme Postmodernist thought, the sense of reaction from it we now sense in the world of ideas, is a sign of this pragmatic correction. (Though it is instructive to note that Dewey and James faced similarly outraged audiences as Postmodernism has recently.) But this would be a problem to be explored not just decried for Dewey. The fear of losing all foundations was not one that moved him. It is also useful to recall his demand for recognition of the particularity – what William James called the "plural" aspect – of the world of inquiry. Ultimately, according to Dewey, all we have to depend upon in this process is our own active participation in the problems and rewards of knowing:

> Under such circumstances there is danger that the philosophy which tries to escape from the form of generation by taking refuge under the form of eternity will only come under the form of a by-gone generation. To try to escape from the snares and pitfalls of time by recourse to traditional problems and interests – rather than let the dead bury their own dead. Better it is for philosophy to err in active participation in the living struggles and issues of its own age and time than to maintain an immune monastic impeccability, without relevancy and bearing in the generating ides of its contemporary present.
>
> (Dewey 1908: 132)

Notes

I would like to thank John Davis, John Duca, Wade Hands, Elias Khalil, Frank Ryan, Stanley Fish and John Wood for insightful discussions and comments concerning this chapter.

1   Dewey himself, in one of his rare introspective pieces, recommends reading *Democracy and Education* as a place where "my philosophy, such as it is, is most fully expounded." (Dewey 1930: 1).

2   Dewey and Bentley 1949: ch. XI, "A Trial Group of Names." The insertion of the qualifier "Trial" offers some hint that, even here, Dewey and Bentley meant the list as an experiment. So for instance: "The reader will understand that what is sought here is clarification rather than insistent recommendation of specific names; that even the most essential postulatory namings serve the purpose of 'openers,' rather than of 'determiners;' that if the distinctions herein made prove to be sound, then the names best used to mark them may be expected to adjust themselves in the course of time," etc. (1949: 289).

3   Perhaps this is a good place to note that the few papers I am directly using here are representative of many that offer a similar view of knowledge, reality and the epistemological problem. Other examples include "Beliefs and existences" (1906), "Reality as experience" (1906), "Pure experience and reality: a disclaimer" (1907), "The postulate of immediate empiricism" (1910) and *Experience and Nature* (1925, especially chapter 7, "Nature, Life and Body-Mind") and "Nature and experience" (1946).

4   This incidentally sounds very much like Lakatos's discussion of "core" theoretical concepts.

5   There is an interesting example of this, regarding a debate between Einstein and Niels Bohr over what the actual reality of physics "really" is, in *Knowing and the Known*, chapter 4, section 4. It is also discussed in a more historical philosophic context in *Experience and Nature* (Dewey 1925: 154–155).

6   I should hasten to preface this simple account of an economics example with the acknowledgment that from around the turn of the century to the 1940s, there existed in the American academy at least two generations of economists who were more or less directly inspired by Pragmatism in general and Dewey in particular. I am of course referring to what became known as the American Institutionalist School of economics. Its great masters, such as Thorstein Veblen and John R. Commons made lasting contributions to the study of economics under the banner of as thoroughgoing a rejection of standard neoclassical economic theory as Dewey's rejection of the dominant philosophy of his day. I do not want in any way to denigrate their achievements, but would add that my own view is that their positive contributions and their critique of neoclassical economic theory are conceptually separate phases of the application of Dewey's thought to economics. Thus, for example, the socially constructed reality of a consumer society, its historical evolution and the habitual adaptions of individuals to its "signs" depicted so masterfully in Veblen's *Theory of the Leisure Class*, is clearly a work that fits squarely within the pragmatist general outlook on inquiry. But Veblen's devastating critiques of marginal utility theory aside, there is no reason that even neoclassical economics, used as a tool in exploring an applied topic, should not also exhibit the common sense adaptive knowing that Dewey saw as the hallmark of successful inquiry. It is just such an example that I wish here to briefly pursue.

7   A very similar breakdown of the demand for more narrowly defined money, cash plus checking accounts, M1, had been established fifteen years earlier; see Goldfeld 1976.

8   See Hendry 2000 for a prominent exception to this claim.

9   For a look at what some monetary economists and econometricians think they
    have learned from this type of modeling experience, along with some insightful
    philosophical comments, the papers by D. Hendry (2000), B.T. McCallum (2000),
    and Mary Morgan (2000), as well as the discussion comments in Backhouse and
    Salanti (2000), "Part II: Monetary Policy," are highly recommended. Estrella and
    Mishkin (1997: 281), using a statistical test of the predictive value of monetary
    aggregates in the USA and Germany find the following: "the empirical relation-
    ships involving monetary aggregates, nominal income, and inflation are not
    sufficiently strong and stable in the United States and Germany to support a
    straightforward role for monetary aggregates in the conduct of monetary policy."

Bibliography

Backhouse, R.E. and Salanti, A. (eds) (2000) *Macroeconomics and the Real World*, Oxford:
    Oxford University Press.

Cagan, P. (1989) "Monetarism," *The New Palgrave: A Dictionary of Economics: Money*,
    London: Macmillan, pp. 195–205.

Dewey, J. (1907) "The intellectualist criterion for truth," reprinted in *The Collected
    Works of John Dewey, The Middle Works: 1899–1924*, vol. 4, pp. 50–75.

—— (1998 [1908]) "Does reality possess practical character?" Hickman, L. and
    Alexander, T. (1998) *The Essential Dewey: Volume 1, Pragmatism, Education and
    Democracy*, Bloomington and Indianapolis: Indiana University Press: 124–133

—— (1925) *Experience and Nature*, New York: Dover.

—— (1929) *The Quest for Certainty: A Study of the Relation of Knowledge and Action*,
    New York: Capricorn Books.

—— (1998 [1931]) "Context and thought," reprinted in Hickman, L. and Alexander,
    T. (1998) *The Essential Dewey: Volume 1, Pragmatism, Education and Democracy*,
    Bloomington and Indianapolis: Indiana University Press, pp. 206–216.

—— (1998 [1940]) "Nature and experience," reprinted in Hickman, L. and
    Alexander, T. (1998) *The Essential Dewey: Volume 1, Pragmatism, Education and
    Democracy*, Bloomington and Indianapolis: Indiana University Press, pp. 154–161.

—— (1998[1930]) "From Absolutism to Experimentalism" pp. 14–21 in Hickman
    Alexander (1998), *The Essential Dewey: Volume 1, Pragmatism, education and
    democracy*, Bloomington and Indianapolis: Indiana University Press.

Dewey, J. and Arthur F. Bentley. (1949) *Knowing and the Known*, Boston: The Beacon
    Press.

Duca, J.V. (1993) "Monitoring money: should bond funds be added to M2?" *The
    Southwest Economy*, Federal Reserve Bank of Dallas, special issue, June.

—— (1995) "The changing meaning of money," *The Southwest Economy*, Federal
    Reserve Bank of Dallas, isssue 6.

—— (2000) "Financial technology shocks and the case of the missing M2," *Journal of
    Money Credit and Banking*, 32 (4): 820–839.

Estrella, A. and Mishkin, F.S. (1997) "Is there a role for monetary aggregates in the
    conduct of monetary policy?" *Journal of Monetary Economics*, 40: 279–304.

Hendry, D.F. (2000) "Does money determine UK inflation over the long run?" in
    R.E. Backhouse and A. Salanti (eds), *Macroeconomics and the Real World*, Oxford:
    Oxford University Press, pp. 85–114.

Hickman, L. and Alexander, T. (1998) *The Essential Dewey: Volume 1, Pragmatism,
    Education and Democracy*, Bloomington and Indianapolis: Indiana University Press

Hicks, J.R. (1967) *Critical Essays in Monetary Theory*, Oxford: Oxford University Press.

Goldfeld, S.M. (1976) "The Case of the Missing Money," *Brookings Papers on Economic Activity*, pp. 683–730.

McCallum, B.T. (2000) "Recent developments in monetary analysis: the roles of theory and evidence," in R.E. Backhouse and A. Salanti (eds), *Macroeconomics and the Real World*, Oxford: Oxford University Press, pp. 115–140.

Morgan, M.S. (2000) "Explanatory strategies for monetary policy analysis," in R.E. Backhouse and A. Salanti (eds), *Macroeconomics and the Real World*, Oxford: Oxford University Press, pp. 141–154.

19 The subjectivist methodology of Austrian economics and Dewey's theory of inquiry

Peter J. Boettke, Don Lavoie,
and Virgil Henry Storr

The environment in which human beings live, act, and inquire, is not simply physical. It is cultural as well. Problems which induce inquiry grow out of the relations of fellow beings to one another, and the organs for dealing with these relations are not only the eye and ear, but the meanings which have developed in the course of living, together with the ways of forming and transmitting culture with all its constituents of tools, arts, institutions, traditions, and customary beliefs. ...

Man, as Aristotle remarked, is a social animal. This fact introduces him into situations and originates problems and ways of solving them that have no precedent upon the organic biological level. For man is social in another sense than the bee and the ant, since his activities are encompassed in an environment that is culturally transmitted, so that what man does and how he acts, is determined not by organic structure, and physical heredity alone but by the influence of cultural heredity, embedded in traditions, institutions, customs, and the purposes and beliefs they both carry and inspire.

(Dewey 1991 [1938]: 48–49)

What are the issues?

Many scholars have questioned the ability of economic science to deliver on its promises of logical determinacy and predictive power. The American cynic Will Rogers once described an economist as someone who can tell you what will happen under any given circumstances and his guess is liable to be as good as anyone else's. It is not so much the jargon of economics that brings on the wrath of the public and other social scientists nor is it the abstract nature of economic reasoning. All specialized disciplines rely on jargon and abstract reasoning. We believe the problem is multi-dimensional. First, some people simply resent the success that economics has had because it calls into question their cherished policy beliefs. Second, there is a perceived arrogance among economists, most obvious in the "economic imperialism" that has emerged since the 1960s where the economic method is exported to the fields of politics, sociology, and even philosophy. However, for the purposes of this chapter we propose that economics falls into disrepute because economics discusses matters which touch on everyday life, yet it seems that economists are talking about something so remote from the world within which we dwell in our everyday life.

As Ronald Coase stated the problem in his original address to the newly founded International Society for New Institutional Economics:

> Economics, over the years, has become more and more abstract and divorced from the events in the real world. Economists, by and large, do not study the workings of the actual economic system. They theorize about it. As Ely Devons, an English economist, once said at a meeting, "If economists wished to study the horse, they wouldn't go and look at horses. They'd sit in their studies and say to themselves, 'What would I do if I were a horse?'"

The implication for Coase is, if economics is going to advance, it must stop doing blackboard economics exclusively and actually look out the window and study the economic system in detail – the underlying property rights structure, the nature of contracts, the operation of firms, etc.

The problem with economics as an academic discipline, then, is that instead of trying to understand the problems of everyday economic life, economists have largely satisfied themselves with playing logical games and solving imaginary puzzles. Over the last few (at least seven) decades, economics has become more and more formal, more and more instrumental, and more and more precise about areas that are of less and less importance to anybody else. Over the last few decades, economists have increasingly special-ized in the production of "kelly green golfing shoes with chartreuse tassels" (McCloskey 2000a: 150). The problem, however, is not that they specialize. Specializing, "sticking to your last" as Smith put it, is sound economics. The problem is that "kelly green golfing shoes" are not in demand (except amongst other economists). Economics as a discipline, thus, seems caught in an institutionalized trap of "conspicuous production" and has come perilously close to becoming "precisely irrelevant."[1]

The more interpretive sub-disciplines of economics have long been complaining about the "puzzle-solving" mentality that infects the mainstream. The new institutionalists, for instance, have argued that the mainstream inade-quately appreciates the formal and informal institutions that constrain the (actual) choices of individuals (North 1990). Similarly, the economic sociolo-gists have criticized the mainstream for representing individuals as atomized, under-socialized creatures, that is, for failing to embed the individual in a context of "ongoing social relationships and structures" (Granovetter 1985). And, the subjectivists (those working in the tradition of Weber, Mises and Hayek) have attacked the mainstream for not being about "purpose," "inten-tionality" and "meaning" (Weber 1978 [1921]; Lachmann 1971; Kirzner 1992, 2000; Lavoie 1991a).

An economics of the world, the subjectivists have asserted, must be thor-oughly focused on the meanings that individuals attach to their actions and their situations. Man lives in a world of radical uncertainty yet he must orient himself to his fellow men if he is to succeed (Mises 1966 [1949]). To understand how he accomplishes this, that is, to understand how he orients himself to his fellows and how he overcomes the problems of time and ignorance, we have to construct an economics of meaning. If economics is to be relevant, if it is to serve the everyman, we have to take seriously the "subjective perspectives" of the individuals we study.

The idea of "subjectivism" appeared, at first, to be only a narrow, technical issue within the field economists call "value theory."[2] But, as Carl Menger suggested from the beginning, and as Ludwig Mises came to emphasize explicitly, the real significance of the idea is much broader. Subjectivism is not limited to a particular technical problem within a field inside of the discipline of economics; it represents a fundamental approach to social theory in general (Mises 1966 [1949]).

The idea of "subjective value" in economic theory, Mises realized, is a specific application of a more general *verstehen* or understanding-oriented approach to the human sciences, that is, the influential tradition of German social thought that is associated with the names Wilhelm Dilthey, Heinrich Rickert, J.G. Droysen, Max Weber, and Alfred Schütz.[3] Mises came to understand Menger's revolution in value theory as amounting to a turn to the *verstehen* approach, which is to say, it is an attempt to find meaning in prices. What Carl Menger was really saying when he undertook a critique of "objectivist" approaches to value theory was that prices provide market participants with a meaningful reading of the economic situation, in terms of the relative scarcities of different, subjectively-valued goods.

Before the so-called subjectivist revolution in value theory, the classical economists' attempts to find the meaning of prices in terms of the historical objective labor hours embodied in them were unsatisfactory. Prices are not arbitrary constraints, representing merely the outcome of some sort of capitalist warfare, as some Marxists would argue. Similarly, Ricardian value theory, in all its variants, mistakes the fundamental nature of price phenomena. What underlies the quantitative ratios we call price phenomena is not something objective, a quantitative property of the goods themselves, but is a quantitative reflection of a set of diverse qualitative judgments. Prices express the relative intensities of diverse "subjective" assessments of value, assessments that are based on radically diverse perspectives on the world. They are unintended resultants of purposeful plans tugging and pulling in different directions. The point in value theory, according to Mises, is that prices are guideposts that help us to orient our plans to one another.

But the traditional Austrian account of subjectivism, like the *verstehen* school with which it was linked, never completely overcame the subject/object dichotomy. It retained a tendency to think of the subjective as in some sense an inaccessible realm, buried inside of individual human minds. We will argue that although subjectivism improved upon mainstream economists in that it was able to at least start from the world of meaning, because of the manner in which it understood "understanding" it was still unable to fully return. One way in which the Austrians could escape from the psychologistic limitations of the *verstehen* approach, we contend, would be for it to take seriously John Dewey's point: inquiry needs to both begin and end in meaningful human experience, in culture.

Objective economics and the Austrian challenge

Much ails mainstream economics. It "cannot explain satisfactorily the dynamics of market activity, let alone the recurrence of macroeconomic crises, the problems of interventionism and regulation, the fiscal crises of democratic welfare states, the failure of development planning and the collapse of socialist regimes in the late 1980s" (Boettke 1994: 603). Amazingly, despite the severity of its illnesses, the mainstream has chosen to ignore the root causes of its problems, preferring instead to treat or rather to mask the symptoms.

Consider, for instance, the problem that entrepreneurship poses for mainstream economics. As Kirzner (1979: 3) pointed out in one of his early salvoes against the mainstream's model of economic activity, the market is a "process" and not a mere "configuration of prices, qualities, and quantities." The mainstream, however, models market activity as a series of instantaneous moves from one equilibrium situation to another. For markets to clear in the mainstream model, that is, for the quantity of a good demanded (desired) in a market to be equal to the quantity of that good supplied to the market, prices must adjust. If the price happens to be below the market clearing price, for instance, the amount of the good people will be willing to buy in the aggregate will be greater than the amount that people are willing to supply to the market. There will be an impending shortage and, consequently, prices will be pressured upward. Nothing within the model, however, explains how this requisite process of adjustment will occur.

Anyone who has tried to teach textbook economics has run head on into this very problem with the standard approach. Most economists compensate for this shortcoming by telling tales of businessmen recognizing the opportunities created by prices being too low or too high to clear markets and acting to exploit those opportunities. Attempts by the mainstream to transform their classroom tales into theoretical improvements, however, have been largely unsuccessful. Most mainstream textbooks barely mention the entrepreneur and little serious work has been done by mainstream economists since Knight's treatment in *Risk, Uncertainty and Profit* (1921).[4]

Why the neglect? Why has the entrepreneur been unable to find a place in mainstream theory? Swedberg (2000), in his volume on entrepreneurship across the social sciences, offers at least three possible reasons for the mainstream's neglect of what should be one of their main characters. First, he contends, "some economists [simply] assume that economic process is automatic or that economies will advance without the help of an entrepreneur."

"Others," he continues, "claim that there is simply no place for the entrepreneur in an equilibrium system; and finally there are those who state that input and output in the firm have to be determined as well as be identical for the theory to work – even though this unfortunately means that the entrepreneur is eliminated" (Swedburg 2000: 21). The entrepreneur is essentially a gadfly, annoying mainstream theory and theorists, who would prefer it to go away.

Economic historian Mark Blaug concurs with Swedberg's analysis. As he contends,

> the growing popularity of general equilibrium theory [in the middle of the last century] set the seal on the possibility of theorizing about entrepreneurship. ... Despite valiant attempts to dynamise microeconomics large parts of modern economics remain trapped in a static framework. Worse than that is the fact that modern economics lacks any true theory of the competitive process; what it actually possesses is the theory of the outcome of that process in an equilibrium state. In short, it emphasizes equilibrium at the expense of disequilibrium. By assuming that all economic agents have free access to all the information they require for taking decisions, decision-making in modern economics is largely trivialized into the mechanical application of mathematical rules for optimization.
>
> (Blaug 2000: 81)

This is extraordinary, especially since most who study entrepreneurship recognize the entrepreneur as the *sine qua non* of the economic process, the principal agent of change in the market.

The subjectivists (those working in the tradition of Weber, Mises and Hayek) are at the fore of the effort to elevate the entrepreneur to his rightful place of prominence. Austrian economist Israel Kirzner (1973: 30), for instance, has recognized that the entrepreneur plays the "crucial role in the market process." As Kirzner argues, "there is present in all human action an element which, although crucial to economizing activities in general, cannot itself be analyzed in terms of economizing, maximizing, or efficiency criteria." The allocative role of the market process cannot be understood, he claims, without reference to this "extra-economic" entrepreneurial element of human action. "A market consisting exclusively of economizing, maximizing individuals," Kirzner continues, "does not generate the market process that we seek to understand. For the market process to emerge, we require in addition an element which is itself not comprehensible within the narrow conceptual limits of economizing behavior."

Profit opportunities indicate that either sellers or buyers have been too pessimistic; buyers have either paid more for their goods than they would have had to pay elsewhere or sellers have sold their wares at a price lower than what they could have charged. For Kirzner (1999: 6) then, the entrepreneurial role in the market process is that of "alertly noticing ('discovering') [earlier] errors" in the course of market exchange and "of moving to take advantage of such discoveries, and thus of nudging the market systematically in the direction of greater mutual awareness among market participants ... the entrepreneurial discovery process is one whose tendency is systematically equilibrative."

More recent treatments of the entrepreneur within the Austrian camp have sought to embed him even more firmly in the real world. Lavoie (1991b: 36), for instance, has recognized (along with Kirzner) that the entrepreneur is not merely a calculative, mechanistic character and has argued (moving beyond Kirzner) that the entrepreneur is primarily a cultural creature:

> Entrepreneurship ... is primarily a cultural process. The seeing of profit opportunities is a matter of cultural interpretation. And like any other interpretation, this reading of profit opportunities necessarily takes place within a larger context of meaning, against a background of discursive practices, a culture.
>
> (Lavoie 1991b: 36)

Chamlee-Wright (1997, 2000a, 2000b), taking her cue from Lavoie, has discussed how Ghanaian (Ga) and Zimbabwean (Shona) cultures have impacted the entrepreneurial practices of market women in those contexts. Similarly, Storr (2002) has examined how the experience of colonialism and slavery has impeded and impaired entrepreneurial efforts in the West Indies.

The mainstream, which does not even register the entrepreneur as a blip on its theoretical radar, is simply unable to appreciate the crucial role of the entrepreneur in the market process, let alone the cultural character of entrepreneurship. Another failing of mainstream economics is its inability to make sense of the collapse of the Soviet system and the failure of the former Soviet countries (particularly Russia) to transition from the rent-seeking system that was communism to an efficient market system. Boettke (2001, 1993) argues that the techniques of aggregate economics masked the underlying structural failings of the Soviet system, and the preoccupation with static efficiency analysis at the microeconomic level also blinded economists to the realities of the political economy dynamics of the Soviet economic system. In the post-communist period, as a result, the reform proposals introduced have often been seriously flawed precisely because they failed to account for the realities of the system actually being reformed, rather than the textbook theoretical image people thought they were reforming. If the transition process is analogous to taking a trip, you need a roadmap to go from "here" to "there." Boettke counters the "shock therapy" versus "gradualism" debate, by arguing that the problem is not so much speed, as misspecification. If we badly define the "here" and leave undefined the "there" we have to arrive at, then why should we be surprised when we get lost on our trip? By focusing on the *de facto* operating principles of the real existing Soviet economic system (rather than either the textbook depiction of a centrally planned economy, or the comparison of aggregate economic statistics), Boettke argues that we can gain a better understanding of why the actual system suffered from systemic failings by exploring the everyday economic life of the people and highlighting what political economy factors must be incorporated into the analysis in order to reform the economic system and eliminate those systemic shortcomings.

Why then, we now ask, have the subjectivists been able to understand the problems of entrepreneurship and transition while many in the mainstream have not? That the subjectivists, in seeking to construct an economics of meaning, have focused on the "subjective perceptions" of the individuals they study and the "real world" (the actual contexts) in which individuals live, act and inquire is, we contend, at least part of the reason. But, there is still something not quite satisfactory about the "subjectivist position," at least as traditionally articulated.

Philosophical traps: subjectivism, objectivism, and the loss of the world

The idea of subjectivism has been interpreted, by some friends as well as foes, as the inaccessibility of the crucial data of the market; it is thought of as being buried in the minds of the participants. As traditionally elaborated, subjectivism often sounds like psychologism. It often sounds as if what is required is that we (somehow) get "into the heads" of our subjects or that we retreat into our own heads (constructing an economics purely through ratiocination). As traditionally articulated, it seems only to be about a mental world, the "subjective perceptions" of (atomized) individuals, and not about the real world. But ours is a world of interconnections and interactions. Human beings are social and political animals. Any science that is to study them must, therefore, study human experience-in-the-world.

When economists talk about something in the economy being "subjective" they are only intending to make reference to the historical debates inside economics over value theory, not rehearsing the debates within post-Cartesian philosophy about the subject/object dichotomy. The economists aren't debating with Descartes, Kant, or Hegel, they are only working on a narrowly technical point in the theory of value, the part of economics that tries to coherently explain price phenomena such as rent, profit, and interest rates. So, one might well suppose that the philosophical connotations of terms such as "object" and "subject" and their derivatives are utterly irrelevant to the economists' uses of these terms. To be called a "subjectivist" is a term of praise among many economists, who understand the term to refer to a particular achievement that marked the transformation of classical into neoclassical economics. The subjectivist or marginalist revolution is widely thought by economists to constitute a major advance in thinking within the field of value theory, an advance through which economists clarified an issue that the previous "objectivist" assumptions in value theory had obscured. It seems only to involve several technical questions in the theory of price, interest, cost, rent, and so forth. To fail to be subjectivist is to revert to a largely discredited viewpoint in value theory.

By contrast, in philosophy to be a "subjectivist" is to somehow be turned inward, in the sense of Descartes' *cogito*, and disconnected from reality. It is almost never deployed as a term of praise, and tends to connote epistemological relativism and solipsism. While the philosophers have had in mind fundamental questions about the nature of knowledge, the economists at least appear to have had in mind only an issue local to certain corners of their own discipline, involving technicalities in value theory within microeconomics.

It is certainly true that when economists deployed this language they were not exactly trying to do philosophy, and that philosophy and economics have had distinct questions in view when using this language of subjects and objects. A closer look, however, suggests that the philosophical issues are more relevant to the economists' discourses in value theory than at first appears. Philosophical problems are often deeply lodged in the culture, embedded in the connotations of words that carry meanings that may go way beyond the self-conscious intentions of the authors. Both classical political economists and neoclassical economists, as they went on imaginative flights aimed at explaining value phenomena, were dragging along more philosophical baggage than fits, so to speak, under the seat in front of them. The philosophical baggage of both terms, subjective and objective, is a burden. The Austrian school's efforts to shake off some of the negative connotations of an objective economics were nevertheless failing to escape from the philosophical hazards of this misleading dichotomy. The connotations of words such as subjective and objective, in the economists' discussions of the theory of value, point beyond value theory to larger questions of the nature of economics and of knowledge.

Perhaps economists should take heed of the kinds of critiques of the dichotomy which the pragmatist philosophers (along with several versions of post-modern philosophy) have developed. If one attends closely to the language economists use to discuss value theory, one can hear the echoes of the philosophical arguments of writers such as John Dewey that challenge Cartesian thinking. The same danger philosophers have seen in the dichotomy shows up here. The notion the Austrians were trying to carve out of "an objective science of subjective phenomena" is misleading on both ends; subjective value phenomena are made to appear too arbitrary, too disconnected from reality, too inaccessibly buried in the realm of the mental. The objectivity of science that the whole *verstehen* tradition, including the Austrians, tended to endorse as some kind of value-freedom, is today thought of by many philosophers as a false ideal. And because of these difficulties, the difference between scientific and everyday knowledge is exaggerated.

The philosophical literature's entanglement with the subject/object dichotomy goes back at least to the work of Descartes, Kant, and Hegel, some say all the way to Plato. We will not rehearse the different versions of this challenge here. Suffice it to say that among contemporary philosophers there is now wide agreement that the dichotomy causes more trouble than it is worth, that both claiming the strict objectivity of science and claiming the subjectivity of non-science (the humanities, practical experience) are highly misleading sorts of claims. Across various otherwise diverse philosophical traditions, from continental, to contemporary analytic, to American pragmatist traditions, philosophers agree that the metaphysical and psychologistic presuppositions behind this way of talking are best left behind. The contemporary analytic tradition has made this point in terms of undermining the presuppositions of the whole mind/body distinction. Likewise one of the main developments of continental philosophy, phenomenology, makes a very similar challenge to this artificial separation of the subject from the object.[5] Virtually all the major figures in philosophy in the twentieth century have come to be wary of the misleading connotations of the dichotomy.

One of the fundamental points of American pragmatism in general, and Dewey's work in particular, was the notion of reconnecting subject and object by turning to the kind of practical knowing involved in the everyday world. The pragmatist John Dewey summed up the problem with the dichotomy in this way:

> [I]t was assumed that … knowledge … is dependent upon the independent existence of a knower and of something to be known; occurring, that is, between mind and the world; between self and not-self; or in words made familiar by use, between subject and object. The assumption consisted in holding that the subject matters designated by these antithetical terms are separate and independent; hence the problem of problems was to determine some method of harmonizing the status of one with the status of the other with respect to the possibility and nature of knowledge.
>
> (Dewey 1989 [1949]: 287–288)

That is, the dichotomy tends to artificially separate the notion of (subjective) meaning from the (objective) world. It lays traps from which the Austrian school never fully disentangled itself.

Subjectivism radicalized: lachmann and the danger of solipsism

Within Austrian economics there has been only a gradual clarification of the principle of subjectivism. It has gone from a narrow, technical point to a larger message involving a fundamental transformation of economic theory, and even social theory in general, and from a psychological or "mental" matter to a broader, philosophical issue about understanding, the nature of meaningful action, and the mutual orientation of plans. This widening has amounted to a linking up of the Austrian work in value theory with the *verstehen* tradition of

German social thought, a group of philosophers and social theorists from whom the Austrians borrowed, and with whom they fought. This linkage brings both some strengths and some weaknesses to the Austrians' work. The main strength in the *verstehen* approach was that it turned the emphasis directly to the study of the meaningful world. But how did it characterize this world? The difficulties in the Austrian school's methodological principle of subjectivism trace to difficulties in the early *verstehen* tradition's own work on the nature of human understanding.

These difficulties are nowhere more evident than in the Austrian school's understanding (and misunderstanding) of Ludwig Lachmann's contribution to the tradition. The Austrian school began with the subjectivist revolution, and had always taken the word "subjectivism" to be a term of unambiguous praise. Until Ludwig Lachmann arrived, that is. Of course he used the word as the term of praise extraordinaire, the main mark of distinction of the Austrian school, of which he counted himself a proud member. But it was Lachmann who prodded the school into having second thoughts about the possibility of "going too far" with subjectivism. When he arrived at Israel Kirzner's Austrian economics program at New York University he challenged the American Austrians by suggesting that they were not thorough-going subjectivists, a charge they couldn't take lightly. Lachmann broadly understood himself as subjectivist in the same sense Mises did, but he was not just subjectivist, he was a self-proclaimed "radical." He was to say that subjectivism advanced as it went from a modest subjectivism of value (Menger) to a broader subjectivism of action (Mises) to a more radical one of knowledge and expectations (Shackle). Whereas Mises linked subjectivism with the *verstehen* school, while insisting on a fundamental distinction between theoretical conception and historical understanding,[6] Lachmann (1977 [1966]: 59–62) rejected the need for this arbitrary distinction, and explicitly called for a " 'verstehende,' or 'interpretative' economics." But what differs between Mises and Lachmann is more their sense of the nature of *verstehen* as their understanding of economics.

Lachmann's "radical subjectivism" was challenged in turn by other Austrians for leading to relativism, or solipsism, or nihilism, that is, the very dangers philosophers think of when they hear the word "subjectivism." In effect he provoked a debate within the American-Austrian school that seemed to pit his "radical" version of subjectivism with the more modest version of Kirzner. Within the Austrian school Lachmann has been criticized for having allegedly gone too far in his radicalized version of subjectivism. Radicalizing subjectivism, then, for the more traditional Austrians, seems to mean turning radically inward, and thereby losing touch altogether with objective reality.[7] We argue that this charge is misplaced, that the danger of solipsism goes way back to the psychologistic formulations of Lachmann's predecessors in the Austrian school, and that the radicalizing direction toward which Lachmann pointed us, if followed to its radical conclusions, is actually a way to avoid the danger. Subjectivism when radicalized doesn't have to mean turning to introspective self-examination, or in any way turning away from the real world. It can mean turning to the "context of inquiry" of market participants within the economy, and also the inquiry of economists who are systematically studying such actors, without having to label either one subjective or objective.

This is how Lachmann sums up the progress of an increasingly radical subjectivism:

> Subjectivism of the first stage in the 1870s was a subjectivism of wants. Different men had different wants and thus were inclined to attribute different values to the same object. Wants were regarded as personal attributes in much the same sense as other attributes, such as weight, body temperature, etc. There was no question of judgements of utility being utterances of the mind, hence problematical.
>
> In Mises's work we reach the second stage. Subjectivism is now a matter of means and ends. "In this sense we speak of the subjectivism of the general science of human action. It takes the ultimate ends chosen by acting man as data, it is entirely neutral with regard to them. The only standard which it applies is whether or not the means chosen are fit for the attainment of the ends aimed at" (Mises 1949: 21). In a world of change the mind of the actor must continuously ponder the adequacy of the means at his disposal, but not the ends themselves which are "given" to it.
>
> (Lachmann 1994: 246)

But this does not go far enough, he says. Since ends lie in the future and are thus always problematical, we have to go beyond the subjectivism of means and ends to the subjectivism of expectations. "We have now reached the third, and thus far highest, stage, the subjectivism of the active mind, and George Shackle, the master subjectivist, has been our mentor." Perhaps owing to the sometimes powerfully evocative language in which Shackle (1972) writes, Lachmann's radical move to emphasize expectations has been controversial. It is widely taken to be the place where the, until then, progressive extension of subjectivism "went too far," stepped over the line, and now, only now, invites the danger of solipsism.

On the contrary, we want to argue that there has always been something unsatisfying about the traditional formulations of the principle of subjectivism. Many statements of the principle, including some of Lachmann's own, but more prevalent in the work of earlier Austrians, exhibit an unfortunate tendency to interpret subjectivity in psychological and/or mentalistic terms, terms that seem to place meaning out of reach of any empirical research.

If what really matters, according to subjectivist theory, is the internal contents of individual minds, then how is it possible to undertake relevant empirical work? Some supporters of subjectivism, such as James Buchanan, confess that they cannot. He tells us we need two branches of economics, an objective empirical science that deals with measurable, observable price phenomena, and a subjective theoretical science that depicts economic phenomena as resulting from the inaccessible contents of minds.

Similarly, Friedrich Wieser (one of the early contributors to the school) referred to the Austrians as the psychological school and contrasted economics from the natural sciences with the notions of knowledge "from without" and "from within." Similarly, Mises and Hayek explicitly pointed to introspection as the method for getting at subjective phenomena. To the extent that subjectivism goes in this direction, there are some serious difficulties here. Laslo Csontos (1998: 86) in an article on Lachmann but actually directed at the whole school, has a point when he charges that this focus on "a kind of a priori and internal knowledge" sounds like it amounts to a form of solipsism. Csontos sums up the classical Austrian position on subjectivism (and offers some of the key citations) when he writes:

> How do we learn about our own mental states and thus how do we get to know the mental states of other people? According to one of the fundamental epistemological postulates of methodological solipsism, we can learn about our own mental states only by way of introspection (Hayek 1955: 44–5, 50, 75–6; Mises 1933: 41, 122). Introspection is a kind of inner perception, independent of any bodily organ of sense, through which we can acquire (so the theory goes) a singularly reliable form of self-knowledge. This introspectively gained self-knowledge, as a result of the basic similarity of the human mind and the commonalities of our mental structures, gives us direct access to those thoughts, concepts, and objectives with the help of which we can understand individual and collective attitudes and actions observable in the world around us.
>
> (Csontos 1998: 86)

Moreover, Csontos says, the subjectivist approach treats the interacting individuals in the market process as if they were isolated atomistic individuals whose only contact with one another is through market signals.

> In their view society is made up of independent and isolated individuals (Hayek 1952: 50–1) who not only lack a common social knowledge or common experiences but who are made even more isolated by their existing knowledge because the latter is scattered, imperfect, specific knowledge based on familiarity with particular circumstances (Hayek 1952: 29–30). Isolated individuals organize into societies as a result of utilitarian considerations, although the emergence of organized societies can be an unintended by-product of their actions. According to the proponents of methodological solipsism, the exchange relationship is the social relation par excellence.
>
> (Csontos 1998: 83)

Some of the earlier Austrians described subjectivism in a manner that certainly invites this reading of subjectivism.[8] The fact that at the time the Austrian school encountered the *verstehen* tradition it, along with most philosophy of the time, was still struggling with the subject/object dichotomy, forced the Austrians into some awkward methodological positions in order to defend the idea of a science of meaningful human action. The main thing the Austrians were trying to do was to provide a general (objective) theoretical framework for the meaningful (subjective) study of economic phenomena. The traditional philosophy of understanding seemed to leave no room for this project. Though sympathetic with the *verstehen* tradition's defense of the study of the world of meaningful action, the Austrians could not (and should not) accept its denial of universality. The way out Mises took was to artificially divorce theory (the general) from history (the particulars) assigning the *verstehen* method only to the particularistic half of the human sciences, in order to hold on to the objectivity that was thought to be required for science. Economic theory could be a body of objective, logical, scientific reasoning, and only history needs to be "tainted" with the personal, with the subjective.

When mainstream economists criticize the Austrians for "going too far" with the idea of subjectivism, or when some more traditional Austrians defend themselves from this charge but criticize Lachmann in turn, for doing so, their concern seems to be expressed in terms of the very dilemmas to which the philosophical literature on the subject/object dichotomy draws attention. Many economists may think they are "subjectivists" in a philosophically harmless sense, but when they voice their concerns about the radicalization of subjectivism they bring out exactly the kinds of difficulties the philosophical literature points to. They fear a loss of what they think is a necessary kind of objectivity; they misread the fundamental nature of subjectivity as some kind of solipsistic, inward, inaccessibility.

Questions arising in the world: Dewey as a remedy for what's ailing economic inquiry

The subjectivists need not remain trapped in the philosophical quagmire of the subject/object dichotomy. Indeed, several different branches of philosophy, including the pragmatist tradition, evolved away from the Cartesian way of thinking we have found in the Austrian and *verstehen* traditions.[9] Philosophy has gradually managed to free itself from the dichotomy and most of its metaphysical baggage. If the phrase "knowledge from within" is still used, the thing human knowing is "inside of" is no longer taken to be an individual person's mind. Rather the point is that in the study of human action we are located within language, within the world of meaning.

As we have argued, in the Misesian assertion that the human sciences are "the objective study of subjective phenomena" both the subject/object terms are problematic when viewed from the standpoint of contemporary pragmatist philosophy. That is, though we can agree with what seems to be the basic point of this formulation, that something like a science of humanly meaningful phenomena is possible, we agree with writers such as Peirce and Dewey that we should give up on the misleading dichotomous language. Perhaps a better way to put it is that economics is a systemic intersubjective study of intersubjective phenomena. The difference, then, between the sort of knowledge achieved in science and everyday life is not a difference in kind.

The study of human action is not objective. It can be systemic, scholarly, open to criticism, etc., but it really can't be objective, in the sense of detached, impartial, or impersonal. Mises, as we have suggested, fudged on this by arbitrarily separating theory from history, claiming objectivity for the theory half, even while admitting that the two halves were inseparable, so that the situatedness of the historian inevitably taints the overall work of the human scientist. In effect, he admits that all knowledge is connected to the phenomena it is about, that applied work in the human sciences is necessarily from the point of view of the researcher. This point of view is not an objective, disconnected representation of the world in itself, but an orientation from a particular context that arises from the articulations of the community of researchers.

The subjective side of this dichotomy is just as misleading. Human action is not subjective in the sense of arbitrary, or private. The "subjective preferences of individuals" sounds like something inaccessible, buried within the skulls of separate atomistic agents. It sounds like it requires a focus on the individual mind, as if it points us to the method of introspection.[10]

But what we are getting at when we refer to the subjective point of view of the agent is really the meaning things in the world have to him, which involves us not in the private, inaccessible world of an individual mind, but rather in the public, social world of language. The point of subjectivism is really the one that sociologists call the social constructivist viewpoint, the recognition that our knowledge is conditioned by the questions we ask, the language we use, the shared meanings within which our meaningful actions take place in the world. Meaning is not buried in individual minds but is publically available in cultural artifacts.

The traditional Austrians were trying to get a perspective on knowledge that doesn't have to accept what philosophers call the subject/object dichotomy. Traditional epistemology has trapped our thinking within the confines of this dichotomy. It forces us to break apart considerations of human meaning, called "subjective," from considerations of "objective" reality.

Can't the underlying message of the "subjectivist" approach to economics be clarified, be made more coherent, and more productive of useful insight, by shaking off this philosophical baggage? How best to make this move away from the (at least apparent) psychologism of Max Weber and the Austrians toward an appreciation of the "real" human experience-in-the-world? How best to make economics be about the meaningful world? How best can it deliver something of value to the general public? These remain open questions. One way to proceed, we conjecture, is by utilizing the philosophy of John Dewey.

Dewey and human experience

Dewey is perhaps the most influential American social theorist. Over his more than seventy-year academic career, he has made significant contributions to everything from the philosophy of education, art and religion to metaphysics and politics. With *Experience and Nature* (1929 [1925]), he humbly set out to repair philosophy. According to Dewey (1929: 8–9), the problem with philosophy and, indeed, with all the philosophical sciences (like economics) is that they are non-empirical or not empirical enough. As a solution, he proposes what he terms the "empirical method."

The attractiveness of the "empirical method" for Dewey (1929: 7) is that it is pragmatic. It forces us to construct philosophies about the world we live in. It forces us to consider actual problems instead of imaginary puzzles. Rather than pushing us to be more precise, the "empirical method" insists that we become more relevant. With the "empirical method," as Dewey correctly asserts, questions arise in the world, that is, they flow from experience. Understanding what Dewey meant by experience-in-the-world is, therefore, critical to understanding the "empirical method" he is promoting.

As John McDermott (1973: xxvi) pointed out in his introduction to a two-volume collection of Dewey's writings, experience stands in Dewey's work for what we might today call culture. In a letter to Arthur Bentley he made some interesting remarks about the misleading connotations of the word experience.

> Commenting on his preparation of a new edition of *Experience and Nature* in 1951, Dewey wrote that he decided to change the title to *Nature and Culture*: "I was dumb not to have seen the need for such a shift when the old text was written. I was still hopeful that the [philosophic] word 'Experience' would be redeemed by [being] returned to its idiomatic usages – which was a piece of historic folly, the hope, I mean. ..." The many critics of Dewey's prose style should be more aware that the gnarled character of some of his writing traces to a determined effort to articulate the character of our experiences in a language faithful to our way of having them and in as rich a descriptive version as possible.

This notion of articulating our experiences "in a language faithful to our way of having them" is not a bad way to sum up what the Austrians have been trying to do in their subjectivist method. Experience, for Dewey (1929: 2), "is no infinitesimally thin layer or foreground of nature." It is not, if you will, mere experience. Rather, "it penetrates into [nature], reaching down into its depths, and in such a way that its grasp is capable of expansion." "It tunnels," as Dewey asserts, "in all directions and in so doing brings to the surface things at first hidden – as miners pile high on the surface of the earth treasures brought from below." Experience, for Dewey, is thus not only the experience of nature but is also experience in nature. As Dewey (1929: 4) notes, "it is not experience which is experienced, but nature – stones, plants, animals, diseases, health, temperature, electricity, and so on." It is "not experience which is experienced" but chairs, tables, computers, friendships, business relationships, factories and offices. It is "not experience which is experienced" but advertisements, money, prices, transaction costs, goods, services and markets. "Things interacting in certain ways," as Dewey remarks, "are experience; they are what is experienced ... they are how things are experienced as well." Indeed, as Dewey contends, experience is experience-in-the-world; "experience reaches down into nature; it has depth. It also has breadth and to an indefinitely elastic extent." Anything in the world can, thus, be added to Dewey's list of "electricity" and "stones" without obscuring what he means by experience.

The contrast between the *verstehen* tradition's subjectivist mind-reading approach and a Deweyan logic of inquiry approach leads to a profound change in the way we describe the differences between the natural and social sciences, and also the differences between the kind of knowing achieved by any scientists and the practical knowing of persons in the society. A Deweyan approach need not insist on the focus on particular circumstances, but can include a discussion of general patterns, or structures. It need not insist that the social scientist's knowing is different in kind from practical knowing of everyday persons. Ultimately it need not cling to either the standard of detached objectivity the earlier *verstehen* tradition thought was required for science or the solipsism and arbitrariness of the notion of subjective meaning that it thought surrounded practical human understanding.

Lived experience, to be sure, "is multidimensional, complicated, laden with memory, emotion, and qualitative judgment" (Boisvert 1998: 17).[11] Dewey recognizes that individuals are church members, employees and employers, husbands and wives, brothers and sisters, friends and acquaintances, community members and outsiders, artisans, civil servants and entrepreneurs.

Like crops in a garden, individuals in Dewey's thought are embedded in a "network of interconnections" (1929: 21). "The crops [in a garden] are rooted in the soil, which is aerated by earthworms. Insects provide the means of pollination for the plants. Rain falls on them, and energy is received from the sun." Similarly, individuals in the world live in homes, commute to work in automobiles, buses and trams, watch television, listen to the radio, shop for books on the Internet and talk to their friends on the telephone. Mainstream economics, as we have said, routinely ignores the social and institutional context in which all economic activity takes place. It routinely treats individuals as disembodied (re)actors motivated only by pecuniary motives. It routinely pretends that individuals have

> no families, are citizens of no countries, are members of no communities and are believers in nothing at all except the pursuit of "hedonistic" utility. Individuals, in the hands of economists, are typically undersocialized, isolated creatures, unaffected by [the] society or [the] polity.
>
> (Boettke and Storr 2002)

When it does take social forces seriously, individuals get treated like social automatons; they are oversocialized creatures (Granovetter 1985). Mainstream economics does not even pretend to portray (real) individuals (interacting) in the world.

Like Dewey and unlike mainstream economics, however, Weber and the Austrians are able to conceive of actual humans. Actors, they insist, are social characters, "affected by, influenced by, even directed by social structures and relations but not determined by them" (Granovetter 1985). They are neither disembodied nor atomistic. As Boisvert (1998: 21) reminds us, "a genuinely inclusive empirical method does not uncover isolated, discrete entities. Ordinary experience reveals entities in varied, multifarious forms of interrelationships." Similarly, a "genuinely inclusive empirical method" recognizes that these "varied" and "multifarious" interrelationships all have a temporal dimension (Boisvert 1998: 22).

Real time

Lived experience takes place in a temporal context. As Boisvert (1998: 20) contends, humans in Dewey's thought "are not primarily disembodied sorts of cogitators. They are embodied individuals, participants in multifarious sorts of interactions with the world that encompasses them." Change, we might say real change, is possible and interactions, varied and multifarious interactions, occur in time. As Dewey argues, temporality is a "quality of experience" (Boisvert 1998: 23). Dewey (1934: 214) argues that "Time as empty does not exist; time as an entity does not exist. What exists are things acting and changing ... a constant quality of their behavior is temporal." As Dewey (1929: 83) asserts, "nature is an affair of affairs." Acknowledging that "nature [is] a scene of incessant beginnings and endings," he continues, "enables thought to apprehend causal mechanisms and temporal finalities as phases of the same natural process."

O'Driscoll and Rizzo (1985) offer both a critique of the superficial manner in which mainstream economics incorporates time into its theories, and an appreciation of the temporality of all action as is displayed by the Austrians. Like Dewey, the subjectivists stress the importance of real time. Time as lived, time as experienced-in-the-world, is not static or inert but is instead, as O'Driscoll and Rizzo (1985: 60) suggest, "a dynamically continuous flow of novel experiences." Genuine surprise and serendipity is possible in the world. In the world, today's experiences necessarily make "tomorrow's perceptions of events different than [they] otherwise would be" (1985: 3). In the world, time is irreversible. The subjectivists, like Dewey, do not, therefore, assume away these characteristics of real time but instead take them seriously, emphasizing the radical ignorance that necessarily conditions human action and, thus, the indeterminateness of human action-in-the-world.

The mainstream, on the other hand, very rarely takes real time seriously (O'Driscoll and Rizzo 1985: 53–59). Indeed, mainstream economists have preferred to analogize time to space (something to be allocated) rather than incorporating time, as it is actually experienced, into their theories. They have preferred a Newtonian conception of time where time is causally inert, homogeneous and only mathematically (not dynamically) continuous. In mainstream economic theories time can elapse "without anything happening" (1985: 54). As O'Driscoll and Rizzo (1985: 55) assert, "a Newtonian system is merely a stringing together of static states and cannot endogenously generate change." Each period (or point) in time is isolated and so time becomes static. In other words, mainstream economists have a radically different conception of time than Dewey and the subjectivists. While the mainstream tries to assume away the problems associated with real time, Dewey and the subjectivists, as we have seen, have no wish to escape "the temporal dimension within which interrelations take place" (Boisvert 1998: 22). Why is this? Why are the Austrians aware of the problems of real time and radical ignorance while many in the mainstream aren't? The answer, we conjecture, is that both Dewey and the subjectivists begin their analysis in the world while the mainstream doesn't.

Indeed, both Dewey's "empirical method" and the subjectivists take as their starting point the life-world where time passes and change is not only possible but inevitable. They take as their starting point the world where learning takes place and radical ignorance conditions all human action. As Dewey (1929 [1925]: 7, emphasis added) asserts, "the subject-matter of primary experience sets the problems and furnishes the first data of the reflection which constructs the secondary objects." Experience-in-the-world sets the problems that our theories try to solve. Questions arise in the world and are answered (through reflection) in the "laboratory" (or in the philosopher's mind). It is not ratiocination that supplies the questions; the "empirical method" does not tolerate logic games or mere puzzle solving. Rather, experience-in-the world "sets the problems" and "furnishes the first data" for philosophical inquiry. "How many angels can fit on a pinhead?" is thus not a valid line of inquiry, as Dewey asserts, unless "primary experience" sets us that question and unless the answer offered allows us to grasp (to better understand) the experience-in-the-world that launched that line of study. As Dewey writes, "the test and verification of [our philosophies] is secured only by return to the things of crude or macroscopic experience – the sun, earth, plants and animals of common, everyday life."

Getting back to the world

Our inquiry should not only begin in the world but should contain a path back to it. The "secondary objects" produced by reflecting on our experiences, should "define or lay out a path by which return to experienced things is of such a sort that the meaning, the significant content, of what is experienced gains an enriched and expanded force because of the path or method by which it was reached" (Dewey 1929 [1925]: 8). Philosophy (and the philosophical sciences) should illuminate aspects of our experience-in-the-world that were hitherto unseen. It should organize isolated details of some everyday experience and impart new meanings. It should search for the keys where they are likely to be, not just under the lamppost (McCloskey 1990b: 73). It should try to serve the everyman.[12]

McCloskey makes a similar point when she speaks of the relationship between metaphors (economic theory) and stories. "It has doubtless been noticed before," McCloskey (1990a: 61) says, "that the metaphorical and the narrative explanations answer to each other." As McCloskey puts it, "a story answers a model. Likewise a model answers a story." If we allow our primary experience-in-the-world (our non-analytical narratives) to inspire our inquiries, we will, as a result, begin to write better poems, develop better theories and tell better narratives.

Mises concurs, making a similar claim about the point of scientific inquiry. "The end of science," Mises (1966 [1949]: 65) asserts, "is to know reality. It is not mental gymnastics or a logical pastime." As a result, Mises continues,

> praxeology restricts its inquiries to the study of acting under those condi-
> tions and presuppositions which are given in reality. It [only] studies
> acting under unrealized and unrealizable conditions ... if such an inquiry
> is needed for a satisfactory grasp of what is going on under the condi-
> tions present in reality.

Experience, for Mises, thus, "directs our curiosity toward certain problems and diverts it from other problems. It tells us what we should explore."

Unfortunately, both the neoclassical and the *verstehen* traditions (in spite of McCloskey's and Mises' chiding) have remained non-empirical or not suffi-ciently empirical philosophical sciences. While the problem with the mainstream is that it is only superficially empirical, opting for precision over relevance, the problem with the *verstehen* tradition (at least as often articulated by the Austrians) is that it shuns any sort of empirical verification. While the blackboard economics of the mainstream does not even pretend to begin in nature, the *verstehen* tradition refuses to return to it. "The charge that is brought against the non-empirical method of philosophizing," Dewey (1929 [1925]: 8) declares, "is not that it depends upon theorizing, but that it fails to use refined, secondary products as a path pointing and leading back to some-thing in primary experience." While mainstream economics is essentially about angels on pinheads, the *verstehen* tradition is enamored with ratiocina-tion and introspection. The non-empirical methods of the neoclassical and the *verstehen* traditions fail on several fronts.

Regrettably, as Dewey asserts, "there is no verification, no effort even to test and check" in the non-empirical sciences. As hinted at earlier, those in the *verstehen* tradition shun empiricism. This is true, even though "an economics of meaning" would seem to force empirical study. How else can you get at the meaning that individuals attach to their situations and their actions except through empirical study? For many in the Austrian camp, however, getting at meaning seems an intractable problem. So, although they insist that experience "set the problems" of inquiry and that it serves as the "primary data" for study, they then all but retreat into their skulls once they begin their inquiries.

Many in the Austrian tradition "strangely" view meaning as something "internal to an individual mind," speaking frequently about the importance of knowledge-from-within. As Lavoie (1991a: 481) complains, meaning in this view, thus, "lies beyond economic science to explain and needs to be taken as given." One consequence of describing subjectivism (their economics of meaning) in this way, Lavoie contends,

> may be a permissive attitude towards abstract theorizing that stays aloof from empirical work. The common opinion of subjectivism is that its importance is strictly theoretical, that if one were to take it seriously in empirical work one would become mired in the problem of how to read people's minds.

Rather than reading people's minds, an absurdly difficult task, the Austrians typically recommend that we interpret the actions of others "on analogy of our own mind: that is, that we group their actions, and the objects of their actions, into classes or categories which we know solely from the knowledge of our own mind" (Hayek 1948: 63). As Lavoie (1991a: 482) points out, however, meaning is not in our skulls but in the world; "it is not [to be found in] an isolated, individual mind, but [in] a communicative process, a discourse." Retreating into our heads, thus, ends with us giving up on accessing the world.[13] Does the mainstream avoid this problem? Does the mainstream test its theories in the world?

On the surface, it seems almost laughable to charge the mainstream with being non-empirical. While many would concede that the mainstream does not begin in the world, most would argue that falsification, testing, checking and verification are the lynchpins of mainstream positivism (the method advocated by Friedman (1953)). As stated before, however, the mainstream is only superficially empirical; by failing to contemplate actual experience, it does not enrich our experience in the world. It does not serve the everyman. Although econometrics (aiming at statistical significance) can be used to "test" economic theories, "the things of ordinary experience do not get enlargement and enrichment of meaning as experience" from most econometric tests (Dewey 1929 [1925]: 8).[14]

Remember that ordinary experience is interconnected and embedded in a temporal world. Econometric models, however, necessarily aggregate and always abstract from the temporal dimension of human interaction. Aggregation, as is often pointed out, abstracts from the heterogeneous and context-specific character of individual interactions. Ordinary experience, on the other hand, takes place in certain places at specific times. And, even time series analysis treats time statically; "time is ... deprived of efficacy and if it does nothing, it is nothing" (Bergson, cited in Rizzo 1994: 115). Relationships are (necessarily) not allowed to change and units of time are (typically) treated as discrete. The mainstream, by failing to begin in the world, is simply unable to return to it.

Perhaps the most unfortunate failure of the non-empirical and the superficially empirical methods, as Dewey notes, however, is that they come to view ordinary experience as either "arbitrary" or "aloof." As Dewey contends,

> The objects of reflection in philosophy [and the philosophical sciences], being reached by methods that seem to those who employ them rationally mandatory are taken to be "real" in and of themselves – and supremely real. Then it becomes an insoluble problem why the things of gross, primary experience, should be what they are or indeed why they should be at all.
>
> (1929 [1925]: 9)

Economics, for instance, makes the world, which is always in disequilibrium, problematic. It cannot explain it but leaves us, in fact, perplexed by it. By beginning with atomized, isolated individuals, by failing to appreciate man's condition in the world, the non-empirical method gives rise to problems, which are, as Dewey complains, "blocks to inquiry, blind alleys; they are puzzles rather than problems, solved only by calling the original material of primary experience, 'phenomenal,' mere appearance, mere impressions, or by some other disparaging name."

The mainstream thus needs a dose of pragmatism; its inquiry needs to be grounded in reality. Similarly, many Austrians are clearly in need of a path out of their heads and back into reality. How can we ensure that our questions arise in the world and that our answers return us to it? Again, we turn to Dewey and, in particular, his theory of inquiry.[15]

Where in the world is the economy?

Dewey in *Logic: The Theory of Inquiry* outlines what he calls "the pattern of inquiry." Inquiry, as Dewey (1991 [1938]: 105) asserts, "in spite of the diverse subjects to which it applies, and the consequent diversity of its special techniques has a common structure ... that is applied both in common sense and science." It is "the controlled or directed transformation of an indeterminate situation into one that is so determinate in its constituent distinctions and relations as to convert the elements of the original situation into a unified whole." By "controlled" or "directed," Dewey simply means that inquiry aims at something. What it aims at are answers to questions that arise in the (indeterminate) world.[16]

To say that the world is an indeterminate situation is simply to concede that it is open to inquiry "in the sense that its constituents do not hang together" (1991 [1938]: 109). In the language of Gadamer, the world presents us with a hermeneutical problem. Our experience-in-the-world is not always unambiguous. Rather, it often needs to be grasped, it often needs to be understood, it often needs to be organized and interpreted (Gadamer 1986: 65). Experience-in-the-world, as Dewey laments, is frequently "disturbed, troubled, ambiguous, confused [and] full of conflicting tendencies." That experience-in-the-world is frequently disturbed is what impels inquiry.[17]

As suggested earlier, the situation that impels inquiry is not only "troubled" in some superficial sense. Indeed, radical, inescapable, inherent uncertainty pervades. Uncertainty that, "cannot be straightened out, cleared up and put in order, by [mere] manipulation of our personal states of mind," exists in the world (Dewey 1991 [1938]: 110). Action-in-the-world, experience-in-the-world is necessarily conditioned by the problems of real time and radical ignorance.[18] As Dewey writes,

> If we call [interaction in the temporal world] confused, then it is meant that its outcome cannot be [fully] anticipated. It is called obscure when its course of movement permits of final consequences that cannot be clearly made out. It is called conflicting when it tends to evoke discordant responses. Even were existential conditions unqualifiedly determinate in and of themselves, they are indeterminate in significance: that is, in what they import and portend in their interaction with the organism.
>
> (1991 [1938]: 110)

One question that now arises is how are individuals able to cope with these problems of time and ignorance? Stated another way, how can inquiry proceed in a world that is confused, obscure and conflicting?

As Dewey (1991 [1938]: 11) contends, the first steps of inquiry are realizing that a situation requires inquiry, that it is problematic, and then formulating (instituting) a problem. Knowing, as they say, is half the battle and a problem well put is a problem half-solved. As Dewey (1991 [1938]: 112) asserts, "to find out what the problem and problems are which a problematic situation presents to be inquired into, is to be well along in inquiry." Defining the problem is all-important. If it is mistaken or incorrectly specified it will send inquiry off into bogus or irrelevant directions; "without a problem, there is blind groping in the dark" (1991 [1938]: 112). If it does not arise out of experience-in-the-world it will start us on a wasteful course; "to set up a problem that does not grow out of an actual situation is to start on a course of dead work ... dead because the work is 'busy work.'" The problem suggests which answers (which hypotheses) should be entertained and which should be dismissed, what data should be investigated and what should be ignored, which paths should be pursued and which should be left unexplored. If the problem is profitably specified and arises from our experience-in-the-world it might lead to the determination of a problem solution.

According to Dewey (1991 [1938]: 112), the next step in the pattern of inquiry is to grope for an answer, that is, to figure out the parameters of the problem situation, to gather data and to formulate and refine our hypothesis. As Dewey notes, to say that a situation is inherently and inescapably doubtful is not to suggest that it is completely doubtful. Action in a completely indeterminate situation would be impossible (Mises 1966 [1949]: 105–119; Lachmann 1971: 37). Similarly, inquiry is not possible in a situation where all the given constituents are uncertain. Recognizing this, the first step in finding an answer to a problem is, therefore, "to search out the constituents of a given situation which, as constituents, are settled" (Dewey 1991 [1938]: 112).

Dewey uses the example of a fire alarm being sounded in a crowded auditorium to illustrate this point. As he suggests, there is much that is indeterminate in this situation; "one may get out safely or one may be trampled and burned." But there is much that is stable (at least regarding the immediate problem). The fire, for instance, is somewhere. The chairs, the aisles, the exit doors are fixed. "Since they are settled or determinate in existence," as Dewey suggests, "the first step in institution of a problem is to settle them in observation." Similarly, the behavior and movements of other people in the auditorium, "though not temporally and spatially fixed," are still observable. "All of these observed conditions taken together," as Dewey (1991 [1938]: 113) contends "constitute the terms of the problem, because they are conditions that must be reckoned with or taken account of in any relevant solution that is proposed."

Lachmann makes a similar point when discussing the role of institutions in enabling human action. Like Dewey, Lachmann (1971: 37) argues that "human action is not determinate, but neither is it arbitrary." Indeed, action is bounded. It is bounded "by the scarcity of means at the disposal of actors." It is bounded "by the circumstance that, while men are free to choose ends to pursue, once they have made their choice they must adhere to it if consistent action with a chance of success is to be possible at all." It is bounded by institutions; these circumscribe "the range of action of different groups of actors, buyers and sellers, creditors and debtors, employers and employees" (Lachmann 1994: 285). And, action is bounded by obstacles. That action is bounded by ends, means, institutions and obstacles and so must be oriented to them in its course, as Lachmann (1971: 37) asserts, is what makes both action and causal explanation possible. The future, as Lachmann frequently asserts, is unknowable but it is not unimaginable.

North agrees with this characterization. Institutions, in North's schema, reduce uncertainty by structuring everyday life, by limiting the range of possible activities and by defining and delimiting the opportunity sets individuals face. "They are a guide to human interaction," as North (1990: 3) asserts, "so that when we wish to greet friends on the street, drive an automobile, buy oranges, borrow money, form a business, bury our dead, or whatever, we know (or can easily know) how to perform these tasks." Accounting for the institutions that constrain and so shape and enable human (inter)action in a particular problem situation is, therefore, a critical stage in pursuing an inquiry.

As more and more of the settled constituents, the points of orientation, the institutions that bound action are observed, that is, once they "come to light in consequence of the being subjected to observation, the clearer and more pertinent become the conceptions of the way the problem constituted by these facts is to be dealt with" (Dewey 1991 [1938]: 113). As more and more is learnt (perceived) about a problem situation, more and more "determinate" (clearly articulated) answers are conceived and a working hypothesis is proposed.

Dewey (1991 [1938]: 115–116) calls the next stage of inquiry reasoning because after proposing a working hypothesis, we test its (internal and external) logic. We see how it holds together. We ensure that it is consistent with the other things that we "know" about the world. We examine its implications. By subjecting our working hypothesis to this sort of critical examination, by engaging in this sort of discourse, we refine and develop our propositions. Finally and critically, we take the "theory" that emerges from this process and attempt to verify it (in the world).

Remember, central to Dewey's thought is the proposition that inquiry should not only begin in the world but that it should also give us a path back to it. He has proposed that we apply the following test to our inquiries,

> Does it end in conclusions which, when they are referred back to ordinary life-experiences and their predicaments, render them more significant, more luminous to us, and make our dealings with them more fruitful? Or does it terminate in rendering the things of ordinary experience more opaque than they were before, and in depriving them of having in "reality" even the significance they had previously seemed to have? Does it yield the enrichment and increase of power of ordinary things which the results of physical science afford when applied in everyday affairs? Or does it become a mystery that these ordinary things should be what they are; and are philosophic concepts left to dwell in separation in some technical realm of their own?
>
> (1929 [1925]: 9)

If our theory passes the test, if we conclude that it serves the everyman, then we should accept it. And, in accepting it, we complete our transformation of the "indeterminate situation" we began with into a "determinate" one.[19] Inquiry, as Dewey argues repeatedly, should neither begin nor end in our skulls. Dewey's pattern of inquiry, thus, presents itself as a mode of study that increases the likelihood that we will produce profitable philosophy by insisting that we both begin and end in the world.

Conclusion

Unfortunately, most economics stopped being about the goings on in the economy a very long time ago. This is bizarre, since the practitioner of political economy is and has always been the everyman (Klein 1999). The practitioners of political economy are and have always been ordinary people. If economics does not aid in our understanding of human (economic) interaction, therefore, it can only be viewed as a logical pastime, as mental gymnastics. It can only be seen as producing "kelly green golfing shoes with chartreuse tassels" (McCloskey 2000a: 150). It cannot be thought of as science.

The Austrians seemed to have been trying to place the emphasis on the issue of meaning, but they didn't quite have a language in which to do this without dragging along some baggage in the form of the subject/object dichotomy. They were called the "psychological school," but their primary concern was never the psyche as such, but the way consumers attach significance to final goods, and the way this significance or meaning is imputed up the structure of production to give us a meaning of producers' goods. Their concern was in fact to make all the value phenomena that are familiar in the world of business (prices, rent, interest, cost, profits, etc.) meaningful in terms of human purposes and plans. Their aspiration was to link the world of meaningful economic action with the world of economic science, but their language trapped them in difficulties familiar to contemporary philosophers.

We have proposed Dewey (and particularly his theory of inquiry) as a path out of this abyss because he pressures us to begin with our experience-in-the-world and to test our theories by returning there. It is quite clear, given Dewey's critique of the non-empirical methods, that a way out is desirable. Economics has lost the world which is particularly bad and, as a consequence, it has also managed to lose the economy.

Notes

1   See Boettke 1996 for an examination of what is wrong with neoclassical economics and what problems remain within the Austrian school of economics. See also Boettke 1997. It is important to note, however, that we in no way intend to implicate economists qua practitioners in this critique. Indeed, we recognize that there are a host of applied economists who cannot be accused of being divorced from the world or of being irrelevant. Instead, we are referring to economists qua academics and to the discipline of mainstream economics.

2   Value theory encompasses the conceptualizations economists have developed to make sense of price phenomena of all kinds, including the nature of accounting cost, capital, wages, investments and profits.

3   We will use the term *verstehen* tradition to refer specifically to the older hermeneutical tradition, not the tradition after it absorbed the radical phenomenological critique of objectivism that was to come later in the Heideggerian tradition. The larger sense of the tradition, including its phenomenological versions, we will call the "understanding" tradition. The distinction between the narrower and broader senses of the tradition is important for two reasons: (1) only the earlier version is susceptible to the Deweyan critique of the subject/object dichotomy that we will summarize later in this chapter; and (2) only the first one made its full impact on the Austrian school. The Austrians had already shaped their sense of the meaning of *verstehen* before the full impact of phenomenology had the chance to transform it.

4 Knight begins by distinguishing between risk (uncertainties for which a probability can be calculated) and genuine uncertainty (for which no objective
   measures can be calculated) and then goes on to describe the entrepreneur as "a
   residual, non-contractual income claimant [who] may make a windfall gain if
   actual receipts prove greater than forecasted receipts" (Blaug 2000 [1986]).
5 Though Edmund Husserl in a sense saw himself as trying to save the Cartesian
   project, he was already in 1900 beginning to challenge the notion of scientific
   objectivity as it is routinely used in everyday language. Since then in the work of
   his followers the challenge to the dichotomy has been deepened in the work of
   Heidegger, Merleau-Ponty, Gadamer, and others.
6 See Mises' *Theory and History* (1985 [1957]).
7 Lachmann was impressively knowledgeable about and interested in institutional
   details of the economy.
8 Although to be fair, they could be read as simply trying to say that in the natural
   sciences we study external things in the physical world, that do not already have
   meaning for us, while in the human sciences we study phenomena that are already
   given meaning by human actors. The way they typically put the point, however,
   was that we are talking about things that are going on within the minds of men
   and women. With the concept of "knowledge from within" they were trying to
   suggest that in this sense we have an advantage in the human sciences, we are
   already inside the world of meaning, but never really clarified their language on
   the subject.
9 In the later developments of the understanding tradition the subject/object
   dichotomy is being gradually overcome. As Alfred Schütz put it, what we are
   inside is an intersubjective communicative process, a culture whose texts are
   publicly available to be interpreted. Or as Hans-Georg Gadamer argues in his
   critique of Dilthey, understanding is to be seen as a phenomenon of mediation
   between a reader and a "text," a spoken or written expression that is publicly
   available for interpretation. It is not a matter of the divination of the original
   intention of the author.
10 Mises inherited this way of talking about the idea of knowledge from within, and
   on this basis sometimes seems to privilege the method of introspection. We are
   supposed to build up the fundamentals of a theory of human action by starting
   with the introspective examination of our own minds. We come to appreciate
   basic concepts of the theory of action through this inward observation. Then,
   from this point of view, we need to make the additional assumption that other
   minds must exist, and that they must work like our own. This whole way of
   talking seems backwards, to me. We come to understand ourselves only through
   our entering into the intersubjective world of language.
11 As Dewey (1929 [1925]: 10) remarks, "'experience' is what James called a double-
   barreled word; Like its congeners, life and history, it includes what men do and
   suffer. What they strive for, love, believe and endure, and also how men act and are
   acted upon, the ways in which they do and suffer, desire and enjoy, see, believe,
   imagine."
12 As Klein (1999) points out, there is "a major difference between political
   economy and such disciplines as physics, chemistry, engineering, and medicine.
   For the latter, experts are appointed to make important decisions … In political
   economy, however, the practitioner is not the expert economist, but every public
   official and ordinary voter – the Everyman." Economics, Klein argues, should,
   thus, serve the everyman.
13 The Austrians' often-expressed and often-chastised insistence that economics is
   universally certain and non-falsifiable, similarly, gives up on the world. This is
   ironic since it was Mises who insisted that we let experience direct our curiosity
   and drive our inquiry. Unfortunately, Mises (1966 [1949]: 65) also insisted that,

"this reference to experience does not impair the aprioristic character of ... economics." The "statements and propositions" of economics, Mises (1966 [1949]: 32) contends, "are not derived from experience. They are, like those of logic and mathematics, a priori. They are not subject to verification or falsification on the ground of experience or facts." Much of the Austrian school, since Mises, has been convinced by these and similar passages in Human Action and so has shunned empirical work. Although the Austrians begin with our experience-in-the-world, they frequently do not return to it.

14 McCloskey (2000a: 220), for instance, argues that although the "main empirical rhetoric in economics" is statistical significance, "statistical significance is bankrupt; all the 'findings' of the Age of Statistical Significance are erroneous and need to be redone."

15 To be sure, Dewey is not the only path forward. See, for instance, Lavoie 1990, 1991b; Lavoie and Storr 2001; Storr 2002, where philosophical hermeneutics is offered as a possible path. See also Boettke 1998; Boettke and Storr 2002, where "a more consistent application of the theories of Weber" is proposed as a fruitful path out of the abyss of economics.

16 Dewey's theory of inquiry belongs, like Gadamer's philosophical hermeneutics, to the dialectic of question and answer. As Grondin summarizes:

> to understand something means to have related it ourselves in such a way that we discover in it an answer to our own questions. ... Every act of understanding, even self-understanding, is motivated, stimulated by questions that determine in advance the sight lines of understanding. A text is given voice only by reason of the questions that are put to it today. There is no interpretation, no understanding, that does not answer specific questions that prescribe a specific orientation.
>
> (Grondin 1994: 116–117)

17 Mises makes a similar point when he notes that action is always impelled by a feeling of uneasiness:

> we call contentment or satisfaction that state of a human being which does not and cannot result in any action. Acting man is eager to substitute a more satisfactory state of affairs for a less satisfactory. His mind imagines conditions which suit him better, and his action aims at bringing about this desired state. The incentive that impels a man to act is always some uneasiness.
>
> (Mises 1966 [1949]: 13)

In the same way, inquiry is only necessary when a situation is disturbed.

18 As O'Driscoll and Rizzo (1985: 2) argue, "a world in which there is autonomous or creative decision-making is one in which the future is not merely unknown, but unknowable. There is nothing in the present state of the world that enables us to predict the future state because the latter is underdetermined by the former."

19 By "determinate," Dewey does not mean to imply that the question is answered once and for all. Instead, the situation is only "cleared up, unified and resolved" with respect to the problem at hand; the answer, to be sure, is a tentative one. Since inquiry ends in the world, the settling of one question may (indeed necessarily) leads to new concerns and questions.

Bibliography

Baetjer, H. (1997) *Software as Capital*, Los Alamitos: IEEE Computer Society.

Blaug, Mark (2000) "Entrepreneurship before and after Schumpeter," in Richard Swedberg (ed.), *Entrepreneurship: The Social Science View*, New York: Oxford University Press.

Boettke, P.J. (1993) *Why Perestroika Failed: The Politics and Economics of Socialist Transformation*, New York: Routledge.

—— (1994) *The Elgar Companion to Austrian Economics*, Northampton: Edward Elgar.

—— (1996) "What is wrong with neoclassical economics (and what is still wrong with Austrian economics)?" in F. Foldvary (ed.), *Beyond Neoclassical Economics*, Aldershot: Edward Elgar.

—— (1997) "Where did economics go wrong: modern economics as a flight from reality," *Critical Review*, 11: 11–64.

—— (1998) "Rational choice and human agency in economics and sociology," in H. Giersch (ed.), *Merits and Limits of Markets*, Berlin: Springer-Verlag.

—— (2001) *Calculation and Coordination: Essays on Socialism and Transitional Political Economy*, New York: Routledge.

Boettke, P.J. and Storr, V (2002) "Post classical political economy: polity, society and economy in Weber, Mises and Hayek," *American Journal of Economics and Sociology*, 61: 161–191.

Boisvert, R.D. (1998) *John Dewey: Rethinking Our Time*, Albany: State University of New York Press.

Campbell, J. (1995) *Understanding John Dewey*, Chicago: Open Court.

Chamlee-Wright, E. (1997) *The Cultural Foundations of Economic Development: Urban Female Entrepreneurship in Ghana*, New York: Routledge.

—— (2000a) "Economic strategies of urban market women in Harare, Zimbabawe," unpublished paper, Beloit College.

—— (2000b) "Entrepreneurial response to 'bottom-up' development strategies in Zimbabwe," unpublished paper, Beloit College.

Cowan, R. and Rizzo, M. (1994) "The genetic causal moment in economics," Kyklos.

Csontos, Laslo (1998) "Subjectivism and Ideal Types: Lachmann and the methodological legacy of Max Weber," in Roger Koppl and Gary Mongiovi (eds), *Subjectivism and Economic Analysis: Essays in Memory of Ludwig M. Lachmann*, New York: Routledge.

Dewey, J. (1966 [1916]) *Democracy and Education*, New York: Free Press.

—— (1929 [1925]) *Experience and Nature*, Chicago: Open Court.

—— (1929) *The Quest for Certainty: A Study of the Relation of Knowledge and Action*, New York: Minton, Balch & Co.

—— (1934) *Art and Experience*, New York: Minton, Balch & Co.

—— (1973) *The Philosophy of John Dewey* (Two Volumes in One): 1. The Structure of Experience, 2. The Lived Experience, Chicago: University of Chicago Press.

—— (1989 [1949]) *Knowing and the Known*, Boston: Beacon.

—— (1991 [1938]) *Logic: The Theory Of Inquiry, The Later Works, 1925–1953*, vol. 12, Carbondale: Southern Illinois University Press.

Friedman, Milton (1953) *Essays in Positive Economics*, Chicago: University of Chicago Press.

Gadamer, H. (1976) *Philosophical Hermeneutics*, trans. D.E. Linge, Berkeley: University of California Press.

—— (1986) *The Relevance of The Beautiful and Other Essays*, New York: Cambridge University Press.

Granovetter, M. (1985) "Economic action and social structure: the problem of embeddedness," *American Journal of Sociology*, 91: 481–510.

—— (1992) "Economic institutions as social constructions: a framework for analysis," *Acta Sociologica*, 35: 3–11.

Grondin, J. (1994) *Introduction to Philosophical Hermeneutics*, trans. J. Weinsheimer, New Haven: Yale University Press.

Hayek, F.A. (1948) *Individualism and Economic Order*, Chicago: University of Chicago Press.

Kirzner, I. (1973) *Competition and Entrepreneurship*, Chicago: University of Chicago Press.

—— (1976) "On the method of Austrian economics," in E. Dolan (ed.), *The Foundations of Modern Austrian Economics*, Kansas City: Sheed, Andrews and McMeel.

—— (1979) *Perception, Opportunity, and Profit: Studies in the Theory of Entrepreneurship*, Chicago: University of Chicago Press.

—— (1992) *The Meaning of Market Process*, New York: Routledge.

—— (1999) "Creativity and/or alertness: a reconsideration of the Schumpertarian entrepreneur," *The Review of Austrian Economics*, 11: 5–17.

—— (2000) *The Driving Force of the Market Economy*, New York: Routledge.

Klein, D.B. (1999) *What Do Economists Contribute?*, New York: New York University Press.

Lachmann, L.M. (1971) *The Legacy of Max Weber*, Berkeley: Glendessary Press.

—— (1977 [1966]) *Capital, Expectations, and the Market Process: Essays on the Theory of the Market Economy*, Kansas City: Sheed Andrews and McMeel, Inc.

—— (1994) *Expectations and the Meaning of Institutions: Essays in Economics by Ludwig Lachmann*, London: Routledge.

Lavoie, D. (ed.) (1990) *Economics and Hermeneutics*, London: Routledge.

—— (1991a) "The progress of subjectivism," in M. Blaug and N. de Marchi (eds), *Appraising Modern Economics: Studies in the Methodology of Scientific Research Programmes*, Gloucestershire: Edward Elgar.

—— (1991b) "The discovery and interpretation of profit opportunities: culture and the Kirznerian entrepreneur," in B. Berger (ed.), *The Culture of Entrepreneurship*, San Francisco: Institute for Contemporary Studies.

Lavoie, D. and Storr, V. (2001) "As a consequence of meaning: rethinking the relationship between thymology and praxeology," paper presented at the 71st Annual Meeting of the Southern Economic Association, Tampa, November.

McCloskey, D.N. (1985) *The Rhetoric of Economics*, Madison: University of Wisconsin Press.

—— (1990a) "Storytelling in economics," in D. Lavoie (ed.), *Economics and Hermeneutics*, London: Routledge.

—— (1990b) *If You're So Smart: The Narrative of Economic Expertise*, Chicago: University of Chicago Press.

—— (2000a) *How to Be Human: Though an Economist*, Ann Arbor: University of Michigan Press.

—— (2000b) *Economical Writing, Prospect Heights*: Waveland Press.

McDermott, J.J. (1973) *The Philosophy of John Dewey*, Chicago: University of Chicago Press.

Mises, L. (1966 [1949]) *Human Action: A Treatise on Economics,* 3rd revised edition, Chicago: Henry Regnery Company.

—— (1985 [1957]) *Theory and History: An Interpretation of Social and Economic Evolution,* Auburn, AL: The Ludwig von Mises Institute.

Morgenbesser, S. (1977) *Dewey and His Critics: Essays From The Journal of Philosophy,* New York: Journal of Philosophy, Inc.

North, D.C. (1990) *Institutions, Institutional Change, and Economic Performance,* Cambridge: Cambridge University Press.

—— (1995) "The new institutional economics and third world development," in J. Harriss, J. Hunter and C. Lewis (eds), *The New Institutional Economics and Third World Development,* London: Routledge.

O'Driscoll, G.P. and Rizzo, M.J. (1985) *The Economics of Time and Ignorance,* New York: Columbia University Press.

Rizzo, Mario J. (1994) "Time in economics," in Peter J. Boettke (ed.), *The Elgar Companion to Austrian Economics,* Northamton, MA: Edward Elgar.

Shackle, G.L.S. (1972) *Epistemics and Economics,* Cambridge: Cambridge University Press.

Storr, V. (2002) "All we've learnt: colonial teachings and Caribbean underdevelopment," *Journal des Economistes et des Etudes Humaines,* 12.

Swedberg, Richard (ed.) (2000) *Entrepreneurship: The Social Science View,* New York: Oxford University Press.

Weber, M. (1978 [1921]) *Economy and Society: An Outline of Interpretive Sociology,* 2 vols, Berkeley: University of California Press.

—— (1930) *The Protestant Ethic and the Spirit of Capitalism,* London: Routledge.

—— (1947) *The Theory of Social and Economic Organization,* New York: The Free Press.

—— (1999) *Essays in Economic Sociology,* Princeton: Princeton University Press.

20 After the "New Economics," pragmatist turn?

William Milberg[1]

Introduction

In the past five years there has been an empiricist turn in economic research, a reaction against the "New Economics" that developed in the late 1970s. The New Economics was itself a reaction to the era of general equilibrium, in which economic knowledge was understood to progress through mathematical proofs of the existence, stability and uniqueness of a general equilibrium set of prices and quantities which appealed to successively weaker sets of assumptions. The New Economics was a response to the widely perceived irrelevance of the general equilibrium approach. By reversing the hypothesis generation process from a strict hypothetico-deductive formula to a creeping inductivism, and adding imperfect competition, increasing returns to scale technology and strategic behavior by firms and states to the analysis of markets, the New Economics became more relevant but less robust than the general equilibrium models of the previous era had been. The lack of robustness was a problem for those interested in drawing policy conclusions from the models. Equally important was the growing sentiment that the models were *ad hoc* and could be used to model any pre-determined outcome.

The response to the weaknesses of the New Economics in the late 1990s was an empirical turn. In this era, hypotheses are often rooted in simple economic logic, intuition, or even as a response to current events, and emphasis is placed instead on the sophistication of the measurement of variables and the correlations among them. The move is reminiscent of the work by Burns and Mitchell in the 1940s that was attacked by Koopmans (1947) as "Measurement without Theory." One reading of the current methodological turn is its de-emphasis of theory, and in the conclusion of the chapter I take up the issue of whether this turn constitutes an embrace of pragmatism or simply naïve falsificationism. Inductivism is not necessarily pragmatism, but pragmatist considerations have resurfaced in research methodology across an array of otherwise differing theoretical tendencies. The gradual erosion of the narrow deductivist criterion for the generation of hypotheses has created a broadening of the acceptable criteria for hypothesis generation. There exist today an array of tendencies in economics – both within and outside the mainstream – each of which claims as a strength its pragmatist methodology. I argue that it is not obvious which of these tendencies, if any, will become the mainstream of a future economics but that, in any case, economics may be headed for a more pluralist era, in which debates over the most appropriate form of pragmatism figure prominently.

Knowledge from mathematical generalization: the case of general equlibrium analysis

General equilibrium analysis has a long tradition in economics, dating back in some accounts to the writings of the Physiocrats, exemplified by Francois Quesnay's "Tableau Economique" of 1758.[2] While the marginalist revolution of 1871 ushered in the utilitarian problem of the simultaneous satisfaction of given and heterogenous, subjective individual preferences, the general equilibrium approach to the theory of prices and resource allocation did not become dominant among economists until after the Second World War.[3] Its ascendency in academic circles was spearheaded by Americans, most significantly, Kenneth Arrow, Paul Samuelson and Gerard Debreu.[4] Interestingly, this rise of a strict hypothetico-deductive method followed an era of theoretical pluralism in which institutionalism had a prominent place. The rise of mathematical formalism and general equilibrium analysis in economics at this time has been attributed to the rise of scientism generally, the success of linear programming and operations research methods for the purposes of wartime planning, and the increasingly free-market ideological climate during the Cold War.[5]

Axiom-based hypothesis generation

General equilibrium analysis begins with a set of axioms describing the behavior of rational individual agents operating in perfectly competitive markets and with complete information, and derives the properties of a set of commodity prices and quantitities such that all agents are optimizing their objective functions and all markets clear. Proof of the existence of such an equilibrium was of course a prerequisite to any attempt to prove the equilibrium's uniqueness and stability. But equally important was the welfare implication showing the optimality of the decentralized market system.

In the era of general equilibrium analysis, economic knowledge was understood to progress through repeated proofs of existence, uniqueness and stability of general equilibrium with appeal to successively weaker sets of assumptions. That is, an economic model was understood to generate new knowledge if it provided a proof of a known result, but required weaker, that is more general, assumptions than did existing proofs of that same result. For example, if the abiding proof of the existence of general equilibrium relied on concave utility functions, then a proof that assumed preferences to be quasi-concave constituted progress in knowledge. Similarly, the assumption of weakly transitive, instead of transitive, individual preferences in a proof of existence or optimality is another example of how the robustness of the knowledge increased.

The great strength of this methodology was the clarity of its criterion for establishing the progress of knowledge – increased mathematical generality, or robustness, of its proofs.[6] Given the general equilibrium school's equation of mathematical generality with theoretical progress, it is not surprising that the era of the dominance of general equilibrium analysis is often characterized by its emphasis on mathematical formalization. However, the era was not simply one of the greater use of mathematics in economic modeling, but one in which a particular mathemematics – based on the axiomatic method – came to dominate the development of theory. According to E. Roy Weintraub: "'mathematization' of economics is not quite the right description. ... It was the dominance of axiomatics, not rigor *per se*, that characterizes modern neoclassical economics. Applied economics is also mathematical and rigorous" (Weintraub 1998: xx)

The axiomatic method followed a narrowly construed, hypothetico-deductive approach to knowledge. Our description of knowledge and its progress in this era has, so far, not referred at all to empirical testing. This is because empirical evidence did not figure in the knowledge-generation process. Economics textbooks during this era continued to insist that knowledge in economics hinged on the testing (verification or falsification was usually not specified) of its deductively generated hypotheses. But academic economic research and journals did not consider such testing to be important. Mark Blaug (1980) critically referred to this era as one of "innocuous falsification," in which the generation of testable hypotheses was the prime role of economic research.

The demise of competitive general equilibrium analysis as the dominant modeling methodology resulted not directly from its failure to empirically test its implications, but from its aridity, that is, its insulation from institutional and historical detail. The insulation was conscious and was considered essential to the rigor of the project. In the preface to his 1959 monograph, *The Theory of Value: An Axiomatic Analysis of Economic Equilibrium*, which would later earn him a Nobel Prize, Gerard Debreu states that while the problem of general equilibrium had been approached by others in the past, they were insufficiently rigorous. He states:

> The theory of value is treated here with the standards of rigor of the contemporary formalist school of mathematics. ... Allegiance to rigor dictates the axiomatic form of the the analysis where the theory, in the strict sense, is logically entirely disconnected from its interpretations.
>
> (Debreu 1959: x)[7]

"Interpretations" would typically refer to how the model relates to the workings of actual market economies. The separation of "logic" from "interpretations" could be found in the early work of the marginalists, in particular in Walras' distinction between "pure" and "applied" analysis, the former referring to the "natural science" of the determination of "value in exchange" and the latter relating to "the organization of industry under a system of the division of labor" (Walras 1954 [1871]: 76). For Walras, "given the pure theory of economics, it must precede applied economics" (Walras 1954 [1871]: 71). The distinction would not have been emphasized by the marginalists until the arrival of the American general equilibrium school. Arguably, the initial phase of acceptance of neoclassical economics was due to Alfred Marshall's insistence on merging theory and application into an economics for the common businessman. As Robert Heilbroner writes:

> Marshall gives voice simultaneously to two approaches to economics. One of them is unquestionably that of marginalism, to which he made contributions of great importance. The second is a very un-, even anti-marginalist conception of economics as intrinsically sociological, or, to say the dreaded word, moral. Throughout the text the two approaches intertwine, not always for the best from the viewpoint of logical clarity, but unfailingly to the interest of those who see in the economy a subject that may have law-like "natural" attributes, but which also possess a core for which there is no counterpart in the world to which science directs its gaze.
>
> (Heilbroner 1996: 228)

The intellectual crystallization and professional dominance of the Walrasian approach would not come until after the Second World War, and from American academics. Criticism of the general equilibrium project – Marshall's contributions were in the area of partial equilibrium analysis – would come soon after Arrow and Hahn's (1972) broadening of the concise presentation in Debreu's 1959 monograph. In a review essay of the Arrow and Hahn book, Alan Coddington (1975) compared the contribution of general equilibrium theory to the understanding of actual economies to "the contribution of flatness to mountaineering." This sarcastic comment was a response to the standard defense of general equilibrium theory that it represented a benchmark of an ideal, fully decentralized, private enterprise system, useful as a standard against which actual and "imperfect" economies could be assessed. Coddington went on to criticize general equilibrium theory for being hermetically sealed off:

> [W]e can see clearly the Procrustean temptations that are held out to the structure of general equilibrium: to consider the arguments not on their own merits, but only to the extent that they can be reformulated within the general equilibrium framework.
>
> (Coddington 1975: 555)

Recently, historians of economic thought have attempted to explain the demise of this technically powerful paradigm. Blaug identifies misplaced rigor as part of the cause of the decline:

[T]he most rigorous solution of the existence problem by Arrow and Debreu turns general equilibrium theory into a mathematical puzzle, applied to a virtual economy that can be imagined but could not possibly exist, while the extremely relevant "stability problem" has never been solved either rigorously or sloppily. General equilibrium theory is simply a research program that has run into the sands.

(Blaug 2001: 160)

Colander (2000) notes that the demise of general equilibrium theory was its inability to lead to applied analysis. He writes:

In the 1950s and 1960s, it was hoped that practical models would be guided by general equilibrium theory. Thus, when Arrow/Debreu proved the existence of a general equilibrium in 1957, there was hope that the pure science of economics would progress in tandem with the practical application of that science. By the 1970s economists recognized that the Arrow/Debreu general equilibrium work was not going to get to the promised land.

(Colander 2000)

Colander notes that this disgruntlement with general equilibrium theory led to a new generation of economic models for which general equilibirum was not the core, guiding principle. He writes that the new generation of theory "freed economists to deal with practical policy models that were inconsistent with general equilibrium theory" (Colander 2000). The criticisms from Coddington, Blaug and Colander, an ideologically diverse but largely mainstream group of economists, are representative of the views of the profession as they evolved over the last quarter of the twentieth century.

Creeping inductivism and the "New Economics"

Poor predictive power has never led to the demise of a dominant paradigm in economics, and the reason for the professional decline in status of general equilibrium analysis must be found elsewhere.[8] The answer seems to be at a stage prior to prediction, that of hypothesis generation itself – that is, in the "context of discovery" as opposed to the "context of justification." A new approach to economics began to develop in the late 1970s in response to a growing perception of irrelevance of the hypotheses generated by general equilibrium analysis. This development – what I will refer to in this chapter as the "New Economics" – arose in a series of sub-fields in the profession, including international economics, labor economics, industrial organization and macroeconomics.[9]

These new approaches had some common features across sub-fields, including an emphasis on imperfect market competition (rather than perfect competition), asymmetric information (rather than symmetric information), on increasing returns to scale technology (rather than constant returns to scale), on strategic behavior by firms and governments (as opposed to optimization independent of rival behavior). While these new sets of assumptions are typically identified as the chief characteristics of the New Economics, methodologically speaking, the important shift was the move away from the strict hypothetico-deductivism of general equilibrium analysis and toward a vaguely construed inductivism. It became increasingly recognized that the questions being raised by general equibrium theory were out of touch with "real world" concerns.[10] I will show in the next section, using the example of the New International Economics, that the New Economics did not cause an abandonment of rational choice mathematical modeling (and in the case of New Keynesianism actually increased it – see footnote 9), but it constituted the beginning of a reversal of the direction of the relation between observation and hypothesis, that is in the accepted conventions for producing economic knowledge.

The New International Economics

The demise of the neoclassical general equilibrium model of international trade began over twenty years ago, partly in response to the model's failure to predict some commonly observed phenomena such as the large volume of intra-industry trade and the cases of successful government intervention along the lines of export-oriented industrial policy, especially in Japan and South Korea. In fact, the issue goes beyond predictive failure. These developments in the international economy in the 1970s were not imaginable given the Procrustean nature of the established, general equilibrium-based theory of international trade. Thus the established theory was of little use even in developing the hypotheses to test. By assuming deviations from the perfect competition, Pareto-optimal general equilibrium model – for example, by assuming the prevalance of imperfect competition, increasing returns to scale technology, strategic interaction among firms or even among governments – the "New International Economics" was able to logically derive the predictions mentioned above about intra-industry trade and the welfare-enhancing effects of "strategic trade policy."

An important feature of the new models was their flexibility: they could be used to "explain" almost anything. This was initially seen as a strength. Phenomena casually observed but inexplicable with the traditional model – Germany's simultaneous import and export of automobiles, Korea's export-generating system of subsidies and trade protections, subsidy competition between the US and EU governments in support of their respective aerospace industries – could now be rooted in the "rigorous" rationality of utility- and profit-maximizing microeconomic agents. In this sense it represented an inward turn of research: providing rational, microeconomic models of casually observed phenomenon was important mainly to the economists themselves.

"Outward" embrace of the theory proved a disaster. The models of increasing returns and imperfect competition showed that state intervention (e.g. subsidy or quota) in international trade or technology development could raise national welfare. Much to the horror of the new international economists, the theory was used as intellectual support by policy makers and political scientists making the case for interventionist trade policies. Such a policy stance, however, was at odds with the longstanding free-trade position of most economists, and some economists responded that because of its lack of robustness, the theory could not effectively be applied in reality.[11]

This generation of economic models had another important feature. Because of the particular functional forms assumed on preferences and technology, proofs of Pareto optimality became mathematically intractable or structurally impossible. Welfare analysis focused increasingly on the capture of rents by national firms or governments, sometimes at the expense of other nations' firms or governments, representing a distinct break from the Paretian tradition. The rents resulted from the market power created by clever intervention that depended on the particular demand or technological conditions.[12]

The flip side of the flexibility was the growing sentiment that the models of the New Economics were *ad hoc* and could be used to model any outcome.[13] This raised some important questions for the scope of research. In particular, what outcomes would be deemed acceptable? Or, put differently, from where should hypotheses come? Unlike the era of general equilibrium in which the name itself characterized the outcome under scrutiny, in the era of the New Economics, "rigorous" or "casual" observation could serve as the initial basis for a prediction. Sometimes the observation related to policy, and thus the model served to explain the rationale for the policy.[14] Sometimes the outcome was based on an observation of a phenomenon that appeared to contradict standard theory.

With a wide range of outcomes to "predict," economic modelers were forced to adopt particular, as opposed to general, assumptions, and highly stylized model structures. This led to a sense of *ad hocery* in economic modeling. According to Colander (2000), "Modern applied microeconomics consists of a grab bag of models with a model for every purpose." For Colander, what distinguishes this era of economics is not its tendency toward formal modeling. He describes this era as one dominated by "applied policy models" as distinct from the "pure theory models" of the general equilibrium period. The shift is a change "in the nature of the modeling." The economists of the New Economics would be best described, he asserts, as "*Ad hoc* modelers, or eclectic modelers" (Colander 2000: xx).

Closely related to the ad hocery of the models was their distinct lack of robustness: because of the stylized mathematical structure of the models, a change in a single assumption often led to a completely different

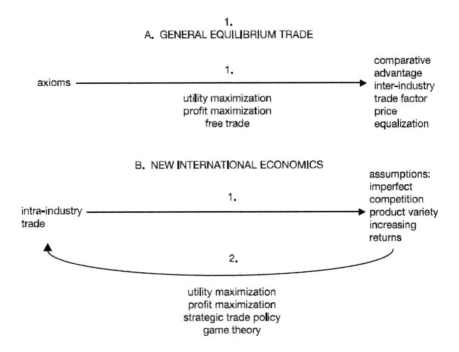

1.
A. GENERAL EQUILIBRIUM TRADE

B. NEW INTERNATIONAL ECONOMICS

Figure 20.1

prediction.[15] As I have argued, robustness, in the sense of mathematical generality, had been the hallmark of the general equilibrium, marginalist tradition. Progess of knowledge was synonymous with the increasing robustness of the hypothesis. In the New International Economics, by contrast, the hypothesis was often identified in an *ad hoc* manner and the model constructed precisely in order to generate the hypothesis. The distinction is depicted in Figure 20.1 which compares the relation between assumptions and predictions in the traditional general equilibrium approach to international trade (Heckscher-Ohlin-Samuelson) and the New International Economics. It shows how this relation was reversed: in the general equilibrium era, assumptions led to hypotheses. In the New Economics, the inductive basis of hypotheses created the need for partic-ular assumptions in order to deductively reconstruct the original hypothesis.

The reversal of the relation between prediction and assumptions created the need for very particular assumptions on behavior, conjectural variations, or even functional forms. Consider the completely general functional form of the utility function assumed in the general equilibrium tradition:

$$U = U(x_1, x_2, x_3, \ldots, x_n)$$
where U = utility
$\qquad x_i$ = good i and $i = 1, \ldots, n$

Now consider the utility function that dominated theory in the New International Economics, the so-called Dixit-Stiglitz utility function:

$$U = (\Sigma x_i^\theta)^{1/\theta},$$

where U and x_i are defined as above and θ is a parameter reflecting the elasticity of substitution, that is the consumer's willingness to substitute one good for another in response to a change in their relative price.

The Dixit-Stiglitz utility function dominated the literature because it implies that utility rises with more product variety, even though it also implies that all goods are equally substitutable in consumption with all other goods. Paul Krugman (1979), in one of the early and pioneering works in the New International Economics, noted that "This is a restrictive functional form which appears to be necessary if the model is to have a steady-state equilibrium in Sec. III below." He goes on:

> Something should also be said about the assumption that all goods enter demand symmetrically, this is clearly unrealistic: There is no reason why mopeds and toothbrushes should have identical demand functions. It also assumes away all differences in substitutability among goods, making all goods equally good subsitutes for one another. The only justification for the assumption is its simplifying power which allows us to analyze economies producing many goods.
>
> (Krugman 1979: 256)

It appears that in the New International Economics, mathematical tractableness had replaced robustness as the criterion for the choice of functional form.

The ad hocery and unrobustness of the New Economics models was reinforced by the difficulty economists had in conducting empirical tests of their hypotheses. The peculiarities of the model specifications made the models difficult to operationalize in a standard multiple regression framework. Researchers turned instead to simple correlation analysis and simulations based on calibration to benchmark data. Neither of these techniques was sufficiently compelling to give a sense of broad empirical support for the models.[16]

One interpretation of the New Economics is that it represents a further generalization of the existing general equilibrium tradition, adding in considerations of market power, non-constant returns to scale and strategic behavior by firms and states.[17] This is both wrong and an understatement of the methodological significance of the New Economics. Imperfect competition is not a generalization of the assumption of perfect competition and increasing returns to scale is not a general representation of technology that comprises constant returns to scale as a special case. To argue that the general equilibrium tradition and the New Economics tradition are methodologically identical is to accept the symmetry thesis concerning prediction and explanation. Beyond the philosophical criticisms of the symmetry thesis (see Blaug 1980: 5–7), economists themselves have viewed the New Economics as a distinct break from the general equilibrium trajectory. Krugman (1983) and Greenwald and Stiglitz (1987) both argue that their work constitutes a distinct break from competitive equilibrium analysis of trade and macroeconomics, respectively – both in terms of model construction and hypothesized results. Krugman (1983: 346) offers that the new theory is "of some use for thinking about issues – including important policy issues – which cannot be handled by traditional theory." Colander (2000) argues that the New Economics (what he calls the era of "applied policy models") breaks so completely from the concern with general equilibrium that it should not even be characterized as "neoclassical economics."

The move to empiricism: pragmatist turn or naïve falsificationism?

The result of the perceived ad hocery and unrobustness of the New Economics has been to discredit any claims its practitioners may have made for its hypothetico-deductive foundations and to gradually legitimate the inductivist pursuit of economic knowledge. The legitimacy crisis of the New Economics has opened a new era in mainstream economics. International economists, for example, may now ask simple, open-ended, experientially relevant questions, and apply sophisticated statistical techniques to answer them. For example: Does trade liberalization raise employment (Levinsohn 1999)? Does foreign direct investment raise wages in host developing countries (Aitken *et al.* 1996)? Does international outsourcing by US firms raise US wage inequality (Feenstra and Hanson 1997; Slaughter 2000)? Is democracy associated with higher wages (Rodrik 1999)? Utility and cost functions do not even appear in these works, and the specific empirical results provided as an answer to the research question posed do not necessarily "test" a particular theory. Sophisticated and careful variable construction and statistical analysis do appear, however, and these are research methods acceptable for publication in leading mainstream economics journals.[18]

The new, empiricist, wave of economic research carries the creeping inductivism identified in the New Economics to a new level. There is less insistence on rational choice microfoundations. Hypotheses are often rooted in simple economic logic, intuition, or current events, and emphasis is placed instead on the sophistication of the measurement of variables and the techniques used to show correlations between and among variables. The New Economics and general equilibrium theory shared a common "context of justification," in particular an insistence on rational choice microfoundations. The recent empirical move constitutes a break from this methodological concern. However, the New Economics had already broken from the general equilibrium tradition in its "context of discovery" and the empirical turn described here grew as an extension of this tendency that began with the New Economics. Both the New Economics and the recent empiricism are defined by broader criteria for the generation of relevant hypotheses, including completely *a posteriori* observation.[19] Some economists appeal to very simple supply and demand theory, but casual empiricism, common sense and introspection – rather than axiomatics – have also motivated the recent research.[20] In sum, there appears to be a further loosening of the already loose set of criteria for hypothesis generation. A new set of rules, a new context of discovery, is forming, with a clear, if unconscious, pragmatist bent. Before we assess whether the new trend is pragmatist or simply naïve falsificationism, we consider briefly some examples of recent research that characterizes the new trend.

Gordon Hanson on subsidies and foreign investment

An important research paper by Gordon Hanson, Professor of Economics at the University of Michigan, on the question of whether or not government subsidies, in the form of tax breaks or subsidized credit, are effective in inducing transnational corporations to invest, relies heavily on case studies for its evidence and conclusions (Hanson 2000). The question is motivated by the observation that subsidies are commonly used to attract foreign capital – their prominence is central to the debate over a possible "race to the bottom" that they may spur. Hanson does rely on a formal microeconomic model to develop a list of conditions under which subsidies to foreign direct investment are warranted. But it is on the basis of three case studies of actual subsidies – for Ford Motors and General Motors in Brazil and Intel in Costa Rica – that Hanson concludes that "there is little basis for subsidizing foreign direct investment." The source of information for the case studies is mainly industry trade journals, newspaper and magazine accounts, and published onsight accounts. While data on subsidies are presented for descriptive purposes, the analysis relies on no statistics to come to its unambiguous and bold conclusion.

Dani Rodrik on democracy and wages

Dani Rodrik of Harvard University is one of the leading development economists today. His 1999 article, "Democracies pay higher wages" in the *Quarterly Journal of Economics* – one of the most prestigious economics journals in the world – takes up the question of how the level of political freedom in a country relates to its wage levels. This grand question is motivated by the observation that labor productivity – the standard predictor of wage levels – deviates from wages to a much greater extent in Mexico than in the United States. If productivity is not a good predictor of wages, then, Rodrik proposes, "it is possible that the political context in which labor markets operate shapes behavior in these markets and influences wage outcomes" (1999: 708). The second section of the paper, following the introduction, is "Data Sources." Not only does the paper not contain a mathematical model – microeconomic or macroeconomic – developing the idea, the hypothesis in the paper is not linked in any but the loosest way to traditional economic theory. Only after the statistical correlation between democracy and wages is established does Rodrik ask "Why does democracy matter to wages?" He sets up a simple (one equation) game theoretic framework, but provides only "the intuitive solution" (Rodrik 1999: 727), and turns quickly to regression analysis of wages with political competition and participation as independent variables – an exercise largely delinked from the game theory intuition. Rodrik concludes that "it would be desirable to sort out some of the causality issues in greater detail. Is there perhaps a two-way relationship between wages and democracy?"

Alan Krueger on class size and student performance

Alan Krueger of Princeton University has produced a series of highly regarded research papers in which formal economic models play almost no role. In 1995 he co-authored a book entitled *Myth and Measurement: The New Economics of the Minimum Wage* (Card and Krueger 1995), which provided a highly detailed test of the relation between the minimum wage and employment based on evidence from the fast food industry in New Jersey. The book contains enormous detail on the statistical relation between these two variables, but the theoretical model tested is the same supply and demand diagram shown in all first-year economics textbooks. And the authors' intent is to show the irrelevance of that diagram, not to provide support for it. Only in the last chapter do the authors seek a theoretical explanation for the 354 pages of evidence preceding this chapter that refute the received view. As with Rodrik's work discussed earlier, the hypotheses offered at the end are heavily influenced by the authors' understanding of the evidence from New Jersey's fast food industry.

More recently, Krueger has produced two papers – one in the *Quarterly Journal of Economics* and one a working paper of the National Bureau of Economic Research – on the question of whether class size matters to student performance (Krueger 1999; Krueger and Whitmore 2000). While the question implies an attempt to determine the conditions for maximum student performance, the hypothesis is not generated with appeal to utility-maximizing agents, or by any formal economic model. Instead, Krueger is interested in testing the commonly held view that smaller class size allows teachers to give more attention to each student, thus raising student performance. Beyond this intuition, there is no prior economic theory about the relation between class size and student performance. The work is also motivated by the availability of a large database on an experiment with various class sizes for kindergarten through third grade performed in Tennessee between 1985 and 1989. In fact, the main claim for the originality of the research is the "well-designed experiment" (Krueger 1999: 528) that produced the data set and the statistical techniques used to capture the benefits of smaller classes. There is almost no attempt, beyond the intuition described above, to explain the relation between class size and student performance. Krueger (1999: 529) concludes that "more research is needed to develop an appropriate model of student learning."

Krueger's work on class size and student performance also gives a new twist to the fears of economics as "imperialism" in the social sciences.[21] This imperialist tendency is often attributed to the adoption of a methodological individualist rational choice model for the study of phenomena outside the standard scope of economic inquiry – Gary Becker's study of marriage being the classic example. It now appears that economics' imperialism may result instead from its pragmatism, that is its willingness to ask intuitively appealing questions and apply sophisticated statistical analysis to answer those questions.

"Measurement without theory" or revival of pragmatism?

The recent empiricist turn is reminiscent of the work by Burns and Mitchell that was criticized by Koopmans (1947) in his paper "Measurement without Theory." Burns and Mitchell's work on business cycles has been understood as heavily influenced, as was much of American institionalist economics, by pragmatist considerations of description and explanation rather than prediction and falsification. The recent empirical turn, while not consciously pragmatist, shares some features of the Burns and Mitchell research project, including broad attempts to find regularities, and careful empirical filling out of well-developed accounting or taxanomic schemes.[22] Empirical research skills and computing techniques have improved considerably since the 1940s, but there is also heightened awareness of the limitations of regression analysis and thus greater acceptance of other types of empirical evidence, including case studies. Despite advances in times series analysis (with the advent of cointegration analysis) and a retreat from unfounded claims of causality (with the common adoption of vector autoregression techniques), economists have still not overcome the sense, among both economists and non-economists, that regression results are simply not compelling enough to settle an argument.[23] In particular, economists have not resolved the issue of "data mining," in which only selective empirical tests are performed or presented. A debate over the merits and demerits of data mining has clarified some issues, but there has been no broad agreement on how to remove the sense of "con" in econometrics, as Leamer (1983) put it in his widely-read article. Still, multivariate regression analysis remains the main statistical technique used in published research.

Does the new trend in mainstream research constitute a pragmatist turn or simply a naïve empiricism? Pragmatism would indicate a deeper inductivism than currently practiced in today's mainstream empirical research. But the recent research has, unconsciously perhaps, embraced the pragmatist notion that observation is central to hypothesis formation. A few researchers have begun to conceive the observation process itself more broadly.[24] Peircean abduction more aptly describes the hypothesis generation process in some contemporary work than simple deduction or induction. Deweys' logic, according to Hirsch (1998: 101):

> encourages extensive observation, using whatever theoretical frameworks are available or seem to be called for by the observations. Such extensive observation is considered desirable in this way of thinking because Dewey encouraged reasoning from observed facts to formulated theoretical concepts.

The new research constitutes a clear break from neoclassicism in its general equilibrium form and, I have argued, even from its New Economics variant. In the neoclassical tradition, observation plays little role in formulating economic questions because the scope of such questions has been narrowly molded in the confines of a mathematical model of rational individual choice. Silberberg (1982), for example, defines "economic questions" as those that can be addressed with the techniques of marginalism. While the New Economics was concerned with the *ex post* construction of rational individual choice theoretic foundations,[25] much of the recent mainstream work I have cited makes no appeal to a formal mathematical model but moves quickly into sophisticated measurement and statistical analysis. It is not obvious that this new trend will continue, much less grow to dominate the mainstream. Still, its emergence at this time is neither an accident, nor an isolated move, as we will see in the next, and concluding, section.

The coming fight for the mantle of pragmatism

In fact, the tendency to pragmatism in mainstream economics comes at a time when a number of other schools of thought claim pragmatism as their philosophical foundation.[26] Some groups, including Friedmanian monetarists and American institutionalists, have long identified themselves as the representatives of pragmatist thought within the field of economics. Others, including feminist economists and complexity theorists, are relative newcomers on the scene. In this concluding section, I briefly review each of these views of a pragmatist economics and then speculate on the outcome of this sudden coincidence of multiple, self-proclaimed pragmatist approaches to economics.[27]

Institutional economics was born out of a commitment to pragmatism by its founders, Veblen, Ayres and Commons. Institutionalism dominated the American economics profession in the early twentieth century (including the formation of the American Economics Association) and fell out of favor with the rise of neoclassicism after the Second World War. But institutionalism has seen a resurgence of late, inspired in part by a growing mainstream search to understand economic evolution and institutional change and by an embrace by European economists of the ideas of institutionalism.

American institutionalists, perhaps justifiably, have long claimed to be the true practitioners of pragmatism in economics. Veblen, for example, wrote passionately on the incompatibility of pragmatism with the individual rational choice methodology. Others argue that the mainstream also includes research that is heavily influenced by pragmatism, especially the work of Milton Friedman and other old Chicago school economists.[28] Hammond (1995: 34), for example, identifies Friedman with the well-grounded theoretical school of Alfred Marshall rather than the hypothetico-deductive tradition of general equilibrium marginalism. And Hirsch and DeMarchi (1989) explain at length the pragmatist foundations of Friedman's work. They argue that Friedman's greatest contributions (to economics and to pragmatism) come from his adherence to the Deweyan principle of working back "from observed regularities taken to be implications to hypothetical premises." They continue:

> What we learn from Friedman's working experience is that many of the hypotheses that suggest themselves in the process of inquiry involve unobservables – like permanent income and utility functions – and that it is diffiucult to make the connection between the hypothesized premises and observed implications and thereby derive theory whose implications can be meaningfully tested with further data.
>
> (Hirsch and DeMarchi 1989: 147)

Institutionalism and old Chicago neoclassicism have both resurfaced and claimed the pragmatist mantle. But two theoretical newcomers have also made their claims. Nelson (2003) argues that feminist economics requires a pragmatist approach to knowledge, a "feminist-process view" of understanding, which involves an alternative ontology that would remove the science/value split and call on new empirical methods involving experience. In this view, "reality" is not objectively given or even fixed, but a function of subjective experience. Knowledge, in this case, embodies values as well as facts. Nelson writes:

> In a universe conceived as open, the question of knowledge must be reframed. Our knowledge is not just about reality, in process thought. Rather, it creatively adds to reality. ... Values and morals are of the same fabric as science and economics; not merely incidental. ... The feminist-process view ... sees the world, including the economic world, as unfinished and evolving, and sees knowledge adding to that world, for better or for worse. Science is, thus, intrinsically a matter of value.
>
> (Nelson 2003: 11, 24)

Feminist economics, then, draws on a pragmatist conception of knowledge. At the same time, a feminist perspective also provides an explanation for why pragmatism, process-oriented knowledge and institutionalism have been so widely dismissed: they are "in conflict with ideals that have been historically, socially, and psycho-sexually associated with masculinity" (Nelson 2003: 2)

Finally, the other emerging school of thought that seems influenced by pragmatism is so-called complexity theory, which gets its name precisely because of its resistance to techniques that give simple closure to economic models and embrace instead nonlinearities and path dependencies that potentially create explosive or chaotic outcomes. Complexity thinking, Nelson argues, shares feminism's resistance to reductionism. Thus, she points out, their coincidental rise in economics is of note. Colander (1999, 2000) sees complexity-based economics as the next dominant paradigm. In an amusing and insightful article written from the perspective of the year 2050 and describing the evolution of economic thought to that year, Colander (1999: 6) writes that around the turn of the millennium economics saw "the fall of loose-fitting positivism and the rise of pragmatism." Colander writes:

> In 2050, the belief of economists in derived analytical models has given way to a belief that underlying reality is too complex to be understood with these sorts of models. [I]n New Millennium economics, "proofs" in economics rely much more heavily on empirically determined economic patterns that have developed through simulation work, experimental work and economic modelling built on generally accepted observed patterns. ... Economic models will be "grown" from observations, rather than from assumptions.
>
> (Colander 1999: 9, 11)

Hirsch (1998) proposes that "Dewey can help us ... to formulate the rationale of aposteriorism in a way which makes sense even to those who are not disciples of aposteriorism." Hirsch's faith in methodological discussion in economics is impressive since I can think of no pure methodological argument that has ever brought a significant change in economic thinking. Moreover, the writings of classic pragmatism provide no single set of instructions on what constitutes pragmatist economic research. Bernstein (2001) notes that "pragmatism provides no blueprint for how to do social science."

It is unclear which of these pragmatist tendencies will come to dominate economic research in the future, or if a new era of pluralism will emerge. The new mainstream economic research is quite compatible with most of the other pragmatist tendencies and it is not hard to imagine that pragmatism will serve as a loose methodological core for varieties of economic research.[29] In any case, it is clear that an opening has been created and, consciously or not, a pragmatist sensibility is likely to be influential in molding the future of economic thought.

Notes

1 I am grateful to Elias Khalil, Michael Lawlor, Ahmet Tonak, and James Webb for comments on the first draft and to Luca Fiorito, Duncan Foley, Stephen Gelb, Wade Hands, Geoff Hodgson, Ann Mayhew, and Michael Piore for general discussion of the issues addressed here. All remaining errors are mine.

2 See Walsh and Graham 1980.

3 My colleague Robert Heilbroner recalls that as an undergraduate economics major at Harvard in the mid-1930s, he was assigned the textbook by Alfred Marshall – the 1898 *Principles of Economics*, best known for its detailed partial equilibrium analysis of markets. Utilitarian at its core, Marshall's book makes no more than one or two passing references to the work of the earlier, general equilibrium, marginalists.

4 Debreu 1959; Arrow and Debreu 1954; Samuelson 1965.

5 Morgan and Rutherford's 1998 volume, *From Interwar Pluralism to Postwar Neoclassicism*, contains a superb collection of essays exploring this subject. Mirowski (2002) focuses on the role of computerization, both as a method for research and increasingly as a model of rationality. Spiegel (1994) attributes the mathematization to the multi-ethnicity of American culture at the time. In Milberg (2001a), I argue that the post-war appeal of neoclassical general equilibrium theory resulted from its allegorical role as an ideal of ethnic assimilation.

6 This criterion of the generality of a proof was slightly different from that evoked by Keynes in his *General Theory* of 1936. Keynes claimed theoretical superiority not because his more general set of assumptions gave the same result as did previous theories. He argued that his distinct theory gave a more general result, that is, in which the previously held result was a special case.

7 Weintraub and Mirowski (1994) trace this tendency to extreme abstraction to the influence of Bourbakism.

8 Here I am referring not to prediction of the future, but of any "if, then" hypothesized relation.

9 On the New International Economics, see the next section. Industrial organization theory was transformed more narrowly along the lines of game theory although it has also been influenced by the "complexity" school. And labor economics already had a strong inductivist tradition, although now even its mainstream has moved in this direction. The New Keynesian macroeconomics is typically understood as a response not to the failure of general equilibrium theory but to the lack of rational choice microfoundations in Keynesianism. I would argue that while this interpretation is valid, the New Keynesian economics fits the methodological pattern of the other sub-fields in terms of the shift within the context of discovery.

10 Colander (2000) writes that "shedding some light on a problem is all that the practical track of modern economics requires." Robert Solow writes that "model-building economists tend to be natural-born, loose-fitting positivists." See Solow (1997: 50).

11 On the "inward turn," see Heilbroner and Milberg (1995). For the debate over "international competitiveness" in *Foreign Affairs*, see Krugman (1994), and subsequent responses in that journal as well as my discussion in Milberg (1996).

12 See Milberg (2001b).

13 Greenwald and Stiglitz (1987: 131), for example, write that the choice of model assumptions "must be dictated by the phenomenon to be studied."

14 Thus Colander (2000) refers to this method as rooted in "data mining."

15 In fact this feature was one reason given by the New International Economics theorists themselves to oppose the actual adoption of the policy conclusions of the models. The other reason given was that governments were not sufficiently

precise to be able to implement the (theoretically) welfare improving interventions. See Milberg (1996) for an overview.

16 The diversity of approaches in the essays in Feenstra 1988 reflects some of these difficulties.

17 I am grateful to Michael Piore for raising this as a possible interpretation of the New Economics.

18 Stephen Gelb has pointed out in discussion that at the same time that there has been a decline in the status of hypothetico-deductivism, there have occurred heightened debates over the measurement of basic economic variables (e.g. GDP growth, consumer price inflation) and of the notion of causality underlying multiple regression techniques (i.e. with the rise in use of vector autoregression).

19 With the introduction of non-convexities in functional forms in the New Economics, there was less ability to generate traditional welfare results based on Pareto optimality. This quiet disappearance of the traditional criteria for social welfare has led to the adoption of intuitively appealingly proxies for welfare as outcome variables (as opposed to axiomatically given behavior in general equilibrium and some New Economics analysis), including wages, productivity and skills attainment, with only a tacit understanding of their role as proxy for welfare. This tendency has created a parallel looseness in the criteria for choice of outcome variable. According to Wade Hands, this is reminiscent of the work on business cycles by Geoffrey Moore and others in the 1940s, in which it was unclear which variables should be the foucs of study.

20 See, for example, Card and Krueger (1995), regarding employment effects of changes in the minimum wage; Feenstra (1998); Levinsohn (1999), regarding the effects of trade on relative labor demand.

21 For a discussion, see Harcourt (1978).

22 For example, see Rodrik (1999) on investment and economic development, on the relative importance of forces driving trade growth or Slaughter (2000) on trade and wage shares.

23 Mirowski and Sklivas (1991) show the enormous variation across estimates of economic "constants." The point about the effectiveness of econometrics in settling a debate is made eloquently by Summers (1991) who, interestingly, cites the simple time series data presentation in Friedman and Schwartz's Monetary History of the United States – now viewed by some as a classic pragmatist work in the field – as the most compelling form of empirical argument.

24 NBER Working papers now include a number of case studies and of course experimental economics has attracted attention from mainstream theorists.

25 Krugman (1995) goes further, arguing that knowledge does not exist in economics until it is established within a mathematical model.

26 Renewed interest in pragmatism goes beyond economics. The Dewey conference is testament to the renewed interest in pragmatism among philosophers. This extends to law and cultural studies as well. In these fields it is seen as a potential middle ground between modernist foundationalism and postmodernist relativism. Hands (2001) makes this case for pragmatism in the field of economic methodology. I have argued here that in economics the motivation is different, although there may be an analogy if the New Economics is read as a postmodern moment in economic thought.

27 In fact, economic methodologists seem in disagreement over the relation between pragmatism and the hypothetico-deductive methodology that defines general equilibrium analysis. Blaug (1980: 2), on the one hand, identifies American pragmatism (along with the Vienna Circle) as important to the creation of this model of scientific explanation. Hands (1998: 377), on the other hand, identifies pragmatism in American institutionalism as one of the few alternative "philosophical visions" to positivism in the history of economics. Both are no doubt correct

since pragmatism has had multiple and even contradictory influences. See, for example, the discussion of Peirce versus Dewey in Mounce 1997.

28 Those seeking to rehabilitate Milton Friedman based on his pragmatist method-ology include Hirsch and DeMarchi (1989) and Hammond (1995). Even McCloskey's rhetorical interpretation of economics has been associated (by McCloskey and others) with the pragmatism of Friedman, Stigler, Knight and others in the old Chicago school.

29 Similarly in the field of economic methodology, Hands (2001) sees the opening of a new eclectic era in which the "Received View" of hypothetico-deductivism no longer serves as a criterion for theory appraisal, but is replaced instead by a looser and more diverse set of methodological tools.

Bibliography

Aitken, B., Harrison, A. and Lipsey, R. (1996) "Wages and foreign ownership: a comparative study of Mexico, Venezuela, and the United States," *Journal of International Economics*, 40: 345–371.

Arrow, K. and Debreu, G. (1954) "Existence of an equilibrium for a competitive economy," *Econometrica*, 20: 265–290.

Arrow, K. and Hahn, F. (1972) *General Competitive Analysis*, San Francisco: Holden Day.

Bernstein, R. (2001) "John Dewey and the pragmatic century," paper presented at conference on "Pragmatism: Modernism, Postmodernism and Beyond," Simon's Rock College, July.

Blaug, M. (1980) *The Methodology of Economics, or How Economists Explain*, Cambridge: Cambridge University Press.

—— (2001) "No history of ideas, please, we're economists," *Journal of Economic Perspectives*, 15(1): 145–164.

Card, D. and Krueger, A. (1995) *Myth and Measurement: The New Economics of the Minimum Wage*, Princeton: Princeton University Press.

Coddington, A. (1975) "The rationale of general equilibrium theory," *Economic Inquiry*, 13: 539–558.

Colander, D. (1999) "New millennium economics: how did it get this way and what way is it?" *Journal of Economic Perspectives*, 14(1): 121–132.

—— (2000) "The death of neoclassical economics," *Journal of the History of Economic Thought*, April.

Debreu, G. (1959) *The Theory of Value: An Axiomatic Approach to Economic Equilibrium*, New Haven: Cowles Foundation Monograph.

Feenstra, R. (ed.) (1998) *Empirical Methods for International Trade*, Cambridge, MA: MIT Press.

Feenstra, R. and Hanson, G. (1997) "Foreign direct investment and relative wages: evidence from Mexico's maquiladoras," *Journal of International Economics*, 42: 371–393.

Greenwald, B. and Stiglitz, J. (1987) "Keynesian, New Keynesian and New Classical Economics," *Oxford Economic Papers*, 39: 119–132.

Hammond, J.D. (1995) *Theory and Measurement: Causality Issues in Milton Friedman's Monetary Economics*, Cambridge: Cambridge University Press.

Hands, D.W. (1998) "Positivism," in J. Davis et al. (eds), *The Handbook of Economic Methodology*, Cheltenham: Edward Elgar.

—— (2001) *Reflection without Rules*, Cambridge: Cambridge University Press.

Hanson, G. (2000) "Should countries promote foreign direct investment?" *Working Paper*, G24 research program, Geneva: UNCTAD.

Harcourt, G. (1978) *The Social Science Imperialists and Other Essays*, London: Routledge and Kegan Paul.

Heilbroner, R. (1996) *The Teachings of the Worldly Philosophy*, New York, W.W. Norton.

Heilbroner, R. and Milberg, W. (1995) *The Crisis of Vision in Modern Economics*, Cambridge: Cambridge University Press.

Hirsch, A. (1998) "Dewey, John," entry in J. Davis et al. (eds), *The Handbook of Economic Methodology*, Cheltenham: Edward Elgar, pp. 100–103.

Hirsch, A. and DeMarchi, N. (1989) *Milton Friedman: Economics in Theory and Practice*, Ann Arbor: University of Michigan Press.

Koopmans, T. (1947) "Measurement without theory," *Review of Economic Statistics*, XXIX(3): 161–172.

Krueger, A. (1999) "Experimental estimates of educational production functions," *Quarterly Journal of Economics*, 114(2): 497–532.

Krueger, A. and Whitmore, D. (2000) "The effects of attending a small class in the early grades on college-test taking and middle school test results: evidence from Project Star," *Working Paper* 7656, National Bureau of Economic Research, April. Online at: http://www.nber.org/papers/w7656

Krugman, P. (1979) "A model of innovation, technology transfer, and the world distribution of income," *Journal of Political Economy*, 87: 253–266.

—— (1983) "New theories of trade among industrial countries," *Amercian Economic Review*, 73 (May): 343–348.

—— (1994) "Competitiveness: a dangerous obsession", *Foreign Affairs*, March/April: 28–44.

—— (1995) *Development, Geography and Economic Theory*, Cambridge, MA: MIT Press.

Leamer (1983) "Let's take the con out of econometrics," *American Economic Review*, 73: 31–43.

Levinsohn, J. (1999) "Employment responses to international liberalization in Chile," *Journal of International Economics*, 47: 321–344.

Milberg, W. (1996) "The rhetoric of policy relevance in international economics," *Journal of Economic Methodology*, 3(2): 237–259.

—— (2001a) "Allegories of ethnic assimilation in American economic thought," mimeo, Department of Economics, New School University.

—— (2001b) "The end of welfare (economics) as we know it," mimeo, New School University (reprint forthcoming in *Rethinking Marxism*).

Mirowski, P. (2002) *Machine Dreams: Economics Becomes a Cyborg Science*, Cambridge: Cambridge University Press.

Mirowski, P. and Sklivas, S. (1991) "Why economists don't replicate (although they do reproduce)," *Review of Political Economy*, 3: 146–163.

Morgan, M. and Rutherford, M. (eds) (1998) *From Interwar Pluralism to Postwar Neoclassicism*, Durham, NC: Duke University Press.

Mounce, H.O. (1997) *The Two Pragmatisms: From Pierce to Rorty*, London: Routledge.

Nelson, J. (2003) "Confronting the science/value split: notes on feminist economics, institutionalism, pragmatism and process thought," *Cambridge Journal of Economics*, 27(1): 49–64.

Rodrik, D. (1999) "Democracy pays higher wages," *Quarterly Journal of Economics*, 114 (3).

Samuelson, P. (1965) *Foundations of Economic Analysis*, New York: Atheneum.

Silberberg, E. (1982) *The Structure of Economics: A Mathematical Analysis*, New York: McGraw-Hill.

Slaughter, M. (2000) "Production transfer within multinational enterprises and American wages," *Journal of International Economics*, 50: 449–472.

Solow, R. (1997) "How did economics get that way and what way did it get?" *Daedalus*, 126(1): 39–58.

Spiegel, H. (1994) "Ethnicity and economics," *International Social Science Review*, 1/2: 3–12.

Summers, L. (1991) "The Empirical Illusion in Macroeconometrics," *Scandinavian Journal of Economics*, 93(2): 129–148.

Walras, L. (1954 [1871]) *Elements of Pure Economics or the Theory of Social Wealth*, trans. William Jaffe, Philadelphia: Orion Editions.

Walsh, V. and Graham, H. (1980) *Classical and Neoclassical Theories of General Equilibrium*, New York: Oxford University Press.

Weintraub, E.R. (1998) "From rigor to axiomatics: the marginalization of Griffith Evans," in M. Morgan and M. Rutherford (eds), *From Interwar Pluralism to Postwar Neoclassicism*, Durham, NC: Duke University Press.

Weintraub, E.R. and Mirowski, P. (1994) "The pure and the applied: Bourbakism comes to mathematical economics," *Science in Context*, 7(2): 245–272.

Index

For Product Safety Concerns and Information please contact our EU
representative GPSR@taylorandfrancis.com
Taylor & Francis Verlag GmbH, Kaufingerstraße 24, 80331 München, Germany

www.ingramcontent.com/pod-product-compliance
Ingram Content Group UK Ltd.
Pitfield, Milton Keynes, MK11 3LW, UK
UKHW021623240425
457818UK00018B/711